BABY MARKE

From Michael Jackson and Madonna to Nadya Suleman and Jon and Kate Gosselin, creating families can no longer be described by heterosexual reproduction in the intimacy of a couple's home and the privacy of their bedroom. On the contrary, babies can be brought into families through complex matrixes involving lawyers, coordinators, surrogates, so-called brokers, donors, sellers, endocrinologists, media agents, and publicity teams, and without any traditional forms of intimacy. Mostly, these baby acquisitions are legal, but in some cases, black markets are involved. In direct response to the need and desire to parent, men, women, and couples – gay and straight – have turned to viable, alternative means. The marketplace for creating families spans transnational borders and encompasses international adoptions with exorbitant fees attached to the purchasing of ova and sperm and the leasing of wombs. For as much as these processes are in public view, rarely do we consider them for what they are: baby markets.

This book examines the ways in which Westerners create families through private market processes. From homosexual couples skirting Mother Nature by going to the assisted reproductive realm and buying the sperm or ova that will complete the reproductive process, to Americans traveling abroad to acquire children in China, Korea, or Ethiopia, market dynamics influence how babies and toddlers come into Western families. Equally, some contributors in this book push back at the notion that markets appropriately describe contemporary adoptions and assisted reproduction. Michele Bratcher Goodwin and a group of contributing experts explore how financial interests, aesthetic preferences, pop culture, children's needs, race, class, sex, religion, and social customs influence who benefits from and who is hurt by the law and economics of baby markets.

Michele Bratcher Goodwin, BA, JD, LLM, is the Everett Fraser Professor of Law at the University of Minnesota, where she holds joint appointments in the Law School, Medical School, and the School of Public Health. In 2008, she was a visiting professor at the University of Chicago Law School. She has been a visiting scholar at Berkeley School of Law in the Center for the Study of Law and Society. She was a postdoctoral Fellow at Yale University, conducting research on the antebellum politics of sex and law. Her op-ed commentaries have appeared in *The Los Angeles Times*, *The Washington Post*, *The Houston Chronicle*, *The Christian Science Monitor*, *The Chicago Sun Times*, and *Forbes* magazine.

Louise Brown was born at the threshold of a genetic renaissance, where biotechnology would once again transform modern medicine. During that time, *in vitro fertilization* (IVF) became a universally recognized term. But what does *in vitro fertilization* really mean – or, for that matter, the term *test-tube baby*? A study conducted in 1986 revealed that when Americans were asked about the meaning of IVF, 54 percent could not identify what the technology involved. Nearly a quarter century later, the odds that Americans are more insightful about the process are not much better. This statistic is meaningful as it indicates that Americans, although demonstrably more inclined to embrace reproductive technologies, are still unaware of the process and, presumably, the risks. Socially, IVF is understood as a process involving the making of babies in laboratories or clinics; the children born through clinical fertilization are understood to be the test-tube children. (Courtesy of Express/Express/Getty Images.)

Baby Markets

MONEY AND THE NEW POLITICS OF CREATING FAMILIES

Edited by

Michele Bratcher Goodwin
Schools of Law, Medicine, and Public Health, University of Minnesota

CAMBRIDGE UNIVERSITY PRESS
Cambridge, New York, Melbourne, Madrid, Cape Town, Singapore, São Paulo, Delhi, Dubai, Tokyo

Cambridge University Press
32 Avenue of the Americas, New York, NY 10013-2473, USA

www.cambridge.org
Information on this title: www.cambridge.org/9780521735100

First published 2010

Printed in the United States of America

A catalog record for this publication is available from the British Library.

Library of Congress Cataloging in Publication data

Baby markets : money and the new politics of creating families / edited by Michele Bratcher Goodwin.
p. cm.
Includes bibliographical references and index.
ISBN 978-0-521-51373-9 (hardback) – ISBN 978-0-521-73510-0 (pbk.)
1. Adoption – Law and legislation – United States. 2. Human reproductive technology – Law and legislation – United States. 3. Child welfare – United States. 4. Intercountry adoption. 5. Family planning – Evaluation. 6. Family policy. 7. Human reproduction – Political aspects. 8. Human reproductive technology – Moral and ethical aspects. I. Goodwin, Michele.
KF545.B33 2010
346.7301′78–dc22 2009034804

ISBN 978-0-521-51373-9 Hardback
ISBN 978-0-521-73510-0 Paperback

For Evelyn, Patricia, and Ben

I looked down at my naked thigh, trying to find an area of skin that hadn't been bruised. It proved quite hard. I was getting genuinely tired of looking like I was a heroin addict each time I went though the donation process. How come I could never ever learn how to perform this simple task correctly, this chore I had performed on so many occasions by now? . . . I was now to do my ninth donation, though technically, it was my tenth since my previous one . . . had been terminated. . . . They paid me 1,000 for the trouble.

– Julia Derek

Ordinarily, potential gains from trade are realized by a process of voluntary transacting – by a sale, in other words. Adoptions could in principle be handled through the market and in practice, as we shall see, there is a considerable amount of baby selling.

– Elisabeth Landes and Richard Posner

Contents

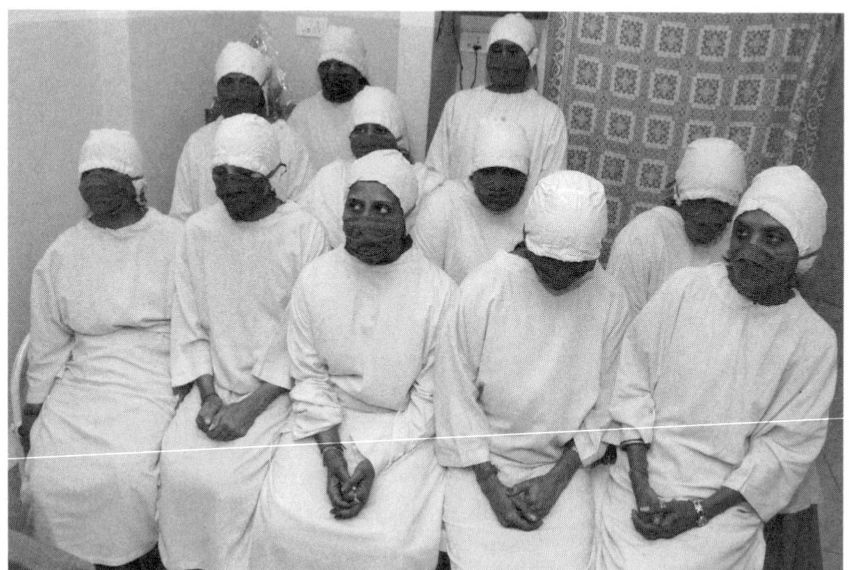

Women in India leasing their wombs. Some with their heads cast down, or nearly fully covered with breathing cloths, these women rent biological space to Americans and others urging them to export their reproductive process to other parts of the globe. These women are paid sums they otherwise would never see and are offered safe, clean housing and food. Most of them know – and even count on – never seeing the babies they will birth ever again. (Ajit Solanki/AP.)

Preface

Applying the laws of supply and demand to babies and children attracted strident criticism thirty years ago, when a University of Chicago Law School professor and an emerging business scholar penned a provocative article titled "The Economics of the Baby Shortage."[1] The article was dismissed as an outrageous package of assumptions; children are not widgets or pieces of property to be reduced to economic analysis. Landes and Posner surmised that white babies were in demand, but that we could all agree that there was a "glut of black babies" for adoption. They hinted that the surplus in black babies had something to do with "the very high ratio of illegitimate black births."[2] The article placed a spotlight on what they referred to as "baby selling," which they claimed was already occurring. Landes and Posner described these transactions as "black market" exchanges because "public policy is opposed to baby selling."[3] Their article offered an elegant analysis of what critical legal scholars might have referred to as an emerging crisis: too many children, especially black babies, were in foster care, and most with no hope of ever being adopted.

But why the backlash? The Landes–Posner collaboration was, after all, grounded in strong empirics. To some, the thought of baby selling or baby markets rekindled images of slavery, which is considered by many the darkest period in U.S. history. The notion that children might be placed with families according to subtle bidding and aggressive negotiating was disturbing – too closely resembling the repulsive practices of slavery, where teeth, skin quality and color, and emotional disposition figured into the market evaluation of men, women, and children.[4] In that old model, a prospective owner could push up the value of a child in a fashion similar to that of bidding on a fine work of art or unique piece of furniture. Auction houses and slave depots were profitable enterprises, specializing in the trade of slaves, including children. According to Richard Wade, "sales took place both at depots and auction centers. The purchasers could drop by the premises, examine the stock and bargain on the spot."[5]

The value of children was accordingly assessed. How sturdy, industrious, and healthy would that child be? The negotiations were serious, and buyers "quizzed the slave as to age, experience, and capacity; he stripped the blacks, male, or female, looking for imperfections or diseases; then, if satisfied, he began haggling over price."[6] Mild temperaments were a plus, and good musculature indicated that a bargain was at hand, for these children were needed most in the cotton and tobacco plantation fields, but also as prospective breeders. Intellect counted, but the abilities to read and write were distracting and a liability. Spirited competition between bidders was encouraged by auctioneers. Unimportant to these transactions was parentage. Indeed, sometimes children were sold by their fathers, reflecting the very ignobility of being born to a slave mother and a plantation-owner father.

Thus, when Landes and Posner revived a discussion about baby selling, many ignored the nuance in their work, but reflected on the horrors of slavery. For nearly thirty years after the publication of *The Baby Shortage*, scholars avoided thinking about the dynamics of reproduction, conception, and adoption through the lenses of supply, demand, and markets. The backlash against Landes and Posner was palpable, especially from left-leaning scholars. In a prolific verve, Posner went on to apply a law and economics framework to other social problems, and babies and markets were left behind.

In truth, Landes and Posner struck a nerve, causing discomfort among many. Baby markets are part of a legacy yet to be fully unfolded in U.S. consciousness and sociolegal and economic discourse. Quite apart from the sophisticated and sterile practices (compared to haggling over slaves two centuries ago) of contemporary baby markets, the slave market reminds us of how slippery parentage can be and the awkwardness of applying market language to human beings and human relationships. Equally, the spectrum of ownership of any human being, which is the usual outcome of a purchase, conflicts with modern parlance, self-perception, and the ways in which we identify adoption and assisted reproduction.

This book came about from my reflections on current family creation dynamics reconciled against images from the past. In my office hangs an aged advertisement for an auction in a rural Kentucky town. The advertisement promises the public a lively atmosphere with "plenty to eat and drink." That is usually what strikes many people who see this announcement. Others note, with some shock, that in bold lettering, slaves are for sale. To this, most voice dismay or sorrow. Yet, in the more than a decade of its framing on my office wall, none of the hundreds who have entered and exited my office comment on the part that is most chilling to me: "two mulatto wenches for sale." When I mention it to colleagues and others, there is a blank stare.

To me, the earliest forms of baby markets were the selling of biological children into slavery. This was a common practice in the United States, but one that is lost in a racially tense abyss. After all, it was more than a century after Thomas Jefferson's death that his family publicly recognized that he could be the father of the enslaved mulatto children who ran amok on his plantation. Born from Sally Hemings, his known slave mistress, whom he took to Paris, these children and their legacy fought for recognition from their father and his family. In some quarters, it seemed easier to believe that an immaculate conception had taken place with Sally than to acknowledge and accept that Jefferson had sex with his slave and fathered her children.

The poster on my wall starts a conversation about paternity, family ties, privacy, the right to return, inheritance, liberty, freedom, miscegenation, blended families, interracial sex, and interracial parenting. Discussions about the law, social status, cultural norms, and values all spring from interracial girls being sold in the antebellum South. Who was their father? What really creates family ties? Did their father love his daughters? At what point is it more important to sell your children than to keep them?

These are questions that haunted my family, and their rather unique and somewhat dysfunctional "baby-keeping" story. Unlike the girls for sale in the poster, my grandfather's dad, Aben, lived with his father and was his most loyal companion until his death. Aben was born a slave, but his Irish father refused to let him go. Deceived for all his life, Aben believed that he was never legally a slave because he was his father's closest ally. Census records informed us of Aben's mistake. But his story is that unlike some, after all, his father built a school for him, traveled with him, and refused to treat him significantly different from his white siblings. But the law had a different status for Aben, and it was one that his father was unwilling to change. Aben was a slave until the Thirteenth Amendment freed him. For Aben, this might have been a minor point had he been aware that government records completed by his father listed him as a slave. In Aben's mind, he was never owned, simply loved by his father. To Aben, his mother was the slave, and forever, she was disowned and disavowed by him. It was a strange twist of fate. Somehow, he was right – by law, his mother did not own him and did not belong to him per se. Within their story are complications too prickly and nuanced for anyone to really pick apart fully and analytically – for they are long gone – but our questions remain.

In these times, we have the opportunity to understand history as it is written, to consider the plight of infertile couples desperate to conceive, to reevaluate social and legal frameworks that restrict gay parenting, to parse out so-called good baby selling from the bad, and to move forward with exactitude and deference as we shape the language to be applied to baby markets. Here is a time for honest discourse, disagreement, and social introspection. This is the space where the language of law meets contemporary family making.

Today, even a cursory survey of so-called child acquisition in the United States reveals a broad landscape of baby demand and the multitudinous ways in which the hunger for babies is satisfied. To be sure, there is not a U.S. shortage in babies, particularly given the surplus in black babies and children in foster care; rather, what becomes apparent are two things, which we can all agree on: the menu of legal and illegal options by which adults can satisfy their cravings for children is expansive, and race, gender, nation of origin, genetic connection, and religious orientation matter to would-be parents. But are the dynamics of the marketplace always in the best interests of children, or do they simply satisfy adult needs? Often it is a bit of both.

– Michele Bratcher Goodwin

NOTES

1 Elisabeth Landes and Richard Posner, *The Economics of the Baby Shortage*, 7 J. Legal Stud. 323 (1978).
2 *Id.* at 325.
3 *Id.* at 324.
4 *See* Richard Wade, Slavery in the Cities: The South 1820–1860 (1964).
5 *Id.* at 200.
6 *Id.*

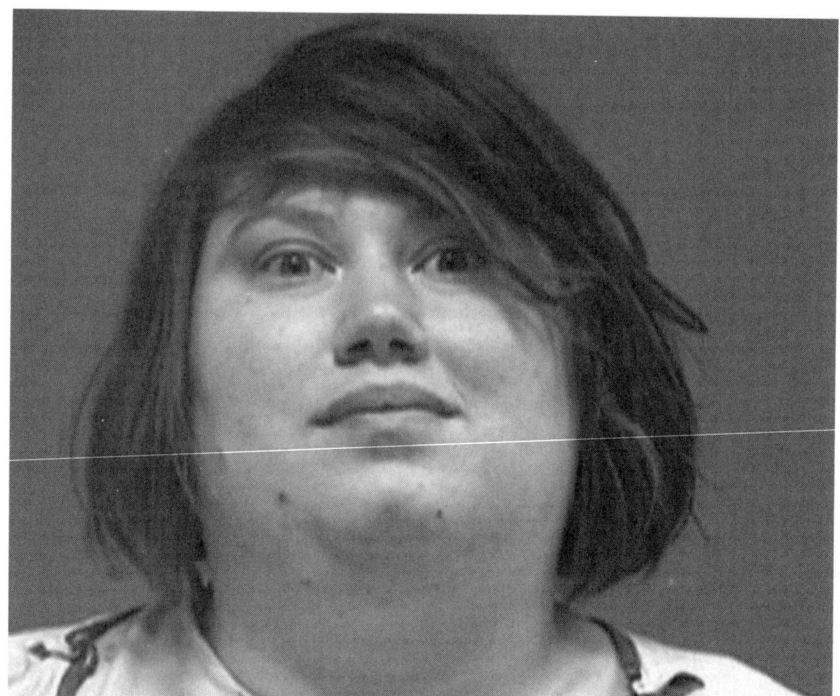

Mug shot of Korena Roberts. The urge to mother became overwhelming for Korena. Typical adoption fees would certainly have been beyond her reach. Korena was so desperate to become a mother that she murdered her friend and carved the baby from the woman's womb. Her friend was later found dead in the kitchen cupboard. (Washington County Sheriff's Office.)

Acknowledgments

This book began as a project about how children come into families and whether the law has an expressive or functional role in responding to social and cultural norms about adoption and assisted reproduction. Its central feature was an economic analysis of how aesthetics matter in adoption and assisted reproduction and, in turn, how characteristics associated with race, ethnicity, and education often drive up or down the financial costs associated with acquiring a child or the building blocks to create one. It was important to me that the twin issues of adoption and assisted reproduction be wedded in this project as the similarities are undeniable and prior works tended to treat the issues in isolation.

Supporting this vision for *Baby Markets* was my editor, John Berger. I am forever in his debt and grateful for his commitment to this project and patience with seeing it through.

In the process of my research, this project took me on a journey through my family and its rugged American tale of antebellum interracial love, power, and coercion. Helping me to excavate and examine that complex story involving my forebears – some of whom sold their children, and others of whom lost them, through the slave market – was my uncle, Charles Mays.

Projects such as this are virtually impossible to complete without the assistance of talented research assistants. Mary Cloutier and Grisel Ruiz provided invaluable research assistance, and I am most grateful to them.

As with most academics, my work takes me far and wide. As I conclude this book, I can only reflect with gratitude on stops along the way. I am most deeply indebted to several individuals and institutions that provided support for this project, especially Glen Weissenberger, who funded an important roundtable from which this project bloomed. Glen's generosity was matched by that of Saul Levmore, my former colleague and dean at the University of Chicago Law School, where the core of this project was developed during a research leave from the University of Minnesota.

I am grateful to the faculties at Dartmouth College, Barnard College, George Washington Law School, the University of Chicago, Cumberland Law School, St. Louis University Law School, and Columbia University Law School for inviting me to present chapters from this work. This book, and my contributions, in particular, have benefited from engaging conversations with some of my dearest friends in the academy, including Mary Anne Case, Richard Epstein, John Paris, Dorothy Roberts, Debora Spar, and Patricia Williams.

This project would not have been possible without the thoughtful contributions in this collection. I thank each of the contributors for participating in this project, for their excellent essays, and for their intellectual generosity to participate in a project that addresses very sensitive procreative issues.

And to Patricia and Ben, thank you for allowing me to share your journey and for being there. Finally, this book is dedicated to Evelyn Marie, who truly remains the last one standing. Your unflappable dignity, uncompromising integrity, wisdom, and warmth are the guides by which I live. Thank you, Grandmother.

MBG

Iris Botros and her husband, **Louis Andros**, detained in a Cairo, Egypt, courtroom on charges that they bought and trafficked children in Egypt. The couple, from North Carolina, thought they were adopting twins and only paying a service fee. (Courtesy of CNN.)

Introduction

MICHELE BRATCHER GOODWIN

In recent months, we have witnessed the lengths to which infertile women and men, celebrities, single persons, and those with nefarious motivations may go to obtain a child. From Madonna's wrangling with the government in Malawi to adopt a little girl (and skirt the residency requirement), to Nadya Suleman and her craftily orchestrated plan to conceive multiples and birth octuplets, to those spine-numbing cases like that of Korena Roberts, who murdered her pregnant friend and claimed the baby she carved from the woman's womb to be her own, we are witnessing the lengths to which people will plan, connive, donate, pay, or kill to adopt, conceive, or acquire a child.

In May 2009, standing in a cage, seemingly more suitable for cattle or dogs, an American couple, Iris Botros and her husband, Louis Andros, pleaded for release. This was the image of the couple shown throughout the world: hands gripping bars, sweat dripping down their foreheads, clothes that appeared slept in, and the look of fear indelibly marked on their faces. Their dream of bringing a child back home with them to Durham, North Carolina, was a distant plan, even fantasy. Now, in a courtroom in Egypt, they wait in a portable prison cell. Botros and Andros thought they would bring twins back home to North Carolina. Instead, the couple, accused of attempting to purchase children, awaited a trial with religious, political, and criminal law implications.

To their sympathizers, Iris and Louis are scapegoats, pawns in a larger political dynamic involving a backlash against Christian adoptions in Egypt.[1] For them, this is not a story involving baby selling, fraud, and manipulation; rather, this couple (along with other similarly situated Americans on trial in Egypt) wanted to adopt Christian children in a country where Islamic law forbids adoption. Because the twins were not Muslim, the couple believed the adoption was permissible, even if facilitated under less than transparent means. The twins whom they planned to bring home, some lament, will otherwise be condemned to life in an orphanage. According to Iris's aunt, "I can't believe this is a crime."

Yet their story is not so clear-cut to some, as indeed, international adoptions in general are complicated by financial exchanges, geography, politics, economics, race, religion, and class. Their case is no exception, for it was U.S. government officials who contacted the Egyptian authorities after the couple sought passports for the twins. On investigation, it appeared that the couple's documents claiming that Iris had given birth to the twins were forged and that they paid nearly five thousand dollars (as a service fee) to the orphanage that housed the babies. During the summer of 2009, the couple awaited the conclusion of their trial on charges of child trafficking, child smuggling, and forging documents, their court appearances taking place behind metal bars in separate cells. The couple passed communications through their lawyers. The orphanage, now closed by Egyptian police, transferred the twins to an overcrowded facility with sixty children.

But Iris and her husband are not alone, symbolically or legally, in Egypt. Another couple, Suzan Hagouf and her husband, Medhat Metyas, faced similar charges of forging papers in the adoption of their child, through the same agency, and although their cases differ in scale – Hagouf and her husband have resided in Egypt since 2003 and donated only seventy dollars – U.S. officials found the pattern similar enough to turn both couples over to Egyptian authorities. On September 17, 2009, both couples were convicted by an Egyptian court. The couples faced up to ten years in jail, and their recently adopted children will return to lives of poverty. And although the judge issued a more lenient sentence of two years each and fines amounting to nearly $20,000 USD each, these husbands and wives will not see each other or the children they came to love.

Nations struggle to develop protocols that respond to the best interests of children, while simultaneously enacting policies that may burden the efficiency of child placements. These efforts collectively attempt to avoid trafficking, abduction, and sexual exploitation of children. Nonetheless, fault lines sometimes appear. The demand for intercountry adoptions remains high. Guatemala, a nation that ranks among the top four in the number of children who are adopted from there into the United States, recently clamped down on transnational adoptions, responding to a fear that children were being stolen from their parents, exploited in sex rings, and trafficked for their organs. Nearly one child for every hundred in Guatemela ends up in a U.S. home. According to one report, "Guatemalan adoptions used to be so quick and hassle-free that the nation of 13 million became the world's second-largest source of babies to U.S. couples, a $100 million-a-year industry managed nearly entirely by lawyers with almost no government oversight."[2] In the past twenty years, nearly 30,000 children have been adopted from Guatemala by couples in the United States.

True or not, the perception that Westerners abuse their wealth and status to obtain children with limited government oversight reached its peak for Guatemalan officials. Prior to its recent legislation, the Guatemalan adoption process could be seamlessly facilitated through a notary, and the bureaucracy that typically accompanies the international adoption process was avoided. Transparency need not become the victim to efficiency, but in the Guatemalan context, officials could no longer ignore the concerns that children were being stolen and trafficked.[3]

This book examines who benefits from and who is harmed by the market structures that more frequently govern reproductive and adoption processes. Quite purposefully, I wanted to engage scholars in a dialogue about contemporary child acquisition. That conversation urged a serious engagement between those who write about assisted reproductive technology (ART) and those who study adoption laws and regulations. It was apparent, when I first began this project, that those two communities did not speak to each other.

Furthermore, both in scholarship and practice, ART had taken off and left the nuances, frameworks, considerations, and controversies involving adoption to another realm. On consideration, that approach was unwise. After all, some of the controversies and policy considerations that now dominate discussions on ART were first articulated with adoption law and policy, including issues of genetic privacy, parental disclosures to children, and biological health concerns.

Thus began this project, which started with a roundtable that I hosted at the University Club in downtown Chicago. The roundtable brought together scholars from the worlds of ART and adoption, to actually discuss, debate, and speculate about where the fields were headed and, most important to this project, how children were ultimately affected by the supply, demand, and market aspects of both domains. It became clear that there are lessons to be learned from the rapid growth of transnational adoptions and the proliferation of assisted reproductive clinics. This book offers a conversation between the two spheres, particularly as both domains lead to parenting and have an impact on the lives of children. The two spheres of baby acquisition are, by their nature and services offered, different, and we should avoid conflating them. At the same time, there are sufficient similarities beyond financial exchanges to warrant a more critical look at how adoption and ART systems operate within societies, and whether the best interests of children are always, or only sometimes, at the forefront of those exchanges.

This book examines demand-side issues, including the ways in which technology provides venues for gay men and women to become parents, when the laws of nature limit that possibility, and the ways in which racial, class, and other preferences in ART and adoption might lead to positive or negative social impacts. The book also considers supply-side issues and contemporary controversies, particularly the overpopulation of black children in foster care and the crowding out of working- and middle-class individuals from adopting white babies, and speculates whether adoption policies in the 1960s and 1970s that advocated against white families adopting black children are the cause of a legacy – the surplus of black children in foster care – that seems difficult to repair.

Baby Markets takes seriously the question of markets for reproductive services and adoption. Its authors consider whether anything is to be done about the status quo of baby acquisition; after all, as one contributor notes, if we do not decry obstetricians being paid for their services, why would we deny the same to surrogates, egg donors, or any number of people involved in natural or assisted births? What we can take away from all this is the deeply contested and complicated nature of becoming a parent. Wealth and status influence reproduction and adoption far more than we might like to believe or acknowledge. It is because of this significant influence that adoption and reproductive services in the United States generate multibillion-dollar-per-year revenues for those industries. This book offers readers a broad view of the landscape of becoming a parent in contemporary times.

NOTES

1 According to their family members, Iris and Louis attempted to conceive for fifteen years. Their unsuccessful attempts, largely blamed on his age (seventy), led the couple to Egypt, and specifically to the Christian community from which Iris hails.

2 *See* Juan Carlos Llorca, *Guatemala Adoptions under New, Painstaking Scrutiny*, The Virginian-Pilot, June 20, 2008, at Q3.

3 *See* Ines Benites, *Guatemala: New Law to End Adoption Business*, Inter Press Service, Dec. 11, 2008. According to Hector Dionisio, legal counsel to Covenant House's Latin American branch, "Adoption has become a business here. Children are produced for export, distorting the meaning of adoption, which is to benefit children who do not have a family."

Madonna in Malawi. On a littered, red-dirt field, the pop star, bedecked in white, holds the ear of a little, dark-skinned boy and peers attentively into his face. On this trip, she might rescue another impoverished African child from a fate that will likely be like so many others in his homeland: joblessness and poverty. Madonna and other celebrities have made Africa their cause, some by adopting children from that region, even when it skirts the law. (Shavawn Rissman/AP.)

PART ONE. WHAT MAKES A MARKET? EFFICIENCY, ACCOUNTABILITY, AND RELIABILITY *OR* GETTING THE BABIES WE WANT

> Although economists have studied extensively the efforts of government to regulate the economy, public regulation of social and personal life has largely escaped economic attention. With the rapid development of the economic analysis of nonmarket behavior, the conceptual tools necessary for the economic study of social (as distinct from narrowly economic) regulation are now at hand. Nor is there any basis for a presumption that government does a good job of regulating nonmarket behavior; if anything, the negative presumption created by numerous studies of economic regulation should carry over to the nonmarket sphere.
>
> – Elisabeth Landes and Richard Posner

Part One of this book examines the economic contours of baby making and adoption. This section critiques the ways in which market dynamics have become central to creating families. Assisted reproductive technology is now a multibillion-dollar industry, which thrives on market principles. Not to be overlooked, however, are the ways in which adoption is a global industry, promoted and sustained by economic exchanges between individuals, agencies, and foreign governments. To overlook these contours is to ignore the sociocultural nuances of family making in the twenty-first century. Authors in this section consider the upsides and also the pitfalls of baby markets. They examine who benefits from and who is harmed by the ways in which baby creating and baby sharing operate in the United States and globally.

1 Baby Markets

MICHELE BRATCHER GOODWIN

> Watt and her husband, Jason Hillard, residents of Athens, Ohio, wanted to adopt a child. When they saw Jolie on that magazine cover with her adopted daughter, their decision to raise a child from Ethiopia was clear.[1]

> And with that magical stroke of the pen, the door to a whole world of plentiful, newborn, brown-skinned little boys . . . opened up to me from behind the curtain marked, "Doesn't Care."
>
> – Patricia Williams

The recent backlash against famed pop musician and actress Madonna in her attempt to adopt a little girl from Malawi highlights a growing social tension and cultural criticism in transnational adoptions. In that case, the celebrity was criticized for using her status to skirt the country's stricter adoption criteria, which includes a yearlong residency requirement. Madonna's public life perhaps offers an unfair advantage to critics, who can trace her lifestyle and travels through the Internet, Twitter, and newspapers. To them, international residency requirements are a farce, especially when celebrities can circumvent such routine protocols by exploiting the financial weaknesses of governments. By donating funds to the state or establishing charities in those countries, celebrities can seemingly expedite the adoption process in ways that middle-class people, who wait years, cannot.

Clearly, with photos emerging of Madonna and her newest lover in South America and the United States,[2] she has not been spending much personal or professional time in Malawi. But should that matter, so long as a child is relieved from poverty? Do residency requirements serve any purpose beyond the symbolic in transnational adoptions as the children will depart without much memory of their native countries and grow up in the West?

Understandably, adoptive parents find market comparisons to the adoption process offensive. The free market in children, as a concept, is rejected based on what it symbolizes, including its argued resemblance to slavery or the auction block.[3] Yet, according to David Smolin, a professor of law and an adoptive parent, directly and indirectly, market forces or economic considerations influence adoptions in the United States to a greater extent than traditionally acknowledged. Recent celebrity adoptions and subsequent international pushback tell a complicated story about adult desire, children's needs, and the mishmash of state and international laws in the adoption realm.

Celebrities figure significantly in the public's perception about contemporary adoption. Often at the center of public focus are Hollywood celebrities and music moguls like Angelina Jolie or Madonna, who seem to defy the bureaucratic necessities that regular people endure such as wait lists, residency requirements, and stable homes. Cambodia, Malawi, and Ethiopia are among the countries where governments have accommodated celebrity adoptions. In turn, celebrities and the countries from which they adopt bring attention to the devastating conditions of children in orphanages, who desperately need families. In the words of one adoptive mother interviewed by *ABC News* in 2005, "In the grand scheme of things, she changed our lives. It's kind of hilarious to think of, but yeah, Angelina Jolie probably brought us an African child."[4] It is not entirely clear who changed the adoptive mom's life – Angelina or the child – but the Ohio couple now have an Ethiopian daughter, just like Brad Pitt and Angelina Jolie.

Perhaps because of the celebrity gloss on adoption, a broader chorus of critics is beginning to raise alarm bells. They wonder about the children in the United States whose urgent need for safe homes seems overlooked not only by celebrities, but by middle-class Americans who adopt abroad before considering domestic children from less exotic locations like Milwaukee, Detroit, and Newark. To those critics, celebrities and middle-class Americans who adopt abroad contribute to an international baby market. Commentators argue that the high cost of adopting children abroad and schemes to subsidize the costs for adoptive parents are evidence of baby markets.[5]

A. CONVENTIONAL WISDOM

Conventional wisdom and early legislation held the best interests of children at the center of all adoptions.[6] In 1851, Massachusetts passed the first adoption law in the United States. That law served as a model for other states – and each emphasized the best interests of the child. Adoptions functioned as a child welfare model for abandoned, abused, neglected, and orphaned youth.[7] Adoptions resolved a social crisis as well as a public health nightmare, as abused, neglected, and homeless children were often malnourished and in need of medical treatment. The charitable function of adoption removed children from desperate situations and repositioned them within families – thereby fulfilling a public service.

Contemporary adoption services expose more complicated motives, from multiple (although nonetheless well-meaning) players. Aesthetic characteristics such as race, hair texture, eye color, and other market variables determine the welfare of children, or at least their likelihood of placement.[8] Between two ends of a spectrum, the first representing child welfare and the other "adult needs," the latter influences U.S. adoptions far more than imagined.[9]

This chapter scrutinizes financial considerations involved in adoption, including so-called baby valuing and rationing, and suggests that those transactions illustrate the market nature of adoptions in the United States. Certain parallels to assisted reproduction are apparent in the adoption realm but are not dealt with here. Other chapters in this volume capture and contest the extent to which market dynamics exist within the assisted reproduction realm. I leave to those chapters the task of unpacking markets in that domain.

This chapter illuminates market consciousness in the adoption process, arguing that economic interests influence adoption more than we might like to acknowledge.[10] It demonstrates that the adoption process is more like a market than less so. Section B frames the adoption market debate, arguing that current adoption indeed resembles a free market. It describes current adoption processes in the United States, which are governed by factors of availability, race, class, and aesthetic preferences. Section C scrutinizes the moral and ethical obstacles to recognition of a market in adoption: the degradation of personhood, the charitable roots of child placement, and the social costs associated with adoption. Section D examines alternative adoption models, including price caps and taxation alternatives, and suggests that each model tramples on established values. It argues for greater transparency and information in the adoption process and proposes a different model to effectuate adoptions in the United States.

B. THE POSNER PARADIGM

1. The Market Debate

Thirty years ago, Elisabeth Landes and Richard Posner encountered strident criticism from scholars concerned that their 1978 publication on adoption, colloquially known as the "baby-selling article," endorsed a market in babies.[11] In that article, Landes and Posner proposed evaluating the efficiency of adoption through a market analysis.[12] They applied a law and economics framework to study the pros and cons of incentives in adoption as well as mechanisms that could increase the matching of babies to couples.[13] Ironically, their article attracted criticism about incentive models that preexisted the article's publication.[14] Opponents decried the language of efficiency in evaluating adoptions, suggesting that it reduced children to objects in a mechanical economic analysis.[15]

Posner's critics characterized the article, "The Economics of the Baby Shortage," as promoting the introduction of financial incentives in the adoption allocation process, thereby suggesting that Landes and Posner were tainting an unflawed and otherwise purely (or primarily so) altruistic process. Transaction fees received by adoption agencies were believed to be so negligible at the time or infrequently present as to pose insignificant ethical problems. Some critics thereby dismissed the resemblance between transactional fees, indirect incentives, and payments. They refused to entertain the proposition that an adoption "market" already existed.

Refusal then and now to acknowledge financial incentives in adoption does not negate the free market's existence and influence in adoption services. In other words, a community preference that adoptions are free from financial transactions does not mean that it is so.[16] Nor does it mean that financial transactions in these spheres necessarily bring about offensive externalities. However, financial transactions and interests govern the adoption process both directly and indirectly. Financial exchanges, including exorbitant fees paid to adoption agencies, medical payments for birth mothers (or surrogates in the case of in vitro babies), transportation costs, and living expenses,[17] although characterized under the umbrella of "transactional costs," resemble payments in most other spheres.[18] Some commentators, including Posner, describe these payments as part of the adoption "black market."[19] To be clear, there seems to be very little that is *illegal* about these transactions, which is implied by the *black market* terminology[20]; rather, exorbitant transaction fees and direct payments to parents and their attorneys are evidence of a de facto, largely unregulated adoption free market.[21]

2. The Free Market: Direct and Indirect

a. Deregulation. Several factors give indication of the free market in adoptions. First, adoption services are largely unregulated and an entrepreneurial enterprise in a growing number of cases.[22] Deregulation is a key factor in free market economics. Robert Horowitz explains that deregulation of a given market must occur to obtain a truly free and competitive marketplace.[23]

Babies are routinely adopted indirectly through the free market by way of an agency process. Some agencies are licensed, and others are not. In the agency setting, fee bundling often occurs, and an adoptive couple pays one fee, which supports salaries for staff, medical expenses for the birth mother, and transportation costs.[24] Babies can also be adopted directly through the free market, by way of independent agents who facilitate the process, including lawyers, pastors, and doctors.[25] Unlike agencies, independent agents may be interested in only one specific adoption. These processes are not monitored by any federal agency, nor are there special exams or classes that agents must take before earning money for facilitating adoptions. State laws govern part of the adoption process but are generally inadequate in addressing the interstate and transnational aspects of adoption. Thus, even with the best intentions of promoting child welfare, children become exposed to free market dynamics. In the free market realm, supply, demand, and aesthetic preference factor significantly in the cost of a baby.[26]

Distinctive adoption practices can be seen prior to and after 1973, the year of the landmark *Roe v. Wade* decision. In 1973, 2.3 percent of women adopted; twenty years later, that percentage dropped to 1.3 percent.[27] Prior to 1973, abortions were illegal, and single motherhood and unwed pregnancies were taboo. Almost 20 percent of unwed white women placed their children for adoption prior to 1973. Since 1973, researchers estimate that as few as 1.7 percent of white unwed mothers place their babies for adoption. Some commentators attribute the low surrender rates to the legalization of abortions (i.e., women are choosing to abort rather than endure pregnancies and have babies). On the other hand, single parenthood is less stigmatized now among certain classes of Americans than prior to 1973.

According to a recent report by the National Center for Health Statistics, nearly 40 percent of births in the United States are to unwed mothers. In raw numbers, this means that 1.7 million children were born to unwed parents – a 25 percent rise in just five years.[28] This trend is most noticeable in black and Latino communities, where 72 percent and 51 percent of births are to unwed parents, respectively. Paula England, a Stanford professor, points out, however, that her study, which tracked unwed parents of color over five years, revealed that 80 percent remained in committed relationships with their children's other parent, and 50 percent lived together.[29] Thus single parenting and abortion add to the debate on child availability for adoption but do not fully explain the financial variations and costs distinguishing adoption fees for white versus black children in the United States.

b. Race-based baby valuing. Second, baby valuing indicates that racial and genetic preferences determine or can help to predict adoption costs and fees. Consider the following: couples may spend upward of fifty thousand dollars to adopt a healthy white infant.[30] Black infants, however, are adopted for as little as four thousand dollars.[31] Adoption agencies attempt to clarify this discrepancy by explaining that black children are more difficult to place than white children,[32] and therefore the costs associated with adopting white children are higher. This logic appears flawed, even though it is true that black children wait longer for permanent placements.[33] Why would it cost more to do less, if transaction costs were based *purely* on the labor and transactions involved?[34] If placing white children is far easier than placing black babies, it would seem that *less work* would result in *less pay* and lower fees. Instead, fee structures based on race give evidence that adoption is subject to the free market forces of supply, demand, and preference.[35] In this market, racial preference matters; biracial children also attract higher fees than black babies.[36]

The National Association of Black Social Workers. The impact of the National Association of Black Social Workers's (NABSW) urgent call against white families adopting African American children cannot be ignored. In the 1970s, the organization campaigned against transracial or interracial adoptions. The focus of their concern was a question that persists in international adoptions, namely, will the adopting parents prepare (or be capable of preparing) their new sons and daughters for healthy, well-adjusted lives in a racially divided society, where social interactions – even within their families – might sharply differ?

Members of the organization, including Charles Mays, suggest that NABSW's position must be understood within the context of the time. Deep patterns of housing, employment, and education segregation meant that African American children adopted into white families in the 1970s and 1980s were isolated and lacked the opportunity to interact with children or role models who resembled them. Equally, it seems, NABSW's leadership feared that white parents would be unable to cope with racism and social stigma experienced by their children, ultimately undermining the children's self-esteem and trust. According to NABSW,

> understanding the historical experiences and their impact on a group of people is essential to developing relevant support services. People of African ancestry have distinct traits and characteristics that are important to raising healthy children of African ancestry. These experiences are typically absent from assessment models and practice decisions.[37]

David Eng explores these dynamics in transnational adoptions of Asian children by white American parents. In a lecture at Barnard College in spring 2009, Professor

Eng suggested that the early transracially adopting parents were oblivious to the unique and often traumatic encounters their new children experienced.

On November 9, 2009, the Evan B. Donaldson Adoption Institute published what is likely to be the "most extensive" study on identity development in adopted adults in the United States. The study, which involved 468 adopted adults, sheds light on interracial and transnational adoption. Findings from the study were immediately picked up by the *New York Times* and other media likely because this was the first time that a study focused on adults rather than children. Most compelling were the narratives of adult adoptees from South Korea (179 participated in the study). Most of the study's participants were adopted as babies or toddlers and grew up in two-parent, white families. Here is what they reported:

> Eighty percent [experienced] discrimination from strangers and 75 percent from classmates. Nearly half (48%) reported negative experiences due to their race in interaction with childhood friends. A notable finding was that 39 percent of Korean respondents reported race-based discrimination from teachers.[38]

Nearly 80 percent of South Korean adoptees grew up thinking of themselves as or wishing they were white. The study participants also disclosed considerable pushback from their white parents when they disclosed the desire to learn more about their ethnic identity. According to one woman, later interviewed by the *New York Times*, her adoptive parents saw her desire to go to Korea as a sign of rejection, she revealed "my adoptive mother is really into genealogy, tracing her family to Sweden, and she was upset with me because I wanted to find out who I was."[39] Her story was echoed by other study participants.

Ironically, NABSW's early concerns about transracial adoptions are reverberating after the Evan B. Donaldson Adoption Institute report. The Institute's recommendations are somewhat in line with early statements issued by NABSW. For example, the Institute calls for the expansion of "parental preparation and post-placement support for those adopting across race and culture," and the "development of empirically based practices and resources to prepare transracially and transculturally adopted youth to cope with racial bias."

Nonetheless, NABSW's critics blame the organization's leadership on the low rates of black adoptions. The seemingly intractable problems that accompany black placements are alarming to critics and the organization. On their Web site, NABSW reminds readers that African American children wait longer in foster care than all other ethnic groups and represent 40 percent of all children in foster care, which is staggering considering that African Americans are less than 15 percent of the total U.S. population.

Measuring the impact of NABSW's position on contemporary adoptions remains difficult. Fifteen years ago, the federal government enacted the Multi-Ethnic Placement Act and, soon after, the Interethnic Placement Act and the Adoption and Safe Families Act, in 1996 and 1997, respectively. These legislative efforts directly promote interracial adoption by requiring agencies to look beyond race and ethnicity in an effort to remove as many children from foster care as possible and place them in loving homes. Thus, as a matter of law, Congress has made a very bold attempt to urge the placement of African American children into homes that will embrace them. As a result, some scholars are skeptical about whether NABSW's 1972 position detracts from whites adopting African American children. For them, white families simply do not want to adopt African American children, even though they are abundantly available.

Racialized adoptions. Although an "estimated 2 million American families" are looking to adopt, the majority will pass over black babies for children from abroad.[40] A recent study published by the National Center for Health Statistics reveals the ways in which race matters in adoption.[41] Whereas 86.4 percent of black women would accept a white child, only 72.5 percent of white women would accept a black child, and only 1.8 percent of white women expressed a preference for a black child.[42] Most notably, more women expressed a preference for adopting a child with severe physical or mental disabilities than a preference for adopting a black child.[43]

In reality, adoption agencies and so-called independent adoption agents establish fees with adoptive parents based on characteristics of children in the adoption supply pool such as race, gender, and supposed genetic strengths, including the parents' intellectual aptitude.[44] In U.S. adoptions, white children are more highly valued than black children by both adoption agencies and, obviously, by those who seek to adopt them.[45] A *Chicago Sun Times* report found that "babies who have two white parents cost the most and those who have two black parents cost the least."[46] Adoptive parents are acutely aware that competition is involved in free market adoptions.[47] Thus, those serious about adopting a white baby, and with the resources to do so, realize that balking at the high costs associated with those adoptions would prove futile.

But for the racialized nature of adoption, the market in babies and children might be less detectable. If U.S. adoptions were primarily focused on child welfare and charity, rather than adult need and desire, the costs associated with adopting white children would not exceed that of black children. A child welfare focus in adoption that emphasizes the best interests of *all* children might avoid artificial values attaching to racial characteristics. Why spend more to adopt a white child if, in fact, the social and moral motivations are the same – to serve the best interests of a child?

Thus, pursuit of the best interests of children in adoptions is modest fiction. Even if the rate of adoption for white babies exceeded that of their black counterparts, black children might nevertheless be second in line to foreign adoption if the fulfillment of the best interests for U.S. babies was the reality. But sadly, it is not. According to the Department of Health and Human Services, many couples wait more than eighteen months, and spend as much as thirty thousand dollars, to adopt children from abroad,[48] bypassing the less "expensive" and less desired black babies.[49] In fact, according to a recent report, adoption of black children can be facilitated in less than three weeks.[50]

c. Social valuing

> If the mother wanted to show a commitment to her daughter, then she should learn English to the extent that her daughter had.[51]

The third factor that provides evidence of a free market in U.S. adoptions is the use of financial status of adoptive parents in the child allocation process. In this capacity, judges and social workers play significant roles. Adoptive parents' social status, including household income and family type, figures significantly in adoption decision making.[52] Angela Kupenda, Zanita Fenton, Kim Forde-Mazrui, and other child welfare law scholars provide an interesting race-based critique of the challenges faced by families of color seeking to adopt.[53] According to these scholars, black families encounter greater obstacles in qualifying for child placements.[54] They suggest that the prevalence of single-parent households weighs against black families, as does lower income status.[55] Thus, potentially, black adoptive parents are comparatively less competitive players in the free market for children; they will lose more often than white parents, even if their goals are to adopt black children.[56]

More recently, immigration status, regardless of legal or illegal residency, might affect whether parental rights are protected or possibly terminated.[57] A Tennessee court recently removed an eleven-year-old girl from the custody of her mother, a Mexican migrant worker, and placed her with a family that "lives in a brick ranch house with a basketball hoop in the driveway, a swimming pool in the backyard."[58] One of Linda's teachers took a special interest in her and petitioned for her adoption.[59] The case attracted considerable attention as Judge Barry Tatum demanded that the mother, Felipa Berrera, *learn to speak English* before visitations would be permitted with her daughter, whose first language is Spanish.[60] Ironically, Linda Berrera Cano was never surrendered by her mother to the state, nor was she in foster care when she was placed with the Patterson family.[61] Instead, Linda was simply a poor, migrant worker's child who missed some days of school to care for her siblings. It is more than likely that Linda suffered from the conditions that poverty typically produces. But is it unreasonable to address the underlying conditions of poverty through the arbitrary displacement of children from their parents?

Tennessee law provides for direct petition to courts in cases of child abuse and neglect. Most would view this law as progress and in the best interests of children; after all, it avoids removal delays. Deciding, however, whether this case and its aftermath were about the welfare of the child or the desires of the adults is more complicated. The facts of the Berrera case seem unique, thereby leaving us with the impression that the case itself is an aberration from traditional adoption practices. Nevertheless, this unique case provides limited precedent for wealthier individuals to directly petition courts to adopt handpicked children. Poverty, immigrant status, limited political clout, and limited English proficiency may factor significantly in one's ability to effectively compete for a child, despite a biological connection and preexisting close relationships.[62]

d. Unrestrained international market. Finally, private, transnational adoptions, including celebrity adoptions (e.g., Madonna and Angelina Jolie), provide evidence of market competition. Foreign adoptions figure significantly in U.S. adoption services,[63] with interesting growth on three fronts. First, the exotification of Africa and the colonizing of black wombs provide an interesting Petri dish of topics to unravel. Celebrity adoptions in Africa are hailed for giving attention to the plight of Africans but also illuminate the tension of domestic adoptions. As one commentator recently noted, Africa, but not Alabama . . . why? Second, overwhelmingly, white couples who are unable to locate white babies for adoption in the United States are increasingly looking for and adopting children from abroad, including China, South Korea, Guatemala, Russia, and eastern European countries.[64] Couples who decide to adopt from abroad pay far more than the costs associated with adopting black children in the United States, including international transportation fees, transactional costs with foreign governments, and fees locally and abroad.[65] In this way, they exercise another key component of free markets: choice.[66]

Third, a notable trend is affecting the lives of African American children. Canadians, Germans, Swedes, and other predominantly white ethnic groups are adopting black children from the United States.[67] With open adoptions, there are no restrictions on the adoption of American children to foreign couples, as long as they can meet the requirements and fees established by adoption agencies and birth parents.[68] Of the many ironies, one which has not escaped the scrutiny of commentators is the dramatic difference in costs associated with these adoptions. The adoption of African American children and babies usually costs about four thousand dollars per child – between 8 and 13 percent of the costs associated with adopting a white baby in the United States or a child from abroad.[69]

C. MARKET PITFALLS AND CONVENTIONAL WISDOM

According to conventional wisdom, the needs and best interests of children would always prevail over the special interests of the adults seeking to adopt them.[70] After the enactment of the first modern state adoption statute in 1851, adoption in the United States evolved as both a state judicial process and a specialized child welfare service to promote the best interests of children in need of permanent homes. Quite correctly, systems were developed to guard against a child being placed into an abusive family or one that sought to exploit the child's labor, sex, or talent. In reality, however, adoption has never been a flawless system.[71] Adoption is no longer a domestic welfare service that attends primarily to the needs of children born in the United States.

That more than five hundred thousand children live in foster care arrangements gives some indication of the strain on the current child welfare system to serve the needs of all kids. But as interesting is what such statistics reveal about potential parents. Each year, thousands of children are adopted from abroad, often through cumbersome, complicated processes that can take years before a foreign child arrives. The irony is that many Americans would like to (and will) adopt, and many children in the United States need adoptive families but will be passed over. Sixty-seven percent of all those in the public foster care system are children of color.[72] Children of color will wait considerably longer for adoption than their white counterparts. For example, in Michigan, white children are three times more likely to be adopted from foster care than their black counterparts.[73]

Adoption is a multimillion-dollar transnational service, in which aesthetics and genetic traits are significantly scrutinized.[74] However, there are pitfalls in the free market model, in which wealth and the ability to navigate complicated systems with the aid of sophisticated lawyers may prevail over child welfare. In such cases, the best interests of children are subordinate to adult preferences.

Critics of the free market in adoption rightfully illuminate the tensions arising from financial considerations of "sensitive subjects," or what Professor Margaret Radin refers to as the "market inalienable."[75] For example, Professor Radin argues that our very "personhood" is threatened by the rapid expanse of commodification in our daily reality. Yet what even the most insightful critics fail to grasp is the diminution of value according to race and social hierarchies that becomes apparent in the current free market model. In other words, opponents criticize overt commodification regimes within adoption but tend to overlook the less obvious or subtle forms of commodification, including that which places different values on children based on racial aesthetics.

The free market model is not like slavery, but according to some scholars, it does reproduce the class and social distinctions found in the legacy of American slavery.[76] Free market opponents seemed to have advanced two distinct ideological criticisms of free markets in adoption. First is that a market analysis was always inappropriate to the study of human subjects.[77] Second, critics suggested that although costs are involved in the adoption process, it is unfair and inaccurate to characterize those fees in market terms.[78] In other words, to imply that the adoption process is subject to market forces of supply, demand, and preferences would tarnish the reputation of the industry.[79]

Unfortunately, financial incentives in adoptions cannot be easily dismissed, nor can we pretend that by ignoring class and the considerable costs involved in domestic and international adoptions, a market has not developed. To ignore the less attractive nuances of adoptions is to presume that adoption services in the United States operate entirely in the best interests of children and that adult interests are *always* subordinated to those of children. Were the best interests of all adoptable children served by unacknowledged market considerations, there would be very little need for further scholarship scrutinizing the mechanics of adoption. After all, adoption is a very sensitive process that involves vulnerable children and adults, as both groups have an interest and a deep psychological desire to be part of a loving family.[80]

D. VALUES AND SOCIAL IMPACT

I have argued that a free market in adoptions already exists and that altruism as a primary goal in adoption has been overshadowed by acquiescence to parental desires. Financial incentives, payments to mothers, exorbitant fees provided to adoption agencies, and the robust enterprise of independent, direct adoptions provide evidence of free market forces in adoption. Determining, then, whether the state has a future role in shaping the adoption market or whether it should be allowed to freely exist without state interference is a relevant and timely question. Because parental autonomy has been so strongly guarded within the common law and constitutional law tradition, we may tend to overlook the government's arguable affirmative duty to be involved in the "sensitive" legal issues involving children.

Unconsciously, individuals often make choices that have significant – sometimes grave – implications for social policy. The method that individuals use to make decisions with regard to acquiring children can have both positive and negative social consequences. To the extent that those individual decisions can negatively impact society, economically, morally, or by burdening social services, arguably, the state has a role in regulation. In the reproductive context, the case of Nadya Suleman provides a telling example on this point. The birth of her octuplets involved more than forty doctors, numerous nurses, and medical expenses that she could not afford to pay. In the context of adoption, individuals make choices that can have significant implications for a broader society, about which we should be concerned. If the by-products of free adoptions are two-tiered racial systems or racial hierarchies, might it be an issue worth greater social scrutiny? Beyond race, we might also be concerned about the crowding out of middle-class whites (and other groups) as they are priced out of the market for white babies, which has a double negative effect.

If the market responds only to the highest bidder with regard to white babies, is it possible that white babies will only be placed with wealthier families? The problem created by the free market is the legitimizing of a troubling normative view that adoption should only be among the wealthy, ignoring class diversity in the United States. This could have a deterrent effect on so-called class-diverse adoptions. In other words, well-meaning, altruistic white parents capable of and well positioned to share their homes and love with another child, although not so wealthy as to own a pool and live in a gated community, could be shut out of the adoption free market. Finally, there is the question as to social involvement in shaping the lives of adoptees. Should we, as a society, be concerned that a special class of adoptees is created through free market adoptions? After all, wealth-based adoptions could lead to children being funneled into an elite class. But what are we to do about it?

How we address the free market in adoption or individual decision making in adoption will have a significant social impact. There are several options we might weigh, and each is burdened by what might be considered undesirable consequences by market proponents. To the extent that agents are needed to service the adoption process, financial transactions will always be involved. Our challenge is to determine a proper balance between promoting and fulfilling the needs and best interests of children, the taste for government regulation, and respect for individual autonomy.

There are several options we might consider in responding to the market dynamics in adoption. They include price caps, taxation, and information. None of these options is perfect. Each is burdened in some manner as all institutional choices carry certain constraints and limitations.

1. Price Caps

One option is to regulate the service fees associated with adoption. Under this plan, service fees could be capped by the state to achieve affordability, uniformity, efficiency, and predictability. In this scenario, all adoptions would ultimately cost the same, regardless of aesthetics such as the child's race, gender, religion, or other physical characteristics, including eye color, hair texture, and complexion.

In this context, the price cap could be established by the state with consultation from adoption agencies and other key players such as prospective parents, adoptive parents, and adult adoptees. To establish an equitable price cap that takes into account operating expenses and other institutional costs, empirical data would be needed. Although most price caps take into account supply and demand, in this instance, the purpose of the price cap would be to avoid scarcity of a particular type that deeply influences the costs of adoption. In other words, real overhead should be the focus here, rather than wealth maximization because of the third-party effects and externalities involved in this particular level of market exchange.

The upside of price caps is that they institutionalize standard pricing, which, in turn, promotes greater predictability, consumer knowledge, and bargaining based on quality, weeding out the inference that costs equate with quality. In other words, it might be inferred in the current adoption process that black babies are valueless because the fees associated with placing them are so low. In turn, such assumptions reify problematic social perceptions, which, although hailing from slavery, have a surprising tenacity in contemporary times.

Price caps in this sphere would tell Americans what is reasonable to pay in service costs to an agent or agency handling adoptions. Price caps provide a reasonable balance between operating costs and profits. In this instance, the distinguishing characteristics between adoption firms, such as quality of communication, reputation in the field, treatment of the children or babies, and rapport with the prospective parents, would help to distinguish one agency from the others.

Of course, there are disadvantages associated with price caps, including the slippage in quality control. Price caps do not necessarily incentivize industries to invest in the products they bring to the market. Thus, price caps are not the ultimate consumer protection; they do not guarantee that firms will operate at the same quality level.

To the extent that even with price caps, the adoption of some children would be unaffordable, there could be adjustments. Critics would likely eschew this option as it interferes with individual autonomy (and the free market). Others might oppose such an option because it unveils what we would otherwise want unrevealed, which is the free market in adoptions.

2. Taxation

A second option to monitor and control the social impact of individual decision making is through taxation. The purpose of taxation would be to reduce the government's subsidization of social programs to address the externalities resulting from individual decision making, which, in these cases, pose certain harmful social costs to children. There are two types of taxation model that could be considered: a progressive tax and a luxury tax. Taxation options are used by governments to address markets that have negative social impacts, such as alcohol and tobacco, and at other times, luxury items.

Under the first taxation model, all adoptions with transaction fees could be assessed a progressive tax, meaning that the government-imposed fee would not be capped, but rather, proportionate to the adoption fee. *Progressive* describes the distributional effect of the state-imposed tax. Under this proposal, all adoptions would have a 10 percent fee attached. Operationally, a potential parent looking to adopt a child who arrives with a four-thousand-dollar service fee pays only four hundred dollars in taxes, bringing the fees associated with that adoption to forty-four hundred dollars. An adoption that would otherwise cost fifty thousand dollars would have a five-thousand-dollar tax attached, thereby bringing the cost of that adoption to fifty-five thousand dollars. A progressive tax avoids the government subsidizing the negative impacts resulting from high-end preferences or tastes.

It can be argued that progressive taxes help to achieve vertical equity, accomplish utilitarian goals, and stimulate lower-income (or lower-fee) markets. According to Adam Smith, in *The Wealth of Nations*,

> The necessaries of life occasion the great expense of the poor. They find it difficult to get food, and the greater part of their little revenue is spent in getting it. The luxuries and vanities of life occasion the principal expense of the rich, and a magnificent house embellishes and sets off to the best advantage all the other luxuries and vanities which they possess. A tax upon house-rents, therefore, would in general fall heaviest upon the rich; and in this sort of inequality there would not, perhaps, be anything very unreasonable. It is not very unreasonable that the rich should contribute to the public expense, not only in proportion to their revenue, but something more than in that proportion.[81]

Progressive taxes help to incentivize markets in low-demand goods and services – in this case, adoptions. Under progressive tax regimes, the propensity to engage in the market increases, or the disincentive to participate in the market is mediated. In adoption contexts, potential parents might be incentivized to adopt those children for whom fees and taxes are less. The price gap becomes intensified under a progressive tax regime, which benefits children at the lower end of the service fee–cost spectrum.

Progressive taxes operate in a nonlinear manner, rising according to the cost of a particular item. Adoptions that typically cost more will cost even more under a progressive tax regime. Thus, there is an inherent disincentive to pay for higher-end items, which will likely drive those service fees down. Adoption agencies are unlikely to hold out for higher fees when the lives of children are at stake. On the other hand, to the extent that the market for higher-fee children remains robust, those who participate in those markets will absorb those costs.

The fairness of progressive taxes can be debated. For example, the economic burden is most felt on those who can afford to pay the tax. On the other hand, progressive taxes disproportionately burden the wealthier. To be sure, the wealthy can avoid high-end progressive taxes by adopting children, rather than babies, as they tend to have lower fees attached, or by adopting black babies and children, who are quite affordable.

An alternative to imposing a progressive tax to address social impacts of contemporary adoption would be to implement a luxury tax. Luxury taxes are generally associated with the purchase of extravagant purchases. Most people will think of expensive vehicles, jewelry, or real estate as luxury tax items – and they would be right. Luxury taxes serve a symbolic purpose – they are usually imposed on purchases or items that people can live without.

However, at times, luxury taxes are applied to the purchase of goods that are not so luxurious but that lead to negative social impacts and externalities such as cigarettes and alcohol. Although there has been pushback against cigarette taxes, the impact of cigarette smoking, including lung cancer, emphysema, and secondhand smoke, are often thought to justify the state making smokers pay for those externalities. In other words, third parties are affected by the decisions people make to smoke. Luxury taxes could also be called *disincentive taxes* – they aim to shape social behavior and values by discouraging the purchase or acquisition of certain goods. The problem with luxury taxes is that they may not discourage the behavior the state seeks to regulate. Consumers seem willing to purchase cigarettes even at a higher cost, but complain about it later.

The correlations to a social harm may be more difficult to understand when applied to luxurious cars, homes, jewelry, or babies. After all, who is harmed by the purchase of a luxury car? And adoption, by its nature, is perceived as achieving a positive social good. Yet the disincentive effect of luxury taxes can serve an important function. In this case, the state would wish to disincentive adoption agencies overpricing or driving up the costs associated with adopting white children. A second goal for the state would be to establish equity in the costs associated with adopting children. Thus, driving down the inflated costs associated with adoption would achieve a social good.

Alternatively, adoption fees over a reasonable dollar amount could be taxed at a higher, luxury rate. Adoption taxes would help to generate state and federal funds, which could be used to promote the social welfare of children in foster care and adoption centers, thereby facilitating a positive social impact. For example, taxation on free market adoptions could be used to provide better care for children who are more difficult to place, including children with disabilities, older children, and black children. Funds generated through taxation could also help to fund private foster care or permanent placements. Critics might equally be troubled by this model and suggest that it detracts from adoptions of so-called desirable babies by taxing well-meaning couples out of the adoption arena. Moreover, they could argue that individual autonomy is compromised through government taxation on adoption.

3. Information

A final option to address the negative social impact of adoption free markets is information. Government-sponsored information campaigns are used to promote organ donation, forward antismoking, entreat mothers to avoid alcohol consumption during pregnancy, reduce abortions, and promote abstinence. In the context of abortion, some states mandate a waiting period and that information be provided to the woman or girl seeking an abortion. Could this model be used with free market adoptions?

Information is a powerful tool in influencing behavior, whether inspiring patriotism, encouraging philanthropy for important causes, or deterring certain conduct. The power to influence behavior through the sharing of information in adoption cases would undoubtedly be true. Adoption agencies that service foreign placements invest in information sharing. Sometimes that information resembles advertising, but most often, it provides stories about the plight of children living abroad. Those stories resonate with well-meaning individuals, especially those open to welcoming children into their homes. The same models should be applied domestically, with one exception. The information model should be pushed further in the United States. Potential parents should be made aware of the social costs associated with passing over American babies and children. These externalities include high dropout rates for children in foster care, higher rates of involvement in the criminal justice system, intergenerational poverty, and sometimes physical and sexual abuse while in foster care.

Providing information to potential parents presumes their concern for the best interests of all children. Information mandates are predicated on the belief that those who receive the information are inclined to be sensitive and rational about the impacts of their behavior within the broader contexts of adoption and society. The benefit of information mandates is that they can achieve an important social good with minimum burden and economic cost imposed on citizens. It is unknown whether information mandates in the context of free market adoptions would be effective in educating potential parents as to the impact of their decision making. Even if parents become aware of the social consequences resulting from their child seeking, it does not follow that information will change their behavior. This is an empirical question that should be pursued.

Currently, adoption agencies provide information to prospective parents, but perhaps there is an additional role for government to the extent that adoptions are not in isolation, but impact society. This third option of greater governmental involvement through providing information as to the social impact of race-based decision making in adoption is perhaps the least invasive of the three options.

E. CONCLUSION

If market forces exist in adoptions, should there be state-based regulation? Even Posner agrees that the vulnerable status of children requires some level of state participation and oversight in the adoption process to prevent the exploitation and denigration of children. How should the fine line of state responsibility and prospective parental autonomy be balanced? Greater state involvement in adoptions could create bureaucracies plagued by inefficiencies that ultimately deter or disincentivize adoptions. Children who otherwise would be adopted might wait longer than anticipated. It is important to keep in mind that although there are certain potential drawbacks or pitfalls to governmental involvement, with attention to those particular issues, externalities can be overcome.

The attacks on marketplace inquiry in the realm of adoption generated by the Landes–Posner baby-selling article unintentionally served to obscure less altruistic adoption practices and ignored relevant questions in the supply and demand of children. The backlash, to some extent, stifled dialogue about the realities of adoption in the United States. Until that point, and not much since, scholars have not rigorously scrutinized the market nature of adoptions and child supply. Greater dialogue is needed on this question, which constructively examines the roles of government, judges, adoption agencies, and independent agents. This chapter is an attempt to generate dialogue on market nuances of contemporary adoption.

NOTES

1 *Angelina Jolie Inspires International Adoptions*, ABC NEWS, Oct. 1, 2005.

2 Richard Simpson, *Will Madonna Make Toyboy Jesus Luz Husband No. 3?* THE DAILY MAIL, SEPT. 28, 2009.

3 David M. Smolin, *Intercountry Adoption as Child Trafficking*, 39 VAL. U. L. REV. 281, 287 (2004) (arguing that adoption practices resemble the purchase of human beings, which is analogous to slavery practices).

4 *Angelina Jolie*, *supra* note 1.

5 The high cost of adopting children (especially those in higher demand) is often evidenced through schemes to subsidize the costs for adoptive parents. *See* Laura Bailey, *Execs Expand Their Families through Adoptions*, CRAIN'S DETROIT BUSINESS, Nov. 1, 2004, at 22 (describing a system of tax credits for adoptive parents of both foreign and American children to ease the often hefty financial burden of adoption); Joe Manning, *More Firms Helping Staff with Costs of Adoption*, MILWAUKEE JOURNAL SENTINEL, Aug. 23, 2004, at D1 (detailing how many employers are providing benefits to aid employees with fees associated with adoption, which have been described as "staggering"); Tess Nacelewicz, *More Love Than Money*, PORTLAND PRESS HERALD, Sept. 27, 2004, at A1 (describing a family wishing to adopt two additional Haitian children; the community organized fundraisers to help the family raise money for the adoption fees); Sylvia Slaughter, *Penny for Your Thoughts of Samuel*, TENNESSEAN, Oct. 23, 2004, at 1 (describing a charity project in which residents collected change to help defray the costs of adoption for a local family).

6 *See* Ruth Arlene Howe, *Adoption Laws and Practices in 2000: Serving Whose Interests?* 33 FAM. L.Q., 677 (2000).

7 *See* Jehnna Irene Hanan, *The Best Interest of the Child: Eliminating Discrimination in the Screening of Adoptive Parents*, 27 GOLDEN GATE U. L. REV. 167, 174 (1997).

8 Smolin, *supra* note 2, at 282 (stating that "the adoption system has become so intertwined with market behavior as to, in theory and practice, frequently permit child selling as a form of adoption"); *see also* Patricia J. Williams, *Spare Parts, Family Values, Old Children, Cheap*, 28 NEW ENG. L. REV. 913, 918 (1994) ("And with that magical stroke of the pen, the door to a whole world of plentiful, newborn, brown-skinned little boys . . . opened up to me from behind the curtain marked, 'Doesn't Care.')".

9 Howe, *supra* note 6.

10 Smolin, *supra* note 2, at 306 ("the effect is to create a market in babies, with high-demand characteristics of the infant [race, youth, and health] . . . being allocated to the highest bidder. This contradicts the legal conception that adoption is guided principally by the best interests of the child.").

11 *See, e.g.*, Elisabeth Landes & Richard Posner, *The Economics of the Baby Shortage*, 7 J. LEGAL STUD. 323 (1978) [*hereinafter* Landes & Posner]; Ronald A. Cass, *Coping with Life, Law, and Markets: A Comment on Posner and the Law-and-Economics Debate*, 67 B.U. L. REV. 73 (1987).

12 Landes & Posner.

13 *Id.*

14 *See* J. Robert S. Prichard, *A Market for Babies?* 34 U. Toronto L. Rev. 341 (1984).
15 Cass, *supra* note 10, at 76–7.
16 *See* Francesco Parisi & Ben W. F. Depoorter, *Continuing Tributes to the Honorable Richard A. Posner – Private Choices and Public Law: Richard A. Posner's Contributions to Family Law and Policy*, 17 J. Contemp. Health L. & Pol'y 403, 411 (2001) (arguing that the "selling" of babies already takes place legally).
17 National Adoption Information Clearinghouse, U.S. Department of Health & Human Services, *State Regulation of Adoption Expenses: State Statute Series* (2005), http://naic.acf.hhs.gov/general/legal/statutes/expenses.cfm.
18 Smolin, *supra* note 2, at 304 (likening payment of birth-related expenses to birth mothers to financial consideration for a right of first refusal if the birth mother ultimately decides to place the child in an adoptive home).
19 *See* Landes & Posner.
20 *See, e.g.*, Donald J. Boudreaux, *A Modest Proposal to Deregulate Infant Adoptions*, 15 Cato J. 117, 119 (1995) (describing that state laws govern monetary compensation given to birth mothers, which is allowed for out-of-pocket expenses related to the birth and prenatal care).
21 *See* Danielle Saba Donner, *The Emerging Adoption Market: Child Welfare Agencies, Private Middlemen, and "Consumer" Remedies*, 35 U. Louisville J. Fam. L. 473, 490 (1996–7) (arguing that the shift to a fee structure in the adoption process is a response to market forces).
22 Data are often inconsistent and unreliable because there is not a specialized agency responsible for data collection. *See, e.g.*, National Adoption Information Clearinghouse, U.S. Department of Health & Human Services, *How Many Children Were Adopted in 2000 and 2001?* (2004), http://naic.acf.hhs.gov/pubs/s_adopted/index.cfm.
23 *See, e.g.*, Robert B. Horowitz, *Understanding Deregulation*, 15 Theory & Soc'y 139 (1986) (explaining that deregulation of a given market [*e.g.*, telecommunications] must occur to obtain a truly free and competitive marketplace).
24 National Adoption Information Clearinghouse, U.S. Department of Health & Human Services, *Adoption Options: A Fact Sheet for Families* (2003), http://naic.acf.hhs.gov/pubs/f_adoptoption.cfm.
25 *Id.*
26 See Marianne Bitler & Madeline Zavodny, *Did Abortion Legalization Reduce the Number of Unwanted Children? Evidence from Adoptions*, 34 Persps. Sexual Reprod. & Health 25 (2002); Mark F. Testa, *When Children Cannot Return Home: Adoption and Guardianship*, 14 Future Children 115, 118 (2004).
27 Anjani Chandra, Joyce Abma, Penelope Maza, & Christine Bachrach, *Adoption, Adoption Seeking, and Relinquishment for Adoption in the United States*, 306 Adv. Data 1–16 (1999).
28 See National Center for Health Statistics, *Out of Wedlock Births*, http://www.cdc.gov/NCHS/fastats/unmarry.htm.
29 See Paula England, Unmarried Couples with Children (2007).
30 *See* Bonnie Miller Rubin, *Adoption Bill Targets Legal Loopholes*, Chicago Tribune, March 27, 2005, at Metro 1 (describing how the price of a [presumably white] American infant can "hit the $50,000 mark").
31 *See* Dusty Rhodes, *Baby Trade*, Illinois Times, Feb. 17, 2005, http://www.illinoistimes.com.
32 *See, e.g.*, Judith K. McKenzie, *Adoption of Children with Special Needs*, 3 Future Children, 62, 62 (1993) (characterizing children of color as having "special needs," resulting in more difficult placement into an adoptive home).

33 *See, e.g.*, Carla M. Curtis & Ramona W. Denby, *Impact of the Adoption and Safe Families Act (1997) on Families of Color: Workers Share Their Thoughts*, 85 FAMILIES SOC'Y 71 (2004) (stating generally that children of color wait longer in foster care to be adopted than do their white counterparts).

34 To the extent that discrimination was legally enforced and social values, with regard to reproduction, were delineated according to race and socioeconomic status, adoption services were affected just as any other social institution. Thus the best interests of young black children were, at best, limited to a model that restricted those adoptions to black families, a model that the National Association of Black Social Workers would later endorse. *See* Larry Elder, *Exporting Black/White Adoptions*, LONG BEACH PRESS-TELEGRAM, Feb. 28, 2005, at A15 (noting that "according to the National Adoption Center, government still allows agencies to use variables to calculate the 'best interest of the child.'"); *see* Hanan, *supra* note 7, at 176–7 (describing the NABSW's objection to interracial adoption as negatively affecting the formation of the child's racial identity). As a contemporary model, the disproportionately low adoption rate for black children in foster care gives some indication of the continued illusory nature of adoption as a specialized child-focused welfare service model. *See* Richard P. Barth, *Effects of Age and Race on the Odds of Adoption versus Remaining in Long-Term Out-of-Home Care*, 76 CHILD WELFARE 285, 288 (1997) (noting that white children in the Michigan foster care system are three times more likely to be adopted than black children).

35 *See, e.g.*, Martha M. Ertman, *What's Wrong with a Parenthood Market? A New and Improved Theory of Commodification*, 82 N.C. L. REV. 1, 10 (2003) ("Children who are racial minorities, such as African-American children, are sometimes cheaper to adopt than white children, a differential that seems to turn more on supply and demand than on agencies expending more money to place white children.").

36 *See* Rhodes, *supra* note 31 (describing how some adoption agencies charge more for biracial children than African American children).

37 *See* National Association of Black Social Workers, Preserving Families, http://www.nabsw.org/mserver/PreservingFamilies.aspx.

38 *See* Hollee McGinnis et al., *Beyond Culture Camp: Promoting Healthy Identity Information in Adoption*, http://www.adoptioninstitute.org/research/2009_11_culture_camp.php.

39 *See* Ron Nixon, *Adopted From Korea And in Search Of Identity*, N.Y. TIMES, Nov. 9, 2009, at A9–11.

40 *See Born in USA; Adopted in Canada*, 60 MINUTES (CBS television broadcast, March 10, 2005).

41 Anjani Chandra, Joyce Abma, Penelope Maza, & Christine Bachrach, *Adoption, Adoption Seeking, and Relinquishment for Adoption in the United States*, 306 ADV. DATA 1–16 (1999), http://www.cdc.gov/nchs/products/pubs/pubd/ad/301-310/ad306.htm.

42 *Id.*

43 *Id.*

44 *See* David Ray Papke, *Pondering Pasts Purposes: A Critical History of American Adoption Law*, 102 W. VA. L. REV. 459, 469 (1999) (framing modern adoption in the era of consumption; "In addition to purchasing their share of conventional consumer goods, many also seek to obtain the child held out by advertising and general cultural imagery as central to a good, successful life."). Furthermore, several cases bear out the assumption that adoption has become a market governed by the laws of economics and that the adoptive parents' wishes to obtain a healthy, genetically desirable child are paramount in the adoption process. The adoptive parents are considered "consumers" who have a right to be informed. *See* Donner, *supra* note 20, at 518–24. For example, in the case

of Michael J., the court awarded judgment to adoptive parents of a child with a genetic disorder. Michael J. v. Los Angeles County Department of Adoptions, 247 Cal. Rptr. 504 (Cal. App.2 Dist. 1988). The child possessed symptoms of the disease at the time of his adoption (manifested in a visible port wine stain birthmark), but the adoption agency took no further action to investigate the underlying cause of the child's condition. The court "implicitly applied an economic analysis of the adoption process" and implied that the "allocation of risk on adoptive parents [was] unconscionable." The case of M. H. also illustrates how the adoptive parents' interests are being served by the courts in deciding adoption cases. The court awarded judgment to the adoptive parents of a child when the adoption agency failed to disclose that the child was a product of incest. M.H. v. Caritas Family Services, 488 N.W.2d 282 (Minn. 1992).

45 See Mary Mitchell, *Adoption Swamp Grows Murkier with Drug Charges*, Chicago Sun Times, March 22, 2005, at 14 ("the fees at a lot of adoption agencies [are based on] the color of the baby's skin").

46 *Id.*

47 *See* Gay Jervey, *Priceless*, Money, April 1, 2003, at 118 (a couple describes the lifestyle changes they underwent when they decided to adopt: "[My husband] took a 'real job.' . . . To adopt, we had to appear to be solid, and we also needed the money. . . . Unless you're independently wealthy, you have to fit the norm.").

48 National Adoption Information Clearinghouse, U.S. Department of Health & Human Services, *Intercountry Adoption* (2001), http://naic.acf.hhs.gov/pubs/f_inter/f_inter.cfm.

49 In researching for this chapter, the highest fee associated with black adoptions was nineteen thousand dollars. The lowest fees included nearly free permanent placements involving children from foster care. *See, e.g.*, Gabrielle Glaser, *The Price(s) to Adopt*, The Oregonian, July 4, 2004, at L01 (a couple adopting an African American child can expect to wait between one to nine months and pay twelve thousand to nineteen thousand dollars); *see, e.g., Adoption Options*, *supra* note 23 (children can be adopted from foster care without the adoptive parents incurring any, or very few, costs).

50 *Born in USA*, *supra* note 40.

51 Amanda Crowell, lawyer for the couple petitioning to adopt Linda Berrera Cano, quoted in Shaila Dewan, *Two Families, Two Cultures, and the Girl between Them*, N.Y. Times, May 12, 2005, at A1.

52 *See, e.g.*, Randall B. Hicks, Adopting in America: How to Adopt within One Year 12 (4th ed. 2004) (describing the importance of adoptive parents' ability to demonstrate financial security to adoption agencies, including those agencies that place an emphasis on a permanent stay-at-home parent).

53 These scholars also suggest that black families tend to adopt within their families, which avoids the costly transaction fees imposed by agencies. *See* Zanita E. Fenton, *In a World Not Their Own: The Adoption of Black Children*, 10 Harv. BlackLetter L.J. 39 (1993) (describing the slavery origins of informal adoption by extended family members, which is still common within African American communities). *See also* U.S. Census Bureau, *Adopted Children and Step-Children: Census 2000 Special Reports* 3 (Oct. 2003), http://www.census.gov/prod/2003pubs/censr-6.pdf. (The informal adoption of children is more common in certain cultural groups, including the Inupiaq in Alaska, blacks, and Hispanics. Because of the structure of the adoption identification category, the data from the 2000 census cannot differentiate among different types of adoption, including informal and formal adoptions).

54 *See* Angela Mae Kupenda, *Law, Life, and Literature: Using Literature and Life to Expose Transracial Adoption Laws as Adoption on a One-Way Street*, 17 Buff. Pub. Int. L.J. 43, 49–50 (1998–9) (citing problems such as the frequency with which black families are

rated as "unqualified" to adopt, the scarcity of black professionals employed by adoption agencies, the presence of hefty adoption fees, and the lack of adoption subsidies).

55 *See* Juan J. Battle, *Education Outcomes for African American Students in Single- versus Dual-Parent Families*, 28 J. Black Stud. 783, 783 (1998) (noting that in 1991, 57.5% of African American children lived with only one parent); U.S. Census Bureau, *People: Income and Employment*, http://factfinder.census.gov ("Black households had the lowest median income. Their 2003 median money income was about $30,000, which was 62 percent of the median non-Hispanic White households.").

56 *See* Ruth G. McRoy, Zena Oglesby, & Helen Grape, *Achieving Same-Race Adoptive Placements for African-American Children: Culturally Sensitive Practice Approaches*, 76 Child Welfare 85, 89 (describing "a National Urban League study of 800 African American families who applied to adopt," and a mere two of the eight hundred were approved for adoption). *See also* Erika Lynn Kleiman, *Caring for Our Own: Why American Adoption Law and Policy Must Change*, 30 Colum. J.L. & Soc. Probs. 327, 359 (1997) (noting that "traditional standards governing parent eligibility are biased against minority parents," which "may be one of the reasons why there is a dearth of minority parents available to adopt minority children").

57 *See* U.S. Census Bureau, *The Foreign-Born Population: Census 2000 Brief 1*, 3 (Dec. 2003), http://www.census.gov/prod/2003pubs/c2kbr-34.pdf (noting that there are 31.1 million foreign-born individuals in the United States, comprising 11.1% of the total population. Naturalized citizens constitute 40.3% of the foreign-born population.).

58 Dewan, *supra* note 51.

59 *Id.*

60 *Id.*

61 *Id.*

62 *Id.*

63 *See Adopted Children and Step-Children*, *supra* note 53, at 12 ("In 2000, 13 percent of adopted children of householders of all ages were foreign born").

64 *See, e.g.*, Dawn Davenport, *Born in America, Adopted Abroad*, Christian Science Monitor, Oct. 27, 2004, at 11.

65 *Adoption Options*, *supra* note 23.

66 *See* Kleiman, *supra* note 56, at 363 (noting the irony in the adoption of foreign children: since many international adoptions are also transracial, the adoptive parents encounter many of the same cultural problems as they would have if they had adopted a ["less expensive"] minority child in the United States).

67 *See* Davenport, *supra* note 60; Anne-Marie O'Neill, Joanne Fowler, & Ron Arias, *Why Are American Babies Being Adopted Abroad?* People, June 6, 2005, at 64 (describing that some American birth mothers simply choose foreign adoptive parents based on the perception that other countries might be less race-conscious than the United States).

68 *See, e.g.*, O'Neill, *supra* note 67 (noting that "looser federal regulations allow even newborns to leave [American] borders").

69 *See Intercountry Adoption*, *supra* note 48 (cost for adopting a child internationally is thirty thousand dollars); Rhodes, *supra* note 30 (cost for an African American child is a mere four thousand dollars); Rubin, *supra* note 30 (cost for a [white] American infant can "hit the $50,000 mark").

70 *See* Hanan, *supra* note 7, at 174 (modern adoption laws beginning in 1851 were designed to serve the best interest of the child, no longer merely to provide adoptive parents with heirs, as did early American adoption laws, based on the Roman model).

71 *See, e.g.*, Administration for Children and Families, U.S. Department of Health & Human Services, *Administration on Children, Youth and Families, Children's Bureau, Preliminary Estimates for FY 2002* (2004), http://www.acf.hhs.gov. For statistics

regarding placement and length of stay of children in foster care, see Children's Bureau, U.S. Department of Health & Human Services, *The AFCARS Report: Preliminary FY 2002 Estimates* (Aug. 2004), http://www.acf.hhs.gov/programs/cb.

72 *See* Kleiman, *supra* note 56, at 366 ("American adoption law- and policy-makers claim to focus on the protection of children's best interests. If this were their true concern, however, adoption laws would facilitate the placement of children with families that want them. Instead, current laws and policies create a strong incentive for American parents to adopt foreign children").

73 *See* Barth, *supra* 34. Yet the adoption of white children may have less to do with early child welfare considerations of the 1850s and social altruism; rather, adult desires factor significantly in this process, meaning children are not necessarily being adopted to simply provide a charitable service; if that were so, fewer African American children would be bypassed for foreign adoptions. Because race matters in adoptions, child welfare may be secondary to the market constraints imposed by the costs of racism in the United States.

74 As mentioned earlier, because the adoption process in the United States is not administered by any single entity, exact data relating to the worth of the adoption industry are not known. *See generally* U.S. Census Bureau, *Industry Series: Summary Statistics for the United States: 2002 Economic Census* (Oct. 2004), http://factfinder.census.gov (data from the 2002 Economic Census estimate that the "child and youth services" industry, which includes adoption, has an annual payroll of 3.3 billion dollars. The data also indicate that revenue of the industry is nearly 9.5 billion dollars). *See also* Glaser, *supra* note 49 ("In 2001, Marketdata Enterprises. . . reported that adoption services were a $1.4 billion industry in the United States").

75 *See generally* Rahel Jaeggi, *The Market's Price*, 8 Constellations 400, 408 (2001); Mario Morelli, *Commerce in Organs: A Kantian Critique*, 30 J.L. & Social Pol'y 315, 318 (1999); Michael Rushton, *The Law and Economics of Artists' Inalienable Rights*, 25 J. Cultural Econ. 243, 248 (2001); Margaret Jane Radin, *Market-Inalienability*, 100 Harv. L. Rev. 1849, 1850 (1987); Margaret Jane Radin, Contested Commodities (1996).

76 *See* Twila L. Perry, *The Transracial Adoption Controversy: An Analysis of Discourse and Subordination*, 21 N.Y.U. Rev. L. & Soc. Change 33, 55 (1993–4) ("To some Blacks, [the placement of Black children in white homes by white-dominated social service agencies] suggest[s] that the disempowerment of enslaved Blacks has continued in modern-day America").

77 *See, e.g.*, Williams, *supra* note 8, at 918 (implying that applying a cold, scientific analysis to something as unscientific as adoption is not appropriate: "I am trying, quite intentionally, to problematize the clean, scientific way in which the subject is often discussed").

78 *See* Ertman, *supra* 35, at 52 (criticizing Landes & Posner's approach: "scholars do not see parenthood and cash as completely commensurable").

79 *Id.*

80 *See* Joan Heifetz Hollinger, *From Coitus to Commerce: Legal and Social Consequences of Noncoital Reproduction*, 18 U. Mich. J.L. Reform 865, 875 (1985) (noting that "women especially have been socialized with the view that their self-esteem, their deepest sense of personhood, depends on their ability to bear a child").

81 Adam Smith, An Inquiry into the Nature and Causes of the Wealth of Nations (1776), book 5, Of the Revenue of the Sovereign or Commonwealth; chapter 2, Of the Sources of the General or Public Revenue of the Society; article 1, Taxes upon the Rent of House.

2 The Upside of Baby Markets

MARTHA ERTMAN

Most people object to markets in babies. I disagree, at least in the case of the gamete markets. I take this position because market mechanisms provide unique opportunities for law and culture to recognize that people form families in different ways. If state or federal law, rather than the laws of supply and demand, determines who can have children using reproductive technologies, then many single and gay people likely will be excluded from this important life experience. Moreover, many children will not have the chance to be born at all. Gamete markets allow some minorities – those who, by virtue of their numbers, are unlikely to obtain legal rights and protections through the legislative process – to skirt the majoritarian morality that would otherwise prevent them from forming families.[1]

Majoritarian hostility to families headed by gay and single parents often finds expression in legislative enactments such as the 1996 Welfare Reform, Defense of Marriage Acts, and popular opposition to decisions such as *Goodridge v. Dept. of Health,* in which the supreme judicial court of Massachusetts overturned the legislative ban on same-sex marriage.[2] Supporters of measures protecting so-called traditional families (and harming so-called nontraditional families) often make moral arguments that heterosexuality and two-parent families are natural, relegating others to the category "unnatural." *Moral* or *natural* are flexible terms that carry multiple meanings such as "inevitable" ("it's only natural") or "mandated by either biology or God" (i.e., designating nonprocreative acts as "crimes against nature").[3] This reasoning often translates to a commitment to traditional gender roles for men and women, especially in families.[4] It could also translate to opposition to reproductive technologies, if so-called natural parenthood is understood as parenthood through coitus rather than with medical assistance.[5] But moral arguments can take other directions.[6]

Market mechanisms present a different moral vision, which gives priority to liberty and innovation, rather than to tradition and divine or biological mandates. Millian liberalism embraces norms of consent, equality, and most important, a liberal commitment to freedom of action absent evidence that one's actions harm someone else.[7] The ideal of freedom of contract imports these norms. Thus framed, the question in the context of baby markets becomes whether the upside of allowing single and gay parents to contract for parenthood is outweighed by a detriment to third parties. Because children are not part of the initial decision to use reproductive technologies, I will treat them as third parties, despite their direct interest, perhaps more than any other, in the transaction.

Reasonable people disagree, as this volume demonstrates.[8] Downsides of alternative insemination include dangers associated with limited access, parental anonymity, eugenics, and objectification. I have argued elsewhere that although these concerns are serious, they do not justify demarketizing sperm either because they are not unique to the alternative insemination market or because addressing the concern will itself trigger other negative effects.[9] Then, as now, I think that the most serious concern is objectifying children.[10]

This chapter revisits my objectification analysis of four years ago, expanding that analysis to explore whether law should recognize, tolerate, or facilitate a market for parenthood through egg and embryo sales. In an article titled "What's Wrong with a Parenthood Market?" I addressed the objectification question in four paragraphs:

> Importantly, purchasing gametes to conceive a child could cause the child to feel that he or she has been purchased like a new car. Radin claims that "conceiving of any child in market rhetoric harms personhood."[11] This statement asks us to consider whether the parenthood market, as manifested through adoption and reproductive technologies, treats children like chattel, thus harming their personhood. It is possible to have a market in parenthood but maintain linguistic mechanisms that mask that reality to reassure ourselves and the children that they are different from Corvettes.
>
> However, this analysis suggests a monolithic market, in which all transactions are interchangeable. Even transactions conventionally understood in market terms, such as insurance, car sales, and housing, are governed by different rules that reflect the different contexts. Ambiguities in insurance contracts, for example, are construed against insurers. For their part, car buyers enjoy the implied warranty of merchantability as well as protection in their contractual relationships with financing institutions. Tenants, in turn, are protected by the implied warranty of habitability. The market for parental rights is just one more market with its own unique rules.
>
> Becoming a parent invokes a raft of obligations quite different from those entailed in car ownership. Legally speaking, parents are obliged to, among other things, feed, clothe, shelter, and educate their child; keep the child out of wage labor; and refrain from discipline that rises to the level of abuse. From an ethical standpoint, parents have the duty to help the child develop a healthy sense of self, become an independent adult, and learn how to be a good citizen. While a car owner is obliged to maintain insurance and refrain from using the car to sell illegal drugs, that owner is also free to destroy the car, if she chooses, or run it into the ground through lack of maintenance. Parents are obviously not free to do the same.
>
> In sum, while one might want to guard against language and transactions that treat children as chattel, the mere existence of a market in parenthood does not pose that particular danger. If it did, wage labor would be akin to chattel slavery. Indeed, wage labor is the opposite of slavery, an insight that shows how slavery is problematic as an instance of both overcommodification (treating people as things for exchange) and undercommodification (refusing to pay people for their labor). In both labor and parenthood markets, the market's character depends on the obligations and rights built into it. The mere fact of market rhetoric's presence (or absence), or money changing hands, does not provide us with this crucial information.[12]

The preceding excerpt concerned only the case for marketizing sperm, which is, I think, the most easily defended element of the market for parental rights. But I think that this reasoning and the other reasoning regarding access, anonymity, and eugenics apply equally well to egg sales. Finding the upside of embryo markets differs somewhat because what is marketed differs – component parts of a baby as opposed to the fertilized egg that matures into a baby – and because the interests served by the market differ. However, to the extent that the objections to the embryo market reject contractualizing family relationships, I continue to view them as misguided. I elaborate this argument subsequently, trying to harmonize the plurality of family forms with the wisdom in guarding against objectification concerns that arise when we treat children as chattel.

Overall, I contend that many dangers of marketization can be countered by taking advantage of the fact that marketization takes various forms. Thus, law and culture can shape parenthood markets to maximize benefits and minimize dangers. We could cabin the downsides of, say, an embryo market by controlling the mechanisms of the sale. For example, one might say that auctions are inappropriate because of their associations with slavery. Moreover, we could recognize the effectiveness of private regulation. eBay already has a policy against posting humans and body parts. In short, the mere fact of exchanging money does not answer the question of whether markets are good, bad, or indifferent.[13] Money itself can express connection or separation.

For example, if a lesbian couple wants to have a child, the two women could divide their labor in a way that reflects the joint nature of the endeavor. One partner might gestate the child, conceived by alternative insemination with an anonymous donor, because health or age considerations make this the most appropriate choice. The other, nonbiological mother might signal her engagement in the family by finding a doctor, making medical appointments, researching medical procedures as they arise, searching the Web for sperm banks, and paying for the sperm. The language they – and we – might use to describe these efforts as reflecting the nonbiological mother's "investment" and "buy-in" to the family arrangement indicates the rhetorical power of marketized thinking to express connection as well as separation. Assume now that the women were friends, instead of lovers. In that case, expenditures of time and money might express something different. Assume further that the birth mother's eggs were unsuitable for fertilization and that she paid her friend for her eggs. That payment could signal that the birth mother, not the egg donor, is the intended mother. Now assume that the women are romantic partners, intending to create a family together. The genetic mother would give, not sell, her eggs to her partner, and the partner would gestate the child. In this instance, they could both be mothers, at least in California.[14] In short, we need to know more than the mere fact of marketization, and contractualization, to reach normative conclusions on gamete and embryo markets.

This insight, that contract can facilitate connection as well as separation, relates to a theoretical point regarding default rules. A liberal commitment to freedom assumes that contracts are permissible, unless there is a reason to think otherwise. A communitarian commitment to dignity, solidarity, and equality, in contrast, takes the reverse default position, assuming that demarketization of contested commodities (such as sex, body parts, and babies) is appropriate, unless there is reason to think otherwise. The falseness of the choice between these antimonies has led commodification theory to travel on fixed rails, with one line of thought concluding that baby selling is bad and another one asserting its benefits.[15] But we need not remain stuck on these fixed rails. We can transcend the false choice between freedom, on one hand, and dignity, solidarity, and equality, on the other, by asking a different question than whether to commodify parental rights.

Asking who controls and benefits from the transactions provides more satisfying answers.[16] It also makes sense since the role of law is largely expressive in this context. Willing buyers and sellers create markets regardless of legal prohibitions, only they are black markets (as in illegal drugs, stolen art, and the flourishing, if shameful, slave trade in human beings). If the law cannot abolish markets, it can create incentives and protect some vulnerable parties from some dangers they would face in a black market.

Baby markets present a modal case for expressing law's role in markets, along with prostitution and body parts. While prostitution is the oldest profession, these other markets – babies and organs – invite futuristic visions.[17] Baby markets especially invite expressive function in law. Who, in the public imagination, is more worthy and in need of protection than a baby? Moreover, babies and children represent the future. If we worry about the future, and expanding the role of markets in that future, baby markets present the perfect context for expression of how far contract, and markets, should go in that future.[18]

As a positive matter, the parenthood market is flourishing, through adoption as well as reproductive technologies. An Internet search under the terms "sperm bank" and "egg bank" demonstrates that there are plenty of willing buyers and sellers for gametes. Currently, reproductive technologies, including egg and sperm sales, are largely unregulated in the United States, creating a relatively free, open market in which most middle-class people can participate.[19] In short, the legal question is largely normative because the market will likely continue to exist regardless of what legal doctrine dictates.

A rich literature weighs in on the question of how law should regulate markets in babies, much of it critical. In defending the upside of the baby market, I am swimming upstream against the following currents:

- Harvard political theorist Michael Sandel, who objects to markets in human gametes and surrogacy on the ground that they corrupt the communal value of human life[20]
- Vassar political scientist Mary Lyndon Shanley, who supports a ban on human gamete sales because of eugenic concerns, concluding that we do not own our body parts, but rather hold them as stewards for the next generation[21]
- Social conservative David Blankenhorn, who critiques gamete markets for creating fatherless families[22]
- Northwestern family law and critical race theorist Dorothy Roberts, who wonders why legal and social mechanisms should facilitate white people creating babies at any cost, where African American women lack access to reproductive technologies and, moreover, face public hostility to their fertility through policies aimed at minimizing the number of black babies born[23]

- Harvard Business School economist Debora Spar, who calls for increased regulation of reproductive technology to protect the interests of parents as well as children[24]
- Stanford property theorist Margaret Jane Radin, whose canonical critique of marketization of body parts, sex, and babies is better described as commodification skepticism than commodification revulsion; still, she unequivocally asserts that "conceiving of a child in market rhetoric harms personhood"[25]

Departing from this center of gravity, my position may be closest to Elisabeth Landes and Richard Posner, who argued in 1979 for marketizing adoption to create incentives for pregnant women not to terminate their pregnancies and move children out of foster care into permanent homes.[26] But I disagree with their comparison of foster children to unsold inventory in warehouses, and think that it is bad to have a racialized valuation of children in adoption markets.[27] My analysis picks up where Landes and Posner leave off. Although Landes and Posner support a limited market in *babies* (refusing to support a market in children and limiting remedies for breach of contract in baby sales), they do not draw a precise line for where the market stops. Here, I make a modest attempt to sketch this line by defending the marketization of sperm and eggs as well as exploring the extent to which this analysis also supports marketizing embryos.

A succinct way of drawing this line is to say that I do not support posting a baby on eBay. But why stop at the eBay baby, and where should law intervene in markets short of the eBay baby?

Although Posner and Landes wrote their article decades before eBay existed, I suspect that they, too, would have refrained from supporting the posting of a baby on eBay. Legal and social grounds support this conclusion. Legally, the Thirteenth Amendment abolishes slavery and involuntary servitude, and putting a child on an auction block, electronic or otherwise, is simply too close to treating a person like a thing, which is the defining characteristic of slavery. Socially, the Millian principles of harm come into play most strongly once a child is born.[28] A person is not greatly harmed by knowing that her mother paid for the sperm to conceive her because medical care and child care are already, and uncontroversially, marketized. Moreover, this child would not be alive but for that transaction, and presumably, the fact of life is worth something in the analysis. On this reasoning, marketizing sperm is unproblematic. But things get more complex as we expand our vision to allow for marketizing eggs and embryos.

A. EGGS AND EMBRYOS

Why not allow a market in eggs and embryos? Although little federal regulation exists regarding sperm, egg, and embryo transfers (other than record keeping and donor testing requirements),[29] nearly half the states restrict the sale of eggs or embryos to some extent. For example, Louisiana flatly prohibits "the sale of a human ovum, fertilized human ovum, or human embryo."[30] Indiana criminalizes the sale of human eggs or embryos but allows egg donors to be paid up to three thousand dollars for "recovery time" as well as expenses for lost work and travel time.[31]

Virginia, in contrast, excludes "ova . . . and other self-replicating body fluids" from its statute criminalizing the sale of body parts, but also allows for expense reimbursements.[32] Maryland takes yet another approach, making selling "unused material" in fertility treatments a misdemeanor.[33] The Maryland statute, like much of the other state legislation regarding the sale and use of human eggs and embryos, seems aimed to prevent commodification for research, rather than fertility, purposes.[34] It is telling that my research did not yield any statute prohibiting the sale of sperm, a difference that may raise constitutional issues.

But perhaps there is a legitimate reason to regulate sperm differently than eggs. Maybe egg sales harm the parties and society in more severe ways than sperm sales. On the other hand, the different regulation of men and women in this context may be invidious. Gametes are one of the few things that women command a higher price for selling than men do. Whereas men may get paid seventy-five dollars for a sperm donation, women get, on average, four thousand dollars for each egg donation.[35] The popular press trumpets stories of egg sales, often noting that elite college newspapers feature advertisements offering up "tens of thousands" of dollars for egg donations.[36] A feminist reader with a chip on her shoulder might suspect that this legal and cultural wrangling about women getting paid too much for selling their eggs smacks of patriarchal desire to control and/or protect women. Indeed, egg sales are one of few contexts in which women of color enjoy even higher compensation because of the scarcity of their eggs in the donor pool.[37] But egg extraction can be painful and involves hormone treatments that might pose danger to the donor's short- and long-term health.[38] That difference, coupled with the limited supply of eggs compared to the nearly infinite supply of sperm, explains the price differential. But paternalism and/or perpetuation of traditional gender roles may play a role in limits on egg prices. A review of the leading communitarian critique of expansive commodification reveals how this may occur.

Michael Sandel proposes a two-part analysis to evaluate markets in contested commodities, looking to whether marketization evidences either coercion or corruption of fundamental social interests or values.[39] Applying his methodology to egg and embryo markets, I conclude that there is insufficient reason to interfere with the egg market by banning payment or otherwise. Embryos present a harder case, both because Sandel's corruption argument is stronger and because counterarguments in defense of intentional families are weaker.

Sandel worries about coercion and corruption. If a sale is coerced, he reasons, as when a poor person is forced by economic desperation to sell his kidney, then we should not tolerate it.[40] But even if the kidney sale is fully voluntary, making the coercion argument inapplicable, we still might prohibit the sale if it corrupts something that society holds sacred (such as human life or human bodies).

Applying this analysis to egg sales leads me to a different conclusion than Sandel reaches. He opposes such sales.[41] In contrast, I do not see problems with coercion and view any corruption of the sacred quality of human life as outweighed by other aspects of human life, notably the equality considerations of allowing gay and single people to become parents, and the interests of children in these families coming into being.

Coercion is an easy case. It is hard to say that college women donating their eggs are coerced into doing so, at least in ways that differ from other kinds of employment. Although it is tempting to say that the high price for eggs could create incentives for young women to sell what they would otherwise keep, this argument does not hold up under scrutiny. Certainly the temptation is there.[42] But if generous remuneration is problematic for socially controversial employment, perhaps prize fighters should not get paid (or only reimbursed for their medical expenses and lost wages). The same reasoning would caution against paying Halliburton for its contributions to the Iraq War, which was controversial from the start and has proved financially, politically, and internationally disastrous.

Corruption is the harder case, in part because of social distinctions between fatherhood and motherhood. This is where feminist concerns about equality and dignity come into play. The relative lack of fuss about the sperm market in either law or the wiser culture may reflect the different expectations of fathers than mothers as well as the relative ease with which sperm is separated from the human body. Men donate sperm in a transaction that is painless, and that may even involve sexual pleasure. Egg extraction, in contrast, involves a minor surgical procedure and powerful drugs. Moreover, sperm donation does not deprive the donor of much because sperm is regenerated every three months. In contrast, females are born with their store of eggs for life so that each donation leaves a woman with fewer eggs with which to create her own family, and any harm extraction causes to her reproductive system might jeopardize reproduction entirely. Thus, perhaps law should regulate egg sales more stringently than sperm sales.

Further analysis indicates, however, that these matters are insufficient justification for banning egg sales or capping the prices on those sales. Both constitutional norms and contemporary notions of formal equality indicate that law should not make distinctions between men and women absent good reason to do so, framing the question as to whether there is sufficient reason to more closely control egg sales. Coming from a position of Millian liberalism, which defends formal equality (and trumpets the dangers of treating men and women differently), I would be inclined to let the market determine the relative value of eggs and sperm, rather than cap egg prices out of concern that young women will be tempted by high prices to sell what they otherwise would not. The very dangerousness of the procedure argues for higher compensation, rather than limiting it. Fortunately, existing doctrines offer models for addressing some concerns associated with either coercion or corruption in a more nuanced way than a blunt ban on payment or an incoherent distinction banning payments and allowing reimbursement for expenses, including Indiana's "recovery costs" capped at three thousand dollars. The following section fleshes out this argument, parsing out the corruption-related dangers of eggs sales related to access, anonymity, eugenics, and objectification that I used to evaluate the sperm market.[43]

Starting with access, one can argue that the egg market corrupts notions of universal access to social goods because not everyone can afford to enter the market. Certainly, fewer buyers have access to the egg market than to the sperm market, given the higher price of eggs. However, the buyers may themselves have more money to spend, on average. First, heterosexual couples may buy eggs if the woman in the couple cannot conceive with her own eggs. And gay men may buy the eggs to be used with their own sperm in a gestational surrogacy arrangement. Because men enjoy higher wealth and income than women, they are better able to afford the prices. Moreover, to the extent that couples of various types and single people are priced out of the market, this pattern is not unique to the parenthood market. These same people may be priced out of expensive cars or beach vacations, as well. In sum, even with the higher relative price for eggs, there is little reason to single out reproductive technologies for special sanction on the grounds of being elitist.

The second possible concern turns on how anonymity in the egg market might corrupt family relations. It has more gravity than the first because it implicates the interests of children as well as parents. Mothers differ from fathers both culturally and biologically. Culture expects mothers to stick around, and of course, gestation marks the first nine months of doing just that. Indeed, the benchmark of loneliness is set by songs like "Sometimes I Feel Like a Motherless Child."[44] Fathers, in contrast, can do their essential work in a matter of minutes, and often, they do just that. Under this reasoning, one could argue that the sperm market is fine, whereas the egg market violates crucial cultural and emotional components of motherhood by allowing a child to be raised by people who are not genetically related to him or her. Moreover, children benefit from being raised by and knowing their genetic parents, and also from the material support and kinship networks these people provide. However, this reasoning gives way under pressure. Law has long recognized adoption, which generally involves being raised by genetic strangers. Moreover, anonymity is not a foregone conclusion. Just as open adoptions have become the norm in some contexts, gestational and genetic mothers may retain contact with children that are raised by the "intended parents."[45] Finally, although it is nice for a child to know his or her genetic heritage, and to enjoy those parents' financial and emotional support, lots of children do not have this benefit. To demand that the children of reproductive technology have gold-standard family environments, when coitally conceived children live with a range of circumstances, is to unfairly burden this one kind of parenthood. Thus anonymity, as with sperm sales, does not provide sufficient reason to ban or sharply limit marketizing parenthood through egg sales.

Eugenics, representing the corruption of moral norms of racial and other forms of diversity, suggests a third reason for limiting egg sales. If people buy and sell some people's eggs for higher prices, and other people's eggs do not have a price on the market at all, then patterns of reproduction may tend toward the breeding of a master race. Certainly the reproductive market is racialized, as other markets are, such as car sales and organ transfers.[46] But my limited review of the inventory of a major sperm bank indicated that the percentage of donors who were men of color was not wildly out of sync with those groups' prevalence in the general population, other than a slight underrepresentation of white donors, an underrepresentation of black donors, an overrepresentation of Asian donors, and a seeming lack of Hispanic donors.[47] The discrimination seems to occur at the level of buyers, and it is hard to see how law can interfere with that process. People select mates for racial, educational, and other characteristics that they deem optimal for a coparent, and legal efforts to intervene are constitutionally problematic.[48] People conceiving with medical help should be entitled to the same level of protection for their choices in creating a family.

Screening for disabilities poses a different kind of danger. Preimplantation genetic diagnosis is now routine in the United States for in vitro fertilization (IVF) procedures so that patients wanting to prevent their child from having Down's syndrome, Tay-Sachs disease, or Huntington's disease can screen embryos for the genes and implant only those with the desired genetic makeup.[49] As Spar observes, "no-one wants to live in a brave new world in which parents peruse a catalog of traits and carefully select their perfect child: a clever cellist, perhaps, with hazel eyes, brown hair, and a left-side dimple."[50] Dorothy Roberts notes, in a similar vein, that such genetic diagnosis shifts the burden of care and responsibility. Without the technology, genetic defects are unfortunate incidents that society accommodates by paying for medical care, establishing special education programs, installing ramps in buildings and on sidewalks, and so on. When, however, these diseases are preventable, parents who do not screen for the genetic mutations, or who do not terminate the pregnancy when they occur, might be seen as responsible for the illness. This line of thinking might transfer, wrongly in Roberts's view, ethical, financial, and social responsibility for genetic illnesses away from God or fate and onto the parents.[51]

However, like the access consideration, eugenics is either an overblown concern in the embryo market or not unique to that market. First, not that many people will use IVF. As one medical expert put it, given the choice between preimplantation genetic diagnosis accompanying IVF and the more conventional way of conceiving a child, "most people would rather have sex."[52] Even if increased access of the embryo market translates to more babies being born by that method, those babies are more likely to be racially diverse, at least, if the prices go down and allow a wider range of people to conceive that way. Reproductive technologies such as preimplantation genetic diagnosis would likely accompany an embryo market, decreasing the incidence of genetic diseases in the resulting children. But reproductive technologies themselves create other physical disabilities in children. Men with low sperm count, for example, can conceive using a technique that injects sperm directly into an egg. The sons born as a result may share their father's low sperm count, necessitating the same treatment once they reach reproductive age.[53] Additionally, and more seriously, fertility drugs and IVF often lead to multiple births, which themselves create health risks for the children (as well as burdens on both parents and the larger society).[54] Reproductive technologies, and thus egg markets, could have a broader social and medical impact than one would expect given the relatively small number of people who conceive this way. Indeed, Liza Mundy contends that it has had as big an impact as the birth control pill in the 1960s and legal protections for abortion in the 1970s.[55] In short, while eugenics concerns may be misplaced or overblown, there may be real social concerns associated with reproductive technologies, especially IVF. Prior to sorting how law might respond to those concerns, I address the most serious concern in the egg market: objectification.

The fourth and final factor, the corruption of the sacredness of being human itself by treating people as objects – objectification – plays out differently in egg and sperm sales. With sperm sales, as I described earlier, marketization need not result in children being treated like Corvettes merely because their parents expended funds in creating the parent–child relationship. Indeed, law carefully regulates different kinds of contractual relationships to protect the interests of systemically vulnerable parties like buyers of goods and residential tenants. In the egg sale context, we may worry about objectification of the donor as well as objectification of the resulting child.

Women as donors are more likely to suffer from objectification because their status as full citizens and legal subjects is relatively recent and, moreover, according to some accounts, remains incomplete.[56] Thus law might worry if egg sales risked turning women into egg factories, or if they lacked the power to fully consent to the transactions. However, the dangers of paternalism seem to outweigh the benefits of protectionism in the prior instance. Furthermore, women now have more opportunities than ever for market participation that does not involve selling intimate parts of themselves. Whereas American law has deprived married women of contractual capacity on the grounds of either vulnerability or cognitive inability through the doctrine of coverture, Married Women's Property Acts long ago began the process of whittling away the vestiges of coverture and recognizing women as full subjects, capable of voting, contracting, and other acts of citizenship.[57]

On the question of objectifying the children, the same analysis applies as with sperm sales. Parents who reproduce coitally obtain prenatal care by paying doctors for ultrasounds and office visits and pharmaceutical companies for prenatal vitamins. Adoptive parents pay agencies a fee to obtain parental rights. None of these payments change the parents' obligations to love, feed, educate, clothe, shelter, and otherwise care for their children, nor to refrain from abuse. In short, the children are not rendered thinglike, or objectified, by virtue of their parents acquiring parental rights and obligations over gametes.

Even if the dangers are greater in gamete sales than in coital reproduction, those concerns could be addressed in marketlike regulations without unduly limiting access to these markets. Anthropologists recognize the ways that commodification can be controlled by dictating the terms of the sale.[58] Pharmaceutical drugs are marketized, but in a controlled way that limits who can authorize the sale (physicians) and who can dispense the drugs (pharmacists). Egg and sperm sales might be regulated in a similar fashion if there are health risks to sellers akin to risks associated with drugs.

Just as minors generally lack the capacity to contract, very young women (and men) are likely barred from donating their gametes. If the donation of eggs poses particular dangers to long-term reproductive health, perhaps legal doctrine could further limit the conditions of the sale. If people cannot contract to buy alcohol until they are twenty-one, perhaps they could be barred from selling their gametes until that age. In the alternative, we could mirror the age limit imposed by many car rental companies and require gamete sellers – both male and female – to be twenty-five years old. None of these interventions interferes with the fundamental choice of people purchasing gametes, which is the most serious danger posted by public regulation of reproductive technologies.

B. EMBRYOS

Embryos present a harder case because they are closer to human beings, raising concerns regarding the crucial cultural dividing line between people, which are not for sale, and things, which generally are. Sperm banks, such as the California Cryobank and the Fairfax Cryobank, store embryos for a fee.[59] But storage is a far cry from sale, a fact illustrated by the newspaper coverage, across the globe, of the expansion of parenthood markets into sale of formed embryos (as opposed to egg and sperm) by a small company, the Abraham Center of Life, in San Antonio, Texas.[60] The outcry seems to have nipped the market in the bud, as a recent visit to the Abraham Center of Life's Web site reports that it discontinued its "human embryo bank" because it was not cost-effective.[61] That market may have barely existed. Jenalee Ryan, who founded the Abraham Center, admitted that "it's a bank without anything in it"[62] during the height of the media flurry in January 2007 that surrounded her founding of the company. Although the embryo market may remain hypothetical, at least for the moment, it represents a significant step in marketizing parenthood beyond the commodification of eggs and sperm.

As discussed earlier, I believe that the benefits of marketizing gametes – eggs as well as sperm – outweigh the downside of the market in gametes. Most important, I think that the higher toll on women of egg sales – compared to the toll on men from sperm sales – actually justifies marketization. However, analogical reasoning, in addition to intuition, cautions against automatic extension of the market for parental rights to human embryos. Applying the four negative elements I explored in relation to gamete sales supports this line of thought. The following discussion addresses access, anonymity, eugenics, and objectification in turn.

Access is a double-edged sword. On one hand, assuming that Jenalee Ryan, the Abraham Center's founder, makes IVF markedly more accessible by reducing the price for an embryo nearly 50 percent, to as little as twenty-five hundred dollars for an embryo and ten thousand dollars for each attempt at pregnancy,[63] lowering prices means that people who are now excluded from the market could participate – not poor women, certainly, but many middle-class people, and also many people of color, given racialized income and wealth disparities in America. It seems that the most likely customers of an embryo bank would be heterosexual couples and older single women. Gay men are less likely to buy fertilized eggs as they would like to use their own sperm to have genetically related children. Lesbians, likewise, are likely to buy sperm and use their own eggs. Allowing older people to become parents through an embryo bank seems reasonable given longer life expectancies. Moreover, other bodies of law allow older people to become parents such as adoption rules and the famous law school estates and trusts class case of the fertile octogenarian.[64]

However, this increased access also triggers a larger impact on the general culture. If more people can participate in IVF, then more people – children, parents, relatives, coworkers, classmates – are affected. It seems premature to worry about designer babies in such a world, where most babies are conceived coitally, often unintentionally.[65] However, if prices go down sufficiently, then a former luxury item can have a broader social impact. As Debora Spar points out, the reproductive technology business exhibits a different relationship between supply and demand than other contexts in that the "quest to conceive" can become "an endless, bottomless demand," leading would-be parents to "take out a second mortgage, wipe out their savings, or give up a lucrative job."[66] Given that reproductive technologies are often a gamble, especially for the older women likely to use them, and that gambling is a highly regulated industry to protect people from harming themselves, one might argue that the state should step in to keep reproductive technologies sufficiently expensive that only people who can afford to pay can play. But such reasoning collapses pretty fast. It ignores the widespread availability of credit cards that can, and do, finance all kinds of things that are beyond the purchasers' means. Moreover, it interferes with a fundamental premise of the liberal state, namely, that individuals are generally better situated to determine their own best interests than the state, especially in matters of child bearing and child rearing.

Second, anonymity might present a fatal downside of the embryo market. Unlike the gamete market, where a child is likely to know and grow up with one genetic parent, the embryo market presupposes total anonymity – no knowledge, no social, financial, or emotional support. However, like the preceding analysis regarding egg sales, this is no different from adoption, except that children are conceived with the knowledge that they will not grow up with either genetic parent. This may be a crucial difference. In adoption, young people get pregnant unintentionally, and adoption makes the best of a bad situation for both children and birth parents. An embryo market, in contrast, creates that situation. This difference might be one ground for a court or other regulatory body to regulate embryo markets more closely than other markets.

Eugenics, the third corruption-based possible objection to the embryo market, also overlaps with the analysis of the egg market. Like the previous factors, eugenics similarly seems to cut both ways as we evaluate the embryo market. But like the anonymity concerns, it may be that there are greater eugenic dangers in the embryo market than in the market for gametes. On one hand, and apparently different from the gamete market, the fledgling embryo bank business evidences the tendency to create embryos from blue-eyed blondes, where at least one genetic parent has an advanced degree and neither exhibits mental or physical illness.[67] Moreover, the prefab nature of the business may tend to create a lowest-common-denominator inventory that undercuts human diversity, just as Wal-Mart may undercut diversity in the retail world. However, the embryo market, like the egg market, is unlikely to be as ubiquitous as Wal-Mart. People would, after all, most likely rather have sex than pay twenty-five hundred dollars for an embryo and a total of around ten thousand dollars for a round of IFV.

Fourth and finally, embryo markets may raise objectification dangers in a more serious way than either sperm or egg sales. First, what is being sold is an entity that, given the right conditions, could mature into a human being. Eggs and sperm, in contrast, are component parts of a human, and thus the markets are more thinglike than personlike. Second, the prefab nature of the ordering process, which is necessary to make the market more cost-effective than existing markets for egg and sperm, where would-be parents engage in separate transactions to acquire each element of the reproductive process, may itself be more objectifying. Reasoning by analogy, one might say that we allow the sale of fertilizer, and gasoline, and nails, but not the bombs that are made up of these things. Still, it is hard to see how the embryo market is so different from the gamete market, especially if the same banks sell eggs and sperm separately.

Assuming one or more of the preceding objections holds sway with lawmakers, the question becomes how law should step in to regulate this impact. As Fran Olsen pointed out, even refusal to regulate has regulatory impact because it leaves the parties to the bargains they strike.[68] The possible regulations span from private to public law. At the highly private end of the spectrum is the agreement within the industry to follow particular rules and norms. John Robertson supports this level of regulation, a method and level that Robert Ellickson has documented in other contexts such as ranchers and farmers.[69] On the highly public end of law, Mary Lyndon Shanley proposes banning payment for gametes, and Marsha Garrison would allow the state to limit the purchase of gametes by gay men and lesbians and mandate disclosure of donor identity.[70] In between these lie proposals like that of Debora Spar, who supports limited state regulation of reproductive technologies, such as preimplantation genetic diagnosis, to allow its use to select against traits such as Tay-Sachs but not to select for desired traits.[71] Analytically, it is hard to enforce Spar's proposal because a desire to choose against deafness is also a choice for hearing. My own proposal would lie closer to the private side of regulation.

Forms of public law could include a limit on embryo sales on the grounds that objectification is more of a concern for embryos than for gametes. Where that line is drawn, and the very existence of the ban, of course, is on a collision course with abortion debates about when life begins. If a sixteen-cell embryo is enough like a person to preclude its sale (an argument sure to be made in socially conservative circles), then what justification remains to protect a woman's right to decide whether to terminate a pregnancy during the first trimester? A line of case law declines to treat embryos as "persons." In *Jeter v. Mayo Clinic for Reproductive Medicine*, the Arizona Court of Appeals held that the Center for Reproductive Medicine was not liable for wrongful death by losing eight-celled frozen embryos. The court did, however, recognize the viability of the Jeters' claim for negligent loss or destruction of property, breach of fiduciary duty, and breach of a bailment contract.[72] Other case law, however, limits the ability of parties to contract regarding the use of frozen embryos. Generally speaking, contractual agreements authorizing a clinic to destroy leftover embryos are enforceable, but courts have refused to enforce agreements that would force someone to become a parent against his or her will. In *Davis v. Davis*, the leading case, the Tennessee Supreme Court declined to award a divorcing wife frozen embryos the couple had created in hope of conceiving a child together because the now ex-husband objected.[73] This extension of some, but not unlimited, contract rights is consistent with other doctrinal areas.

In UCC Article 9, for example, lenders and debtors can agree to many provisions regarding their relationship, but contract law, through the UCC, provides a floor under which lenders cannot force debtors to go. One plank of the floor is the duty of good faith, defined as honesty in fact and compliance with reasonable commercial standards of fair dealing in the trade.[74] Attempts to waive the duty of good faith are unenforceable.[75] Another plank, specific to debtors and creditors under Article 9, is the right of debtors to redeem repossessed collateral before the lender liquidates it.[76] Any attempt by a secured creditor to include a waiver of the right to redeem in the security agreement is unenforceable.[77] In short, contractualization is not entirely laissez-faire. Different transactions are governed by different rules. This reasoning supports the idea of treating egg and sperm sales differently from embryo sales. If the benefits of gamete sales are greater than those of embryo sales, then perhaps the latter transactions might be more closely regulated to protect against downsides of the embryo market such as objectification.

One way to protect against objectification might be through methods of sale and advertising. Lawyer advertising is regulated, as is advertising for liquor, cigarettes, and pharmaceutical drugs.[78] Pharmaceutical drugs provide a nice analogy in that only licensed medical professionals can order the sale of drugs, and only pharmacists can sell them. This kind of controlled commodification might be used for the sale of embryos. The banks selling them might agree among themselves on standards for advertising and sales, perhaps even agreeing to price caps.[79] Still private, but moving along the continuum toward public law, might be tort or contract liability for losses incurred during the IVF process.[80] Further into the realm of public law, one might see a public accommodations statute mandating that providers of alternative reproductive medicine offer their services to anyone seeking it, regardless of race, sex, disability, marital status, or sexual orientation. In the unlikely event that this public accommodations statute were passed,[81] other public regulation may become more tenable. But until that happens, I think that the benefits of a laissez-faire treatment of reproductive technologies, including embryo sales, outweigh the dangers of big brother determining intimate family matters along the lines of majoritarian morality. As a matter of political theory, I prefer a narrow vision of the state's police or parens patriae powers in many areas of intimate life, including the embryo market. Once public law is in the business of regulating any of the reproductive technologies, it is hard to see that it will do a better job than the industry or the parties themselves (or private law). Moreover, it is hard to see why the state that interferes with intimate decisions that happen to occur with medical assistance to reproduce cannot similarly interfere in decisions of who to marry or otherwise have a child with by coitus.[82]

C. CONCLUSION

Reproductive technologies are largely unregulated in the United States. I think this is a good thing, in part because I suspect that if legislatures were to start deciding who is worthy of having children, they would only allow heterosexual, married couples to become parents. This would leave out lots of people because recent census figures indicate that married households comprise a minority of the U.S. population.[83] Without gamete markets, it would be much harder for single and gay people to become parents, and lots of children would not be born.

Moreover, the very limitation would defeat the market's ability to facilitate family formation on the basis of intent and function, rather than heterosexuality and biology.

Whether these arguments apply to embryo markets is a closer call. Gay people as a class are more likely, I suspect, to buy gametes (gay men supply their own sperm and lesbians supply their own eggs). Thus the likely embryo buyers are older heterosexuals, with infertility in both partners, as well as older single women. Older heterosexuals are likely to get protection from legislation and thus are less likely to need markets to skirt majoritarian moral disapproval. But single older women would need markets, just as gay men and lesbians have been able to become parents in large numbers by virtue of the largely free, open market in American reproductive technologies. Thus, especially with controls for over-the-top marketization (i.e., posting embryos on eBay or other auctions or advertising), the benefits of embryo markets may well outweigh the dangers.

NOTES

1 Racial minorities, whether single, gay, or heterosexual and coupled, paradoxically have had less access to reproductive technologies, despite higher rates of infertility. Dorothy Roberts, Killing the Black Body (1997).

2 The Personal Responsibility and Work Opportunity Reconciliation Act of 1996, codified as 42 U.S.C. §1305 (2000); The Defense of Marriage Act, 1 U.S.C. §7 (1997); and Goodridge v. Dept. of Health, 798 N.E.2d 941 (Mass. 2003).

3 Paradoxically, nature is also contrasted with civilization so that some kinds of "unnatural" affiliations might be viewed as "too natural," even feral, in opposition to the orderly world of heterosexual marriage. Martha M. Ertman, *The Story of Reynolds v. U.S.: Federal "Hell Hounds" Pursuing Mormons for Treason*, *in* Family Law Stories (Carol Sanger ed., 2007).

4 One defect in this reasoning lies in the fact that what constitutes the so-called natural family changes over time. Anthropologists view family through the lens of kinship and note how kinship exists on the border of nature and culture by providing the cultural context for biological functions of procreation. Marilyn Strathern, Reproducing the Future: Essays on Anthropology, Kinship, and the New Reproductive Technologies 17 (1992). Strathern notes that over the course of the twentieth century, "nature" increasingly became biologized, which has in turn biologized the idea of natural kinship. *Id.* at 19.

5 Strathern suggests that *natural parent* may be understood in the future to mean "one for whom no special techniques are involved and the one on whose behalf no special legislation is required." Strathern, *supra* note 4, at 20.

6 Moral arguments regarding organ donations often focus on altruism, an analysis that often ignores other moral considerations such as the way that race and class issues affect the rights and obligations of both donors and recipients. Michele Goodwin, Black Markets: The Supply and Demand of Body Parts (2006).

7 John Stuart Mill, On Liberty (1859).

8 Naomi Cahn's chapter in this volume (Chapter 10) previews her book Test Tube Families (2009).

9 Martha M. Ertman, *What's Wrong with a Parenthood Market? A New and Improved Theory of Commodification*, 82 N.C. L. Rev. 1, 26–34 (2003).

10 If white, blonde, blue-eyed children have particular market cachet, then other children are implicitly devalued. Moreover, the very nature of treating the acquisition of parental rights and responsibilities as a market transaction blurs the crucial cultural distinction between things and people.

11 Margaret Jane Radin, Contested Commodities 139 (2001).

12 Ertman, *supra* note 9, at 33–5 (citations omitted [other than Radin quote]).

13 Viviana Zelizer, The Purchase of Intimacy (2005).

14 K.M. v. E.G., 117 P.3d 673 (Cal. 2005).

15 Martha M. Ertman & Joan Williams, *Preface*, *in* Rethinking Commodification 2–5 (Martha M. Ertman & Joan C. Williams eds., 2005).

16 For a fuller statement of this point, *see* Joan Williams & Viviana Zelizer, *To Commodify or Not to Commodify: That Is Not the Question*, *in id.* at 362.

17 Fictional, and dystopic, renditions of these markets include Margaret Atwood, The Handmaid's Tale (1985), and Kazuo Ishiguru, Never Let Me Go (2005).

18 Strathern, *supra* note 4.

19 See the Fertility Clinic Success Rate and Certification Act of 1992, 42 U.S.C. 263a-1 (2000); 21 CFR 1271 (2006); Ertman, *supra* note 9.

20 Michael Sandel, What Money Can't Buy: The Moral Limits of Markets (1998); Michael J. Sandel, *The Case against Perfection*, Atlantic, April 2004, at 52.

21 Mary Lyndon Shanley, Making Babies, Making Families 92–95 (2001). She does allow for reimbursement of expenses in making donations.

22 David Blankenhorn, Fatherless America (1995).

23 Roberts, *supra* note 1.

24 Debora L. Spar, The Baby Business: How Money, Science, and Politics Drive the Commerce of Conception (2006).

25 Radin, *supra* note 11.

26 Elisabeth Landes & Richard A. Posner, *The Economics of the Baby Shortage*, 7 J. Leg. Stud. 323 (1978). For other robust defenses of marketizing parenthood through reproductive technologies, *see* Lori Andrews, Between Strangers: Surrogate Mothers, Expectant Fathers, and Brave New Babies (1989). *See also* John Robertson, Children of Choice: Freedom and the New Reproductive Technologies (1994).

27 Prices of adoption, too, vary on the basis of race already. Ertman, *supra* note 9; Patricia J. Williams, *In Search of Pharaoh's Daughter*, *in* Rethinking Commodification, *supra* note 15, at 68.

28 Posner recognizes as much. Landes & Posner, *supra* note 26.

29 See the Fertility Clinic Success Rate and Certification Act of 1992, 42 U.S.C. 263a-1 (2000); 21 CFR 1271 (2006).

30 La. Rev. Stat. 9:122 (2007).

31 Ind. Code Ann. 35–46-5–3(a) (2007) ("A person who knowingly or intentionally purchases or sells a human ovum, zygote, embryo, or fetùs commits unlawful transfer of a human organism, a Class C felony"). The statute does not prohibit paying a "woman donor of an ovum" for lost earnings, travel expenses, and up to three thousand dollars for recovery time in a "procedure to enhance human reproductive capability" such as IVF. *Id.* at 35–46-5–3(b).

32 Va. Code 32.1–289.1 (2007). Like the Indiana statute, it allows for "reimbursement for expenses associated with the removal and preservation of any natural body parts for medical and scientific purposes."

33 Md. Code 83A, 5–2B-10 (2007).

34 *See* National Conference of State Legislatures, *State Embryonic and Fetal Research Laws* (updated Jan. 19, 2007), http://www.ncsl.org/programs/health/genetics/embfet.htm.

35 Spar, *supra* note 24, at 30, 39.

36 Roni Caryn Rabin, *As Demand for Donor Eggs Soars, High Prices Stir Ethical Concerns*, N.Y. Times, May 15, 2007, at F6.

37 Lynn Harris, *Bionic Parents and Techno-Children*, Salon.com, May 9, 2007.

38 *See, e.g.*, Julia Derek, Confessions of a Serial Egg Donor (2004).

39 Sandel, *supra* note 20.

40 Michael Sandel, *What Money Can't Buy: The Moral Limits of Markets in* Rethinking Commodification, *supra* note 15, at 122.

41 Michael Sandel, Tanner Lectures on Human Values at Oxford University (1998); *see also* Spar, *supra* note 24 (referencing Sandel's opposition to such sales).

42 *See, e.g.*, Derek, *supra* note 38; Rabin, *supra* note 36 (describing a twenty-three-year-old woman's egg sale for seven thousand dollars to pay off her student loans, a transaction she would not have engaged in but for the payment).

43 Ertman, *supra* note 9.

44 Wishbone Ash, Motherless Child (Talking Elephant 2006).

45 *See generally*, Intended Parents, Inc http://intendedparents.com/Info/Surrogate_Moms.asp

46 Goodwin, *supra* note 6; Williams, *supra* note 27; Roberts, *supra* note 1. Ian Ayres, Pervasive Prejudice? Unconventional Evidence of Race and Gender Discrimination (2001).

47 Ertman, *supra* note 9, at 310–11 (describing California Cryobank inventory from May 2001 with 68% Caucasian donors, 17% Asian donors, 11% "mixed race or unique racial designation," and 4% African American donors, and noting that the 2000 census reported that the general population, in contrast, was 75% Caucasian, 4% Asian, 3% mixed race and American Indian and Alaskan Native, and 12% black or African American).

48 Loving v. Virginia, 388 U.S. 1 (1967); Palmore v. Sidotti, 466 U.S. 429 (1984).

49 Spar, *supra* note 24, at 112–17.

50 *Id.* at 123.

51 Roberts, *supra* note 1.

52 Spar, *supra* note 24, at 126, 112 (quoting Mark Hughes, a pioneering researcher in preimplantation genetic diagnosis at Baylor College of Medicine in Houston).

53 Liza Mundy, Everything Conceivable, 78–9 (2007).

54 *Id.* at 213 (noting that one child in thirty-three born is a twin), 217 (noting increased challenges faced by twins and other multiples, including prematurity, low birth weight, and cerebral palsy).

55 Harris, *supra* note 37.

56 Linda Kerber, No Constitutional Right to be Ladies (1998).

57 This progress is not always direct or complete. Reva Siegel, *Why Equal Protection No Longer Protects*, 49 Stan. L. Rev. 1111 (1997).

58 Arjun Appadurai, *Introduction*, *in* The Social Life of Things (1986), *reprinted in* Ertman & Williams, Rethinking Commodification, *supra* note 15.

59 California Cryobank homepage, http://www.cryobank.com; Fairfax Cryobank Home Page, http://www.fairfaxcryobank.com.

60 *See, e.g.*, Osagie K. Obasogie, Op-Ed, "*Walmartization*" *of Embryos*, Boston Globe, Feb. 1, 2007, at A9; Rob Stein, *Embryo Bank Stirs Ethics Fears: Firm Lets Clients Pick among Fertilized Eggs*, Washington Post, Jan. 6, 2007, at A1; Carol Midgley, *Embryos for Sale*, The Times (London), Jan. 12, 2007, at 4.

61 Abraham Center of Life home page, http://www.theabrahamcenterforlife.com/index4.html.

62 Joe Palca, *Adoption Agency Offers Up Embryos to Couples*, http://www.npr.org/templates/story/storypho?storyID=6749036. Other news coverage detailed Ryan's production of twenty-two embryos from a twenty-something egg donor in Arizona and a six-foot-tall blonde lawyer whose sperm she purchased from the Fairfax Cryobank, and two pregnancies that apparently resulted from her arrangements with a New York fertility clinic.

63 Stein, *supra* note 60, at 1.

64 *See* Black's Law Dictionary (8th ed. 2004) ("fertile-octogenarian rule," "The legal fiction, assumed under the rule against perpetuities, that a woman can become pregnant as long as she is alive").

65 A baby conceived coitally by a heterosexual couple likely to be unintended. John Santelli *et al., The Measurement and Meaning of Unintended Pregnancy*, 35 Persp. Sexual Reprod. & Health 94, 94 (2003) (noting that 49% of pregnancies in 1994 were unintentional, down from 57% in 1987).

66 Debora Spar, The Baby Business 32 (2006).

67 Stein, *supra* note 60.

68 Fran Olsen, *The Family and the Market*, 96 Harv. L. Rev. 1497 (1983).

69 John Robertson, *Commerce and Regulation in the Assisted Reproduction Industry*, 85 Tex. L. Rev. 665, 694 (2007); Robert Ellickson, Order without Law (1991).

70 Shanley, *supra* note 21; Garrison, *infra* note 82.

71 Spar, *supra* note 24, at 126.

72 Jeter v. Mayo Clinic, 121 P.3d 1256, 1261 (Az. App. 2005).

73 842 SW.2d 588 (Tenn. 1992).

74 UCC 1–201(b) (20); 1–203; 2–103.

75 *See, e.g.*, First Texas Service Corp. v. Roulier, 750 F. Supp. 1056 (D. Colo. 1990). However, parties can define what constitutes compliance with the duty of good faith, such as written notification within ten business days to take a particular action. *See, e.g.*, Q.C. Onics Ventures, LP v. Johnson Controls, Inc., 2006 U.S. Dist. LEXIS 45189 (N.D. Ind. June 21, 2006).

76 *In re* Cilek, 115 B.R. 974 (Bankr. W.D. Wis. 1990)

77 *In re* Schwalb, 347 B.R. 726 (Bankr. D. Nev. 2006).

78 3 Am Jur 2d Advertising §16 (2007).

79 Recent Supreme Court jurisprudence suggests increasing tolerance for price fixing under antitrust laws. Leegin Creative Leather Prods. v. PSKS, Inc., 127 S. Ct. 2705 (U.S. 2007).

80 Joshua Kleinfeld, *Tort Law and In Vitro Fertilization: The Need for Legal Recognition of "Procreative Injury,"* 115 Yale L.J. 44 (2005).

81 Legislatures faced with the question of recognizing the right of gay couples to form families overwhelmingly tend to reach the opposite conclusion by passing Defense of Marriage Acts that refuse to recognize alternative families. Fla. Stat. §63.042

82 For an extended argument that law should regulate parental rights and responsibilities the same for children conceived with reproductive technology and coitally, *see* Marsha Garrison, *Law Making and Baby Making*, 113 Harv. L. Rev. 835 (2000).

83 Sam Roberts, *It's Official: To Be Married Means to Be Outnumbered*, N.Y. Times, Oct. 15, 2006, at A14.

3 Price and Pretense in the Baby Market

KIMBERLY D. KRAWIEC

Few proposals generate the moral outrage engendered by a suggestion that babies – or, more accurately, but less vividly, parental rights – should be traded on the open market. More than anything else, baby selling seems to fly in the face of our deeply held convictions that some items are too priceless to ever be bought and sold. Throughout the world, in fact, baby selling is formally prohibited. And throughout the world, babies are bought and sold each day. As demonstrated in this chapter, the legal baby trade is a global market in which prospective parents pay, scores of intermediaries profit, and the demand for children is clearly differentiated by age, race, special needs, and other consumer preferences, with prices ranging from zero to more than one hundred thousand dollars.

Yet legal regimes and policy makers around the world pretend that the baby market does not exist, most notably through proscriptions against so-called baby selling – typically defined as a prohibition against the relinquishment of parental rights in exchange for compensation. As a result, fees, donations, and reimbursements take the place of purchase prices. Although large sums of money change hands and many market intermediaries profit handsomely from the baby trade, compensation to some of society's most vulnerable suppliers is legally restricted, and despite the successful addition of new sources of supply, the number of available so-called desirable children continues to fall far short of demand.

Until recently, the most visible and contested debates regarding baby markets primarily addressed the normative desirability of an open-market baby exchange, largely assuming that formal bans against baby selling relegated the baby trade to the black and gray markets. Recent analyses, however, persuasively document the legal, but highly imperfect, baby market, rendering (in some circles, at least) assertions regarding the existence of legal baby markets so widely accepted as to be almost mundane.

This chapter explores the costs of societal pretense that legal baby markets do not exist. Those costs include scarcity, forgone opportunities to address market failures, an inability to develop regulations designed to further particular public policies unlikely to be advanced solely through the goal of profit maximization, and the promotion of rent seeking. This chapter focuses specifically on the rent seeking problem, arguing that although frequently defended by those who contend that commercial markets in parental rights commodify human beings, compromise individual dignity, or jeopardize fundamental values, bans against baby selling (at least as currently written and enforced) serve little purpose other than enabling anticompetitive behavior by the most economically and politically powerful baby market participants.

Section A of this chapter defines the baby market, demonstrating both its similarities to and differences from other types of commercial markets. Section B argues that a systematic failure to acknowledge the full depth and breadth of the baby market extracts a high price from the market and its participants. That price includes forgone opportunities to improve market functioning, as discussed in section B1, and an inability to address potential tensions between public policy and collective action concerns, on one hand, and market forces and individual choice, on the other hand, as discussed in section B2. Section C, however, addresses the highest price imposed by legal pretense regarding baby markets – a romanticization of the baby market and its distribution networks enables politically and economically powerful market participants to cloak private wealth transfers as public-interested regulation. Section D concludes.

A. DEFINING THE MARKET

To say that a baby market exists, of course, indicates relatively little about that market, either normatively or descriptively. As a descriptive matter, the baby market resembles other common markets in some ways and not in others. As a normative matter, the baby market poses many of the standard regulatory concerns presented by other commercial markets, including issues arising from unequal bargaining power or access to information such as fraud; anticompetitive behavior such as price fixing and barriers to market entry; and collective action problems such as the "race to the courthouse" in bankruptcy. Yet the important public policy issues raised by trafficking in human lives suggest that the baby market raises special regulatory concerns, as well. Understanding these similarities to, and differences from, other markets – along with the baby market's unusual political dimensions – provides insight into the regulatory concerns raised by the baby market.

1. Common Market Attributes: Industry Segmentation and Price Differentiation

Like many other markets, the baby trade can be divided into distinct market sectors. A robust and growing commercial market exists in each of these sectors, including the three-billion-dollar assisted reproductive technology (ART) industry; the so-called donation of sperm and eggs for prices ranging from less than one hundred dollars to more than one hundred thousand dollars; the controversial, but growing, surrogacy industry; and the adoption market, including the highly commercial international and private domestic adoption sectors.

Although the product supplied in each sector of the baby market differs – ranging from the hope of a future child in the ART sector to a fully formed, already existing child in the adoption sector – effective regulation of the baby trade necessitates a unified, holistic approach to the market. This is not to imply that a one-size-fits-all legal regime is suitable for the varied sectors of the baby market. To the contrary, each market sector poses vastly different legal and public policy issues.

But because each industry sector can act as an imperfect substitute for the others, regulation that limits supply in one sector will channel consumers into another. In other words, prospective parents determined to have a child may be forced into the next best substitute, say, adoption, when their first reproductive choice, say, ART, has been fully exhausted without success or becomes otherwise unavailable. As a result, regulations and market failures that limit the egg trade will force prospective parents into the adoption market, and vice versa. Moreover, a holistic approach to the baby market that encompasses each of its various sectors facilitates an analysis of an important commonality across those sectors – the extent to which societal pretense regarding the existence of for-profit market exchange obscures anticompetitive behavior by economically and politically powerful baby market participants.

A second point of commonality between baby markets and traditional commercial markets is price differentiation based on consumer preferences. The extent of this price differentiation depends on the particular baby industry sector in question. Although some baby market sectors exhibit relatively low levels of price differentiation based on perceived quality, others exhibit enormous variation. In the gestational surrogacy market, for example, the surrogate bears no genetic relation to the child. Intended parents, therefore, have relatively basic requirements such as the surrogate's willingness to live a healthy lifestyle and the probability that she will relinquish the child at birth. As a result, although there is some price differentiation, gestational surrogacy compensation tends to vary within a relatively narrow range within specific geographic markets.

Egg market pricing, in contrast, is highly differentiated according to the perceived genetic quality and traits of the egg donor. As the market has become more commercial, the demand for particular genetic preferences has increased. Although the baseline rate for eggs in 1999 was twenty-five hundred to five thousand dollars, depending on geographic region, donors with traits that are particularly rare or desired command significantly higher prices.[1] For example, East Asian and Jewish eggs command a price premium because they are rarer, as do the eggs of Ivy League college students, women with high SAT scores, women with athletic ability, and women with extraordinary physical attractiveness.

Similarly, the adoption sector is price differentiated based on race, age, special needs, and other consumer preferences. Minority, older, and special needs children can be adopted from the foster care system for prices ranging from zero to twenty-five hundred dollars, thanks to a variety of federal and state adoption assistance programs and subsidies. The healthy, white infants acquired through private agency and independent adoption, by contrast, typically command placement fees ranging from ten thousand to forty thousand dollars, although prices as high as one hundred thousand dollars have been reported.[2] In addition, adoptive parents of these children frequently must pay birth parent expenses, including medical and living costs, legal representation, and counseling.[3]

In the international adoption market, prospective parents can select children from thirty-nine different countries, each of which provides a different product and price structure. For example, in China, the available children are almost exclusively girls, generally between the ages of ten and seventeen months. Although Russia has both boys and girls available, there is a much larger supply of older children than of infants, which are in short supply and costly. In Guatemala, the children are generally very young and of Mayan decent. Choosing a country, therefore, involves choosing your child's race, age, and other characteristics, with prices varying accordingly.[4]

In summary, the exchange of parental rights operates in many ways like any other market. Despite formal bans on baby selling, in the United States alone in 2001, roughly forty-one thousand children were born through assisted reproduction, six thousand of whom were created through the use of donated eggs and six hundred of whom were carried by surrogates.[5] In 2003, Americans adopted 21,616 children through international adoptions and gave birth to 30,000 babies using commercially purchased sperm.[6] Each of these children was purchased, usually at great cost.

2. Distinct Market Attributes: Public Policy, Inelasticity, Substitutability, and Consumer Desperation

The baby market differs from many other commercial markets in important ways, however. First, and most obviously, the fact that the so-called product in question is a human being (or future human being) raises difficult public policy issues not implicated by commercial exchange in other markets. The baby market can, and should, never be identical to the markets for bonds, cars, or pets, and nothing in this chapter is intended to suggest otherwise. Nor do I mean to suggest that other regulatory goals should take precedence over the best interests of the children and future children traded in this market. Yet, as elaborated in the section and elsewhere, societal pretense regarding the existence of legal baby markets is not a necessary component of a legal regime that holds the best interests of children paramount. Indeed, the contrary is true: pretense regarding legal baby markets thwarts the development of sound public policies designed to protect the best interests of children.

Second, the baby market exhibits the characteristics of a market in which demand is inelastic with respect to price.[7] Demand in the baby market often knows no limits. For some prospective parents, the desire for a family is so strong that they will stop at virtually nothing to procure a child – they will take on a second job, mortgage their house, incur massive debt, deplete their savings account, and sell other assets. In short, attempts to acquire a child often stop only when success is attained or access to funds runs out. Although demand in the baby market is not completely price-insensitive (customers do care about price and do purchase fewer services when prices rise), "frequently, people buy on hope rather than on performance, and they base their spending largely on their available resources."[8]

Third, and relatedly, for three reasons elaborated here, the role of substitutes is tricky in the baby market, reducing the downward price pressure created by close substitutions in many other markets. First, other markets supply no suitable substitute products. For most prospective parents, a puppy is not an acceptable substitute for a baby.

Second, the baby market exhibits significant product differentiation across its various industry sectors. As previously discussed in section A1, prospective parents may be forced into a second-best reproductive option when their first reproductive choice is foreclosed. Yet such forced substitutions do not diminish the extent of product differentiation in the baby market. For example, although some parents are indifferent as between the choice of genetic offspring and an adoptive child, others will turn to substitutes only when all hope of a genetic heir to one or both parents has run out.

Third, within most baby market sectors (gestational surrogacy, as previously noted, being a possible exception), babies and baby-making components tend to be highly differentiated, even within an industry segment. Parents desiring a healthy infant, for example, are unlikely to accept an older or special needs child, absent extraordinary circumstances. Similarly, many parents desire – and are willing to pay a premium for – a child matching their own ethnic background.

Commentators frequently consider the level of product differentiation in analyzing market regulation because the unwillingness of consumers to switch to a competitor's product reduces the incentives for sellers to compete on price. As a result, product differentiation increases the market power of individual sellers and can result in higher consumer prices. At the same time, however, product differentiation may thwart some types of producer collusion by complicating the ability to set prices.

Finally, infertile couples understandably do not view themselves as purchasing a baby or, perhaps, even entering into a market transaction, and their behavior as consumers in the baby market tends to reflect this, differing from consumer behavior in other types of transactions. Prospective parents, for example, frequently do not engage in extensive price comparison or bargaining over fees; change providers only reluctantly, even when faced with a lack of success through a given provider; and behave like desperate parents, rather than rational consumers, when weighing their purchasing options. As discussed in section B2, these – and other – distinct features of the baby market suggest that, despite the baby market's many similarities to other commercial markets, it also poses unique regulatory issues that distinguish it from other markets.

B. THE COSTS OF REGULATORY PRETENSE

The failure to acknowledge the full breadth of the legal baby market imposes severe costs on the market and its participants. Those costs include the forgone opportunity to develop legal policies designed to improve the functioning of the market, as discussed in section B1, and forgone opportunities to further particular public policies unlikely to be advanced solely through the goal of profit maximization, as discussed in section B2. This is not to suggest that legal oversight is a panacea without costs of its own. Greater government involvement means that costs are likely to rise, some services that people desire may be prohibited, and certain types of customers – for example, older parents, single parents, and gay and lesbian parents – risk being legislated out of the market. These are the costs that must be weighed against attempts to improve the baby market.

The primary focus of this chapter, however, as discussed in section C, is not the forgone opportunity for the development of sound legal policies, but rather, a failure to properly understand the purpose and effect of existing legal rules. Specifically, the romanticization of the baby market and a failure to understand its market participants and distribution networks enables economically and politically powerful market actors to extract private benefits from the state under the guise of public interest regulation.

1. Improving Market Functioning

A regulatory failure to recognize markets as markets may prevent those markets from operating at their full potential. As detailed in section C, for example, the regulatory exclusion of many suppliers from the substantial profits shared by other baby market participants reduces the available supply.

Moreover, microeconomic theorists have identified a variety of conditions necessary to the competitive functioning of markets, and regulatory regimes governing other commercial markets frequently seek to promote those conditions. For example, the legal regime may seek to reduce transaction costs, information asymmetries, externalities, monopolies, and barriers to the provision of public goods. Toward those ends, some commentators have advocated disclosure-based baby market regulations such as those governing the securities markets. Others have looked to the markets for luxury goods, organs, or health care for regulatory guidance. Societal pretense regarding the baby market's very existence, however, renders many such regulatory analogies politically impractical.

2. Other Public Policies

In addition to impeding the development of legal policies designed to ensure the efficient functioning of the market, the insistence on treating exchanges in an impersonal, profit-centered market as if they were motivated by something else – altruism or personal preference, for example – thwarts the development of legal rules designed to further particular public policies unlikely to be advanced solely through the goal of profit maximization. Disparate access to the baby market, for example, implicates troubling issues of class and race that deserve – and largely fail to receive – the attention of commentators and policy makers. Common defenses of limitations on compensation to birth parents, surrogates, and egg donors, for example, rest on claims that a legalized baby market would convert poor and (particularly in the case of gestational surrogacy) minority women into handmaidens for their wealthier counterparts, and that a market pricing system would unambiguously highlight the extent to which Americans value black children less than white children. Yet this is the reality of the baby market as it currently exists: women of color act as surrogates for white women with increasing frequency,[9] rarely use ART to redress their infertility,[10] and disproportionately face the involuntary termination of parental rights.[11] Moreover, only those determinedly ignorant of the differentiated pricing in the adoption market could fail to appreciate the fact that Americans' preference for white children is already obvious.

At the same time, however, the anticompetitive capping of egg donor compensation and laws limiting birth parent compensation in the adoption market to reasonable living expenses primarily affect the earning power of egg donors and birth parents with the most highly valued genetic and other traits. In other words, legal pretense regarding baby markets in these industry sectors primarily harms women who are attractive, white (or, in the case of the egg market, of a particularly desired ethnic ancestry such as East Asian or Jewish), and intelligent.

In addition, technological and other baby market innovations create a potential tension among public policy goals, market forces, reproductive freedom, and parental rights that troubles many baby market observers. For example, concerns over eugenics plague the sperm and egg sectors of the market, while differential access to and the potential uses of preimplantation genetic diagnosis (PGD) raise other important public policy issues.

To illustrate, in the absence of universal access to PGD, poor mothers may be more likely to give birth to a child with a genetic disease than an affluent mother who can afford to have her embryos screened. As a result, those families least able to afford the special needs of a child with a genetic disease may be most likely to give birth to such children. Moreover, because white women currently are more likely to use ART, including PGD, than black women, if this trend continues, genetic diseases may be disproportionately borne by racial minorities.

Other contested uses of PGD include embryo selection for a genetic match to an existing child so that the new child can be a stem cell donor; the use of PGD to screen embryos for adult-onset diseases such as Alzheimer's; and screening for mutations indicative of a heightened, but uncertain, risk of some diseases such as breast cancer. Finally, many disability advocates worry about the potential implication of PGD that individuals with disabilities – many of whom lead happy, productive lives – would have been better off never being born.

Nonmedical uses of PGD are even more contested. For example, gender selection is a quickly growing and controversial use of PGD that is legal in the United States but banned in most other countries.[12] In addition, although not currently scientifically possible, many scientists consider it "not completely implausible" that technology may someday enable parents to select other genetic advantages for their children – advantages that will accrue only to those who can afford PGD.[13]

These and other issues posed by the baby market may pit market forces and individual choice against public policy and collective action concerns because, in the abstract, respondents report high levels of discomfort with many of these scientific and market advances, including embryo purchases and the creation of customized children who meet the specific genetic preferences of their parents.[14] But on an individual basis, parents do exactly what parents have always done – they spend whatever is necessary to endow their families with the advantages that money and modern technology can provide. As a result, many customers are willing to buy – and many suppliers are willing to sell – a girl to the family who, through natural means, has managed to produce only boys; a child who is the perfect donor match to a sibling dying from a fatal illness; and, if it becomes technologically possible, a child with straight hair, blue eyes, high SAT scores, or natural musical aptitude.

The point here is not to argue for or against any of these commercial possibilities. But recognizing the baby trade for what it is – a market driven by profits and in which supply will inevitably grow to meet demand – is essential to understanding the tensions raised by this industry.

C. BABY-SELLING BANS AS RENT SEEKING

As discussed in section B, societal pretense regarding the baby market poses a price in the form of the lost opportunity for sound lawmaking. The greater price, however, may be that the romanticization of the baby market obscures the impact of existing laws dictating the allocation of parental rights. The most obvious incarnation of this regulatory pretense is the legal rule prohibiting baby selling, typically defined as a prohibition against the relinquishment of parental rights in exchange for compensation. Frequently defended by those who contend that commercial markets in parental rights commodify human beings, compromise individual dignity, or jeopardize fundamental values, such bans, in fact, have more in common with the rent seeking by powerful market actors seen in other commercial markets than with normative statements about the sanctity of human life.[15]

The notion that the government's power to regulate may be used to provide private benefits by restricting market entry, policing cartels, and legitimizing price-fixing tactics is a phenomenon well documented in other industries.[16] In fact, George J. Stigler argues that every industry with sufficient political power to harness the state's coercive machinery will seek to use that authority to (1) control market entry by new competitors and (2) police cartels and price-fixing agreements.[17]

Baby-selling restrictions arguably serve both these goals. As discussed in this section, a wide array of fertility specialists, agents, brokers, facilitators, lawyers, and other middlemen (hereinafter called *baby market intermediaries*) legally profit handsomely from the baby market. As public choice theory would predict, these baby market intermediaries are more economically and politically powerful than those suppliers of babies and baby-making components whose market access is legally restricted. Not coincidentally, baby market intermediaries have also agitated actively for legal and industry restrictions that impede the ability of birth parents, gestational surrogates, and egg donors (hereinafter called *baby market competitors*) – quite literally, the mom-and-pop producers of this industry – from collecting the market clearing price for their services, thus reducing competition and capping the price of their required inputs.[18] Not surprisingly, then, supply in these sectors of the baby market frequently falls far short of demand.

1. Controlling Market Entry

As discussed previously, baby-selling restrictions, adoption regulation, and legal uncertainty regarding the enforceability and payment terms of surrogacy contracts complicate the ability of birth parents and surrogates to collect the market clearing price for their services. Such rules thus deter independent market entry, preserving the division of profits among established baby providers and enhancing the role of baby market intermediaries (particularly incumbent intermediaries who have already established market position and reputational capital).

To illustrate, the adoption sector can be broadly divided into the international and domestic markets. The domestic market, in turn, has both a private component, through which nearly all healthy white infants available for adoption in the United States are placed, and a state-run (foster care) component, in which older, minority, and special needs children are disproportionately represented.[19] Both the international sector and the private domestic sector are distinctly commercial. In the private domestic market, adoption agencies, brokers, and facilitators typically command placement fees ranging from ten thousand to forty thousand dollars, although prices as high as one hundred thousand dollars have been reported.[20]

Similarly, the majority of international adoptions in the United States are carried out through licensed agencies, which, in most states, have few limits on the fees and expenses charged to prospective parents. The domestic charges in international adoptions typically include an application fee, a home study fee, and a program fee. Overseas charges include a required so-called donation to the child's orphanage and fees to the agency's facilitator, drivers, and interpreters. These charges vary by agency and home country.[21]

Finally, adoptive parents in international and private domestic adoptions frequently pay birth parent expenses, including medical and living costs, legal representation, and counseling (costs of adoption). However, international law, as well as the laws of all fifty states, forbid payments to birth parents in exchange for the relinquishment of parental rights.[22]

A variety of murky – and manipulable – state statutes govern these adoption-related fees. Although no state permits baby selling, few states specifically cap or otherwise restrict permissible payments for medical, living, and other expenses of birth parents, allowing some latitude to those eager to evade such restrictions. At the same time, because such payments must be justified as reasonable living or other expenses, the restriction does deter very large payments and acts as a de facto price-fixing agreement that may prevent particularly desirable birth parents from collecting the market clearing price for their services.

In addition, nearly all states ban finders' fees to intermediaries, but most permit reasonable payments to intermediaries for services rendered in connection with the child's placement. Although the level of control and oversight over intermediary fees can vary significantly across jurisdictions, few states impose specific limits on such fees, providing a similar latitude to those eager to evade the ban on finders' fees.

Baby market intermediaries in the adoption sector, such as state-licensed adoption agencies, have long sought to protect their market positions through active agitation for prohibitions against baby selling, with exceptions for their own activities. Those efforts have met with mixed success in restricting market entry by private agencies and brokers who enjoy the political support of lawmakers, whose constituents value the larger supply and shorter waiting times associated with private adoption. These anticompetitive efforts, however, have been quite successful against birth parents desiring to profit from the baby trade, nearly all of whom are funneled into the baby trade through a baby market intermediary, rather than as direct suppliers.

Finally, legal uncertainty regarding the enforceability of surrogacy contracts and the permissibility of surrogacy payment terms in many jurisdictions channels some parents into less risky sectors of the baby market, causes those who remain in the surrogacy sector to charge a risk premium for the surrogate's risk of nonperformance, and enhances the role of intermediaries (particularly incumbent intermediaries), whose reputations and profits depend on the repeated delivery of surrogates who will perform under the terms of the contract. The effect of each of these outcomes is to stymie the direct provision of surrogacy services and deter independent market entry.

2. Cartelization and Price Fixing

As discussed in section C1, legal bans on baby selling that prevent compensation to birth parents for the relinquishment of parental rights, while permitting baby market intermediaries free reign in setting placement fees and other expenses, make independent entry into the baby market less attractive for many baby market competitors, thus restricting market entry. Less obviously, as discussed in section C2, the insistence that baby market competitors are, and should be, motivated primarily by altruism, rather than by profit, enables explicit and implicit price fixing by baby market intermediaries seeking to cap the price of their inputs. This produces two related results: (1) inefficiently low supply and high consumer prices and (2) distributional concerns stemming from the distorted division of profits between baby market intermediary and competitor.

When babies, eggs, or the use of a womb are characterized as donative or altruistic transfers from a baby market competitor, rather than as inputs into the final product (a child) offered for sale by baby market intermediaries, it is easy to overlook the fact that such intermediaries have an economic interest in artificially depressing the price of that input. Of course, capping input prices reduces the available supply for both baby market intermediaries and consumers. As in the traditional oligopsony model, however, baby market intermediaries accept reduced access to inputs in exchange for a lower purchase price.[23] In other words, assuming that the marginal cost of any unit of a good is the price paid on all prior units, an oligopsonist will fail to purchase some units whose value to the oligopsonist exceeds their costs, to cap the purchase price of prior units. As a consequence, oligopsony power (like oligopoly power) produces inefficient supply levels. The end result, as seen in all sectors of the baby market, is product scarcity. More difficult to observe – but inherent in the oligopsony model – is the distorted division of profits between producer (baby market competitor) and middleman (baby market intermediary) produced by baby-selling restrictions.

Confusion regarding the economic effects of monopsony markets has sometimes led courts and policy makers to conclude that monopsony is not a concern of antitrust law, which seeks a goal of low consumer prices. Such an approach, however, incorrectly assumes that the savings from low input prices in a monopsony market will be passed on to consumers. Instead, a monopsonist who sells into a competitive market will charge consumers the same price as a nonmonopsonist but will supply a lower amount of the good. In contrast, a monopsonist buyer who also enjoys monopoly (or cartel) power over consumers will sell to consumers at a higher price than a nonmonopsonist.[24] Monopsony markets, therefore, never benefit consumers and create a deadweight efficiency loss, as do monopoly markets, because some market actors engage in a second-choice transaction that produces less social value than their first choice.[25]

This intuition has been employed in a growing body of work in labor economics, which posits that – in contrast to competitive employment models, which assume a mass exodus of employees if the employer cuts wages – employers may enjoy significant market power over their workers in some cases.[26] That market power may derive from a variety of sources, including employer differentiation, moving costs, job search costs, an inability of rival employers to absorb additional employees quickly, and – most relevant for the baby market – employer collusion.

Although empirical research documents numerous examples of collusion attempts (both successful and unsuccessful),[27] cartels are, in fact, difficult to organize and even more difficult to maintain. Incentive problems encourage cheating among cartel members, and the possibility of supernormal profits encourages new market entrants, who compete with and destabilize the existing cartel. Consequently, successful cartels must have a credible enforcement mechanism to punish defectors and a mechanism for preventing new market entrants, who would eat up any cartel profits. Legal rules can – and, in the case of baby markets, do – decrease the private costs of cartel formation and enforcement, and of policing market entry.

As previously discussed, baby-selling restrictions perform this input capping function of the buyers' cartel in the adoption and surrogacy sectors of the baby market. In the egg industry, input price capping is accomplished, instead, through explicit price-fixing agreements in the form of professional standards. Yet the anticompetitive nature of these agreements rarely elicits comment or controversy, perhaps because the persistent dialogue of altruism and donation that characterizes the egg business distracts observers from the true nature of the industry.

For example, the American Society for Reproductive Medicine Ethics Committee Report recommending caps for financial incentives to egg donors, together with the published list of egg donor agencies that have signed an agreement with the Society for Reproductive Technology to abide by the committee's recommendations governing egg donor payments, closely resembles the same type of price-fixing agreements that have been deemed *per se* illegal in other industries.[28] Similarly, fertility clinics and doctors would likely not be so forthcoming in discussing with the press their informal attempts to limit prices paid for eggs in the New York metropolitan area if they were given a reason to fear the reactions of policy makers and the public.

Ironically, such legal rules and the anticompetitive behavior that they enable are frequently defended as a means of preventing the commodification and commercialization of human beings, women's labor, or motherhood. As demonstrated, however, the costs of these rules are borne primarily by baby market competitors, who are disproportionately young, female, and in financial need.[29] The benefits, meanwhile, are disproportionately enjoyed by wealthier and more politically powerful baby market intermediaries. Similar arguments have been made regarding the perverse effects of the ban against unconscionable contracts,[30] protective women's labor laws,[31] and laws and rhetoric opposing the commodification of women's, particularly poor women's, labor.[32]

D. CONCLUSION

Commentators and policy makers have spent much time romanticizing or ignoring the baby market and fretting over an impending commercialization or commodification that, in fact, took place long ago. In today's legal regime, rules prohibiting baby selling have little to do with grand normative statements about sacred values and, instead, accomplish little more than impeding market access by baby producers.

Societal pretense regarding the baby market is exhibited most clearly by the ban against baby selling. As demonstrated in this chapter, this supposed ban merely prevents full compensation to certain suppliers and does not (and is not designed to) prevent commercial transactions in children. Therein lies the harmful hypocrisy of baby-selling bans. Were Americans serious about their refusal to attach price tags to children, the law would ban all commercial transactions in babies, rather than merely restricting compensation to baby market competitors.

But baby market critics should not delude themselves about either the probability or the costs of a real baby-selling ban. First, a true baby market ban would entail high costs, as demonstrated by the experience of those countries that have eliminated commercial exchange in some sectors of the baby trade. Were the United States successfully to prohibit commercial transactions in children, supply in the baby market would be even further reduced.

Second, banning the baby market is politically infeasible in the United States. Consumer demand is simply too strong and too deeply felt, and unlikely to be sated through substitutes outside the baby market. In addition, baby market consumers and intermediaries are too economically and politically powerful and have too much at stake in the baby market to permit its abandonment.

Perhaps, in the absence of a sufficient number of healthy, white infants, prospective parents would be forced into the only sector of the baby trade that, sadly, does not suffer from a shortage of supply – the state-run foster care system, through which a disproportionate number of older, minority, and special needs children are available. Such substitutions arguably have positive effects such as providing homes to children who otherwise would remain in state care or altering American norms about what constitutes a desirable child. Cross-racial adoptions, however, are controversial for a variety of reasons, and many child advocates worry about promoting, through scarcity, the adoption of special needs children by parents who are ill equipped to handle the challenges.

This chapter encourages the recognition of the baby trade for what it is – a market, with similarities to and differences from other markets. As with other markets, the legal regime may seek to improve competitive conditions and should be suspicious of attempts to use the state's power to extract private benefits under the guise of public interest regulation. Trafficking in human lives, however, poses some public policy issues that may be best addressed by political forces, rather than by market ones. Pretending that legal baby markets do not exist accomplishes none of these objectives.

NOTES

1 American Society for Reproductive Medicine Ethics Committee, *Financial Incentives in Recruitment of Oocyte Donors*, 74 Fertility & Sterility 216 (2000).
2 Debora L. Spar, The Baby Business 178–9 (2006).
3 Evan B. Donaldson Adoption Institute, *Costs of Adoption* (2006), http://www.adoptioninstitute.org/research/costsadoption.php.
4 Spar, *supra* note 2.
5 *Id.* at IX.
6 *Id.* at X.
7 The price elasticity of demand is "the percentage change in the quantity of a good demanded that results from a one percent change in price" but is rarely constant across all ranges of demand and price. Robert Frank, Microeconomics and Behavior 122 (1999). Demand for a good is said to be elastic with respect to price if price elasticity is less than –1, and it is said to be inelastic if price elasticity is between –1 and zero. A variety of factors impact the price elasticity of demand, including the availability of substitutes, the product's share of total expenditures, and the effect of income. *Id.* at 130–1. Other commonly invoked examples of markets in which demand is inelastic with respect to price include addictive and life-saving drugs.
8 *Id.* at 32.
9 *Id.* at 82–3.
10 Dorothy Roberts, Killing the Black Body: Race, Reproduction, and the Meaning of Liberty 250–64 (1997).
11 Extrapolating from the data available from the U.S. Department of Health & Human Services for 2001 on the children whose parents have had their parental rights terminated, and assuming a similar distribution among children in foster care and parents whose parental rights have been terminated, suggests that black (non-Hispanic) and white parents are represented roughly equally among parents with involuntarily terminated parental rights (37% vs. 38%, respectively), despite the greater percentage of whites in the population. This extrapolation is necessary because although statistics on children whose parents have had their parental rights terminated are readily available, information is not collected on the parents whose rights are terminated. Mary O'Leary Wiley & Amanda L. Baden, *Birth Parents in Adoption: Research, Practice, and Counseling Psychology*, 33 Counseling Psychologist 22–3 (2005).
12 Rob Stein, *A Boy for You, a Girl for Me*, Washington Post, Dec. 14, 2004, at A1.
13 Kathy L. Hudson, *Pre-implantation Genetic Diagnosis: Public Policy and Public Attitudes*, 85 Fertility & Sterility 1638, 1642 (2006).
14 Genetics and Public Policy Center, *IMAGN! Increasing Minority Awareness of Genetics Now!* (2005), http://www.dnapolicy.org/pub.reports.php?action=detail&report_id=11); Genetics and Public Policy Center, *Reproductive Genetic Testing: What America Thinks* 38 (2004), http://www.dnapolicy.org/pub.reports.php?action=detail&report_id=6).
15 This chapter does not attempt to rehash the voluminous literature debating the expressive function of baby-selling bans. Instead, I argue that, even assuming that baby-selling

bans provide some expressive benefit, such benefits are substantially diminished by the reality of legal baby markets. Moreover, such expression extracts a high price by using the dialogue of public interest to mask private wealth transfers from less powerful baby market suppliers to more powerful baby market intermediaries. *See* Kimberly D. Krawiec, *Altruism and Intermediation in the Market for Babies*, WASH. & LEE. L. REV. (2009) (discussing this at greater length).

16 *See, e.g.*, GEORGE STIGLER, CITIZEN AND THE STATE: ESSAYS ON REGULATION (1975); Jonathan R. Macey, *Commercial Banking and Democracy: The Illusive Quest for Deregulation*, 23 YALE J. ON REG. 1 (2006); Jonathan R. Macey, *Promoting Public-Regarding Legislation through Statutory Interpretation: An Interest Group Model*, 86 COLUM. L. REV. 223 (1986).

17 Stigler, *supra* note 16, at 5–6. Stigler also contends that industries with sufficient political power will seek state assistance in encouraging the production of complements and discouraging the production of substitutes. *Id.* at 6. As previously noted, the role of substitutes in the baby market is complicated.

18 For similar arguments in the context of organ markets, *see, e.g.*, Michele Goodwin, *The Free-Market Approach to Adoption: The Value of a Baby*, 26 B.C. THIRD WORLD L.J. 61 (2006); Julia D. Mahoney, *The Market for Human Tissue*, 86 VA. L. REV. 163 (2000). For influential discussions of the relationship between organ-selling restrictions and the organ shortage, *see* LLOYD R. COHEN, INCREASING THE SUPPLY OF TRANSPLANT ORGANS (1995); Henry Hansmann, *The Economics and Ethics of Markets for Human Organs*, 14 J. HEALTH POL. POL'Y & L. 57 (1989); RICHARD A. EPSTEIN, MORTAL PERIL: OUR INALIENABLE RIGHT TO HEALTH CARE? chapters 9–12 (1997).

19 An estimated one-half to two-thirds of U.S.-born healthy, white infants are placed directly by birth parents with adoptive parents through the assistance of an intermediary such as an attorney, doctor, clergy, or other facilitator, but estimates vary because states are not required to report private domestic adoptions. *Id.* The remainder are placed through for-profit or nonprofit adoption agencies that are licensed by the state. *Id.*

20 Spar, *supra* note 2, at 178–9.

21 *Id.* at 176–86.

22 *Id.*

23 The term *monopsony*, meaning "a single buyer," was first coined by Joan Robinson. JOAN ROBINSON, THE ECONOMICS OF IMPERFECT COMPETITION 215 (1933). Given that single-buyer models are unrealistic as applied to modern markets, economists instead employ models of oligopsony, or "competitive monopsony," in which buyer market power persists despite competition among buyers. The term *oligopsony* refers to the market power of buyers and not their number, which need not be small. V. Bhaskar et al., *Oligopsony and Monopsonistic Competition in Labor Markets*, 16 J. ECON. PERSP. 155, 156 (2002).

24 As noted in section C1, legal restrictions and uncertainties impose a variety of barriers to entering the baby market, creating market power among industry incumbents.

25 A difficulty with antitrust analyses of monopsony markets, however, is distinguishing low input purchase prices stemming from monopsony from those stemming from reduced transaction costs or the elimination of upstream market power. *See* HERBERT HOVENKAMP, FEDERAL ANTITRUST POLICY AND THE LAW OF COMPETITION AND ITS PRACTICE 16 (2005).

26 *See* DAVID E. CARD AND ALAN B. KRUEGER, MYTH AND MEASUREMENT: THE NEW ECONOMICS OF THE MINIMUM WAGE (1995); David E. Card & Alan B. Krueger, *Minimum Wages and Employment: A Case Study of the Fast-Food Industry in New Jersey and Pennsylvania: Reply*, 90 AM. ECON. REV. 1397 (2000); ALAN MANNING, MONOPSONY

IN MOTION: IMPERFECT COMPETITION IN LABOUR MARKETS (2003); David Neumark & William Wascher, *Minimum Wages and Employment: A Case Study of the Fast-Food Industry in New Jersey and Pennsylvania: Comment*, 90 AM. ECON. REV. 1362 (2000).

27 *See* Margaret C. Levenstein & Valerie Y. Suslow, *Studies of Cartel Stability: A Comparison of Methodological Approaches*, *in* HOW CARTELS ENDURE AND HOW THEY FAIL 9–50 (Peter Z. Grossman ed., 2004).

28 *See* American Society for Reproductive Medicine Ethics Committee, *Financial Incentives in Recruitment of Oocyte Donors*, 74 FERTILITY & STERILITY 216 (2000); American Society for Reproductive Medicine, *Egg Donor Agencies*, http://www.asrm.org/Patients/eggdonor_agencies.pdf; Kimberly D. Krawiec, *Sunny Samaritans and Egomaniacs: Price-Fixing in the Gamete Market*, L. & CONTEMP. PROBS. (2009).

29 "Financial need" should not be interpreted as synonymous with poor, although some baby market suppliers – e.g., birth parents in the international adoption market – may be poor. But many egg donors, in contrast, are college students anxious to earn extra money to defray educational or other expenses. *See* Kimberly D. Krawiec, *Altruism and Intermediation in the Market for Babies*, WASH. & LEE. L. REV. (2009).

30 *See* Richard A. Epstein, *Unconscionability: A Critical Reappraisal*, 18 J.L. & ECON. 293 (1975).

31 *See* JULIE NOVKOV, CONSTITUTING WORKERS, PROTECTING WOMEN: GENDER, LAW, AND LABOR IN THE PROGRESSIVE ERA AND NEW DEAL YEARS (2001); David E. Bernstein, *Lochner's Feminist Legacy*, 101 MICH. L. REV. 2401 (2003).

32 See Mary Anne Case, Pets or Meat, 80 CHI.-KENT L. REV. 1129 (2005); Naomi R. Cahn, *The Coin of the Realm: Poverty and the Commodification of Gendered Labor*, 5 J. GENDER RACE & JUST. 1 (2001); Katherine Silbaugh, *Turning Labor into Love*: Housework and the Law, 91 NW. U. L. REV. 1 (1996); JOAN WILLIAMS, UNBENDING GENDER: WHY FAMILY AND WORK CONFLICT AND WHAT TO DO ABOUT IT (2000).

4 Bringing Feminist Fundamentalism to U.S. Baby Markets

MARY ANNE CASE

The central claim of this chapter should not be a controversial one. The claim is simply this: that our nation's fundamental constitutional commitment to the equality of the sexes, and to the instantiation of that equality in the repudiation of "fixed notions concerning the roles and abilities of men and women,"[1] should apply with full force in any legal intervention into the baby markets, including intervention in adoption and child custody disputes, as it does whenever the state necessarily intervenes in family matters.

What makes the claim more controversial than it should be is that many who are themselves personally and professionally committed to sex equality in American law and life are also committed to honoring other values, including religious freedom, cultural diversity, personal and family autonomy, and sharp limitations on governmental interference in private life and individual choice. Properly interpreted, however, existing U.S. law already commits us as a nation to sex equality as a priority, as I will demonstrate. I call the position I am seeking to vindicate *feminist fundamentalism*, by which I mean an uncompromising commitment to the equality of the sexes as intense and at least as worthy of respect as, for example, a religiously or culturally based commitment to female subordination or fixed sex roles.[2] Both individuals and nation-states can have feminist fundamentalist commitments relevant to the legal regulation of the baby markets. Before considering the claims of individuals, including both parents and children in custody and adoption disputes, let me first review the constitutional law that commits the United States as a nation to a particular kind of feminist fundamentalism when it intervenes in the baby markets.

Although both religious freedom and family autonomy are protected by the Constitution of the United States, the Supreme Court has also made clear that

> the family itself is not beyond regulation in the public interest . . . and neither rights of religion nor rights of parenthood are beyond limitation. . . . Acting to guard the general interest in youth's well being, the state as parens patriae may restrict the parent's control by requiring school attendance, regulating or prohibiting the child's labor and in many other ways. Its authority is not nullified merely because the parent grounds his claim to control the child's course of conduct on religion or conscience. . . . Parents may be free to become martyrs themselves. But it does not follow they are free, in identical circumstances, to make martyrs of

their children before they have reached the age of full and legal discretion when they can make that choice for themselves.[3]

When the state does exert its regulatory power over the family, it must do so consistently with its fundamental commitments, including those to equality on grounds of sex as well as race. Among regulations of the family in the public interest are, for example, laws mandating that parents support their minor children. In the *Stanton* case, in 1975, the U.S. Supreme Court held that it would be unconstitutional for Utah to require a divorced father to support his son until age twenty-one but his daughter only until age eighteen. The Court explained,

> A child, male or female, is still a child. No longer is the female destined solely for the home and the rearing of the family, and only the male for the marketplace and the world of ideas.... If a specified age of minority is required for the boy in order to assure him parental support while he attains his education and training, so, too, is it for the girl. To distinguish between the two on educational grounds is to be self-serving: if the female is not to be supported so long as the male, she hardly can be expected to attend school as long as he does, and bringing her education to an end earlier coincides with the role-typing society has long imposed.[4]

In the nineteenth and early twentieth centuries, justices of the Supreme Court had been willing to go along with society's sex-role stereotyping. Concurring in a judgment that the state of Illinois could deny a license to practice law to Myra Bradwell, a married woman, Justice Bradley wrote, in 1873,

> Man is, or should be, woman's protector and defender. The natural and proper timidity and delicacy which belongs to the female sex evidently unfits it for many of the occupations of civil life. The constitution of the family organization, which is founded in the divine ordinance, as well as in the nature of things, indicates the domestic sphere as that which properly belongs to the domain and functions of womanhood. The harmony, not to say identity, of interests and views which belong, or should belong, to the family institution is repugnant to the idea of a woman adopting a distinct and independent career from that of her husband.... The paramount destiny and mission of woman are to fulfill the noble and benign offices of wife and mother. This is the law of the Creator. And the rules of civil society must be adapted to the general constitution of things, and cannot be based upon exceptional cases.[5]

Since the 1970s, however, as the *Stanton* case indicates, the U.S. Supreme Court, interpreting the equal protection clause of the Constitution, has consistently held views such as those expressed by Justice Bradley in the *Bradwell* case to be not only outdated as a descriptive matter, but impermissible as a normative matter as a basis for governmental decision making. More generally, the Supreme Court has held all sex stereotypes to be anathema when embodied in law or in other government action. Not only is the equality of the sexes now firmly established as a fundamental constitutional value, but an unbroken line of Supreme Court precedent has consistently articulated as our constitutional orthodoxy a particular vision of sex equality – not the equality of separate spheres, but rather, a fundamental opposition to "fixed notions concerning the roles and abilities of males and females."[6]

In one of his last important opinions, *Nevada Department of Human Resources v. Hibbs*,[7] Chief Justice Rehnquist reaffirmed that we in the United States have so strong and well established a constitutional orthodoxy on matters of sex and gender – an orthodoxy not simply of sex equality, but of no governmentally endorsed sex-role differentiation in all matters, including those related to family and child rearing – that Congress has prophylactic power under Section 5 of the Fourteenth Amendment to enforce it on the states. Accordingly, to fight the long-standing, now heretical, "pervasive sex-role stereotype that caring for family members is women's work,"[8] Congress can impose on the states as employers the Family and Medical Leave Act (FMLA), which mandates that persons of both sexes, not just women, can get leave from their employers for what Martha Fineman[9] would call their inevitable or derivative dependency, that is to say, for their own illness or that of close family members as well as to care for their young children.

The *Hibbs* opinion completes the circle opened in *Stanton*: when Justice Blackmun's *Stanton* majority opinion declared, "no longer is the female destined solely for the home and the rearing of the family, and only the male for the marketplace and the world of ideas," there was a subtle lack of parallelism in the formulation ("only the male," not "the male only"). Women, the *Stanton* court held, were welcome in both the public and private spheres, but what of men? "Women's activities and responsibilities are increasing and expanding," Blackmun continued. Indeed they were, but were men's to the same extent? In his majority opinion upholding the FMLA, Rehnquist perfects the parallelism, holding, in effect, that it is no longer "solely . . . the female [who is] destined . . . for the home and the rearing of the family."[10] According to Rehnquist, Congress has prophylactic power to target, through the FMLA, "the fault line between work and family – precisely where sex-based overgeneralization has been and remains strongest"[11]:

> Stereotypes about women's domestic roles are reinforced by parallel stereotypes presuming a lack of domestic responsibilities for men. Because employers continued to regard the family as the woman's domain, they often denied men similar accommodations or discouraged them from taking leave. These mutually reinforcing stereotypes created a self-fulfilling cycle of discrimination that forced women to continue to assume the role of primary family caregiver.[12]

Although Rehnquist ordinarily gave great constitutional weight to federalism and states' rights and was, as a result, reluctant to extend congressional powers under Section 5, he saw the need for such power to combat "stereotype-based beliefs about the allocation of family duties."[13] This is further evidence of the fundamental place that not only sex equality, but its instantiation in the repudiation of sex stereotypes, has in the U.S. constitutional order. The equality of the sexes, together with racial equality and the nonestablishment of religion, ranks now among the very few commitments the existing U.S. constitutional order makes binding on government whenever it acts or speaks.

The strength of our constitutional commitment to racial equality has led to constitutionally mandated limitations on government tolerance of and participation in private discriminatory acts, including those affecting baby markets. Just as the *Stanton* case established that state actors cannot take societal sex-role stereotypes into account in setting child support obligations, so the 1984 Supreme Court case of *Palmore v. Sidoti* prohibited any racial discrimination in custody decisions, even when the best interests of an individual child might call for it.[14] The child in question was the young daughter of divorced white parents in Florida, whose father sought to gain custody when her mother married a black man. The Supreme Court acknowledged, "There is a risk that a child living with a stepparent of a different race may be subject to a variety of pressures and stresses not present if the child were living with parents of the same racial or ethnic origin."[15] It nevertheless held that the courts were precluded from taking racial prejudice into account in determining custody:

> The Constitution cannot control such prejudices but neither can it tolerate them. Private biases may be outside the reach of the law, but the law cannot, directly or indirectly, give them effect.[16]

I have argued elsewhere that, just as it does with racial equality, government as decision maker must also act consistently with its commitment to sex equality. The equality of the sexes is now, like racial equality and the nonestablishment of religion, something it is incumbent on the government to follow through on in all fields – in its hortatory pronouncements, in its funding decisions, and in its necessary interventions into the private sphere such as its custody and adoption decisions.[17] Thus, although government as speaker, actor, and dispenser of subsidies is free to take a variety of positions, among the positions it may now no longer take nor promote is, for example, that of Justice Bradley in *Bradwell v. Illinois*, to the effect that "the natural and proper timidity and delicacy which belong to the female sex evidently unfits it for many of the occupations of civil life,"[18] notwithstanding that such a position may still be fervently held by many people of faith.

What it might mean in practice for sex-equality norms to operate as a necessary constraint on state action is particularly tricky when that state action involves children. But, as has been clear for some time when it comes to state laws governing matters such as alimony and child support,[19] sex-equality norms also should constrain government on those occasions when the state necessarily adjudicates concerning the family. In the remainder of this chapter, I will work through examples of what this might mean, some more controversial than others. Among the questions I will consider is to what extent government, in its adjudication of custody as between already recognized parents or its placement of children for adoption, should take commitment or opposition to women's equality into account. Before readers protest that I am proposing massive governmental intervention into constitutionally protected parenting choices, it is important for me to stress that I am focusing my attention here on situations where there is already, of necessity, governmental intervention. In such situations, a policy of noninterference in the family or of leaving things up to autonomous individuals to decide for themselves simply is not an option. A custody dispute between two divorcing parents, for example, must be resolved – if neither parent is unfit, a court must decide between them in the best interests of the child.

In deciding such cases, evidence of commitment to sex equality should be at least as assiduously inquired into and at least as positively weighted as a prospective adoptive or custodial parent's commitment to providing a child with religious training, something many decision makers in adoption and custody cases seem to inquire into and weigh favorably, often without much apparent attention to the substance of the religious beliefs. It is notoriously difficult to determine what is actually happening as a general matter in family law cases, given how few result in reported decisions and how manipulable and vulnerable to judicial bias, conscious or unconscious, the relevant standards, such as "best interests of the child," are. From the few reported cases, it appears, however, that when repressive religious beliefs are pitted against secular feminist ones, the religious beliefs often begin with a presumption to respect I want to insist is even more deserved, but I realize is often not granted, to the feminist ones. Consider, as a frightening example, the case of Laurie April Wang, who left her husband after his church subjected her to an exorcism, as it had another woman, to "to rid herself of the 'evil, unsubmissive spirits,' the spirits which caused her to speak up for herself and to exercise authority rather than completely submit to her husband."[20] A court adjudicating her custody dispute was unwilling to consider whether her husband's religious convictions and his efforts to pass them on to his son might adversely affect her relationship with her son, apparently because it "took the position that religion is beyond the pale of the court's scrutiny."[21]

Even courts that do, in the end, rule against parents who claim religious authority for the sexist beliefs and practices those parents seek to impose on their children often do so without giving any explicit consideration to the role constitutional norms of sex equality should play in their decision making. Thus, in *Roberts v. Roberts*,[22] a Virginia judge did terminate a father's visitation with his son and daughter after hearing testimony by a clinical psychologist that the daughter "is particularly at risk of psychological damage because of [her father's] telling her that women should not strive to accomplish what men accomplish and that they are supposed to be subservient to men." Evidence that the daughter, an "excellent student," did "better in school this academic year, during which no visitation has occurred, than she did last academic year, when there was visitation," and evidence that the father had told both children that they and their mother, whom he called "a sinner" and "of the devil," would all go to hell, caused the judge to conclude that visitation with the father was causing "serious psychological and emotional damage to the children," in no small part because "the values being taught to the children by [their father] are different from the values being taught to the children by [their mother]."[23] Among these conflicting sets of values were that the mother "encourages the children to be whatever they want to be. [The father] tells [his daughter] women cannot do what men do."[24] But, even with respect to these values, the court insisted only, "Whichever set of values is right, and the court makes no judgment on which set of values is right, they are irreconcilably at odds." It may well be true that, as between "tolerance" and "fire and brimstone" – another of the enumerated conflicts in values between these particular parents – a court can make no judgment, but I would argue that a court is constitutionally compelled to choose encouragement of a daughter's choice of occupation over a fixed and subordinating message that "women cannot do what men do." That is not to say that the parent who most favors sex equality should always prevail, but simply that a court must not remain viewpoint-neutral as between sex equality and its opposite; it must put a thumb on the scales in favor of the parent who would give a daughter the same encouragement, liberty, and opportunity as a son.

If the son or daughter makes use of this liberty to develop interests and ambitions traditionally and stereotypically not associated with his or her sex – if he develops an interest in nursing or she in engineering – this should not be seen as a harm, but as a vindication of our commitment as a constitutional culture not to enshrine "fixed notions concerning the roles and abilities of men and women." Sociologist Judith Stacey has reported data suggesting that among the few differences between children raised in lesbian households and other children is that those raised in lesbian households, particularly girls, are somewhat more likely to "behave in ways that do not conform to sex-typed cultural norms," have a "greater interest in activities associated with both 'masculine' and 'feminine' qualities and that involve the participation of both sexes," and a have greater interest in pursuing careers in fields traditionally dominated by the opposite sex.[25] If these reported differences are to play any role at all in governmental decision making about lesbian parenting, they should cut in favor of, not, as some opponents of gay rights have argued, against, recognition of lesbian parents.

Although my take on cases like *Wang* and *Roberts* is consistent with the analysis of scholars such as James Dwyer, who has written extensively about religious exemptions to child welfare and education laws as denials of equal protection to children of religious objectors,[26] it is directly at odds with that of many scholars of the First Amendment. Most notably, in 2006, Eugene Volokh argued that the First Amendment requires that views such as those articulated by Wang and Roberts not be stifled.[27] The hierarchy of constitutional values is not as Volokh suggests, however. It is not the free exercise or free speech clause that is on a par with equal protection on grounds of race and sex when it comes to the extent of the limitations it places on government action; it is the establishment clause, and, in cases such as Wang and Roberts, the prohibition on government's establishing a religion and the guarantee of equal protection on grounds of sex that cut in the same direction – against the parent insisting on a religiously grounded commitment to female subordination.

One of the reasons the First Amendment may be seen to complicate the analysis in cases like *Wang* and *Roberts* is that both involved conflicts over gender ideology reflected largely in the fathers' discriminatory speech, rather than in any other alleged discriminatory treatment of children on grounds of sex. Harmful though it may be for Mr. Roberts to tell his daughter that her options are more limited than her brother's, it might have been even easier for a court to see the harm had her father also pulled her out of school in accordance with his ideology.

Some might suggest that the Supreme Court case of *Wisconsin v. Yoder*,[28] in which the Old Order Amish were allowed, as part of their constitutionally protected free exercise of religion, to withdraw their teenage children from school in contravention of school attendance requirements, stands in the way of the argument I am making here. But subsequent decisions have made quite clear that the *Yoder* case will be essentially limited in its application to the Amish. Moreover, although the Amish resisted higher education for their children, they apparently did not distinguish between boys and girls in doing so, giving both sexes similar training. Scholars who studied them at about the time of the *Yoder* decision reported,

> Although the Amish girls always wear dresses and the little boys, after they are toilet-trained, wear trousers, there is little difference in the tasks they are taught to perform. Boys are encouraged to like horses and machinery, but children of both sexes accompany their father around the farm and help their mother with simple household tasks.[29]

Had the Amish insisted on pulling only their daughters out of school without a high school diploma, while also insisting on sending their sons to college, the case would be more on point here.

Because religious liberty claims played such a central role in decisions such as *Yoder*, there is every reason to believe, as a matter of law, that a parent who limits a daughter's education or loads her down with chores will get less respect from a court for this decision if it is only culturally, and not also religiously, grounded. Indeed, courts, many dealing with immigrant families in which not only gender-role ideology, but a parent's genuine pressing need for help around the house, may keep a girl out of school, generally seem to have fewer problems favoring the parent who equalizes educational opportunity when religion is not at issue. This causes consternation among some scholars, but I think it was, for example, perfectly appropriate of a Nevada court that awarded custody of a young Mexican girl to her U.S. resident father in preference to her illegal immigrant mother to take into account, among other things, that while in her mother's custody, the girl had been forced to assume substantial care-giving responsibilities for her disabled brother.[30] Similarly, I think it appropriate that a court considering a teacher's petition to remove eleven-year-old Linda Berrero Cano from the custody of her migrant Mexican mother and to adopt her considered, among other things, how many school days the girl had unwillingly missed to care for her siblings.[31]

Linda's case was drawn to my attention by Michele Bratcher Goodwin's contribution to this volume, "Baby Markets" (Chapter 1). Goodwin is critical of a judicial system that removes a child from her mother's poor, unassimilated, Spanish-speaking home to place her with a family that "lives in a brick ranch house with a basketball hoop in the driveway, a swimming pool in the backyard." But Goodwin lists as the factors that determine the loser in competition for Linda only "poverty, immigrant status, limited political clout, and limited English proficiency," nothing connected to sex and gender roles. I agree with her that there is cause for concern when a judge in a custody dispute overvalues the material and cultural advantages of growing up in a wealthy, assimilated, English-speaking household, and I know too little about the facts of the case to be in a position to evaluate its bottom line result, but, in apparent contrast to Goodwin, I think Linda's being unwillingly kept out of school to perform household labor is an important factor for the judge to take into consideration.

Government should disfavor in competition for children those who, for example, would make a girl do all the household chores, while her brother can study or play. Although the cases that get press attention in this regard tend to feature families that are culturally, ethnically, or religiously exotic, from the polygamous Fundamental Church of Jesus Christ of Latter-Day Saints (FLDS) to Muslim and Mexican immigrants, recently released data on the chores performed by children show that even in mainstream American families, girls in many households do in fact spend far more hours on household chores than boys, leaving boys more time to play and to study. Moreover, the chores girls are given to do are less likely to be paid and less likely to be marketable than those assigned to boys.[32] Notwithstanding that, as Viviana A. Zelizer points out in her contribution to this volume (Chapter 18), in the nineteenth century, families often took in foster children principally to have an extra pair of hands for farm chores and household tasks, we would today find unthinkable the adoption of a black child to be, in effect, a household servant for his or her white adoptive siblings. We should feel similarly about a girl expected to do likewise for her brothers.

I also agree with Goodwin that it is noteworthy that Linda Berrero Cano "was never surrendered by her mother to the state nor was she in foster care" when her teacher sought to adopt her. Unlike custody disputes between two already recognized parents, or adoption decisions, when there are multiple prospective adoptive parents, Linda's case did not have two contenders for custody who began on a presumptively equal plane. For the teacher to prevail over the mother ordinarily would require a finding of parental unfitness, a much higher standard.

The case for feminist fundamentalism being outcome-determinative in custody or adoption decisions is, other things being equal, stronger (1) when those competing for a child begin with presumptively equal rights in that child, as occurs in a custody fight between two recognized parents or an adoption decision, when there are multiple qualified adoptive parents; (2) when both ideology and actions are discriminatory; (3) when only culture, not religion, is used to justify the antifeminist contender; (4) when the child is a girl, although, as the *Wang* and *Roberts* cases show, a son can also be at risk; and most important, (5) when the antifeminist acts or speech rise to the level of child abuse, so as potentially to justify a finding of parental unfitness. Even those who may find the examples I have thus far cited in this chapter unpersuasive would surely agree that there is some point on the continuum at which a parent's speech or action in support of a commitment to female subordination or rigid sex roles would cross the line into abuse. For example, those who might not agree that it should count against a parent that he tells his daughter her place is in the home doing housework might feel differently if he kept her chained there day and night, an illiterate drudge, and might then favor state intervention, even if there was no recognized competitor for his daughter's custody.

Unfortunately, the fact that sex-role differentiation, with its roots in female subordination, seems so "familiar" inhibits support for state intervention to combat it.[33] Consider, for example, the reaction to the state of Texas's April 2008 attempt to remove more than four hundred children from parents who were members of the FLDS, living on the Yearning for Zion Ranch. The state's intervention was prompted by reports that a sixteen-year-old girl was being forced to marry a forty-nine-year-old man. The state did find that "more than 30 of the 53 girls from 14 to 17 who were at the ranch are pregnant or have children."[34] A quick overview of public commentary on the state's action reveals that few other than representatives of the state of Texas itself and self-identified survivors of polygamy have been quoted in support of the state's action, however. Pundits on both the left and right condemned the state's intervention into the family and the community. I agree that the strict preconditions Texas law sets before children can be removed from their homes on an emergency basis were not satisfied in this case and that the Texas courts therefore had little choice but to order the children's prompt return.[35] But I am disturbed by the dismissive way in which the Texas Court of Appeals, whose decision that the children should be returned was upheld by the Texas Supreme Court, treated the Texas Department of Family and Protective Services's allegations of danger to the children.

The department took the position that "due to the 'pervasive belief system' of the FLDS, the male children are groomed to be perpetrators of sexual abuse and the girls are raised to be victims of sexual abuse."[36] But the Texas Court of Appeals repeatedly insisted that the department had made no showing of "any risk to them other than that they live in a community where there is a 'pervasive belief system' that condones marriage and child-rearing as soon as females reach puberty," as if this in itself were no big deal.[37] To help clarify why I find the court's attitude so disturbing, imagine that instead of the "pervasive belief system" of the FLDS concerning adolescent female sexual activity with older males, the court had instead been faced with the pervasive belief system of the Sambia of New Guinea, who, as documented by anthropologist Gilbert Heard, held and acted on the view that if young boys did not regularly fellate older males and ingest their semen, thereby replacing mother's milk with male milk, they would never grow up to be proper men themselves.[38] Would the court have sent young boys back to their families so promptly after finding that they "were in [no] physical danger other than th[ey] live . . . among a group of people who have a 'pervasive system of belief' that condones," not "polygamous marriage and underage females having children,"[39] as did the FLDS, but underage males regularly fellating older males, as did the Sambia? Surely not. Perhaps this is because the FLDS's "umbrella of belief" that, for girls, "having children at a young age is a blessing" is more "familiar and agreeable" to the Texas courts than the Sambian "umbrella of belief" that, for boys, ingesting semen at a young age is a comparable blessing.

It remains unclear where in the cycle of socialization into an "umbrella of belief," such as that of the FLDS, courts are prepared to intervene so as to protect young girls. If the age of consent remains unchanged, impregnating them remains a crime. But does the after-the-fact possibility of long sentences for statutory rape for men who have sex with young girls trained to believe they risk their salvation if they do not cooperate actually prevent harm to the girls? Should not some efforts be made to intervene earlier, before the girls are pregnant?

Yet even when one parent strongly objects to socialization into underage polygamy, courts seem reluctant to rule in favor of that parent. Consider the Pennsylvania Supreme Court's disposition of the custody dispute between the divorcing Shepps.[40] Their divorce had been occasioned by his conversion to a fundamentalist polygamous variant of Mormonism from the more traditional Mormonism both parents had previously practiced. A lower court had heard evidence that he had told his thirteen-year-old stepdaughter that her salvation depended on her practicing polygamy, and that when she turned fourteen, she should marry him, her stepfather. An intermediate appellate court then "specifically prohibited" him "while [his biological] child is a minor from teaching her about polygamy, plural marriages or multiple wives" because it found that "promotion of his beliefs to his stepdaughter involved not merely the superficial exposure of a child to the theoretical notion of criminal conduct, but constituted a vigorous attempt at moral suasion and recruitment by threats of future punishment."[41] But the Pennsylvania Supreme Court reversed, saying that, even when it came to "religious beliefs, which, if acted upon, would constitute a crime," their promulgation to a child could not be restricted unless it were "established that advocating the prohibited conduct would jeopardize the physical or mental health or safety of the child, or have a potential for significant social burdens."[42] I agree with the dissenting judge that such a showing had clearly been made in the *Shepp* case.

Unfortunately, however, so long as so many judges continue to underestimate the harm even extremely sexist parents such as Shepp, Wang, and Roberts (not to mention those of the FLDS) can do, and to undervalue the voices for women's equality raised against these parents, by, among others, their ex-wives and mothers of their children, our legal system will have failed to live up to its constitutional commitment to offer all persons, including the girls and boys who enter the baby markets through adoption and custody disputes, the equal protection of the law.

NOTES

1 Miss. Univ. for Women v. Hogan, 458 U.S. 718, 725 (1982).
2 I discuss more fully the implications of my concept of feminist fundamentalism in contexts other than the baby markets in my chapters *in* Gender Equality: Dimensions of Women's Equal Citizenship (Joanna Grossman & Linda McClain eds., 2009) and Children and the Discourses of Religion and International Human Rights (Martha Fineman ed., 2009).
3 Prince v. Mass., 321 U.S. 158 (1944). In the *Prince* case, the Supreme Court upheld the application of laws prohibiting child labor against a woman who had taken her nine-year-old niece and ward onto the streets of Brockton, Massachusetts, to preach and distribute religious pamphlets.
4 Stanton v. Stanton, 421 U.S. 7, 10 (1975).
5 Bradwell v. State, 83 U.S. 130, 141 (1892) (Bradley, J. concurring).
6 Miss. Univ. for Women v. Hogan, 458 U.S. 718, 725 (1982).
7 538 U.S. 721 (2003).
8 *Id.* at 731.
9 *See, e.g.*, Martha Fineman, The Neutered Mother, the Sexual Family, and Other Twentieth Century Tragedies (1995).
10 Stanton v. Stanton, 421 U.S. 7, 14 (1975).
11 538 U.S. at 738.
12 *Id.* at 736.
13 *Id.* at 730.
14 Palmore v. Sidoti, 466 U.S. 429 (1984). The strength of our constitutional commitment to racial equality has led to constitutionally mandated limitations on government tolerance of and participation in private discriminatory acts in other fields, as well.

See, e.g., Shelley v. Kraemer, 334 U.S. 1 (1948) (placing constitutional limitations on the court's ability to enforce racially restrictive covenant on private land); Griffin v. County Sch. Bd., 377 U.S. 218 (1964) (placing constitutional limitations on the ability of a county to close public schools and subsidize private ones, rather than desegregate); Norwood v. Harrison, 413 U.S. 455 (1973) (placing constitutional limitations on a state's ability to subsidize private, racially discriminatory schools).

15 466 U.S. at 434.

16 *Id.* at 433.

17 The project I pursue here is an outgrowth of my response to Kathleen Sullivan's Jorde Symposium lecture, in which Sullivan endorsed "normative pluralism" through "constitutional immunity for a private sphere" and sought to reinforce a dichotomy between "judicially enforceable and hortatory norms." *See* Kathleen Sullivan, *Constitutionalizing Women's Equality*, 90 Cal. L. Rev. 735, 755 (2002). In my view, Sullivan overstated, even under existing law, the permissible or desirable scope for normative pluralism on matters concerning women's equality. Mary Anne Case, *Reflections on Constitutionalizing Women's Equality*, 90 Cal. L. Rev. 765 (2002). I set out my argument at greater length in my contribution to Martha Fineman's edited collection Children and the Discourses of Religion and International Human Rights (2009).

18 Bradwell v. State, 83 U.S. 130, 141 (1892) (Bradley, J. concurring).

19 *See, e.g.*, Orr v. Orr, U.S. 440 U.S. 268 (1979) (holding unconstitutional Alabama state law that made wives, but not husbands, potentially eligible for alimony payments incident to a divorce).

20 *In re* Marriage of Wang, 271 Mont. 291 (1995) (Leaphart, J. dissenting).

21 *Id.*

22 60 Va.Cir. 49 (2002).

23 *Id.* at 59.

24 *Id.*

25 Judith Stacey & Timothy J. Biblarz, *(How) Does the Sexual Orientation of Parents Matter?* 66 Am. Soc. Rev. 159 (2001).

26 James Dwyer, *Religious Exemptions to Child Welfare and Education Laws as Denials of Equal Protection to Children of Religious Objectors*, 74 N.C. L. Rev. 1321 (1996).

27 Eugene Volokh, *Parent Child Speech and Child Custody Speech Restrictions*, 81 N.Y.U. L. Rev. 631 (2006).

28 406 U.S. 205 (1972).

29 John A. Hostetler & Gertrude Enders Huntington, Children in Amish Society: Socialization and Community Education 18 (1971).

30 Rico v. Rodriguez, 120 P.3d 812 (Nevada 2005).

31 *See* Shaila Dewan, *Two Families, Two Cultures, and the Girl between Them*, N.Y. Times, May 12, 2005, at A1.

32 *See, e.g.*, Sue Shellenbarger, *Boys Mow Lawns, Girls Do Dishes: Are Parents Perpetuating the Chore Wars?* Wall St. J., Dec. 7, 2006, at D1.

33 *Cf.* Lynch v. Donnelly, 465 U.S. 668 (1984) (Brennan, J. dissenting) (noting, in an establishment clause case, that "because the Christmas holiday seems so familiar and agreeable," the Court's majority is blinded to the "distinctively sectarian" nature of the display of a crèche in the public square).

34 Dan Frosch, *Texas Reports Added Signs of Abuse at Sects Ranch*, N.Y. Times, May 1, 2008, http://www.nytimes.com/2008/05/01/us/01raid.html.

35 I am therefore not suggesting that the bottom-line decision of the Texas courts, that, by law, the children should be returned forthwith to their FLDS parents, was incorrect. There did not seem to be evidence of imminent physical harm to all the children, nor

did it seem that Texas had taken heroic measures to find a solution short of immediate removal, as the law requires. *See*, *In re* Texas Dep't of Family and Protective Services, 2008 Tex. LEXIS 510; 51 Tex. Sup. J. 967 (2008).

36 *Id.*

37 *In re* Sara Steed *et al.*, 2008 Tex. App. LEXIS 3652 (Tex. Ct. App. 2008).

38 *See generally* Gilbert Herdt, The Sambia: Ritual and Gender in New Guinea (1987).

39 *In re supra*, note 31.

40 Shepp v. Shepp, 832 A.2d 1064 (2003).

41 Shepp v. Shepp, 2003 PA Super 140, 821 A.2d 635 (2003) (citation omitted)

42 Shepp v. Shepp, 588 Pa. 691; 906 A.2d 1165, 1174 (2006).

5 Producing Kinship through the Marketplaces of Transnational Adoption

SARA DOROW

You shoulda gone to China. You know, 'cause I hear they give away babies like free iPods. You know, they pretty much just put them in those t-shirt guns and shoot them out at sporting events.

– from *Juno* (Fox Searchlight, 2007)

Sara: What if you'd grown up in the orphanage? What do you think your life would be like?

Lani: A lot different still because being in an orphanage, people would be wanting to [adopt other kids] and so then you would be like "OK, no one is ever going to buy me."

Sara: Oh, ha-ha [*light laugh*]. It's interesting that you used the word *buy*. Do you feel like your mom and dad bought you?

Lani: No, but they adopted me and it's sort of like buying. . . . My mom and dad, my mom and dad had to sign all these forms and so then it's like they're going to be paying for it, so it's like . . . [*comically mimics rapid, panicked breathing*].

– excerpt from a 2003 interview with Lani,[1] an eight-year-old girl adopted from China

Juno and Lani have something in common: they dare to breach the narrow zone that buffers adoptive kinship formation from crass, globalized market forces. They remind us that whether conceived as freely accessible or prohibitively expensive, adoption might run the risk of constructing children as commodities. Responses to their respective comments corroborate that crossing this line is precarious and risky. Juno's snarky adolescent on-screen remark (to a prospective adoptive couple hoping to adopt her unborn child) caused an uncomfortable stir among some audiences of adoptive parents of Chinese girls, and Lani's interview narrative momentarily threw this experienced adoption researcher off guard.

In this chapter, I draw on several years of research on China–U.S. adoption to explore the way in which markets mediate the production of kinship. I will not spend much time asserting that transnational adoption is marketized; it is

Select portions of this chapter are adapted from Sara Dorow, Transnational Adoption: A Cultural Economy of Race, Gender, and Kinship (2006).

perhaps by now a given that most forms of kinship are intertwined with market exchanges of various kinds, without necessarily being reducible to them. And so this chapter proceeds with two particular foci. First, although some of the research on adoption as market exchange emphasizes consumerist or sometimes black market practices, I concentrate here on the more mundane marketlike forces and relations of transnational, transracial adoption that actively *produce* adoptive kinship. Not all forms of market or consumerist activity come to be seen as dangerous, which suggests that it is not necessarily market forces *per se* that are the problem. In fact, some kinds of acceptable market activities are meant to produce adoption in a way that protects it from seeming or feeling overtly commercialized, that is, to protect against the kinds of so-called risky constructions offered by Juno and Lani. For example, a story in *The San Francisco Chronicle* countered Juno's image of Chinese adoption by emphasizing that it is instead complexly regulated and transparently managed – arguably the positive language of market efficiency.[2] And so as its second point of intervention, this chapter explores the relationship between dangerous and banal (or even welcome) market forces, including raced, classed, and gendered.

China–U.S. adoption is an important case for this line of inquiry. For the better part of the decade between 1997 and 2007, it was the most popular form of transnational adoption in the United States. The reasons for its appeal are manifold, including the promise of children that are female, Asian, and relatively young, and the prospect of a process that is predictable, "transparent," and well run. Such a context requires that we consider consumerist desire within the institutionalized practices that structure and produce it. But China–U.S. adoption is also an important case because the people adopted from China are getting older. John Raible has astutely observed that in much of scholarly and popular discourse, "adoptees are positioned as perpetual children."[3] I would add that even critical analysis of so-called baby markets might also unwittingly fix adoptees as (silent, passive) children if we do not also consider the marketlike practices that continue to produce kinship in a variety of ways across the life course of adopted persons and their families.

Given these key facets of China–U.S. adoption, my analysis draws on specific kinds of ethnographic material: first, qualitative interviews and observational research conducted in the late 1990s with the facilitators and agency personnel who so-called broker adoption, and second, a 2008 analysis of some of the Web-based businesses that offer goods and services in the postadoption culture market. I then conclude with some of the ways that school-aged adoptees negotiated the marketplaces of adoption in interviews I conducted in North America in 2004 and 2006. As a whole, my inquiry aims to understand how market forces and practices contribute to the production of kinship and, in the process, how raced, gendered, and classed discourses are circulated and negotiated.

A. THE PRODUCTION AND CONSUMPTION OF ADOPTIVE KINSHIP

Interest in the marketized hierarchies of intercountry adoption owes much to some of the critical work on domestic transracial adoption in the United States. Key figures, such as Dorothy Roberts and Rickie Solinger, have pointed to a stratified market in children, from the so-called less desirable, hard-to-place, and least costly black children in the public welfare system to the so-called more desirable, hard-to-find, and most expensive white children available through private adoption networks; all along this spectrum, including in the realm of intercountry adoption, the quintessential adoptive parent is white. Since the 1990s, the increased size and scope of intercountry adoption programs appears to have exacerbated this complex alchemy of race, class, gender, and nation by offering more choices in the realm of private adoption. Quiroz points to the increasingly competitive and relatively unregulated private adoption industry to ask, "Most arguments about adoption include a market-driven rationale, so why do U.S. citizens incur the added costs involved in international adoption when there are minority programs with reduced fees, shorter wait time, and fewer restrictions, not to mention the lack of comparatively significant travel expenses?"[4]

Ortiz and Briggs have argued that within the transnational racial imaginary of white America, which includes the vilification of poor mothers of color, nonwhite orphans abroad are deemed more rescuable and desirable than domestic nonwhite children; they dub this "resilient (overseas) and toxic (U.S.) childhoods."[5]

The specter of the cross-border exchange of nonwhite babies from poor countries into the hands of white parents in relatively wealthy countries contributes to the construction of adoption as a global market.[6] Nonetheless, intercountry adoption must be analyzed beyond a market versus nonmarket binary. First, the interplay of markets with law and politics is crucial; consider the role of global military action and colonial expansion in the histories of countries that have opened to intercountry adoption, or the codification of the clean break – what Trenka calls "legal orphaning" – that severs children's legal and social ties to birth family and thus facilitates their exchange. Second, the market is never a totalizing force in the exchanges of kinship; rather, personal bonds and layers of social desire work alongside market and consumer practices. Yngvesson demonstrates that although adoption exchange is interlaced with commodity thinking, it can still produce new or unexpected forms of personal and familial "enchainment" across disparate nodes of family, nation, and race.

At the juncture of these multiple differences, the adopted child appears as both object and subject. Her "being object" is fine when she is the object of "protection and enculturation,"[7] the "'gift of love' that makes a family (complete)."[8] On the other hand, her "being object" is deeply problematic when she becomes or threatens to become an object of consumption available in multiple categories from which parents will choose, "contractually alienated from one owner so that it can be attached to another."[9] In her study of constructions of motherhood in online China–U.S. adoption groups, Ann Anagnost observed that

> the anxiety that the child might be a commodity is aroused by the incontrovertible fact that as the child moves from one site of nurture to another, money has to change hands; agencies are established; "baby flights" are chartered; tour packages are assembled. This awareness often takes the form of a refusal and resignification of the meaning of monetary exchanges.[10]

This marshalling of resources to contain or resignify the monetary exchange in China–U.S. adoption is the focus of a following section, where adoption facilitators negotiate the fine line between dangerous and banal forms of the marketized production of adoptive kinship.

But we must also consider the child's "being subject," which, as Eng and Anagnost point out, becomes a problem when it is her raced, classed, and gendered body that is the agent of the production of parenthood and family and nation – when "full and robust citizenship is *socially* effected from child to parent and, in many cases, through the position of the adoptee, its visible possession and spectacular display."[11] While this slippage between object and subject does not disappear as adopted people get older, there has been only limited scholarship that considers the ongoing impact or involvement of market practices in adoption kinship formation beyond its official beginning, as adoptees become more actively speaking subjects.[12]

Jacobsen and Volkman have considered ongoing but shifting practices, including market transactions, that constitute "culture keeping" in postadoptive families. The power of this work is in its move from inter- to transnational adoption, and from the adoption moment to its insistent and unpredictable resignifications. It evidences the struggle to critique the hegemony of market capitalism and, at the same time, account for transformative possibilities, alternative identities, and the personal and agential facets of social exchange in kin relations. Crucial here is the growing corpus of work by transnational, transracial adoptee writers, artists, and filmmakers. *Outsider within: Writing on Transracial Adoption*[13] is a poignant example: in situating the personal experiences of adoption in its broader political economy, this anthology carves out a way to move between the point of adoption and the ongoing lives of adoptees and their families. As the editors put it in the introduction to the text, "even as we learn more about our communities and countries of origin, and the social, political, and economic inequities that mark our journeys away from (and sometimes back to) them, we also struggle with the details of our lives and loves."[14] With this in mind, I turn in the last section to some of the contradictory ways in which market practices produce China–U.S. adoptive kinship through the marketing of culture, and thus contribute to how school-aged Chinese adoptees and their parents might materially and symbolically negotiate and express their kinship.

B. MARKET, STATE, AND CLIENT: CONTEXTUALIZING CHINA–U.S. ADOPTION

A complicated intersection of economic, political, cultural, and emotional labor by the formal facilitators of adoption buffers the production of kinship from the raced, gendered, and classed excesses of marketized relations that would make parent and child into consumer and consumed. Buffering work is especially important because China–U.S. adoption straddles a space between doing business well and just plain doing business, that is, between dangerous and banal forms of globalized market practice. These tensions surface on both sides of the Pacific. Mr. Xin, a former administrator of the China Center of Adoption Affairs

(CCAA) in Beijing, told me that when the Chinese government decided to legislate international (and domestic) adoption in the early 1990s, some government officials felt that China could not take care of all its abandoned children, "so why not let foreigners do it," whereas others felt this was "like selling off children to foreigners." For this reason, he emphasized, standardization of paper work and procedures served to ensure both foreign and domestic observers that families were carefully selected in rational, systematic ways. The universal appeal of modern business efficiencies (one kind of relatively banal market practice) thus rose to the occasion of protecting the sacra of childhood and parent–child relations from the taint of consumption (another less desirable form of market practice).

At the same time, however, efficiency and predictability came with new kinds of market creep. Adoption agency director Lynn Besky worried that they were becoming "China R Us," a sentiment I heard from various agency administrators (another called China "our bread and butter"). Lynn posed a dilemma that haunts the process: it should not be nor seem that parents go out and acquire a child, yet parents request – and agencies push – particular countries or types of children through a program that promises choices, services, or sometimes guarantees. The China program was expensive, at twenty thousand dollars or more, but young, healthy Asian girls were available, all of these being desirable traits. During my research, parents and social workers often compared China to Russia (the second largest sending country of the 1990s), where white but older and less predictably healthy children were available. In these and other intercountry adoption programs, race, gender, age, and health intersected to create a matrix of choices for parents who could afford it.

China's so-called competitive edge must also be understood in conjunction with state policies that have increasingly codified the construction of *adoptable children* and *able-to-adopt parents* since the 1990s. For example, the CCAA announced new stringent rules regarding the age, income, education, health, and marital status (straight couples only) of eligible adoptive parents in 2007, asserting that adopters with these conditions "answer better to the spirit of Hague Adoption Convention and the provisions of adoption law in both adopting and sending countries, and are able to offer the Chinese children adopted the best possible environment to grow in."[15] A complex web of market and governing practices marks the eligibility of certain kinds of bodies for kinship with each other, toward the construction of the so-called natural or real family.[16]

The contractual relations that attend the popular China–U.S. adoption program come with messy contradictions that can perhaps best be summed up in the problem of "two clients" – parent and child. Family Foundations director Marjorie Sessions bluntly told me, "We're *supposed* to say children are the clients," but it is parents that pay the bills and get to make choices. A social worker from another agency, Carrie Betts, insisted that the child remains the primary client, but a kind of phantom ideal client: "It's unknown to us, unmet, and maybe unborn." The (impossible) trick was to keep the child at the center of adoption practice, even as the secondary client was the one directly paying for services.

C. BROKERING AND BUFFERING THE PRODUCTION OF KINSHIP

Managing the production of kinship at the juncture of two clients and two nations falls to a host of agencies, officials, professionals, and technologies, but I especially want to attend to the mediating role of facilitators. Their banal market practices absorb the dangers of the market, ensuring that competitive greed, crass consumptive choice, and obvious exclusion do not trump transparency, efficiency, good service, and formal regulation. Facilitators are quite often Chinese nationals, based in either the United States or China, who are hired or contracted by U.S. adoption agencies to manage the Chinese end of things, including paper work, cultural training, and most substantially, the escorting of parents through their emotional and bureaucratic two-week journey to China to meet and adopt their children. When conducting my fieldwork in both China and the United States between 1998 and 2000, I interviewed and/or observed at some length ten facilitators of adoption. Even as many facilitators did not think that market competition was necessarily anathema to adoption, their good service meant fairly regular negotiation and buffering of its material and symbolic excesses.

One role facilitators find themselves in is buffering parents from exchanges that might make adoption feel like a transaction and children look like commodities. For example, Arthur told me that local administrators sometimes added extra charges at the last minute, which he then had to figure out a way to explain to parents. Larry gave me the example of disgustedly but quietly watching an orphanage director, who knew nothing about the children in his own orphanage, count out the donation money from adoptive parents, then hold up the crisp one hundred U.S. dollar bills to ask semijokingly, "Are these fake?"[17] Larry and Arthur would never relay these experiences to their direct clients: parents who, in the vulnerable moments of exchange, need (pay?) to be protected from signs of a commodified child.

Facilitators also protect adoptive parents from the reactions of Chinese bystanders to their unlikely charges (i.e., groups of white people holding Chinese babies), especially buffering any negative construction of them as global consumers. The ensuing tension is revealed in my notes from a joint informal interview with two facilitators as they took a break at one of the many hotels in China that have become main stopovers for adoption groups:

> Jane says Chinese people are of course very curious about seeing this adoption happen, and will ask what so many foreigners are doing with Chinese children. He interprets this as a kind of pride in being Chinese, in Chinese children being good at so many things. Jane disagrees, and says these observers feel anger and embarrassment that foreigners are adopting Chinese children. Jane tells me it is different for them than it would be for me when I travel with U.S. parents; she and Larry are Chinese, so other people still say bad words to them about these parents, and thus about their work in helping to do this. "They don't understand our work," says Larry; Jane adds, "We need to protect families, *and* protect Chinese feelings."

This is not to say that most facilitators were not gratified by the part they played in producing kinship. Jane put it this way: "At first I thought of it as only a business, but now I do it for the babies and families, because I can feel the love between them." But the coexistence of love and business surfaces the fraught positioning of the child as both subject and object, where salient distinctions along lines of race, health, and age emerge. The mere existence of differentiations among types of children as more or less desirable is, to some extent, a normalized part of the process. Consider that at one adoption agency orientation that I attended, the session leader told the group of prospective adoptive parents gathered there that they should feel free to ask any question, from "Can I ask for a particular gender or shade of skin?" to "Can I reject a child that is not healthy enough?" But these kinds of desires and choices lose some of their seeming innocence when facilitators like Zhuli must personally absorb the cost of their excesses:

> I think the majority of families are very reasonable and they do it with their heart. Just sometimes with a few families I find it is kind of difficult, when they say they want a child really, really, young, and it's not possible. You know, if I have a client who is really demanding, that makes me uncomfortable, when they tell me "Well, I want my child to have this shape face, or that shape eyes." Or "Oh, I don't want my child to have very dark skin." You know, that kind of talk. That's not very common, but it does exist.

Facilitators nonetheless negotiate a way to produce kinship out of complex cases, whether they be direct requests for specific types of children in the preadoption phase or, worse yet, potential rejections of specific children (usually for health reasons) after parents meet them in China. Most facilitators agreed that the latter kinds of excess were rare, but very difficult. As Arthur put it, he had to uphold parents' right to "choose" as business clients, even as he worried what he would do if they decided not to go ahead with the adoption of a child assigned to them: what would he tell the officials and the orphanage, whose good graces were crucial to the ongoing business of adoption?

A final buffer zone filled by facilitators is in the area of Chinese culture, where they are expected to be resources and guides. Facilitators' management of Chinese culture sometimes served to produce kinship in ways desired by adoptive parents. For example, when interacting with orphanages, Zhuli would ask personnel to consider giving the children names that would appeal to American adoptive parents as beautifully and uniquely Chinese (parents were sometimes upset to learn that their children were named after the welfare institution or the place where they had been abandoned and found). In other situations, facilitators worked to protect parents from the strange "too much" of Chinese culture. Even Eddie, who championed good public relations for adoption, expressed disappointment at the occasional family who asked him not to speak Mandarin to their newly adopted child because they thought it might disrupt her smooth transition into new family and culture. And Larry, who was passionate about teaching Chinese culture, was deflated that a group of American parents he was leading did not seem to care about the history and culture of the province from which they were adopting. As I accompanied Larry and this weary new group of parents on the bus to the notary office, they looked out the windows and half-listened while Larry shared historical anecdotes from the front of the bus. But when it came time to fill out the official adoption application forms at the notary office, and parents had to answer the question "Why do you want to adopt from China?" they dutifully obeyed as Larry slowly dictated the words they were to write: "Because I love Chinese culture and the Chinese people." Larry here brokered the official performance of love for Chinese culture, an important service given the CCAA's directive to foreign adopters that they continue to teach their children about Chinese culture after they return home.

D. MARKET MEDIATION OF KINSHIP AND CULTURE

Although the group of new parents on Larry's bus may have been too weary to even perform interest in cultural history, no doubt many of them have gone on to pay for Chinese language lessons, eat regularly at a Chinese restaurant, buy a Chinese doll online, or even return to China with their adopted children on one of the increasingly popular heritage tours. Indeed, Chinese adoption has grown to popularity during a period of increased emphasis within professional and popular adoption circles on honoring or integrating an intercountry adoptee's birth culture into the family narrative,[18] and markets have responded. A niche market of businesses established specifically to facilitate the culture-keeping practices of China–U.S. adoptive families has proliferated in the decade since I began my adoption research, playing an active role in the ongoing production of adoptive kinship and thus extending the culture work done by facilitators. This section considers several aspects of the relatively seamless imbrication of market relations with the cultural production of adoptive kinship.

A good place to start is with *Mei* (Chinese character for "beautiful" and also the first character in the Chinese word for "United States"), a magazine founded by an adoptive couple that is self-described as a "wholesome and age-appropriate magazine with a special emphasis on issues specific to Chinese adoptees age 7 to 15." Not only is it itself a market mechanism for producing kinship, but its pages also advertise the core array of businesses devoted to marketing cultural goods and services to China–U.S. adoptive families with girls in this age group; it is thus a kind of microcosm of the market in question. MoonRattles, Red Thread Gifts, and China Sprout are three Web-based stores[19]; Lotus Travel states that its "current goal is to become adoptive families' first choice when it comes to China Homeland Heritage Tour planning."[20]

Across this array of entrepreneurs, the business of building bridges to Chinese culture is, at the same time, a business of building families; their rhetorical strategies emphasize that families are strengthened either because Chinese culture is brought to them and/or because families are brought to China. The founders of MoonRattles, Red Thread Gifts, and China Sprout (the first two are adoptive parents, and the latter is a Chinese American woman) all refer to their aim of providing cultural tools for families to learn, communicate, and bond. This goal of coproducing family and culture is seamlessly and conveniently embedded in some of the products the businesses offer. China Sprout has an array of jewelry, for example, that features pendants with the Chinese characters for "mother," "mother and love," or "mother and daughter"; the site also offers adoptive families the free service of "giving your child a good real Chinese name" (explaining that most non-Chinese adoptive parents do not or cannot get it right). Red Thread Gifts offers designs that integrate Chinese characters into more recognizable, Western family themes such as "Our First Christmas" ornaments, while MoonRattles sells Chinese heritage activity kits for hands-on family learning that introduces children "to the world . . . right at home." And Lotus Tours offers tours to China, on which activities from kiteflying to rickshaw rides promise to engage the whole family; the company's tag line is "Uniting Families and Connecting Cultures." Some of the customer testimonials posted on these businesses' Web sites in fact highlight the cathecting of kinship accomplished through the purchase of cultural products; this might be especially important given that adoptive kinship continues to hold a precarious nonnormative position in American understandings of kinship:

> Another neat thing about the magazine is then she wants to sit down and read it all the way through with *me*! I find that remarkable![21]
>
> This is a wonderful site for adoptive parents (I especially came for an adoption-related charm). Not only can you trust the translations and the quality, but the products are beautiful and celebrate both Chinese culture and adoption in meaningful ways.[22]

Trust in the cultural products and services offered by China–U.S. adoption businesses is also a matter of their good market practices. Lotus Tours emphasizes reliable customer service, including tours uniquely customized to the needs of clients and led by experts in tourism, culture, and adoption issues. In most of the businesses, this reliable expertise is linked to convenience (a "hassle-free" experience). MoonRattles emphasizes how its products can ease the time and knowledge pressures on adoptive parents to include Chinese culture in their family practices. One adoptive mother's testimonial featured on the site states,

> As a parent of a Chinese daughter, I feel we could use all the guidance we can get, and your kits make it so easy. The concise, easy to use kits take all the stress out of researching, copying, and googling many sites to find just one or two activities. You offer numerous ones in one place that gets shipped to our door! Please keep up the great work, good luck with your business. I hope it continues to grow as we will all benefit from your kits! My bio 11 year old was just as interested as my 4 year old from China! You've succeeded!

Business "success" appears here as the application of sound market practices to the simultaneous production of cultural knowledge and family ties.

The degree to which practices of selling culture challenge and/or reproduce dominant forms of family ties remains an open question. On one hand, these businesses sometimes link culture and kinship in ways that accentuate the enchainment of participants in adoption to people outside the nuclear adoptive family unit, and potentially stretch the comfort levels of their customers. *Mei* magazine emphasizes the sisterhood of Chinese adopted girls to each other as well as the "important lessons to learn from adult adoptees and Asian American role models."[23] The owner of China Sprout, Xiaoning Wang, celebrates the growth of the business as a blurring of boundaries between adoptive kinship and other forms of interracial and intercultural kinship.[24] These enchainments extend to China: *Mei* magazine's April–May 2007 issue featured an article on Mother's Day as "a chance to focus on understanding how you have become a beautiful part of BOTH of your moms," and Lotus Tours recommends that adoptive families "extend their tour for birthplace and orphanage visits." A related form of enchainment is the charitable networks that create kinlike relations to Chinese children who remain in orphanages. For example, the MoonRattles site features jewelry made and sold by eight-year-old Cleo, an adoptee "donating 100% of the net profits to two orphanages in China." But it is the sale and purchase of goods and services that emerges as a prime catalyst for the globalized triangulation of family–culture–charity:

> Two percent of Lotus Travel's China Homeland Heritage Tour cost is donated to the orphanages; by offering these meaningful birth country tours, Lotus Travel helped many orphans and at the same time succeeded in introducing the authentic and inspiring Chinese culture to adoptive parents and their children.[25]

On the other hand, the market-brokered links between cultural goods and services and family building do not necessarily challenge the clean break that separates the here and now of the child's postadoption life from the there and then of her preadoption life. Put another way, we might ask how these businesses produce only limited and safe kinds of enchained kinship through cultural brokering. The reproduction of efficient, trustworthy, custom-tailored, hassle-free market exchange might entail covering over and/or reproducing some of the dangerous excesses of race, class, and gender that attend market exchange.

One key to understanding how excess difference is handled in the marketplace of China–U.S. adoption lies in the treatment of Chinese culture itself. For the most part, the connection offered to Chinese culture is not too heavy-handed. Its difference is rendered fun and accessible. When they visit the Lotus Tours Web site, adoptive families are encouraged to visit the orphanage but are first offered the option of just being tourists, where they can "expect to be enchanted by all that China has to offer: authentic Chinese cuisine, fun, shopping, sightseeing and cultural activities." Family fun with and through so-called cultural authenticity is also part of the heritage kits offered by MoonRattles, while Red Thread Gifts has fun by integrating Chinese characters into authentically American t-shirts, totes, or coffee mugs that say everything from "Coach" and "I Love My Uncle" to "Heartbreaker" and "Girl Power." *Mei* magazine is light on Chinese culture as well, with occasional stories on holiday celebrations that might blend a colorful history on Chinese tea with fun ideas for putting on a tea party with banana sandwiches.[26] China Sprout's products run the gamut, from silk *qipao* dresses to Chinese-zodiac onesies (which come in their own plastic Chinese take-out box package). In these businesses, then, Chinese culture is given its lightness and accessibility in different ways, in some cases via a desirably exoticized (and ancient) authenticity, and in others via a selectively hybrid (and contemporary) form.

The safe handling of Chinese culture in the marketplace does not mean that adoptive kinship itself is treated lightly, and in fact, it may be that the former helps to mitigate the dangers of devaluing the latter. This may be especially important given that the social intelligibility of kinship has not (yet) moved beyond a biological or genetic foundationalism, potentially putting adoptive parents on the defensive. As seen previously, Chinese cultural services and products are especially geared to the production of *adoptive* kinship, without putting too heavy an emphasis on its difference.[27] The fun celebration of culture is the serious celebration of kinship.

But in the case of China–U.S. adoption, kinship difference is compounded by its visibility in race and gender. China Sprout sells books on and encourages discussion in its community forum on the serious issues of how to understand and deal with racism, and *Mei* magazine has featured articles on gender stereotyping of Asian girls and racial discrimination (often drawing on stories of so-called role model Chinese American women and/or adult Asian American adoptees). Yet these concerted attempts to produce adoptive identity within its broader complexities and enchainments sit alongside a world of shopping that threatens to spill over into racialized and gendered packaging. The implicit customer for these businesses is the white adoptive parent and, more than this, the white *mothers* of Asian *girls*. The businesses advertised in the pages of *Mei* sell products that, from one angle, transform adoptive kinship across racial divides and, from another angle, fold the exoticism of Chinese girls into domestic white kinship. Red Thread Gifts markets a reunion logo (for reunions of adoptive families that traveled together to China to adopt) that features an illustration especially legible in popular white market spaces: a girl in black pigtails, in a recognizably "Chinese" outfit, standing in front of a pagoda. One of the more telling examples is the Chinese Silver Take-Out Box offered at http://www.adoptshoppe.com. The site tells readers,

> I saw this in a wedding favor catalog but thought, hey, this works for adoptive parents and adoption day celebrations, too! This silver takeout box has a classic Asian style and is a creative place to store jewelry or trinkets. It can be personalized on the front side of the container.[28]

Class relations are also at work, perhaps most obviously in the cost of some of the goods and services that promise the two-sided coin of education and kinning; tours back to China for the whole family add up, as do Chinese language courses or immersion schools. Even the charity that enchains families to family-less children in China might in some ways assert a (white) globalized class position, especially as it surfaces the uneven marketized choices through which kinship was produced in the first place. And although the consumption of trinkets and t-shirts might seem a fairly ubiquitous practice, its global commodity chains and China's centrality to them might also pose challenges to the identity of the adoptive family. One such example comes from a 1996 Listserv discussion among adoptive parents about how to find and compare the cost of Chinese Barbie: one parent reminded readers that Chinese Barbie is made under exploitative sweatshop conditions in underdeveloped countries, something parents with children from China should be compelled to combat in "this new global community we are joining."

E. COMING TO CONCLUSIONS: THE PRODUCTIVE EDGES OF THE MARKET

Is normalized, white, nuclear family kinship produced through the celebratory consumption of difference, or does the consumption of this otherness press the family into uncharted territories of transnational hybridity? Adoptive kinship would seem to sit at the seams of these possibilities, a space touched and produced by markets. While adoptive families' accession of cultural markets might be read as consuming ethnic identity – in keeping with the increasing social normalization of consumption as a means of expressing identity – I want to emphasize how these practices can and should be understood as producing social relations of kinship. As I have tried to demonstrate in this chapter, this is both a banal and dangerous place. Chinese adoption facilitators deflect or absorb a range of raced and classed excesses – including the dangers of adoption itself as commodified – in their work of efficiently and predictably serving the production of kinship. The businesses that market cultural goods and services to China–U.S. adoptive families in the postadoption years also soften the blow that difference and commodification might deal to the social intelligibility of kinship, even as the very banality of those goods and services might reproduce intersections of race–class–gender difference. And so the quotes from Juno and Lani with which I began the chapter do not so much marketize adoption as point to moments when its banal market practices cannot or do not contain its excesses: when raced, classed, and gendered imaginaries plant themselves in popular, mass-marketed cultural spaces and/or in the self-understanding of adoptees, beyond the ability of parents or professionals to manage them.

But adoptees also do their own kind of culture work through, beside, and against the marketplace. In these concluding pages, I briefly turn to Lani and other school-aged adoptees I have interviewed in recent years to see what their experiences and perspectives suggest about the production of kinship through market exchange.[29] Rather than presuppose that markets violate the sacra of childhood, their stories suggest that children participate in and respond to economic production, distribution, and consumption in meaningful and consequential ways. Just as Lani casually discussed adoption as buying a child (after all, lots of money changes hands), so the stories she told about her room full of stuff (from her "guardian angel" doll to a Chinese storybook about a dragon) seamlessly moved between the joy of buying cultural goods and the value of those objects for her identity and kinship. She looked forward to going to culture camp to learn some Chinese dances and told me that she thought adoption was special because you weren't "just American." At the same time, her reflections on what life might have been like if she hadn't been adopted to the United States focused on cultural knowledge that would not have had to be acquired in the market: "It would be *a lot* different from what it is now. We wouldn't go out to eat so much Chinese food. I would know a lot more about my culture.... And, I probably wouldn't need to go to Chinese language camp."

A number of the girls with whom I spoke were aware of the multiple forms of value and valuation placed on them, but also on Chinese cultural objects and activities. Adoptive sisters Tina and Vicki were nine and eight years of age, respectively, when I interviewed them. When I invited them to draw pictures related to adoption, Tina drew a picture of a blonde woman and brown-haired man standing over cribs of both boy and girl Chinese children (she explained that she had used pink and blue to signal gender and "yellow skin" to indicate that the babies were Chinese). Tina explained, "They're looking at babies. That's the dad trying to decide." This imaginary of choice innocently surfaces the excesses of difference that produce kinship within the marketplace of adoption. But my further conversation with this pair of adopted sisters also shows the significance of the mundane purchase of Chinese objects in the home, where family, class, and cultural identity merge. When I asked the girls if they thought it made a difference that they had Chinese art objects hanging in their house, Tina said that if the big scrolls got taken away, she would be sad "because these two things cost a lot of money." Vicki transformed this market value into a social value by adding, "If there were no pictures like this I would probably not think as much of my heritage."

A number of the girls told stories in which money itself cathected them simultaneously to their adoptive families in America and to people and places in China. Eight-year-old Vivian Babicek had a piggy bank full of Chinese currency that she explained this way: "My, my mom, when she went to China, she got me these money so then, because someday we are going to go to China, when I'm older. . . . We're going to the Great Wall. I'm not just going to go but my sister can go, too." A number of the girls imagined how fun it would be to spend money shopping for cute and cheap clothes and toys in China, even as they were involved in raising and/or giving charitable funds to orphanages. Holly Blackmore, who thought learning Chinese was important so she could go back and help orphanages in China, told me, "I think I'm lucky because the nanny [in the orphanage] could have chose other kids to come, to my mom and dad. There was a 1 percent of a chance that it would be me. There's all those other children that could have gone." The relationship between money and good fortune rides on a marketplace of uneven choices, including around the uses of cultural knowledge itself.

While markets play a key and even welcomed role in the production of transnational, transracial adoptive kinship, they only sometimes absorb or deflect the dangers of commodification. All the acquisition of cultural goods and services in the world cannot fully manage the racialized, gendered, and classed differences that characterize the unequal availability of choices and values. As they get older, Chinese adoptees have to negotiate the market-mediated differences of their kinship and sometimes outright refuse to be interpellated by them. But they also seem aware that markets are not so much totalizing as unevenly implicated in the social making of kin. Their insights call for more work on the role that markets play in producing old or new forms of kinship and in absorbing or reproducing the excess differences of family formation.[30] The practices and narratives of China–U.S. adoptive and postadoptive kinship both corroborate and challenge its construction as a baby market. They especially invite attention to the interweaving of market and nonmarket as well as the personal and the global in the political economy of kinship formation.

NOTES

1 All names used in this chapter are pseudonyms, unless otherwise noted.

2 Reyhan Harmanci, *Some Not Smiling over Juno*, San Francisco Chronicle, Feb. 13, 2008, http://www.sfgate.com.

3 John Raible, *Enduring Impact, Enduring Need, in* Outsiders Within: Writing on Transracial Adoption 182 (J. J. Trenka, J. C. Oparah, & S. Y. Shin eds., 2006).

4 Pamela Anne Quiroz, Adoption in a Color-Blind Society 77 (2007).

5 Ana Ortiz and Laura Briggs, *The Culture of Poverty, Crack Babies, and Welfare Cheats: The Making of the "Healthy White Baby Crisis,"* 21 Social Text (2003) 39–57.

6 The Assembly of the Council of Europe has noted "the current transformation of international adoption into nothing short of a market regulated by the capitalist laws of supply and demand." Council of Europe 2000, *International Adoption: Respecting Children's Rights*, http://assembly.coe.int/mainf.asp?Link=/documents/adoptedtext/ta00/erec1443.htm. In this context, China has been the focus of some debate about the degree to which it has given the more "lucrative" intercountry placement of children priority over domestic adoption (*see* Brian Stuy [2006], http://research-china.blogspot.com/2006/01/domestic-adoption-in-chinas-orphanages.html), despite having ratified the Hague Convention on Protection of Children and Co-operation in Respect of Intercountry Adoption.

7 Sharon Stephens, *Introduction: Children and the Politics of Culture in "Late Capitalism," in* Children and the Politics of Culture 10 (S. Stephens ed., 1995).

8 Barbara Yngvesson, *Placing the "Gift Child" in Transnational Adoption*, 36 Law & Soc'y Rev. 227, 235 (2002).

9 *Id.*

10 Ann Anagnost, *Scenes of Misrecognition: Maternal Citizenship in the Age of Transnational Adoption*, 8 *Positions: East Asia Cultures Critique* 390, 398–9 (2000).

11 David L. Eng, *Transnational Adoption and Queer Diasporas*, 21 Social Text 1, 8 (2003).

12 See Barbara Yngvesson *Going "Home": Adoption, Loss of Bearings, and the Mythology of Roots*, 21 Social Text (2003) 7–27; and Eleana Kim *Korean Adoptee Autoethnography: Refashioning Self, Family and Finding Community*, 16 Visual Anthropology Review 43–70 (2001). Yngvesson has drawn on the experiences and narratives of transnational adult adoptees to reconstruct the routes of exchange and value that continue to produce new forms of identity and kin, and Eleana Kim's recent work traces the "returns" of Korean American adoptees to their birth country, where the Korean state interpolates them in the consumption and production of nationalist culture, and where they encounter as adults the trail of paper work that underwrites their global circulation.

13 Julia Chinyere Oparah *et al.*, *Introduction, in* Outsiders Within, *supra* note 4.

14 *Id.* at 7.

15 China Center of Adoption Affairs 2007, *Priority Rules in the Review of Inter-country Adoption Application Dossiers by CCAA*, http://www.china-ccaa.org.

16 It must also be noted that in 2005, the CCAA established rules regarding the types of foreign-country adoption agencies with which it would cooperate (e.g., only those that have nonprofit status and experience in international adoption), which at least, on the surface, undercut some of the marketized conditions of adoption. This law was most likely aimed especially at the United States, where agencies vary dramatically in size, level of experience, type of screening of and support to adoptive families, etc.

17 Intercountry adoptive parents give a required donation of three thousand U.S. dollars to the local welfare institute. There have been occasional reports of misuse of these funds by local officials.

18 This bit of wisdom intensifies in the case of transracial kinship, even as parents and sometimes adoptive professionals worry about overemphasizing the so-called difference of the child. Jacobsen argues that while Chinese culture keeping is "group oriented, intentional, deep, and public," Russian culture keeping tends to be "shallow, sporadic, and familial." HEATHER JACOBSEN, CULTURE KEEPING: WHITE MOTHERS, INTERNATIONAL ADOPTION, AND THE SOCIAL CONSTRUCTION OF RACE AND ETHNICITY (2006) (PhD dissertation, Brandeis University).

19 *See* http://www.moonrattles.com; http://www.cafepress.com/redthreadgifts; http://www.chinasprout.com.

20 Available at http://www.lotustours.net. This small but growing number of small businesses have been established in large part by adoptive parents and/or ethnic Chinese in the United States and range from one-person operations to having up to a dozen staff in both China and the United States.

21 *See* http://www.meimagazine.com.

22 http://www.chinasprout.com.

23 *See* http://www.meimagazine.com.

24 January 2004 newsletter, http://www.chinasprout.com.

25 http://www.lotustours.net/info/adoption/fund/fund.shtml

26 April–May 2007 issue.

27 It is worth noting that on a couple of the sites, adoptive families are not mentioned as the primary customers, but become implicitly so through the kinds of goods and services offered (including translating adoption documents and providing naming services). *See also* http://www.hometownchina.com.

28 http://www.cafepress.com/redthreadgifts.

29 I conducted in-depth interviews with fifteen children in the United States in 2004 and fifteen children in Canada in 2006, between the ages of eight and sixteen (most were eight to ten years old). The former included a drawing exercise and the latter a video tour of interviewees' homes. I touch here on just a few of the themes that emerged from these interviews.

30 In her work on Korean government-sponsored "homeland" tours for adult Korean American adoptees, Eleana Kim has argued that even as adoptees are hailed as returnees to their lost heritage within the globalized Korean economy, they reimagine kinship via extended transnational communities, including with each other. Eleana Kim, *Wedding Citizenship and Culture: Korean Adoptees and the Global Family of Korea, in* CULTURES OF TRANSNATIONAL ADOPTION (T. A. Volkman, ed., 2005).

Nadya Suleman and her babies. At her new home, purchased with funds from media appearances following the birth of her octuplets, Ms. Suleman begins the life of a single mother of fourteen children. She used assisted reproduction and borrowed sperm to achieve her multiple pregnancies. Ms. Suleman's case became controversial after the world learned that she is jobless and receives food stamps and government aid to care for her growing family. (Polaris Images)

PART TWO. SPACE AND PLACE: REPRODUCING AND REFRAMING SOCIAL NORMS OF RACE, CLASS, GENDER, AND OTHERNESS

Transracially adopted children face challenges in coping with being "different." Many transracially adopted children of color, particularly those with dark skin, express the wish to be White. Several studies have found that transracially adopted children struggle more with acceptance and comfort with their physical appearance than do children placed in-race. Appearance discomfort has been linked to higher levels of adjustment difficulties in transracially adopted children and young adults, and one study found that those raised in heavily White communities were twice as likely as adoptees living in racially mixed communities to feel discomfort with their racial appearance.

– Evan B. Donaldson, Adoption Institute Report, 2008

The reaction to the Harris sextuplets stands in stark contrast to the highly publicized White Iowa septuplets. In addition to a phone call from former President Bill Clinton and an invitation to the White House, the McCaughey family received an offer by Iowa's governor to build a new home, the donation of a new 12-seat Chevrolet van, cover stories in Time and Newsweek magazines, and free advertising in major newspapers for their family assistance fund.

– Nikitta A. Foston, *Ebony Magazine*, October 2003

Race matters in society – but does it have any relevance in families? Part Two of this book explores the contours of race, class, gender, and otherness in contemporary child acquisition and parenting. This part considers whether the social, economic, and cultural push back over intercultural placements and assisted reproduction is overblown or deserves continued scrutiny in society.

6 Adoption Laws and Practices: Serving Whose Interests?

RUTH-ARLENE W. HOWE

After enactment of the first "modern" state adoption statute by Massachusetts in 1851,[1] and the subsequent abolishment of slavery and indentured servitude by the Thirteenth Amendment to the U.S. Constitution, adoption in the United States, for the next 120 plus years, evolved as both a state judicial process and a specialized child welfare service to promote the so-called best interests of children in need of permanent homes. During the last two decades, however, developments such as (1) increased involvement of the federal government in promoting adoption for children in state foster care,[2] (2) the federally mandated elimination of race from all adoption or foster care placement decision making,[3] and (3) the rapid growth of private adoptions of infants as a "business" should force us to ask whether U.S. adoption today is meeting its original child welfare intent, or is rather serving the interests of adults. President Clinton's heralded Adoption 2002 Initiative[4] and the 1993 Hague Convention on Protection of Children and Co-Operation in Respect of Intercountry Adoption[5] declared an intent to promote the best interests of children adopted within the country or from outside the country – but is this happening?

As we move into the second decade of the new millennium, all serious child advocates and responsible professionals working in the field of adoption should question the efficacy of the current federal prohibition against any consideration of race in adoption or foster care placement decision making. Are the short- and long-term needs of the steady numbers[6] of children entering the foster care system adequately being met? How well are the best interests of these children being served, especially African American and other nonwhite children, many of whom have so-called special needs[7] and are not the healthy newborn infants many waiting, approved families seek to adopt? Do current laws serve them well? Have the interests and asserted rights of adults superseded the child-centered purpose of adoption as a child welfare service for children in need of substitute permanent families?

And what are the implications of (1) the growing practice of sending African American infants abroad for adoption by foreign nationals and (2) new state and federal legislative changes that permit for-profit organizations to provide foster care and adoption services? Are such for-profit businesses a positive or negative development for African American and other children of color? Will the U.S. State Department's newly published guidance,[8] which insists that service providers in all intercountry adoptions (ICAs) under the Hague Convention counsel parents about raising a child whose cultural, ethnic, or racial background may differ from theirs, inspire the U.S. Department of Health and Human Services (HHS) to reexamine its policy of eliminating any consideration of race in placement decisions?[9]

A. PARADIGM SHIFTS

Two important paradigm shifts have redefined the concept of power in the field of adoption – that is, who holds it and exercises it, and to accomplish what ends? *Child welfare agency workers*, whether in public or private agencies, once were the dominant professionals who worked to provide the specialized service of adoption for a child in need of a substitute permanent home.[10] *Private adoption lawyers and others* today approach adoption as a profit-making business enterprise to meet the desires of adults who want to parent.[11]

1. The Baby Adoption Business

Because of these paradigm shifts, U.S. adoption is no longer a "specialized child welfare" service. Today, when children are voluntarily relinquished shortly after birth, their adoption is more like a business transaction than a child welfare service. Private adoption of healthy infants can be compared to early Roman adoption law and practices. Roman law accorded adults the right to ensure continuity of a particular family by adopting not a child, but often an adult male.[12] Some assert that the growth and privatization of baby adoptions, especially involving African American and other biracial or mixed youngsters of African descendant, sets the stage for an anachronistic recommodification of African Americans.[13] It also poses a challenge for the future existence of voluntary, nonprofit agencies, which traditionally have been committed to the delivery of quality service, and not to making a profit for shareholders and owners.

Massachusetts governor Mitt Romney, on September 7, 2006, signed a bill that permitted for-profit agencies to place children for adoption and compete for state foster care contracts.[14] The measure, part of an economic development bill, amended the definition of *placement agency*, which previously limited child placements to nonprofit agencies. This provision was passed by the state house and senate in late August, without a public hearing. Massachusetts child advocates were outraged to learn that Massachusetts Mentor, part of a national for-profit human services company, had lobbied extensively for the measure. Massachusetts Mentor has come under intense scrutiny in local child welfare circles because of its role in the March 2005 death of a four-year-old boy, Dontel Jeffers, just eleven days after being placed in the home of a twenty-four-year-old single foster mother, who was hired by Massachusetts Mentor, in partnership with a Newton, Massachusetts, nonprofit agency. Massachusetts Mentor, as reported in an October 7, 2006, article in the *Boston Globe*,[15] has agreed to pay an undisclosed amount to settle the wrongful death case filed by the parents of Dontel Jeffers. Massachusetts Mentor officials have defended their lobbying role and assert that this state bill is a follow-up to the federal legislation[16] that President Bush signed in November

2005, which allows certain for-profit foster care agencies to receive Medicaid funds and direct federal reimbursement. State adoption advocacy groups are moving to have this amendment rescinded.

Whenever demand for a desirable product or service exceeds the available supply in any market economy, a new business opportunity is created for those who can meet the demand. As the number of adults (mostly white) seeking to adopt began to exceed by far the number of available healthy, white infants, many people, frustrated by the long waiting lists of agencies, began, in the 1980s and 1990s, to adopt internationally through reputable agencies. Others obtained babies privately, via independent adoptions arranged by lawyers, doctors, the clergy, or other persons, and sadly, some, to their grief, used the Internet to locate available babies both here and abroad. With advances in assisted reproductive technologies, some fertility clinics now offer embryos for adoption.[17] Indictments and prosecutions for illegal so-called baby selling[18] are on the rise. At some point, pressure for federal regulatory legislation may begin to mount, more perhaps to protect prospective adopters from unscrupulous baby brokers than to protect the welfare of the involved babies.

Another harsh reality of the baby market is that African American babies go for the lowest price to white consumers, who, because of continuing income gaps between white and black Americans, are able to outbid and exclude prospective African American adopters from the marketplace. While U.S. State Department records indicate that international adoptions by Americans have increased more than 140 percent, with couples citing a lack of American babies as the reason for adopting from abroad, an increasing number of American babies (largely black) have begun to be placed for adoption in other countries. Two years ago, the *Christian Science Monitor* reported that

> the US is now the fourth largest "supplier" of babies for adoption to Canada. Adoption by Shepherd Care, an agency in Hollywood, Fla., placed 90 percent of its African American babies in Canada. One-third of the children placed through Adoption-Link in Chicago, which specializes in adoptions for black babies, go to people from other countries.... The exact numbers are not available, but interviews with adoption agencies and families in Canada, Germany, France, and the Netherlands indicate that the US also sends babies to those four countries as well as Belgium and England. Most of the children are black newborns. Most of the adopting parents are Caucasians.[19]

Completely unregulated baby selling by new private adoption business entrepreneurs and the increasing numbers of transracial adoptions of foster care youngsters can contribute to a destructive undermining of the African American family and community, that is, a cultural genocide of sorts.[20] The greatest harm one can inflict on any group is the oblivion that awaits a people denied the opportunity to rear its own children.[21]

2. Agency Adoptions: Public Policy for Nonbabies

From my perspective, there is something very disingenuous about the way transracial adoption (TRA) proponents constantly refer to the plight of black children in foster care, when in fact, most whites who seek to adopt domestically look for healthy infants, not older children with a range of special needs. Although current U.S. statistics on biracial and mixed-race births are not available, the steady increase in such births is commonly acknowledged. I view the push in the mid-1990s to eliminate race from placement considerations as having been a maneuver to enable whites who sought to adopt infants to gain access to the growing number of nonmarital, mixed-race children who were being voluntarily relinquished to public and private agencies; because of the traditional one-drop rule,[22] these biracial and mixed-race infants were deemed to be black and, under a traditional same-race placement preference, not readily available. Thus passage of Interethnic Placement Act (IEPA),[23] which definitively prohibited any consideration of race, enabled white applicants to essentially "garner the market" on the only readily available "crop" of healthy infants.[24]

The ten-year federal legislation prohibiting consideration of race ignores the realities of caste in our society. It encourages participation in a charade that reinforces and perpetuates old prejudicial myths and discriminatory practices. Dangerous stereotypes now float disguised under a new halo of professed righteous concern for the well-being and best interests of African American children in the foster care system.[25] Yet can their true interests be promoted by ignoring something as immutable as skin color and appearance? Race and color still profoundly influence the lives of all Americans, governing the choices a person makes or believes that he or she may have.[26]

Indeed, those who consider the United States to now be a so-called color-blind society in fact take a very blind-sighted approach to race and color issues that prevents acknowledgment of unresolved issues of race and color inextricably intertwined with issues of power, status, and the allocation of resources. This accounts for continuing inequities that make a mockery of America's claims of being a democratic land of equal opportunity for all. Most individuals are not color-blind. Skin color and perceptions of racial difference trigger, within the beholder, unconscious stereotypical expectations and assumptions, which then govern any ensuing social interactions.[27]

Without a doubt, the Adoption and Safe Families Act of 1997 and its subsequent amendments have required courts and child welfare agencies to work on a much faster timetable by mandating that a hearing must be held no later than twelve months after a child enters foster care. But far too little attention has been given to understanding why the number of children in foster care – disproportionately nonwhite – continues to climb. Something systemic is wrong. More macrostudy of the problem is needed, along with a stated national family policy. Rather than mandating a reduced time frame for decision making once a child enters foster care, strategies to preserve families and empower communities should be in place to minimize intervention and removal.

Given both the shortage of trained minority child welfare workers and the overall youth and inexperience of many child protection line workers, a serious question can be raised as to whether the true needs of African American children and their families are being met. Why are greater efforts and resources not made and deployed to help and assist the parents, families, and communities from which children are removed to adequately care for and rear their children? Sadly, from my perspective, entrenched negative stereotypes, assumptions, and beliefs in the inherent inability and incompetence of minority families and communities account for the unquestioning acceptance that elimination of all consideration of race, ethnicity, or national origin from placement decision making could be in the best interests of black children.

It is indeed both ironic and encouraging that a decade after the repeal of the Multiethnic Placement Act of 1994 and a voiding of the initial HHS guidance[28] on permissible considerations of race in making placement decisions, the U.S. State Department, another federal agency, has openly acknowledged that for ICAs under the Hague Convention, it is in children's and parents' best interests to provide a thorough background about each child and how his or her medical, educational, and social history may play out in an adoptive family. One can only hope, given the disturbing increase in the trafficking of children and women around the world, that these State Department directives will not only apply to U.S. parents adopting children from abroad, but may also serve to ensure that the growing number of African American babies leaving the country are placed with appropriate adoptive parents. Furthermore, one can hope that provisions under the Hague Convention requiring the rendering of periodic reports on a child's growth and development are enforced. Otherwise, I worry about what the future may hold for these children, especially if, on adoption, they lose their U.S. citizenship.

B. PERSONAL PERSPECTIVE

On the basis of my academic training in social work and law, and professional experiences working in the field, following are the key considerations and perspective lenses through which I view the questions posed at the beginning of this chapter:

1. Adoption should be a specialized child welfare service offered to meet the needs and promote the best interests of the child without a permanent home or family able to provide adequate care. This service should be provided by either private voluntary or public governmental agencies, staffed by competent child welfare professionals. It should not be a private for-profit business run by those who seek to satisfy the desires of adults with the economic means to "purchase" a child of their choice.
2. Sensitive adoption policies and practice should acknowledge the adopted child's place in a complex family structure that might include both his or her adoptive and birth parents and other relatives. In certain cases of adoption of older children by foster parents, or in cases of so-called open adoption of newborns,[29] I think that contact with birth parents and family members is appropriate. I also believe that case law[30] allowing adult adopted persons access to their records is moving in the right direction.[31]
3. Those who adopt, either via domestic TRA or an ICA, take on a huge responsibility and challenge. Successful parenting requires a lifelong commitment to being involved in continuous learning about human growth and

development to acquire the knowledge and skills necessary to meet the particular needs of one's child. Given the unresolved issues of race and color in American society, successful TRA or ICA parenting requires a special awareness, sensitivity, and knowledge.[32] If adoptive parents encounter difficulties, societal resources and services should be available to assist them.

4. To ensure that qualified persons are entrusted with the rearing of children in need of substitute parents, there must be an orderly, thorough screening process to select the most appropriate placement situations. In light of what is known today about child development and the care a child must receive to develop self-management skills, a capacity to complete demanding tasks, and positive self-esteem and identity, more than loving care given within the private confines of the adoptive home is required.[33] The messages that a transracial or international adoptee receives from the extended familial group of which the family is a part, from the community in which the family resides, and from the larger society are critically important. If these messages convey positive acceptance, the child's self-esteem will grow and flourish. If the messages are negative, the child will feel devalued, rejected, and/or ostracized, and the lifelong emotional impact of these feelings can be devastatingly crippling.
5. Finally, current federal legislation and state enactments modeled on the revised Uniform Adoption Act[34] do not advance any of the long-range objectives I strongly believe practitioners and policy makers in the fields of law and social work should be working toward on behalf of African American children, namely.
   - properly *naming* and *acknowledging* what African American children need to grow up to be successful, contributing citizens in the twenty-first-century United States
   - developing and implementing better policies, practices, and protocols for identifying, recruiting, approving, and sustaining those best able to rear and nurture children of color in need of permanent adoptive homes.

NOTES

1 Massachusetts Adoption of Children Act of 1851, Act of May 24, 1851, 1851 Mass. Acts, ch. 324.

2 Ruth-Arlene W. Howe, *Adoption Laws and Practices in 2000: Serving Whose Interests?* 33 FAM. L.Q. 677, 677 (1999).

3 *Id.*

4 On December 14, 1996, President Clinton announced the goal of doubling "the number of children we move from foster care to permanent homes, from 27,000 a year today, to 54,000 a year by the year 2002." *President's Radio Address*, 32 WEEKLY COMP. PRES. DOC. 2512 (Dec. 14, 1996). *See also President's Memorandum on Adoption and Alternative Permanent Placement of Children in the Public Child Welfare System*, 32 WEEKLY COMP. PRES. DOC. 2513 (Dec. 14, 1996), and U.S. DEPT. OF HEALTH & HUMAN SERVICES, ADOPTION 2002: A RESPONSE TO THE PRESIDENTIAL EXECUTIVE MEMORANDUM ON ADOPTION ISSUED DECEMBER 14, 1996 (Feb. 1997); *President Clinton Announces Expansion of the Internet to Increase Adoptions* (Nov. 24, 1998), http://govinfo.library.unt.edu/accessamerica/docs/adoption.html.

5 In 1988, Hague Conference member states decided to prepare a convention on intercountry adoption that would set reasonable and achievable international standards to protect the children, prospective adoptive parents, and birth parents involved in any intercountry adoption. Hague Conference on Private International Law, *Hague Convention on 29 May 1993 on Protection of Children and Co-operation in Respect of Intercountry Adoption*, 1 May 1995 (entered into force), S. Treaty Doc. No. 105-51, 32 I.L.M. 1134, http://www.hcch.net/index_en.php?act=conventions.pdf&cid=69.

6 U.S. Department of Health & Human Services, *Trends in Foster Care and Adoption*, http://www.acf.hhs.gov/programs/cb/stats_research/afcars/trends.htm.

7 *See* Sanford Katz & Ursula Gallagher, *The Model State Subsidized Adoption Act*, 4 CHILDREN TODAY 8 (Nov.–Dec. 1975); Janet Mason & Carol W. Williams, *The Adoption of Minority Children: Issues in Developing Law and Policy, in* ADOPTION OF CHILDREN WITH SPECIAL NEEDS: ISSUES IN LAW AND POLICY 83 (Ellen C. Segal ed., 1985) (discussing special law and policy challenges regarding black and minority children); Judith K. McKenzie, *Adoption of Children with Special Needs*, 3 THE FUTURE OF CHILDREN 1, (Spring 1993), http://www.futureofchildren.org/usr_doc/vol3no1ART4.PDF.

8 U.S. Department of State Office of Children's Issues, *Intercountry Adoption*, p. 11, http://adoption.state.gov/pdf/Intercountry%20Adoption%20From%20A-Z.pdf.

9 U.S. Department of Health & Human Services, *Protection from Race, Color, and National Origin Discrimination in Adoption and Foster Care*, http://www.hhs.gov/ocr/civilrights/resources/specialtopics/adoption/index.html.

10 Howe, *supra* note 2, at 680.

11 *Id.*

12 *See* J. A. CROOK, LAW AND LIFE OF ROME 90 B.C.–A.D. 212, at 111–12 (1967).

13 I use the term *recommodification* to denote a revival of commodification, construed broadly by Professor Radin to include "market rhetoric, the practice of thinking about interactions as if they were sale transactions, and market methodology, the use of monetary cost-benefit analysis to judge these interactions." Margaret Jane Radin, *Market-Inalienability*, 100 HARV. L. REV. 1849, 1859 (1987) (rejecting two archetypes – universal commodification and universal noncommodification – claiming both fail to recognize market inalienability, i.e., that some things may be given away but not sold). *See also* Ruth-Arlene W. Howe, *Redefining the Adoption Controversy*, 2 DUKE J. GENDER L. & POL'Y 131, 147–9 (1995).

14 Patricia Wen, *For-Profits to Compete in Child Placements*, BOSTON GLOBE, Sept. 17, 2006, at B1. *See also An Act Relative to the Economic Development of the Commonwealth*, CHAPTER 293 OF THE ACTS OF 2006, Sept. 7, 2006, http://www.mass.gov/legis/laws/seslaw06/sl060293.htm.

15 Patricia Wen, *Deal Seen in Death of Boy, 4, in Foster Care*, BOSTON GLOBE, Oct. 7, 2006, at B1.

16 Fair Access Foster Care Act of 2005, Pub. L. No. 109-113, 119 Stat. 2371 (2005).

17 *See, e.g.*, National Embryo Donation Center, http://www.embryodonation.org/index.html; Malpani Infertility Clinic, http://www.drmalpani.com/embryoadoption.htm; California IVF: Davis Fertility Clinic, Inc., http://www.californiaivf.com/adoption.htm.

18 Late in September 1999, a Los Angeles grand jury handed down a nine-count, twenty-one-page federal indictment alleging a widespread scheme to recruit Hungarian women to enter the United States illegally to sell their babies between 1994 and 1996. Janice Doezie, an Orange County attorney, pleaded guilty to charges related to this scheme. *Lawyer Pleads Guilty in Baby-Selling, Fraud Case*, LOS ANGELES TIMES, March 18, 2000, http://articles.latimes.com/2000/mar/18/local/me-10098. Heather Barnett, a Vancouver barrister, was also charged with conspiracy to smuggle pregnant women into the

United States at Blaine Crossing. Scott Sunde, *Conspiracy Charged in Baby-Selling Operation*, SEATTLEPI.COM, Oct. 5, 1999, at B1, http://www.seattlepi.com/archives/1999/9910050072.asp. *See also* Susan Gilmore, *Alleged Baby Sellers Slipped into U.S. at Blaine Crossing*, SEATTLE TIMES, Oct. 4, 1999, at A1.

19 Dawn Davenport, *Born in America, Adopted Abroad*, THE CHRISTIAN SCIENCE MONITOR, Oct. 27, 2004, http://www.csmonitor.com/2004/1027/p11s01-lifp.html.

20 Ruth-Arlene W. Howe, *Redefining the Transracial Adoption Controversy*, 2 DUKE J. GENDER L. & POL'Y 131 (Spring 1995).

21 *Id.*

22 Daniel J. Sharfstein, *Crossing the Color Line: Racial Migration and the One-Drop Rule, 1600–1860*, 91 MINN. L. R. 592, 593 (2007) ("the idea that anyone with any African 'blood' is legally black").

23 Interethnic Placement Act, Pub. L. No. 104-188 § 1808, 110 Stat. 1755 (1996), 42 U.S.C. §1996b (1996).

24 Howe, *supra* note 20, at 147–49.

25 Ruth-Arlene W. Howe, *Transracial Adoption: Old Prejudices and Discrimination Float under a New Halo*, 6 B.U. PUB. INT. L.J. 409 (1997). *See also* A. Leon Higginbotham Jr. *et al.*, *Shaw v. Reno: A Mirage of Good Intentions with Devastating Racial Consequences*, 62 FORDHAM L. REV. 1593, 1630 (1994).

26 Howe, *supra* note 2, at 685. *See also* Lynda Gorov, *Lexington Reexamines Strength of Its Diversity*, BOSTON SUNDAY GLOBE, Nov. 13, 1994, at 1 ("Around suppertime last January, Gerri Weathers' car stalled on a residential street in this town, where she has lived for nearly 20 years. Instead of ringing a stranger's doorbell, the management consultant who is active in community affairs trudged 2 miles in the dark and bitter cold to a public telephone. 'That's right, I did, because I wouldn't take that risk,' Weathers said. 'Being a woman doesn't matter. I'm an African-American, and I wasn't sure how I'd be received.'").

27 *See, e.g.*, Hans J. Massaquoi, *The New Racism*, EBONY, Aug. 1996, at 56 (reporting incidents that illustrate that black VIPs are far from immune to bigotry), and CORNELL WEST, RACE MATTERS x–xi (1993) (recounting his difficulties in hailing a taxicab in New York City).

28 Howe, *supra* note 2, at 684–6.

29 Ruth-Arlene W. Howe, *Adoption Practices, Issues, and Laws 1958–1983*, 17 FAM. L.Q. 178, 191 (1983) ("Hence, 'open adoption' is a concept that encompasses more than just 'opening' adoption records. It is the antithesis of the old adoption mode that attempted to mirror biology. Rather, it harks back to the time of Justinian when all parties of the adoptive triad had to appear before a magistrate and the right to inherit from the biological father was recognized even after an adoption decree.")

30 *See, e.g.*, Doe v. Sundquist, No. 01-S-01-9901-CV-00006, 1999 Tenn. LEXIS 429 (Sept. 27, 1999) (holding that disclosure of sealed adoption records to adopted persons over twenty-one years, as provided in 1995 Tenn. Pub. Acts, ch. 523, as codified at TENN. CODE ANN. § 36-1-127(c), does not impair plaintiff birth parents' right to privacy nor any vested rights in violation of the Tennessee Constitution).

31 *Id.*

32 Howe, *supra* note 2, at 679.

33 *Id.*

34 Unif. Adoption Act (1994) has been adopted by Vermont; *see* VT. STAT. ANN. Tit. 15A, § 1–102 (2007).

7 International Adoption: The Human Rights Issues

ELIZABETH BARTHOLET

Human rights issues are at the core of the current debate over international adoption. Many of us who support international adoption see it as serving the most fundamental human rights of the most helpless of humans – the rights of children to the kind of family love and care that will enable them to grow up with a decent chance of living a healthy and fulfilling life. Many who oppose international adoption, however, argue that it violates the human rights of the children placed and of any birth parents that may exist, and serves only the interests of those who should be seen as having no rights – the adults who want to become parents.

Human rights activists in the international adoption arena have spoken with a relatively singular voice – a voice that is generally critical of international adoption, calling either for its abolition, or for restrictions that curtail its incidence in ways that I see as harmful to children, limiting their chances of being placed in nurturing homes with true families, and condemning even those who are placed eventually for unnecessary months and years in damaging institutions. This voice has had a powerful impact, in part because the international children's rights organizations taking the negative view include such powerful ones as the United Nations Children's Fund (UNICEF) and the United Nations Committee on the Rights of the Child (CRC). Also, opposition to international adoption that purports to be grounded in children's human rights tends to be more politically palatable, and thus persuasive, than arguments grounded in a country's nationalist claims of ownership rights over its children or nationalist pride in not appearing unable to care for its children. It is important for those who care about human rights and about children to think through their position on these issues, rather than simply accepting without question the notion that the children's human rights establishment has a fix on the truth in this area. The future of international adoption, and of many children, is at stake.

In international adoption, adoptive parents and children meet across lines of difference involving not just biology, but also socioeconomic class, race, ethnic and cultural heritage, and nationality. Typically, the adoptive parents are relatively privileged white people from one of the richer countries of the world, and typically, they will be adopting a child born to a desperately poor birth mother belonging to one of the less privileged racial and ethnic groups in one of the poorer countries of the world. International adoption is characterized by controversy. Some see it as an extraordinarily positive form of adoption. It serves the fundamental need for family of some of the world's neediest children. The families formed demonstrate our human capacity to love those who are, in many senses, "other," in a world that is regularly torn apart by the hatred of alien others. But many see international adoption as one of the ultimate forms of human exploitation, with the rich, powerful, and white taking children from poor, powerless members of racial and other minority groups, thus imposing on those who have little what many of us might think to be the ultimate loss.

International adoption grew steadily and significantly over the half-century following World War II, with many thousands of children crossing national borders for adoption each year. But the controversy surrounding such adoption continues, and pro-adoption moves have recently been matched by moves in the opposite direction. In the past three years, adoptions from other countries into the United States have gone significantly down in number.[1] The prior general increase in numbers reflects the opening up of new countries willing to send some of their homeless children abroad for purposes of finding adoptive homes. However, the typical pattern has been for countries that do open up to close down again, either by prohibiting international adoption altogether or by creating restrictions that limit the number of children placed and increase the waiting periods that those children who are placed spend in damaging institutions. This happens without regard to the fact that millions of children in these countries are growing up or dying in horribly inadequate orphanages or on the streets.

The 1993 Hague Convention on Protection of Children and Co-operation in Respect of Intercountry Adoption illustrates the conflict today in terms of directions for law reform. In many ways, the Hague Convention represents a step in the direction of legitimizing international adoption. Most of the countries involved in both sending and receiving children agreed to the terms of this convention, and many have ratified it, with more likely to do so soon. The Hague Convention recognizes international adoption as preferable for children as compared to any in-country placement other than adoption, by contrast to the earlier Convention on the Rights of the Child, which prefers in-country foster care and other "suitable" institutional care to out-of-country adoption. However, the original goals of the Hague Convention included the idea of *facilitating* international adoption and expediting the placement of children in need. International children's human rights organizations succeeded in changing the focus of the Hague Convention negotiations so that this facilitation goal was eliminated and the thrust became more single-mindedly focused on preventing adoption abuses. In addition, the Hague Convention is being used by many adoption opponents to argue for the kind of state monopoly control over international adoption that often functions to effectively close, not open, opportunities for adoption.[2]

UNICEF has played a major role in recent attempts to restrict international adoption.[3] UNICEF's official policy on international adoption makes clear its generally negative attitude. The policy only grudgingly approves of such adoption and places it low on the hierarchy of alternatives for children in need of care, even if perhaps not quite as low as institutional care.[4] It states, in pertinent part,

> For children who cannot be raised by their own families, an appropriate alternative family environment should be sought in preference to institutional care, which should be used only as a last resort and as a temporary measure. Inter-country adoption is one of a range of care options which may be open to children, and for individual children who cannot be placed in a permanent family setting in their countries of origin, it may indeed be the best solution.[5]

UNICEF makes clear in this policy statement and in discussions of its significance that "permanent family" care in the form of foster care in-country is preferred to out-of-country adoption. Of course, there is little to no foster care in most sending countries today, and even in countries like the United States, where foster care is the primary placement for children in state care, it is rarely "permanent," even when it takes the form of kinship foster care. Another paragraph in this policy statement argues that the money involved in international adoption, together with the lack of adequate regulation, has created an industry "where profit, rather than the best interests of children, takes centre stage," and where "abuses include the sale and abduction of children, coercion of parents, and bribery, as well as trafficking to individuals whose intentions are to exploit rather than care for children."[6] UNICEF has, in recent years, issued a variety of statements indicating that large numbers of adoptions from any particular country should be seen as an indication of problems, requiring restrictive action. UNICEF has recently promoted forms of so-called adoption reform law in Guatemala, which have resulted, at least temporarily, in the closing down of international adoption in that country[7]; many think that the proposed reforms will, at a minimum, limit any such adoption in the future to very small numbers. Along with many others, UNICEF has for years claimed that Guatemalan adoptions are plagued by problems, including illegal payments to birth mothers. However, the extent of any illegal activity in Guatemala is subject to debate. Moreover, Guatemala is one of the very few countries that have, in recent years, kept many babies preplacement in decent foster care, rather than in damaging institutions, and one of the few that have placed for adoption in infancy, conditions that are central to the children's prospects for healthy, normal development. Guatemala has also freed up significant numbers of children for placement, ranking second in 2006 for the number of children sent to the United States for adoption, despite its relatively small size.[8]

The European Parliament was, in recent years, dominated by forces taking the position that international adoption was inherently a violation of children's human rights and was committed to making eastern European countries agree to outlaw international adoption as a condition to joining the European Union. Romania, where ongoing poverty and dislocation resulting from the disastrous Ceausescu regime mean that vast numbers of children continue to be relegated to orphanages, which deny them any decent life prospects, was induced by this pressure to enact, in June 2004, a law eliminating international adoption altogether (except for adoption by a child's grandparents).

Overall, as of 2003, almost half of the forty nations that had made the top-twenty list of nations sending children to the United States for adoption within the previous fifteen years were either closed or effectively closed to intercountry adoption.[9]

International adoption is not a panacea. It will never be more than a very partial solution for the problems of the homeless children of the world. There are millions and millions of those children. The best solution, in any event, would be to solve the problems of social and economic injustice that prevent so many birth parents from being able to raise their children themselves. But given the realities of today's world and the existence of so many children who will not be raised by their birth parents, international adoption does provide a very good solution for virtually all of those homeless children lucky enough to get placed. In my view, it also pushes us forward on a path to creating a more just world. At the moment, most of those who matter in determining the world's policies on international adoption see the issues differently.

A. THE POLITICS AND THE POLICY PROS AND CONS

There are three issues at the heart of the debate over international adoption. One has to do with the interests of existing children who need homes and could realistically be placed in international adoptive homes but are unlikely to find in-country adoptive homes. Another has to do with the interests of the larger community, particularly in the sending country, and particularly including birth parents and homeless children with no prospects of international adoptive placement. The third has to do with adoption abuses such as baby buying and other violations of core adoption laws.

Opponents of international adoption range along a broad spectrum from those who believe that it is inherently a violation of human rights and should be entirely eliminated, such as Baroness Emma Nicholson, former rapporteur to Romania for the European Parliament,[10] to those who think it should be treated as a last resort, with the focus kept on improving in-country welfare services and on regulation designed to better ensure against adoption abuses. Supporters of international adoption range along a similarly broad spectrum, from those who think it should be treated as one of the best options for children who cannot expect to be reunited with their birth parents, to those who think that it should at least be kept open and be treated as a preferred option to institutional care in-country. Most of those who count themselves as supporters go along with the idea of a preference for in-country adoption over out-of-country adoption. Essentially all agree with the core adoption law principles ensuring that children made available for adoption have been properly separated from their birth parents, with those parents having consented to adoption without any coercion or payment, and ensuring also that the children are placed with appropriately screened adoptive parents.

I place myself at the most enthusiastic end of the spectrum of supporters. I find it overwhelmingly clear that international adoption serves the best interests of existing children in need of homes. I take seriously the arguments based on larger community interests, but I think, in the end, that encouraging and facilitating international adoption does more to serve those interests than does restricting and closing down such adoption. And finally, in addressing adoption law abuses, I think we need to work to eliminate the abuses but keep the focus on the bigger picture – ensuring that as many children as possible receive permanent, nurturing homes as early in life as possible. We have to avoid, as the saying goes, throwing the baby out with the bath water.

1. Interests of Existing Children in Need of Homes Who Could Be Placed Internationally

Here the case for international adoption rests on the social science and child development expertise that demonstrate how harmful it is to children to grow up on the streets or in institutions[11] and how well children do when placed in international adoptive homes.[12] Children placed early in life in international adoptive homes are likely to do essentially as well in their families and in life as children raised by their biological parents in those receiving countries. Children subjected to terrible experiences prior to adoptive placement, as many international adoptees have been, often show remarkable success in overcoming some of the damage done by these early experiences. By contrast, research on orphanages shows how devastatingly harmful institutional life is for children. Interestingly, even the better institutions have proven incapable of providing the personal care that human children need to thrive physically and emotionally. Research on children who started their early life in institutions demonstrates vividly the damage such institutions do even when the children are lucky enough to escape the institutions at relatively early ages.[13] Age at adoptive placement regularly shows up in adoption studies as the prime predictor of likelihood of successful life adjustment.

Opponents of international adoption argue that children are best served by remaining in their community of origin, where they can enjoy their racial, ethnic, and national heritage. They argue that children are put at risk when placed with dissimilar adoptive parents in foreign countries, where they may be subject to ethnic and racial discrimination, in addition to the basic loss of identity associated with their community of origin. But the opponents' claims are based on extreme romanticism, without any grounding in the available evidence and without support in common sense. Children doomed to grow up in orphanages or on the streets cannot expect to enjoy their cultural heritage in any meaningful way. And the real choice today for most existing homeless children in the countries of the world that are or might become sending countries is between life – and often death – in orphanages or life on the streets in their home country, and for a lucky few, life in an adoptive home abroad. Possibilities for adoption at home in the birth country are drastically limited by the poverty of the population and by attitudes toward adoption in most Asian and many other countries that are more blood-biased and otherwise discriminatory toward adoption than is the United States.

Opponents argue that children might be placed in in-country foster care, and in that way, children benefit from remaining in their country and culture as well as possibly remaining linked, in some way, with their birth family. But foster care does not exist to a significant degree in the sending countries and the poor countries of the world – overwhelmingly, the homeless children of the world are living and dying in orphanages and on the streets. The United States is the country with the greatest experience with foster care – for many decades now, the vast majority of the children committed to state care here have been living in foster care because it has been seen as so superior to institutional care. Even with the resources that the United States has to support foster care, it does not work especially well for children. Social science demonstrates clearly that although foster care works better for children than living in birth families characterized by child abuse and neglect, it does not work nearly as well as adoption.[14] It is extraordinarily unlikely that foster care will work better in desperately poor countries than it has in the United States. Moreover, the bottom line for children who might find adoptive homes abroad now is that foster care, whether good or bad, rarely exists as an option.

2. Larger Community Interests

Here the arguments are more amorphous; social science provides no clear answers, and in the end, one must simply make a complicated judgment call. Opponents of international adoption argue that international adoption constitutes a particularly vicious form of exploitation of the impoverished sending countries of the world by the richer countries of the world and the loss of the poor countries' "most precious resources." I see international adoptive families, in which parents and children demonstrate the human capacity for love across lines of difference, as a positive force for good in a world torn apart by hatred based on racial, ethnic, and national differences. I also question how impoverished communities will in fact be in any way enriched by keeping these children in institutions or on the streets.

Opponents point out that international adoption is, at best, only a very partial solution, providing homes to only a small fraction of the children in need in any sending country. They argue that the funds spent on giving homes to the handful would be better spent improving conditions that would benefit the larger group of children in need. A related argument is that the governments of both sending and receiving countries should do more to change the conditions of poverty and the cultural attitudes that result in children being abandoned and surrendered for adoption, rather than making efforts to facilitate the transfer of such a limited number of children to adoptive parents. Opponents also argue that the huge amount of money involved in international adoption, much of which flows to adoption intermediaries and orphanage bureaucrats in the sending countries, creates pressure to keep the international adoption system going, rather than to build up social welfare institutions that would better support birth parents, enabling them to keep their children.

These arguments raise hard issues. The history of the world has involved exploitation by the United States and some other receiving countries of the world, and it is understandable that many would see international adoption as a continuation of this pattern. Moreover, international adoption is unlikely ever to provide direct help for more than a limited number of children. Even if laws were changed to facilitate such adoption, it is unimaginable that it would ever begin to seriously address the needs for adequate nurturing of any significant percentage of the vast numbers of children in need. There are, after all, said to be some one hundred million children with no available caregivers – sixty-five million in Asia, thirty-four million in Africa, and eight million in Latin America and the Caribbean.[15] UNICEF estimates that at least 2.6 million children worldwide live in institutional care, noting that this is a significant underestimate because in some countries, many institutions are not included in the reporting.[16] In any event, the better, more humane solution would be the elimination of the kind of poverty and injustice that produce so many desperately poor people who are unable to keep and raise the children they bear.

A central question is whether international adoption impedes the goals of helping the larger group of children in need and of addressing global poverty and injustice. It is hard to know for sure. It *could* be that international adoption diverts energy and resources that would otherwise be devoted to these goals. But I see no evidence that this is the case, and I hear no claims by opponents that such evidence exists. Indeed, I hear no developed arguments as to why this likely *would* be the case. Opponents, instead, tend simply to describe with outrage the picture of the rich American swooping in to carry the adoptive baby off to its new, privileged life, paying the thirty thousand dollars' worth of adoption fees to various adoption agencies and other intermediaries, and they talk of all that thirty thousand dollars might mean if were devoted to supporting birth parents or improving conditions in orphanages for the many children left behind. But the fact is that denying that prospective adoptive parent the opportunity to parent that child will not likely provide a substitute contribution of thirty thousand dollars to the sending country's poor parents and children. It will much more likely result in that person deciding to pursue parenting through reproductive technology in the United States, or simply giving up on parenting altogether. It is hard to see how closing down international adoption will likely work in any systematic way to help birth parents and children in poor countries.

It seems to me more likely that allowing international adoption will push us slightly forward on the path to improving conditions for parents and children and otherwise addressing poverty and social injustice in the poor and the sending countries of the world. And there is at least some evidence that this is true. Anecdotal evidence indicates that many international adoptive parents emerge from their experience with a much greater sense of commitment to contribute to social services of various kinds in their children's sending countries. Many of them form new organizations dedicated to providing funds for children and child-oriented social services in those countries. So, for example, adoptive parents of children from China have formed several major organizations that fund a wide range of services for the children left behind in orphanages, including medical and surgical services as well as funding for preschools, fostering, "hugging grannies," and much else.[17] The international adoption experience is also likely to make parents more supportive of efforts by their own government to contribute to foreign countries in need or to international organizations devoted to improving the lot of the world's children and addressing world poverty.

Sending country officials who witness foreign adoptive parents gratefully taking into their homes children of different racial and ethnic backgrounds seem likely to realize new potential for placing these children in adoptive homes in their own country. There is some indication that this has happened in South Korea.[18] The exposure that international adoption brings may provide helpful pressure on sending country officials and on people in the richer countries of the world to improve conditions for children in orphanages and on the streets. International adoption has created a new consciousness throughout the world of China's one-child policy and of the related widespread killing and abandonment of baby girls. It has created awareness of the horrendous conditions in orphanages worldwide, as the media discover and expose the facts, as adoptive parents discover the ongoing problems these children suffer related to orphanage life, and as social scientists document these problems.

International adoption often brings significant new funds to poor orphanages in sending countries. For example, in many countries, international adoptive parents are required to pay fees or make contributions that are designed to go directly to improving conditions in the orphanages from which the children are placed for adoption. In China, there has, for some time, been a three-thousand to five-thousand dollar fee[19] required to be paid to the orphanages in connection with every adoption. Given the sixty-five hundred children adopted into the United States from China in 2006 and the seventy-nine hundred or so adopted in 2005, and assuming a minimum three-thousand dollar contribution, this would have meant some 19.5 million dollars in total contributions to orphanages in 2006 and some 23.7 million dollars in 2005. Many international adoption agencies provide support on an ongoing, systematic basis to a wide range of supportive services for children in sending countries who cannot be placed in adoptive homes.[20] International adoptive parents often found and fund programs to provide services for children in the orphanages or areas from which their children came.[21] In addition, international adoption saves sending countries significant costs by relieving them of the burden of support for the children adopted. Opponents see these kinds of contributions as creating problematic pressure to continue with international adoption, rather than focusing on improving conditions in the sending country, but they fail to document any evidence justifying their concern or to show how closing down such adoption produces any comparable contributions to actually improving those conditions.

In the end, it is hard to know for sure what impact international adoption has on the larger goal of helping address global issues of poverty and injustice, but there are reasons to think that it does more good than harm. Given this, the fact that we *do know* that such adoption radically improves life prospects for virtually all those children who are placed provides a powerful argument for expanding, rather than restricting, international adoption.

3. Adoption Abuses

Here there is dispute as to the extent of abuses and as to what to do about abuses, but not as to whether they are a bad thing and should be eliminated. Opponents and supporters of international adoption agree that basic adoption law principles should apply: children should not be given to adoptive parents unless the birth parents have voluntarily relinquished or abandoned them; adoptive parents should raise children lovingly and not in any way exploit them. Universally applicable laws, including domestic law within sending and receiving countries, and international law such as the Hague Convention and the CRC, prohibit payments to birth parents and other practices that can fairly be characterized as baby buying or selling. They also prohibit any exploitation in connection with adoption and provide for the screening of international adoptive parents to ensure that they will be appropriately nurturing parents.[22]

Opponents make some arguments that are simply absurd but are nonetheless seriously problematic to international adoption because they are sometimes believed and thus give adoption an unjustified bad name. For example, some have claimed that adoption involves the murder of children for their organs so that the alleged adoptive parents can use the organs for their "own" children. Responsible agencies have investigated this rumor on numerous occasions and have always rejected it as without any foundation.[23]

More common are the claims that international adoption regularly involves the kidnapping and the purchase of children from birth parents. There is some proof that on some occasions, kidnapping has occurred. To prevent such abuses, the United States now requires, in some countries, DNA testing to match alleged birth parents with the children surrendered for adoption. There is also good reason to believe that in some countries, payments have, on some occasions, been made to birth mothers in connection with their decision to relinquish children for adoption. Many claimed that this was common in Guatemala, and this was a major argument made by those who called for the current moratorium on international adoption there.

It is impossible to say how extensive abuses such as kidnapping and payments to birth parents are. However, the opponents regularly make very misleading statements. For example, UNICEF links under the same "child trafficking" name tag what it calls "illicit adoption," which presumably includes all forms of illegal adoption, with vicious forms of exploitation of children like kidnapping for the purposes of prostitution, slavery, killing for the removal of organs, and child military service.[24] Yet there is no evidence that even when international adoption involves some illegality, it results in the kind of *exploitation* of children that these other "trafficking" practices systematically do. Any fair-minded observer of international adoption would have to admit that the children overwhelmingly end up in adoptive families where they are loved and nurtured and that they grow up doing as well as most children raised in those same receiving countries, as the research discussed earlier shows. Opponents also tend to equate all adoption with baby buying, citing the large amounts paid by adoptive parents, without regard to the fact that such payments may be, and almost certainly generally are, entirely legal, accounted for by the fees charged by agencies and other intermediaries authorized to receive payment for their services in connection with facilitating adoptions.

Opponents also ignore the distinction between payments made to birth parents, which induce them to surrender children they would otherwise keep, and payments made to parents who would be surrendering in any event. The latter may be illegal, but the former is the problem at the core of the baby-buying prohibition. The idea is to prevent any form of coercion, including the proffer of money, having an influence on the decision whether to keep or surrender the child. It is an idea based on the felt value of enabling birth parents to keep their children and children to grow up with those parents, if at all possible. It is extremely unlikely that much of this core form of baby buying is going on in the world. It is illegal everywhere, under a multitude of overlapping laws – laws of the sending country, laws of the receiving country, and international law. And overwhelmingly, the reasons that birth parents in the sending countries of the world surrender their children for adoption have to do with extreme poverty and social devastation – they simply have no choice. They often will have had no choice in getting pregnant – no access to contraception is typical. They may have a job, if they are lucky, that they would lose if they kept their child. They may have one or two children they are struggling to keep alive and know they are incapable of supporting a third. It is entirely understandable that many of these birth parents might accept money, if offered, or seek money if they know other birth parents are getting it, in connection with surrendering their children. These birth mothers are in desperate need, and everyone else involved in the adoption process, most of whom have no such dire need, are getting paid handsome fees. It may be that we should still make such payments illegal – it would be hard to draw a clear legal line between such payments and the kind of payments that would induce surrender, and you need a clear legal line if you are going to hold people criminally responsible, as we do, for baby buying. But we should not see such incidental payments, payments that accompany but do not motivate the relinquishment of a child, as a terrible evil to be avoided at all costs.

There are no doubt some number of birth parents in sending countries who are getting payments that indeed do function to persuade them to surrender children for adoption that they otherwise might have kept and even to get pregnant to surrender the children born. The latter practice we call surrogacy, and in the United States, it is legal today in almost all states, with an enormous surrogacy industry primed to expand the practice as we move forward to the future. I myself would prohibit commercial surrogacy both here and abroad, and I also believe we should maintain the existing prohibition on payments to already pregnant women designed to induce surrender of the child. However, I think we need to acknowledge that such payments are not the ultimate evil that they are often assumed to be. They may, on balance, be wrong, but they need to be weighed against other evils as regulators decide how to shape policy on international adoption.

Opponents of international adoption never weigh the evils on *each side*. Instead, they focus solely on the evils represented by adoption abuses and then argue for restrictive regulation to address those evils. They do not consider the evils represented by failing to place children in international adoptive homes and the good that comes from placing them. And opponents find a ready audience in policy makers, who have traditionally regulated adoption in a way that focuses on the negatives that come from transferring children from one set of parents to another, and not on the positives.

Adoption opponents and adoption policy makers often respond to alleged adoption abuses by calling for a moratorium on adoption, either temporary or permanent. One example is Romania, where, after international adoption first opened up, it was closed down in 2000 in reaction to baby-buying allegations and remained closed for years, essentially until it was permanently closed by the new law banning all international adoption, except grandparent adoption.[25] The evil represented by the fact that some number of impoverished Romanian birth parents accepted money incidental to the relinquishment of their children, with there likely being only a handful who were motivated by the money to relinquish children they otherwise would have kept, was *minuscule*, in my view, by comparison to the evil represented by the thousands of Romanian children condemned to live and die in horrible institutions, who could have had loving, nurturing adoptive homes. Another example is Guatemala, discussed previously. Whatever evil may be represented by the payments to birth mothers there that allegedly triggered the current moratorium pales, in my view, to the evil represented by the thousands of Guatemalan children per year who will now likely be relegated to institutions, rather than being placed in international adoptive homes (see Appendix B, which shows that 4,135 children were placed in the United States in 2006).

Adoption opponents and policy makers typically argue that if international adoption is to continue, the government in any given sending country should take over the adoption process, eliminating any private lawyers and other intermediaries. So do many others who see themselves as supportive of international adoption but focus on the importance of eliminating adoption abuses. They see the state as more likely motivated to enforce the laws, and the private actors as more interested in facilitating adoption, and thus more ready to do what it takes to make it happen, including making payments to birth parents. This tendency to look to the state – to government – as *the* way to solve human rights problems has been critiqued by Professor David Kennedy in a recent book titled *The Dark Sides of Virtue: Reassessing International Humanitarianism*:

> The conflation of the law with the good encourages an understanding of international governance... that is systematically blind to the bad consequences of its own action. The difficulty the human rights movement has in thinking of itself in pragmatic rather than theological terms – in weighing and balancing the usefulness of its interventions... is characteristic of international governance as a whole.[26]

In the realm of child welfare, we often let private actors solve problems that occur when birth parents cannot care for children, and we often let them do this informally, without any state intervention. There is a powerful tradition in all countries of simply letting birth parents or others arrange for someone in the kinship or friendship group to take in children who need parenting care. The U.S.-sponsored Demographic and Health Surveys carried out in many developing and transition countries routinely show 10 to 20 percent of children under fifteen living in households where their parents are not present, sometimes because they have been orphaned and sometimes – indeed the majority of the time – because their parents simply cannot care for them.[27] Often these arrangements are characterized as informal adoption. In the United States, in addition to such informal caretaking arrangements, private or independent adoption is also common – forms of official court-approved adoption in which birth parents and adoptive parents are directly responsible for making the agreement to transfer the child, with the state role limited largely to ensuring that certain basic rules of the adoption game are satisfied, namely, that no financial or other pressure has been put on the birth parents and that the prospective adopters satisfy basic fitness criteria. There is no reason to think that children would be better off if the government in all these countries and in all the states throughout the United States intervened to control all these informal arrangements and much reason to think that children would be far worse off. There is no significant move worldwide or within the United States to outlaw all these private arrangements, substituting state monopoly power. Yet in the world of international adoption, it is common to assume that state monopoly power is the right answer.

In fact, our experience with international adoption helps demonstrate the danger in assuming that more state power will likely mean more protection for human rights. In many countries, state monopoly power over international adoption means that it grinds to a near or total halt. This has been the case in several countries in South and Central America – where the state has taken over, adoptions dwindle to a small trickle, and children made available are no longer freed up as infants, but rather, only after spending many months, and typically at least two or three years, in damaging institutions.

This is the battle that is now being fought in Guatemala, in terms of future regulation. Guatemala has had some of the most international adoption-friendly rules of any country in recent history. Guatemala had been releasing significant numbers of children for international adoption, as discussed earlier, ranking as one of the major sending countries of the world. It placed many of the children surrendered by their birth parents in foster care immediately after birth and moved many of them to their adoptive families within six to eight months. This is almost unheard of in today's international adoption world, and of course, it meant that the children were spared the horrors of institutional life. These children had a good chance to develop normally, both physically and emotionally, in contrast to most international adoptees, who, by virtue of spending most of their early infancy in institutions, are at high risk for developmental and ongoing problems. However, those who called for the current moratorium on adoptions from Guatemala are insisting that any future regulatory system include a state monopoly over international adoption, the elimination of the private intermediaries who have made foster care possible, and the prompt placement of significant numbers of children.

We do need to pay attention to adoption abuses. We should enforce the laws that already exist making them illegal. In some cases, we may need to redesign laws to make them more effective. But we must keep in mind that the main thing children need is a permanent, nurturing home, and that this is also the main thing most birth parents want for the children they cannot raise themselves, but rather, must relinquish. We should avoid any action that, in the name of eliminating abuses, causes children more harm than good by reducing their chances to obtain a nurturing family.

B. REFORM DIRECTIONS FOR THE FUTURE

Those committed to human rights and to children's rights should focus on the *genuine* and *most significant needs* of children, parents, and communities, rather than engaging in false romanticism. They should also focus on the *genuine* and *most significant evils* that children face. Children need loving, nurturing parents to raise them. They need food and shelter and affection. They need protection from disease and disaster. Large numbers of children in the poorer countries of the world live in truly desperate circumstances. Those in orphanages spend their infancy having bottles jammed in their mouths as they are propped in the corners of their cribs. Left unattended for hours in between bottle-propping events, they learn that screaming their hearts out, or making other demands for human attention, is meaningless. Those familiar with orphanages say that one of the most horrifying things is the silence that characterizes so many because the children have learned not to bother to ask for attention. Largely deprived of the human touch, human affection, and human relationships as they grow up, children who survive physically are unlikely to develop emotionally and mentally in ways that will make it possible for them to relate meaningfully and happily to other human beings or to take advantage of educational and employment opportunities. The longer they spend in such orphanages, the less chance they will have at anything resembling normal development. By contrast, those placed in international adoption live comparatively blessed lives and have an opportunity to overcome even very significant deficits caused by early deprivation, with the age of placement overwhelmingly predictive of the chance for normal life.

Those who believe in children's human rights need to promote children's basic right to be liberated from the conditions under which they live in orphanages or on the street, and to grow up with parents who can provide the loving nurturing that is essential for human flourishing. We should place as many of these children as we can in adoptive homes because adoption generally works better for children than other options such as foster care. There may be instances in which foster care will work better, and of course, there should be room for exceptions to the general rule, but the step taken by the Hague Convention to preference international adoption over in-country foster care as a general rule is a step taken in the right direction.

Should in-country adoption be preferred over out-of-country adoption? Almost all who discuss this say yes. However, there is no evidence that in-country adoption works better for children. While almost everyone tends to assume that children should be placed with birth parents of similar cultural and ethnic background, the issue has been examined fairly extensively in the area of domestic transracial adoption within the United States, and there is not a shred of evidence in the entire body of social science studies following transracial adoptees from infancy into adulthood, and comparing them with control group samples of adoptees placed with same-race parents, that any harm comes to children from being raised by parents of a different racial or ethnic background.[28] One might still find an in-country preference appropriate for a range of reasons, including beliefs that, despite the absence of evidence, children will still likely do best when matched with similar parents, or that in-country parents deserve a preference because of the history of exploitation their group or country may have suffered, or simply that it looks better to those suspicious of international adoption and will therefore help limit opposition. Some might find an in-country preference important to counter the risk that the foreign parents' likely comparative wealth will bias the process against the in-country parent.

But the risk of any in-country preference is that it will function as another barrier to placement, delaying, and perhaps entirely denying, the chance for children to find an adoptive home. The overwhelming number of potential adoptive parents for children in poor countries will be in the more privileged countries of the world. If countries implement an in-country preference by a rule mandating an in-country search before the child can be placed internationally, there is a real danger that this will result not only in delaying adoption, but in denying it altogether. This risk is made worse when the official rule prohibits international placement for a period of time, as some countries have provided. When Russia enacted its six-month waiting requirement, there was no realistic possibility of any but a tiny fraction of Russia's institutionalized children finding an in-country adoptive home during that six months. For almost all those children, the rule translates to a simple requirement that they spend an additional six months in damaging institutional care. Beyond that, it reduces the chances the child will ever be placed, both because older children are harder to place and because risk-averse bureaucrats get the message from such rules that international adoption should be seen as a failure, a last resort that should be generally avoided. India recently adopted a rule requiring that 50 percent of adoptions be in-country, effectively precluding adoption for vast numbers of children, given the limited number of in-country adoption prospects. The history of race-matching policies in the United States, which, for many years, gave a preference to placing black children with black as opposed to white prospective parents, is that such policies resulted in delaying and denying adoptive placement for many black children.[29] It is in large part because of recognition of this fact that Congress, in the 1996 amendments to the Multiethnic Placement Act, eliminated *any preference* for placing children within their racial group.[30]

Ideally, in my view, there should be no in-country adoption preference. Countries should simply place children as soon as possible in any available adoptive homes. But if countries institute such a preference, as, under the Hague Convention, they are required to, they should do so in a way designed to cause *no delay whatsoever* in placement for children. *Concurrent planning* is the term for the adoption program inside the United States that should serve as the model. In concurrent planning, adoption professionals work simultaneously to reunite children in foster care with their birth parents, while they work to prepare for adoption. At the point that a decision is reached not to reunite, the child can immediately move forward to adoption. Adapted to international adoption, this model would mean that adoption officials in the sending country would plan simultaneously for the international adoption, while they checked to see if any domestic placement would be possible, rather than planning the international adoption only after exhausting the possibility of domestic adoption.

All efforts should be made to avoid unnecessary delays in placement for children. Like Dr. Dana Johnson, a widely respected specialist in international adoption pediatrics, I think we should treat keeping children in institutions as an intolerable act of cruelty:

> Putting a child in a long-term institution is an act of abuse. Children in institutional care have deteriorations in many things that we want to see children improve in during the earliest years of their life. . . . Their cognitive abilities are lower, their growth is terrible and their brain development is abnormal as well. . . . *A few days in an institution should be as long as children are asked to endure.*[31]

Assuming that adoption, including international adoption, is made the priority option, policy makers then need to focus on certain key reforms. First, they need to ensure that children who cannot realistically be cared for by their parents are freed for adoption as promptly as possible. UNICEF and others emphasize that most of the children in institutions worldwide are not technically orphans, as if this demonstrates that few should be considered for adoption. But the reality is that almost all of these institutionalized nonorphans can expect to live out their youth or die in these institutions, with few or no visits from their birth parents, unless they are made available for international adoption. Governments should be required to take action either to reunite these children with their birth parents, when that can be done in a way that will be good for the child, or to move them promptly on to adoption. The Adoption and Safe Families (ASFA) legislation recently passed by the U.S. Congress[32] can serve as a model for other countries' domestic laws. ASFA provides that children can be held for no longer than fifteen of the prior twenty-two months in foster or institutional care before either being moved back to their birth parents or on to adoption. It provides for bypassing any efforts to pursue family preservation or family reunification in situations where there is no good reason to think the child will ever again be able to live with his or her birth parents. It provides that reasonable efforts must be made *not only* to keep children with their birth parents, *but also*, in appropriate cases, to move them on to adoption. Most countries have no adequate system for identifying children in need of adoptive homes and freeing them from their biological parents so that they can be placed. Orphanages worldwide are filled with children who grow up with no meaningful tie to their parents except the technical tie that means they cannot be placed with adoptive parents. The same is true for street children. Law reform efforts need to focus on creating systems for identifying and freeing up such children, and they need to create realistic methods of expediting the entire process for children, from birth to placement, so that they are moved to nurturing, adoptive homes as early in life as possible.

Second, policy makers in both sending and receiving countries need to facilitate the adoption process so that it better serves the needs of prospective adopters. The primary reason to do this is not because it will promote their interest in parenting, although that interest should be understood as perfectly legitimate, but because it will maximize the numbers of parents for the children in need. Bureaucratic barriers serve to drive prospective parents away, either away from parenting altogether or into the world of reproductive technology, where they will try to produce new children, rather than giving homes to existing children in need.

Policy makers must also address the baby-buying and kidnapping problems that exist in the international adoption world. International adoption's opponents have grossly exaggerated the scope of these problems, using them deliberately to promote their larger antiadoption agenda. But taking children from loving birth parents by applying financial or other pressures is wrong. And it victimizes not only the particular children and parents involved, but the larger group of children and parents whose opportunities for legitimate international adoption are thwarted by the negative regulation that is so often triggered by adoption abuses.

Finally, policy makers need to link their new adoption reform moves with efforts to improve conditions for the children who will not be adopted and for their birth parents. International adoption's opponents are correct in arguing that it can never provide homes for all the children in need and that we must address the problems of poverty and injustice that result in children being abandoned in large numbers in the poor countries of the world. International adoption provides a natural trigger for such reform efforts. Adoptive parents, agencies, and others in receiving countries become more aware of the problems in the sending countries of the world by virtue of the adoption process. With this knowledge, and with the privilege of caring for these children, comes new responsibility for the children left behind.

APPENDIX A: NUMBERS OF INTERNATIONAL ADOPTIONS IN THE UNITED STATES BY YEAR, 1990–2006

Year	International adoptions
2006	20,679
2005	22,728
2004	22,884
2003	21,616
2002	20,099
2001	19,237
2000	17,718
1999	16,363
1998	15,774
1997	12,743
1996	10,641
1995	8,987
1994	8,333
1993	7,377
1992	6,472
1991	8,481
1990	7,093

Source: U.S. Department of State, *Immigrant Visas Issued to Orphans Coming to the U.S.*, http://travel.state.gov/family/adoption/stats/stats_451.html; *see also*, http://travel.state.gov/visa/laws/telegrams/telegrams_1408.html.

APPENDIX B: COUNTRIES SENDING THE LARGEST NUMBER OF CHILDREN TO THE UNITED STATES FOR INTERNATIONAL ADOPTION, BY YEAR, 1990–2006

Fiscal year 2006
6,493 – China (mainland)
4,135 – Guatemala
3,706 – Russia
1,376 – S. Korea
732 – Ethiopia
587 – Kazakhstan
460 – Ukraine
353 – Liberia
344 – Colombia
320 – India
309 – Haiti
245 – Philippines
187 – China (Taiwan-born)
163 – Vietnam
70 – Mexico
67 – Poland
66 – Brazil
66 – Nepal
62 – Nigeria
56 – Thailand

Fiscal year 2005
7,906 – China (mainland)
4,639 – Russia
3,783 – Guatemala
1,630 – S. Korea
821 – Ukraine
755 – Kazakhstan
441 – Ethiopia
323 – India
291 – Colombia
271 – Philippines
234 – Haiti
183 – Liberia
141 – China (Taiwan-born)
88 – Mexico
73 – Poland
72 – Thailand
66 – Brazil
65 – Nigeria
63 – Jamaica
62 – Nepal

Fiscal year 2004
7,044 – China (mainland)
5,865 – Russia
3,264 – Guatemala
1,716 – S. Korea
826 – Kazakhstan
723 – Ukraine
406 – India
356 – Haiti
289 – Ethiopia
287 – Colombia
202 – Belarus
196 – Philippines
110 – Bulgaria
102 – Poland
89 – Mexico
86 – Liberia
73 – Nepal
71 – Nigeria
69 – Thailand and Brazil
57 – Romania

Fiscal year 2003
6,859 – China (mainland)
5,209 – Russia
2,328 – Guatemala
1,790 – S. Korea
825 – Kazakhstan
702 – Ukraine
472 – India
382 – Vietnam
272 – Colombia
250 – Haiti
214 – Philippines
200 – Romania
198 – Bulgaria
191 – Belarus
135 – Ethiopia
128 – Georgia
124 – Cambodia
107 – China (Taiwan-born)
97 – Poland
72 – Thailand

Fiscal year 2002
6,119 – China (mainland)
4,939 – Russia
2,419 – Guatemala
1,779 – S. Korea
1,106 – Ukraine
819 – Kazakhstan
766 – Vietnam
464 – India
334 – Colombia
260 – Bulgaria
285 – Cambodia
221 – Philippines
187 – Haiti
169 – Belarus
168 – Romania
105 – Ethiopia
101 – Poland
67 – Thailand
56 – Georgia
61 – Mexico

Fiscal year 2001
4,681 – China (mainland)
4,279 – Russia
1,870 – S. Korea
1,609 – Guatemala
1,246 – Ukraine
782 – Romania
737 – Vietnam
672 – Kazakhstan
543 – India
407 – Colombia
297 – Bulgaria
266 – Cambodia
219 – Philippines
192 – Haiti
158 – Ethiopia
129 – Belarus
86 – Poland
74 – Thailand
73 – Mexico
51 – Liberia

Fiscal year 2000
5,053 – China (mainland)
4,269 – Russia
1,794 – S. Korea
1,518 – Guatemala
1,119 – Romania
724 – Vietnam
659 – Ukraine
503 – India
402 – Cambodia
398 – Kazakhstan
246 – Columbia
214 – Bulgaria
173 – Philippines
131 – Haiti
106 – Mexico
95 – Ethiopia
88 – Thailand
83 – Poland
79 – Moldova
60 – Bolivia

Fiscal year 1999
4,348 – Russia
4,101 – China
2,008 – S. Korea
1,002 – Guatemala
895 – Romania
709 – Vietnam
499 – India
323 – Ukraine
249 – Cambodia
231 – Colombia
221 – Bulgaria
195 – Philippines

Fiscal year 1998
4,491 – Russia
4,206 – China
1,829 – S. Korea
969 – Guatemala
603 – Vietnam
478 – India
406 – Romania
249 – Cambodia
236 – Colombia
200 – Philippines
180 – Ukraine
168 – Mexico
151 – Bulgaria
121 – Haiti
96 – Ethiopia
90 – Brazil
84 – Thailand
77 – Poland
76 – Latvia
73 – Bolivia

Fiscal year 1997
3,816 – Russia
3,597 – China (mainland)
1,654 – S. Korea
788 – Guatemala
621 – Romania
425 – Vietnam
349 – India
233 – Colombia
163 – Philippines
152 – Mexico
148 – Bulgaria
142 – Haiti
108 – Latvia
91 – Brazil
82 – Ethiopia
78 – Lithuania
78 – Poland
77 – Bolivia
72 – Hungary
66 – Cambodia

Fiscal year 1996
3,333 – China
2,454 – Russia
1,516 – S. Korea
555 – Romania
427 – Guatemala
380 – India
354 – Vietnam
258 – Paraguay
255 – Colombia
229 – Philippines
163 – Bulgaria
103 – Brazil
82 – Latvia
78 – Lithuania
77 – Georgia
76 – Mexico
68 – Haiti
64 – Poland
63 – Chile
55 – Thailand
51 – Ecuador and Hungary

Fiscal year 1995
2,130 – China
1,896 – Russia
1,666 – S. Korea
449 – Guatemala
371 – India
351 – Paraguay
350 – Colombia
318 – Vietnam
298 – Philippines
275 – Romania
146 – Brazil
110 – Bulgaria
98 – Lithuania
90 – Chile
83 – Mexico
67 – Ecuador
63 – Ethiopia
63 – Japan
59 – Latvia
53 – Thailand
51 – Georgia

Fiscal year 1994
1,795 – S. Korea
1,530 – Russia
787 – China
483 – Paraguay
436 – Guatemala
412 – India
351 – Colombia
314 – Philippines
220 – Vietnam
199 – Romania
164 – Ukraine
149 – Brazil
97 – Bulgaria
95 – Lithuania
94 – Poland
85 – Mexico
79 – Chile
77 – Honduras
61 – Haiti
66 – Ethiopia
49 – Japan

Fiscal year 1993
1,775 – S. Korea
746 – Russia
512 – Guatemala
426 – Colombia
412 – Paraguay
360 – Philippines
331 – India
330 – China
273 – Ukraine
224 – Peru
179 – Honduras
161 – Brazil
133 – Bulgaria
124 – Bolivia
110 – Vietnam
100 – El Salvador
97 – Romania
91 – Mexico
70 – Poland
69 – Thailand
64 – Japan

Fiscal year 1992
1,840 – S. Korea
418 – Guatemala
404 – Colombia
357 – Philippines
352 – India
324 – Russia
309 – Peru
249 – Honduras
212 – Paraguay
206 – China
179 – Chile
138 – Brazil
121 – Romania
117 – El Salvador
109 – Poland
91 – Bulgaria
91 – Mexico
86 – Thailand
73 – Bolivia
68 – Japan
64 – Costa Rica

Fiscal year 1991
2,594 – Romania
1,818 – S. Korea
705 – Peru
521 – Colombia
445 – India
393 – Philippines
329 – Guatemala
266 – Chile
234 – Honduras
190 – Paraguay
175 – Brazil
131 – Thailand
123 – El Salvador
97 – Mexico
92 – Poland
87 – Japan
61 – China
60 – Cambodia
56 – Costa Rica
54 – Taiwan
50 – Dominican Republic

Fiscal year 1990
2,620 – S. Korea
631 – Colombia
440 – Peru
421 – Philippines
348 – India
302 – Chile
282 – Paraguay
257 – Guatemala
228 – Brazil
197 – Honduras
121 – Romania
112 – Mexico
105 – Costa Rica
103 – El Salvador
100 – Thailand
66 – Poland
66 – Taiwan
64 – Haiti
59 – Ecuador
58 – Dominican Republic
57 – Japan

Source: U.S. Department of State, *Immigrant Visas Issued to Orphans Coming to the United States*, http://travel.state.gov/family/adoption/stats/stats_451.html.

NOTES

1 *Numbers of International Adoptions in the United States by Year, 1990–2006*, http://travel.state.gov/family/adoption/stats/stats_451.html. *See* Appendix A. While official statistics for 2007 have not yet been released, the State Department has revealed provisionally that the 2007 total is approximately 19,411, down about 16% from the 2004 total of 22,884. *Foreign Adoptions in U.S. Decline for Third Year*, http://www.msnbc.msn.com/id/22045640/; Mac Margolis, *Who Will Fill the Empty Cribs?* Newsweek, Jan. 28, 2008, http://www.newsweek.com/id/105530.

2 *See infra*, note 20.

3 On UNICEF's role, *see generally* Bartholet, *infra* note 10; Pat Wingert, *When There's No Place Like Home*, Jan. 28, 2008, http://www.newsweek.com/id/105531.

4 *See* UNICEF's position on intercountry adoption, *Inter-country adoption*, http://www.unicef.org/media/media_15011.html.

5 *Id.*

6 *Id.*

7 *See* U.S. Department of State, *Warning: Adoptions Initiated on or after Dec. 31, 2007 in Guatemala*, http://travel.state.gov/family/adoption/intercountry/intercountry_3927.html.

8 *Countries Sending Largest Number of Children to the United States for International Adoption, by Year, 1990–2006*, http://travel.state.gov/family/adoption/stats/stats_451.html. *See* Appendix B. The author has had extensive experience with the Guatemalan situation, including a trip to Guatemala in 2005 to give a keynote speech at a conference addressing the controversy over international adoption. Elizabeth Bartholet, *Keynote Speech* (at conference in Guatemala City, Guatemala, "In the Best Interests of Children: A Permanent Family") (Jan. 25, 2005), http://www.law.harvard.edu/faculty/bartholet/speeches.php.

9 Ethica, *The Statistics Tell the Story*, http://www.ethicanet.org/item.php?recordid=statistics.

10 *See* Emma Nicholson, *Red Light on Human Traffic*, GUARDIAN UNLIMITED, July 1, 2004, http://society.guardian.co.uk/adoption/comment/0,,1250913,00.html (opposing international adoption, claiming, with no substantiation, that "children exported abroad... are often subjected to paedophilia, child prostitution or domestic servitude"). Andrew Bainham, Fellow of Christ's College, University of Cambridge, provided intellectual backing for Baroness Nicholson, serving as special adviser to her in her role as rapporteur for Romania. He takes the position that for any of the modern European democracies, engaging in international adoption "amounts to a fundamental failure... to comply with the requirements of the European Convention [for the Protection of Human Rights and Fundamental Freedoms 1950]," together with the CRC, because international adoption constitutes an admission of failure to provide for their own children, and accordingly, that no country should be allowed to join the European Union so long as they were engaging in such adoption. *See* Andrew Bainham, *International Adoption from Romania – Why the Moratorium Should Not Be Ended*, 15 CHILD & FAM. L.Q. 223 (2003); *see also European Parliamentarians Break the Nicholson Monopoly on International Adoptions*, BUCHAREST DAILY NEWS, March 8, 2006 (discussing Nicholson's position and its current rejection by many members of European Parliament, including her successor as rapporteur to Romania).

11 *See generally, e.g.*, Charles A. Nelson *et al.*, *Cognitive Recovery in Socially Deprived Young Children: The Bucharest Early Intervention Project*, 318 SCIENCE 1937–40 (2007); Nelson, *A Neurobiological Perspective on Early Human Deprivation*, 1 CHILD DEVELOP. PERSP. 13 (2007) (summing up a half-century of evidence demonstrating the damaging impact of institutionalization on children); Charles H. Zeanah *et al.*, *Designing Research to Study the Effects of Institutionalization on Brain and Behavioral Development: The Bucharest Early Intervention Project*, 15 DEVELOP. & PSYCHOPATHOLOGY 885, 886–8 (2003). These articles sum up previous research on deleterious effects of institutional rearing as well as ameliorating effects of early intervention. They also describe the Bucharest Early Intervention Project, an ongoing randomized controlled trial of foster placement as an alternative to institutionalization designed to document scientifically both the effects of institutionalization and the degree of recovery that foster care can provide, and to assist the government of Romania in developing alternative forms of care beyond institutionalization. For other recent research, see the St. Petersburg–USA Orphanage Research Team, *Characteristics of Children, Caregivers, and Orphanages for Young Children in St. Petersburg, Russian Federation*, 26 J. APP. DEVELOP. PSYCHOL. 477 (2005) (giving comprehensive, empirical description of orphanage environments, describing the most salient deficiencies as in the social-emotional environment, and describing harmful impacts on children, all consistent with reports on other countries' orphanages); Bilge Yagmurlu *et al.*, *The Role of Institutions and Home Contexts in Theory of Mind Development*, 26 J. APP. DEVELOP. PSYCHOL. 521 (2005) (documenting the harmful impact of institutionalization on "theory of mind" development of children in Turkey, relevant to

social, cognitive, and language development and psychological adjustment, all related to deprivation of normal adult–child interaction, and all consistent with other research findings).

12 *See* Zeanah, *supra* note 9 (describing earlier research). A meta-analysis of research on international adoptees recently published in the *Journal of the American Medical Association* showed the adoptees generally well adjusted with those living with their adoptive families for more than twelve years to be the best adjusted, and with preadoption adversity increasing the risk of problems. Femmie Juffer & Marinus H. van IJzendoorn, *Behavior Problems and Mental Health Referrals of International Adoptees*, 293 J. Am. Med. Assoc. 2501 (2005). *See also* Elizabeth Bartholet, Family Bonds: Adoption, Infertility, and the New World of Child Production (1999), at 150–60; Elizabeth Bartholet & Joan Heifetz Hollinger, *International Adoption: Overview, in* Adoption Law and Practice 10–11 (Joan Heifetz Hollinger, ed., 2006), at 10-15–10-21.

13 Early results of the Bucharest Early Intervention Project, *supra* note 8, show that placement of the institutionalized Romanian children in specially designed, model foster care had ameliorating effects on their intellectual, emotional, psychiatric, and brain development, with the length of time previously in the institution and the age at which they were removed to foster care being significant factors in their functioning.

14 *See* Elizabeth Bartholet, Nobody's Children: Abuse and Neglect, Foster Drift, and the Adoption Alternative 81–97 (1999).

15 USAID, UNICEF, and UNAIDS, Children on the Brink 2002: A Joint Report on Orphan Estimates and Program Strategies (2002), http://www.dec.org/pdf_docs/PNACP860.pdf, at 22–4.

16 *See* presentation by Aldexandra Yuster, Senior Advisor, Child Protection, UNICEF, New York, *Why Children Are Homeless and Effective Responses – Socio-economic Factors*, at conference, "Looking Forward: A Global Response for Homeless Children," Holt International Children's Services, Eugene, Oregon, Oct. 19–21, 2006.

17 *See, e.g.*, http://www.lovewithoutboundaries.com/; http://www.halfthesky.org/; http://www.altrusa.ws/about_altrusa/about_altrusa_index.htm; http://www.chinaorphans.org/. *See also* Laura Christianson, *International Adoption: Giving Back to Your Child's Country of Origin*, http://adoptionblogs.typepad.com/adoption/2004/11/international_a.html (encouraging readers to give back to countries from which they adopt). *See generally* Laura McKinney, *International Adoption and the Hague Convention: Does Implementation of the Convention Protect the Best Interests of the Children?* 6 Whittier J. Child & Fam. Advocacy 361 (2007).

18 Margaret Liu, *International Adoptions: An Overview*, 8 Temp. Int'l & Comp. L.J. 187, 202–3 (1994).

19 U.S. Department of State, *Intercountry Adoption, China*, http://travel.state.gov/family/adoption/country/country_365.html (noting the required three-thousand to five-thousand dollar donation to the institution where the adopted child was raised); Curtis Kleem, *Airplane Trips and Organ Banks: Random Events and the Hague Convention on Intercountry Adoptions*, 28 Ga. J. Int'l & Comp. L. 319, 324 (2000) (discussing international adoption from China and the required donation).

20 *See, e.g.*, http://www.hfsadopt.org/china/index.php?option=com_content&task=view&id=30&Itemid=84; http://www.chinesechildren.org/Charity/.

21 *See, e.g.*, http://www.fujiankids.org/; https://www.grace-hope.org/index.aspx.

22 So, *e.g.*, baby buying not only violates the laws of all sending and receiving countries, but also a variety of international laws. The CRC prohibits "improper financial gain" and "the abduction of, the sale of or traffic in children" (CRC, Arts. 21(d), 35). An Optional Protocol to the CRC, with 103 states parties, requires contracting nations to criminalize

the improper inducement of consent and to enact laws and institute programs to deter the sale of children. Optional Protocol to the Convention on the Rights of the Child on the Sale of Children, Child Prostitution and Child Pornography, G.A. Res. 54/263, Annex II, U.N. GAOR, 54th Sess., Supp. No. 49, U.N. Doc. A/RES/54/263, Arts. 3, 9–10 (May 25, 2000). One of the major goals of the Hague Convention is to establish safeguards to prevent the abduction, sale, or trafficking of children, and many of its provisions are designed to further these goals, with other provisions designed to ensure against other abuses.

23 Bartholet, *supra* note 10, at 153 (general discussion about mythical concerns of organ harvesting).

24 UNICEF, *Guidelines on the Protection of Child Victims of Trafficking*, Provisional Version 2.1, Sept. 2006, at 9; UNICEF, *Combating Child Trafficking* (2005), http://www.unicef.org/publications/index_33882.html.

25 Bartholet, *supra* note 10, at 162–3.

26 *See* David Kennedy, The Dark Sides of Virtue: Reassessing International Humanitarianism 31–2 (2004).

27 Yuster, *supra* note 14.

28 *See* Elizabeth Bartholet, *Where Do Black Children Belong? The Politics of Race Matching in Adoption*, 139 U. Penn. L. Rev. 1163, 1207–26 (1991); Bartholet, *supra* note 12, 126–8.

29 *See* Bartholet, *supra* note 12, at 126; Bartholet, *supra* note 26, at 1201–7.

30 *See* Elizabeth Bartholet, *Cultural Stereotypes Can and Do Die: It's Time to Move on With Transracial Adoption*, 34 J. Am. Acad. Psychiatry Law 315–20 (2006) (describing decisions by the agency with enforcement responsibility in the Multiethnic Placement Act which make it crystal clear that race is to play no part in agency decision making); Bartholet, *supra* note 12, at 130–1.

31 Mental Disability Rights International, *Hidden Suffering: Romania' Segregations and Abuse of Infants and Children with Disabilities* (2006), http://www.mdri.org/projects/romania/romania-May%209%20final.pdf, at 21 (emphasis added).

32 Adoption and Safe Families Act of 1997, Pub. L. No. 105-89, 111 Stat. 2115 § 102 (amending Title IV of the Social Security Act, 42 U.S.C. 601 *et seq.*).

8 Heterosexuality as a Prenatal Social Problem: Why Parents and Courts Have a Taste for Heterosexuality

JOSÉ GABILONDO

José: Hey, Dick, would you rather have a whole gay baby or a straight one without a little toe?
Dick: Yuck, what a weird question. I don't know. I never really gave it much thought.
Jane: Well... I think that I'd rather have the straight baby. People don't really see your toes... and who needs *two* little toes, anyway?
José: Indeed. How about a whole gay baby or a straight one without a pinkie?
Jane: Gee, that's harder. I mean, you can *see* a missing pinkie.
Dick: Ughghg...
José: So true. Well, then, how about a whole gay baby or a straight one without a thumb?
Jane: A *thumb*! An *opposable* thumb? No way, José. Now you've gone too far. You can't do anything without a thumb... I'll take the gay baby.
Dick: Oh, *jeez*...

Michele Bratcher Goodwin has analyzed the race discount in adoption markets and recommended reforms to mitigate marketized racism in this secondary market for children.[1] Analogizing to her argument, I argue that many – perhaps most – heterosexual would-be parents also have a strong preference for heterosexuality in offspring: what I call the "taste" for heterosexuality. It may seem harmless and even benevolent, given the animus to which sexual minorities are subject at the hands of judges, legislators, deans, teachers, doctors, and even their families. But the taste contributes to the very condition – risk to sexual minorities – which would-be parents often use to justify a heterosexuality offspring preference: "It's for the child's sake, not my own." Indeed, the taste may be a eugenic one because it furthers the conceptual liquidation of a type of people: sexual minorities. It may seem odd to view heterosexuality as a social problem, but from the standpoint of its victims, it is.[2] This chapter investigates the taste for heterosexuality and its judicial expressions.

This chapter proceeds in three parts. First, I describe the heterosexuality offspring preference, show how it is a corollary of much critical theory, and argue that it is the socially constructed symbolic value accorded to heterosexuality that drives much of the demand for it, prenatally and elsewhere. To show how law subsidizes heterosexual reproduction, I discuss some recent state court decisions that provide so-called price support for it, despite judicial findings that heterosexual reproduction often involves disordered thinking and poor planning. Obviously, a more critical rethinking of the microeconomics of the parent–child relationship is in order, not only to protect sexual minority children from parental underinvestment, but also, more generally, to understand the role of projective preferences of would-be parents on demands for children.

A. HETEROSEXUALITY OFFSPRING PREFERENCE

The race discount that Goodwin analyzes is observable in the racialized transaction cost data from the adoption markets, but similar data on secondary markets for sexual minority children are lacking. Therefore, I observe price discovery for heterosexuality informally in what financial economists call "when, if, and as-issued" markets using an auction game to price heterosexuality "futures." I teach about heteronormativity in our school's Women and the Law class, for which I developed a playful – and quite fun, I might add – survey to teach students about conceptual liquidation of sexual minorities.[3] One of the survey questions asks about responses to a friend's joke that one's child might be gay. The auction emerged spontaneously the first time we went through this question. In the game, I assumed the role of an auctioneer and invited the students to act as "purchasers" of their future children. As purchasers, they could bid against alternative reproductive trade-offs in these notional children. I used the preference for heterosexuality in offspring as a unit of account for the bidding. That way, the bidding would reflect the players' relative valuation of heterosexuality against other features. (Play along as you read the following account.)

In round 1, I announce what is going to be priced – "Would you rather have a gay baby or a straight one with ——?" The bidding starts with the extremities, which are divisible, rankable, and easy to compare. I ask whether the players would – all else being equal – prefer a straight baby missing a small toe over a gay one with ten toes. Eventually, someone will say, "Well, who needs *two* little toes?" Fair enough. So I go on to make heterosexuality more expensive by – remember, it is only a game – removing enough of the straight baby's toes until the players prefer the gay one. I look for the price points against what are commonly perceived to be other reproductive trade-offs, for example, sterility, ugliness, blindness, deafness (first in one eye or ear, and then in both), or cleft lip. An opposable thumb seems to be a price point; a mere pinkie, like a small toe, is not. The patterns in these price points made me think that some people might have a taste for having straight children (not a taste that I have or can understand). Moreover, this taste seemed elastic, in the sense that it would yield if the price were right. It is one thing to know that, chances are, your child will be heterosexual; it is another to desire such an outcome.

Several U.S. legal scholars have addressed forms of heterosexual preference, notably Ruthann Robson, Teemu Ruskola, Karolyn Ann Hicks, and Sonia Renee

Martin.[4] The best feminist accounts of straight supremacy also imply the taste for heterosexuality, for example, Monique Wittig's model of the straight mind and Adrienne Rich's analysis of compulsory heterosexuality.[5] Michael Warner's foundational work on queer theory suggests the same.[6] Most recently, Lee Edelman has performed the most sustained (albeit Lacanian) analysis of the symbolic value of heterosexual reproduction, to which I return later.[7]

To understand the microeconomics of heterosexuality offspring preference, I put it in the context of Gary Becker's work on demand for children. He introduced an economic model to explain why heterosexuals, in particular, like to have babies: like other commodities, these babies give their parents income, in the broad sense in which economists use that term.[8] Here, *income* refers not primarily to monetary income (although this is so when children act as an income reserve from which aged parents may draw), but rather, to various forms of psychic income. So he suggests – and it is a refreshing perspective – that reproduction involves a discretionary lifestyle choice by an individual to acquire a good.[9]

His model assumes a pair consisting of a female and a male, typically, but not necessarily, married to each other. According to his model, the total cost (or benefit) of having a child is the present value of all economic outlays minus the present value of all anticipated inflows.[10] This income forms part of a time-discounted dynastic utility function that anticipates the income of future descendants, as well. Unlike most other commodities, however, "children are usually not purchased but are self-produced by each family, using market goods and services and the own time of parents, especially of mothers."[11] The costs of reproduction also involve both money and psychic costs, but children can reduce their net cost to the family unit by providing services or other forms of income.

As with other commodities, Becker asserts that the number and type of children are a function of the would-be parent's tastes.[12] When justifying the "taste for own children" rather than those of others, he posits it as the "distinguishing characteristic of families."[13] However, the taste for heterosexuality may come to displace the "taste for own children," as suggested by the parental disinvestment in sexual minority children discussed later.

My intuition was that it is heterosexuality's socially constructed value that leads to this interesting reversal of the "taste for own children." Lee Edelman's argument in *No Future Queer Theory and the Death Drive* discusses a related issue in his analysis of the symbolic value of heterosexuality.[14] He observes a symbolic conflict in the minds of parents between two primitive categories. First is the Child (capitalization is Edelman's, to emphasize its totemic power).[15] No child-in-fact, this is a when, if, and as-issued child, whose imputed interests reach back from an imaginary future to drive the present expectations of would-be parents, including their interest in containing homosexual influences. The Child "marks the *fetishistic* fixation of heteronormativity: an *erotically* charged investment in the rigid *sameness* of identity that is central to the narrative of reproductive futurism."[16] (Granted, this is not an easy sentence, but it is worth unpacking.) I add emphasis to Edelman's complex clause to point out that these symbolic operations involve the collective regulation of libido – that of the parent, the child, and third parties who bear the social costs and benefits of the parental project.[17] Against the Child, the homosexual emerges symbolized in the death drive, which is not associated with reproduction; it disrupts reproduction.[18] It is clear who wins this fight, as a symbolic matter, anyway.

In some economies, future children provide would-be parents with the expectation of wage returns from labor. However, sociologist Viviana Zelizer has pointed out that although the financial value of many children dropped during the nineteenth century due to child labor laws, they became economically "worthless," but emotionally "priceless."[19] What does that mean about the type of income that children provide to parents in a society like ours? In addition to the other forms of satisfaction they produce for parents, babies and children provide parents with social and symbolic capital by enhancing reputation in valued networks and signaling conformity with widely held norms.[20] (As I say later, the sexual minority does not keep their end of the bargain on this score.) Social economist Thorsten Veblen coined the concept of "status goods" with "positional benefits," in drawing attention to the consumer's social standing.[21] A straight child may be a form of status good for some parents. Adapting Veblen's idea to the current intellectual economy organized in terms of identity, I also suggest that a child may serve as an "identity good" when it produces not only status benefits, but also, more foundational ontological value, that is, confirming the value of a parent's identity.[22] For some, a straight child may also be an identity good.

Indeed, a person may begin to collect symbolic income simply by expressing the intent to have a baby. Visible pregnancy generates income in the form of smiles, expressions of good intentions, parking spaces at the supermarket, and claims in social space to attention. In general, the baby-as-idea (and then later, in fact) invites nonmarket altruism from counterparties who might otherwise treat an individual at arm's length. Much like belonging to the Freemasons, acquiring a baby signals membership in a definite social project.[23] Part of its value as a social signal may be that reproduction suggests that one gives due regard to the claims of the future. Interpreting reproduction as a civic virtue is odd because it seems – and one notices this especially among liberals and progressives – that having babies causes a person to sacrifice public commitments for the priorities of the brood. After all, Becker makes clear that what induces reproduction is the anticipation of private satisfaction – the parent's – rather than any concern for the common wealth.

In a social economy where a child is a commodity, a parent may correctly discount the gay child. Such a child may impair the present value of the parent's dynastic utility function.[24] The gay child may cut off the parent's genetic ambitions, "corrupting the blood" by reducing the likelihood of genetic transmission and accumulation through that child.[25] And the gay child may produce less social capital in networks where the parent may have some explaining to do, for example, with the parents *own* parents, who may now face the annoying prospect of capital impairments of their own against dynastic utility. Law both reflects and creates heterosexuality's social and symbolic value. The next section discusses two state court decisions that have shored up the value of heterosexual reproduction, not only against the challenges from external litigants, but also, against the internal inconsistencies of heterosexual reproduction.

B. THE JUDICIAL TASTE FOR HETEROSEXUALITY

To consider symbolic capital more carefully, I want to point out the special value of Pierre Bourdieu's work, which might be considered sociology of social reproduction.[26] Three of his core ideas explain reproduction as an exercise in gain seeking: the accumulative self; the convertible capitals that it seeks unceasingly; and the exchange markets, where the self converts the capitals in competitive contests with other gain seekers. At the heart of his theory is a notion of a "future-projected, strategizing, accruing, exchange-value self."[27] The self works through the "habitus," a reservoir of skills, tastes, and dispositions that reflect prior learning, including religious indoctrination.[28] Because it drags the past into the present, the habitus is a "structure broker" that mediates between former and future states of the world by reproducing what it knows and has been taught to like into new fields of contest.

At stake in these contests is the accumulation of "multiform and convertible" capital, in the form of social capital, cultural capital, economic capital, or symbolic capital.[29] "Symbolic power is the power to make things with words"; hence its special relevance to the legal academy.[30] "The legal consecration of symbolic capital confers upon a [particular] perspective an absolute, universal value, thus snatching it from a relativity that is by definition inherent in every point of view."[31] (The cases discussed later in this section consecrate heterosexuality.) Symbolic capital also refers to social approval – an accumulation or deficit of it. For essentially the same reasons, then, Bourdieu's socioeconomic model and Becker's rational actor model predict the taste for heterosexuality in a straight-supremacist social economy: a straight child – even one missing a toe or two – may carry more symbolic capital than a gay one.

This taste – like Altoids, curiously strong – finds its echo in two recent appellate state decisions: *Morrison v. Sadler* (Indiana)[32] and *Hernandez v. Robles* (New York).[33] In each case, the courts used substantially the same rationale to reject the state equal protection claims brought by gay and lesbian couples against the gay marriage ban. Each court found that many heterosexuals reproduce recklessly but – like judicial alchemists – went on to convert these findings against heterosexual reproduction into a "rationale" for the gay ban and, with it, an opportunity to reaffirm the symbolic priority of compulsory heterosexuality as a social arrangement.

Morrison does this when considering the plaintiffs' claim that the Indiana Defense of Marriage Act violates the state's equal privileges and immunities clause in distinguishing heterosexual reproduction from that by others.[34] In response, the court first pays a backhanded compliment to reproductive homosexuals, whom it presumes can provide the "stable environments" the state seeks for all children.[35] These homosexual parents are "financially and emotionally" invested, committed to child rearing, and, importantly, good at planning and thinking ahead.[36] According to these courts, the same cannot be said about heterosexuals: they may reproduce "with no foresight or planning" and become pregnant from "one instance of sexual intercourse," with "little or no contemplation of the consequences that might result."[37] Much the same is true in *Hernandez*, which holds that a rational legislature could find that heterosexual relationships are "all too often casual or temporary" and that they "present a greater danger that children will be born into or grow up in unstable homes than is the case with same-sex couples."[38]

For these courts, marriage is the white knight. For example, *Morrison* holds that marriage will encourage heterosexuals "to procreate within the legitimacy and stability of a state-sanctioned relationship and to discourage unplanned, out-of-wedlock births resulting from 'casual' intercourse."[39] How marriage does this is not clear, given that the marriages in question seem to come as afterthoughts to the momentary indiscretions leading to the unintended pregnancies the courts allude to only obliquely. The court avoids addressing the "morning after" function of marriage to manage the effects of coital "accidents." *Hernandez* makes the same move, holding that the purpose of heterosexual marriage is to "create more stability and permanence in the relationships that cause children to be born."[40] And again, *Hernandez* blurs causation in time between the problem (impaired rationality during coitus) and the remedy (marriage ex post), as did *Morrison*. Neither court considers the obvious: if barriers to entry make homosexual reproduction more deliberate, then why not impose transaction costs on heterosexual coitus before the fact to promote deliberation?

The judicial taste for heterosexuality comes out again in the second rationale given in *Hernandez* for why a rational legislature could limit marriage to heterosexuals: children are better off growing in a cross-sex, heterosexual household.[41] "Intuition and experience suggest that a child benefits from having before his or her eyes, every day, living models of what both a [heterosexual] man and a woman are like."[42] But how rational could it be for a legislature to favor child rearing by cross-sex couples whose existence as a married couple may reflect a public law bribe after impulsive coitus? Courts give many reasons for why marriage should belong only to heterosexuals, but in this one, it is their carelessness that founds their title. Rates of unintended pregnancy and abortion suggest that these courts are on to something.[43] Welcome to what Edelman has mockingly called heterosexuality's "Ponzi scheme of reproductive futurism."[44] There is no accounting for taste.

These judicial moves are another example of the diacritical relationship that Janet Halley has pointed out in federal equal protection doctrine, one which previously left heterosexuals unmarked, while marking homosexuals as sodomites.[45] After *Lawrence v. Texas*, however, U.S. courts can no longer use sodomy to mark homosexuals, and these cases reflect the same diacritical relationship. So these courts use reproduction as the basis for the mark: a positive one for homosexual reproduction and a negative one for heterosexuals, but a decision in favor of heterosexual reproduction nonetheless. (The negative mark on heterosexuality consists in recognizing that the state must use its police power to control the so-called mischief intrinsic to heterosexual coitus.)

The gymnastic ability of these courts in sidestepping the foibles of heterosexual coitus to elevate it also illustrates a more general problem with law's symbolic overvaluation of heterosexual reproduction: the denial – and therefore tacit acceptance – of time-inconsistent reproduction. This unreasoned investment in reproduction is so striking that I can characterize it only as *reproductivism.* It is an -*ism*, but because it wields babies-as-ideas as a club against other ways of making meaning in life, all the while denying the real costs of reproduction. Reproductivism consists of several seemingly separate deductive premises, some explicit, some implicit: (1) existence – whatever the subjective qualities of that experience – is generally preferable to nonexistence, as reflected in legal decisions about wrongful life, voluntary euthanasia, suicide, and involuntary sterilization; (2) reproduction tends to further self-interest, including through saving for old age in the form of children's anticipated future support and through the satisfaction of feeling that one has contributed to society; (3) without reproduction, society would perish; and (4) given the foregoing, courts must enable parents to inculcate their children with reproductivist values (as well as many others equally deserving of stricter scrutiny). Reproductivism is what leads to Derek Parfit's "repugnant conclusion" that more unhappy lives are better than fewer happy ones.[46]

What reproductivism obscures, of course, is a frank recognition of the real scope and prevalence of human ambivalence and regret about reproduction. To mitigate the analytical effects of reproductivism, it may be useful to think in terms of an aggregate that measures this ambivalence and regret. I am no economist, but what I want to contribute to this project – as a feminist method in reproduction – is the idea of *counterdemand* for children. Counterdemand connects the dots between behaviors that suggest a preference after-the-fact against babies-in-fact. (*Morrison* and *Fernandez* pointed to counterdemand obliquely, but only to pass over it as part of reaffirming the symbolic value of reproduction.)

Counterdemand adds up the observable preferences of people for back-tracking after getting themselves into reproduction. (In that sense, counterdemand is the sum of time inconsistency in reproduction.) It is nothing more than the routine practice of calculating the *net* implications of reproductive choices by adding up the plusses *and* the minuses.[47] The point is to internalize – as a theoretical matter and in our own consciousness – the *effective* value of reproduction: what traders call the "all-in" effects of a financial item. Counterdemand starts by adding up data about abortion, infanticide, so-called postpartum disorders in women, pregnancy denial, child abuse, pregnancy-related domestic violence, child abuse leading to the death of an infant, abandonment, and giving up one's child for adoption. Packing these into a single concept reveals patterns – and causes – that might escape detection, disaggregating the behaviors. This interim measure may understate counterdemand because it overlooks private parental regrets about reproduction that never rise to the level of a reportable incident. Of course, counterdemand is different from conscious decisions that successfully eliminate the risks of pregnancy ex ante by contraception, avoidance of reproductive sex, and voluntary sterilization.

Of each year's roughly four million births, one million represent unintended pregnancies not terminated.[48] About an overlapping one million of these births involve premature birth, low birth weight, or birth defects (all factors that may impair a real baby's quality of life), and more than 450,000 of the total births were by teenaged females, arguably too young to appreciate how having a baby at that age impacts one's life prospects.[49] In a typical year, about 240,000 pregnant women experience domestic abuse, with 40 percent of this abuse beginning during the couple's first pregnancy.[50] Suggesting counterdemand on the part of fathers, pregnant women are at twice the risk of battery (presumably from partners) than nonpregnant women.[51] Many children also suffer crimes, neglect, and other misfortunes, which may be linked to parental frustration over contact with the realities of child rearing.[52]

Liquidating unwanted children is the ultimate affront to reproductivism (and may suggest a profound degree of time-inconsistent behavior). Reflecting its own situational psychosis on the issue, U.S. law is "remarkably inconsistent" about infanticide, lacking federal or state statutes (unlike the United Kingdom) and giving only begrudging recognition to so-called postpartum psychosis as a legal defense.[53] This inconsistency fails to "recognize the profound similarities that underlie the many contemporary infanticide cases."[54] Postpartum mood disorders may also involve a form of counterdemand. As a formal matter, postpartum depression means only the postnatal mood disruptions that are more serious than the common "baby blues."[55] Even at this high threshold, it is frequent, with some estimates putting it at from 10 to 20 percent of all live births. Postpartum psychosis affects far fewer women, but far more seriously.

Even this primitive construction of counterdemand suggests a more complex picture than simple euphoria about babies-as-ideas suggests. Expressed as a rough ratio of supply (live births) to counterdemand in a year, composed, for argument's sake, from these statistics, for every eight live births (two of which resulted from an unplanned pregnancy), two involve premature birth, low birth weight, or birth defects; one is born to a teenager; one produces postpartum depression; and two abortions occur, exposing women to the health risks of a quite invasive procedure. This is not a great yield on human capital investment, when you consider its all-in costs. Procreative morbidity and mortality abroad are much worse.

A particular mental disorganization of time contributes to counterdemand for children. The reproductivist premises discussed earlier (legal support for more people trapped in existence, regardless of the quality of their lives) involve confusion between the interests of the present and those of the future. Edelman's argument is also about the mental structure of time because, he says, it is the ricocheting backward and forward in time between the imaginary interests of the future Child that may keep some heterosexuals locked in to a time disorder. And as *Morrison* and *Hernandez* note, it may have been coital time inconsistency that got them into this situation.

Trends in behavioral law and economics can help on this score. Research in this field concludes that humans tend to suffer from overoptimism and to overvalue nearer states in time to later ones, called *hyperbolic discounting*.[56] Reproduction (and sexual decision making generally) are good candidates for this type of analysis because the effects of sex and reproduction may have lifelong implications and because sex impulses have a lot of horsepower. In the context of the enforcement of surrogacy contracts, Molly Walker Wilson has persuasively argued that the time variability intrinsic to the gestation cycle may make it legally impossible for surrogates to give meaningful informed consent in a surrogacy contract.[57] More is needed.

C. IMPLICATIONS

Goodwin suggests some worthwhile and feasible reforms to mitigate the effect of marketized racism in the adoption market.[58] In the United States, law is formally committed to ending formal racism, but the same is not true for antigay animus: it is the stepchild of federal and state law. So although it makes little sense for me to suggest legal reforms, let me conclude with some implications of the taste for heterosexuality.

First and foremost, the taste for heterosexuality is as troubling as, and far more universal than, son preference in some cultures. Because it systematically targets the erasure of a people, the taste is eugenic, as Martha Ertman has observed about other preferences in reproduction markets.[59] The ordinary instability of heterosexual pairings cited by *Morrison* and *Hernandez* may be worse for gay children, who may suffer special harms from parent-investors who are not only impulsive, but who are also, now, disappointed when a child's homosexuality reduces the value of the parents' dynastic utility function. For example, the high suicide rate among sexual minority children may reflect a parent's downgrade of a child from investment to subinvestment. And this is not to disregard the real losses felt by parents of a gay or lesbian child. They hurt, too, of course, and their actions may leave them with regret and ambivalence of a different sort. Modest advances in reducing antigay animus have triggered a backlash campaign based on the – quite real and correct – fear that such advances reduce the symbolic value of heterosexuality. They do. Small wonder, then, that parents and others mobilize against this tolerance.[60] In U.S. law schools, activist groups like the Christian Legal Society are on the front lines.[61]

Do homosexuals also prefer heterosexuality in offspring? It would seem that homosexuals might derive the same social and symbolic income from having straight children. Indeed, such income might be more valuable to a homosexual.[62] Public displays of heterosexuality tend to pay instant dividends, whereas comparable expressions of homosexuality (especially between males) may be met with negative reactions, ranging from disapproval and shunning to physical violence and, in the most extreme cases, murder.[63] Expanding on sociologist Erving Goffman's work on identity management by members of stigmatized groups, Kenji Yoshino has noted that homosexuals play down their identity – *covering* – to reduce exposure to this type of hostility.[64] For a gay or lesbian parent, then, having a child – especially a heterosexual one – may yield covering value.[65] And this kind of social and symbolic income may be dearer to the homosexual parent than the straight one, who is already awash in that type of capital.[66]

Much social science research on this question genuflects to conceptual liquidation of sexual minorities by showing that gay and lesbian parents do not "homosexualize" their offspring. The supplicant posture of this research is understandable.

When reaffirming the symbolic priority of heterosexuality, *Morrison* and *Hernandez* nervously suggest that gay and lesbian parents might socialize their children differently. This is obvious. For example, homosexual parents might disapprove of the sex-based institutions that seem natural to some heterosexuals but that have been the bane of their existence. Blocking the transmission of these sex-based institutions may not be such a bad thing, especially if feminist Dorothy Dinnerstein correctly blamed cross-sex child-rearing arrangements for patterned unhappiness in heterosexual life.[67] But another effect of these cases is to ensure that conversations like this do not occur in the context of a legal case. In that sense, these cases provide protectionism for heterosexual reproduction from the kind of competition with gay and lesbian parenting that might show up heterosexual reproduction.

Bourdieu encouraged readers to think hard about their own intellectual agency. Indeed, his work has been called "sociology as therapy" – for the body social, that is.[68] Eradicating the taste for heterosexuality – grotesque as it is – may be impossible, but the project of analyzing it and sounding the alarm about its social costs is an important one.

NOTES

1 Michele Goodwin, *The Free Market Approach to Adoption: The Value of a Baby*, 26 B.C. Third World L.J. 61, 62 (2006).
2 I know the difference between heterosexuality and heteronormativity, but until heterosexuals at large internalize and sustain this working distinction, it may be more effective to collapse the two, as many do. José Gabilondo, *Asking the Straight Question: How to Come to Speech in Spite of Conceptual Liquidation as a Homosexual*, 21 Wisc. Women's L.J. 1 (2006).
3 *Id.* at 39–45.
4 Ruthann Robson, *Our Children: Kids of Queer Parents and Kids Who Are Queer: Looking at Sexual Minority Rights from a Different Perspective*, 64 Alb. L. Rev. 915, 932–48 (2001); Karolyn Ann Hicks, *Reparative Therapy: Whether Parental Attempts to Change a Child's Sexual Orientation Can Legally Constitute Child Abuse*, 49 Am. U. L. Rev. 505 (1999); Teemu Ruskola, *Minor Disregard: The Legal Construction of the Fantasy That Gay and Lesbian Youth Do Not Exist*, 8 Yale J.L. & Feminism 269 (1996); Sonia Renee Martin, *Note, A Child's Right to Be Gay: Addressing the Emotional Maltreatment of Queer Youth*, 48 Hastings L.J. 167 (1996).
5 Monique Wittig, The Straight Mind in the Straight Mind and Other Essays 27 (1992); Adrienne Rich, *Compulsory Heterosexuality and Lesbian Existence*, 5 Signs J. Women & Culture 631 (1980).
6 Michael Warner, Fear of a Queer Planet xxi (1993).
7 Lee Edelman, No Future: Queer Theory and the Death Drive (2004).
8 Gary Becker, *An Economic Analysis of Fertility*, *in* Conference Proceedings of the National Bureau of Economic Research, Demographic and Economic Change in Developed Countries 209–40 (1960).
9 *Id.* at 210.
10 *Id.* at 213.
11 Gary Becker, A Treatise on the Family 38 (1993).

12 *Id.* at 45.
13 *Id.*
14 *See* Edelman, *supra* note 7, at 14.
15 *Id.* at 2–3, 13–14.
16 *Id.*
17 This symbolic operation involves managing sex energy ("erotically," "fetishistic"). The goal of the operation is to reproduce "sameness," hence my corollary that the Child – like the heterosexual parent – is straight, too.
18 *Id.* at 9.
19 Viviana Zelizer, Pricing the Priceless Child: The Changing Social Value of Children 1–5 (1985).
20 The need for social approval is common, but persons in subordinated positions, e.g., women, minorities, and/or the poor, may have pent-up demands for this type of approval, which may not be forthcoming given the persistence and reproduction of patterns of inequality.
21 Thorsten Veblen introduced the concept of a status good. Thorsten Veblen, A Theory of the Leisure Class (1994).
22 With regard to sex identity, e.g., one infertility researcher concludes that infertility leads men and women to revise their own sex self-concept. Gay Becker, The Elusive Embryo: How Women and Men Approach New Reproductive Technologies 29 (2000).
23 This is consistent with the subsequent discussion about Lee Edelman's argument that reproduction by heterosexuals involves "reproductive futurism," a strategy for the mental organization of life that simplifies existential complexity.
24 The strategies of heterosexual parents to "quarantine" a child from potentially homosexualizing influences tacitly reflect the fear that heterosexuality, too, may be at least partially socially constructed.
25 This may be part of what parents "blame" themselves for when a child is gay. *Cf.* Devon W. Carbado, *Straight out of the Closet*, 15 Berkeley Women's L.J. 76, 120 (2000) ("The parents of heterosexuals do not love them 'in spite of' their sexual orientation, and parents do not blame themselves for their children's heterosexuality").
26 His classic text on the subject is Pierre Bourdieu & Jean-Claude Passeron, Reproduction in Education, Society, and Culture (1977).
27 Beverley Skeggs, Exchange, Value, and Affect: Bourdieu and the "the Self" in Feminism after Bourdieu 83 (2004).
28 Pierre Bourdieu, In Other Words: Essays towards a Reflexive Sociology 13 (1990).
29 Craig Calhoun, *Habitus, Field, and Capital: The Question of Historical Specificity*, *in* Pierre Bourdieu Clinical Perspectives 55, 65 (1993).
30 *See* Bourdieu, *supra* note 28, at 138.
31 *Id.* at 136.
32 Morrison v. Sadler, 821 N.E.2d 15 (Ind. 2005).
33 Hernandez v. Robles, 855 N.E.2d 1 (N.Y. 2006).
34 *Supra* note 32, at 21.
35 *Id.* at 24.
36 "[Homosexuals and others] wanting to have children by assisted reproduction or adoption are, by necessity, heavily invested, financially and emotionally, in those processes. Those processes also require a great deal of foresight and planning." *Id.* "Members of a same-sex couple who wish to have a child . . . have already demonstrated their

commitment to child-rearing, by virtue of the difficulty of obtaining a child through adoption or assisted reproduction, without the State necessarily having to encourage that commitment through the institution of marriage." *Id.* at 27.

37 *Id.* at 25.

38 *Supra* note 33, at 8.

39 *Id.* Neither do the other reasons given by the court address the ex ante risks from impulsive coital intercourse.

40 *Id.*

41 *Id.* at 7.

42 *Id.*

43 About half of each year's roughly six million pregnancies in the United States are unintended. Guttmacher Institute, *Facts on Induced Abortion in the United States* (2006) (citing L. B. Finer *et al.*, *Disparities in Unintended Pregnancy in the United States, 1994 and 2001*, 38 Persp. Sexual Reprod. Health 90–6 [2006]). For 2003, the Centers for Disease Control & Prevention recorded more than eight hundred thousand legal abortions, which had been reported voluntarily by health authorities. U.S. Centers for Disease Control & Prevention, Abortion Surveillance – United States, 2003 (Nov. 24, 2006). My use of abortion statistics to support my argument does not involve any criticism of women who seek abortion. Quite the contrary: it is remarkable that at least this many women manage to obtain abortions despite the legal and cultural obstacles. A more so-called abortion-friendly legal system that gave people – especially the young – more options for managing their reproduction might reduce demand for so-called morning-after marriages in response to unintended pregnancy.

44 *See* Edelman, *supra* note 7, at 4.

45 Her point about equal protection analysis should be extended to legal constructions of heterosexuality generally: "Indeed, it seems to me to be at timely moment to argue that equal protection theorizing should focus not, as it has until the last few years, on categories, but on *practices of categorization.*" Janet Halley, The Construction of Heterosexuality in Fear of a Queer Planet 82, 83 (1993).

46 Derek Parfit, The Repugnant Conclusion in the Repugnant Conclusion: Essays on Population Ethics (2004).

47 Considering the net effects of reproductive decisions is the essence of deliberative rationality on this point: "A child does not only generate household costs but revenues as well. . . . There is a calculus of cost and revenue behind it and in some sense we are only really interested in the balance." Bernard Van Praag & Marcel Warnaar, *The Costs of Children and Use of Demographic Variables in Consumer Demand*, *in* 1AR Handbook of Population and Family Economics 241, 245 (1997).

48 *See supra* note 43.

49 American Pregnancy Association, *Statistics*, http://www.americanpregnancy.org/main/statistics.html.

50 *Id.*

51 *Id.*

52 *See* Emily Douglas and David Finkelhor, *Child Maltreatment Fatalities Fact Sheet*, http://www.unh.edu/ccrc/factsheet/pdf/ChildMaltreatmentFatalitiesFactSheet.pdf. In 2004, state child abuse authorities substantiated claims of child abuse and neglect for 872,000 children.

53 Michelle Oberman, A Brief History of Infanticide and the Law in Infanticide: Psychosocial and Legal Perspectives on Mothers Who Kill 9 (2003).

54 *Id.* at 14.

55 Katherine Wisner, *Postpartum Disorders: Phenomenology, Treatment Approaches and Relationship to Infanticide* (*in* Infanticide: Psychosocial and Legal Perspectives on Mothers Who Kill, Spinelli ed. [2003]).

56 Christine Jolls *et al.*, *A Behavioral Approach to Law and Economics*, 50 Stan. L. Rev. 1471, 1524–5 (1998).

57 Molly Walker Wilson, *Precommitment in Free-Market Procreation: Surrogacy, Commissioned Adoption, and the Limits on Human Decision Making Capacity*, 31 J. Legis. 329, 331 (2005).

58 *See* Goodwin, *supra* note 1, at 75–9 (recommending "price caps," taxation, and public education about marketized racism).

59 Martha Ertman, *What's Wrong with a Parenthood Market? A New and Improved Theory of Commodification*, 82 N.C. L. Rev. 1, 26–30 (2003).

60 The constitutional status of religious claims makes them valuable to parents who want to safeguard their investment from the risk of homosexualization. *See, e.g.*, Citizens for a Responsible Curriculum v. Montgomery County Pub. Sch., No. AW-05-1194, 2005 U.S. Dist. LEXIS 8130 (D. Md., S. Div., 2005) (issuing a temporary restraining order against an eighth- and ninth-grade curriculum to which religious fundamentalists had objected because it noted that some fundamentalist religions are more likely to have negative attitudes about gays than other religions).

61 Understandably, Christian Legal Society (CLS) officials worry that antigay animus may come to be viewed as seriously as racism is, as noted in a recent article explaining the CLS's rationale for its litigation strategy. "'Think how marginalized racists are,' said [Christian activist Gregory] Baylor, who directs the Christian Legal Society's Center for Law and Religious Freedom. 'If we don't address this now, it will only get worse.'" Stephanie Simon, *Christians Sue for Right Not to Tolerate Policies: Many Codes Intended to Protect Gays from Harassment Are Illegal, Conservatives Argue*, L.A. Times, April 10, 2006, at A1. Baylor takes pains to reassure members of other minorities that the CLS's litigation campaign targets only homosexuals and not racial minorities or women. *Id.*

62 Heterosexuals and homosexuals face different reproductive economies in general because heterosexuals may choose between coital or other means of reproduction and because homosexuals face significantly higher transaction costs for reproduction. For example, the homosexual would-be parent may face higher costs in the form of legal prohibitions on adoption or marriage.

63 Consider the pleasant surprise felt by this woman who, after decades as a lesbian, began expressing affection in public with a man: "'Whenever we [two women] would hold hands in public, I felt . . . fear, waiting for the customary dirty looks or . . . looking-away.' In place of revulsion [with a man] she was now greeted by strangers with approving smiles. 'I felt suddenly acceptable and accepted and cute, as opposed to queer.'" Guy Trebly, *A Kiss Too Far? For Same-Sex Couples, Simple Displays of Affection Are Fraught*, N.Y. Times, Feb. 18, 2007, at D1.

64 Gays and lesbians sometimes play down their identity to avoid the discomfort of regulatory attention from enforcers of straight supremacy. Kenji Yoshino, *Covering*, 111 Yale L.J. 769 (2002).

65 *Id.*

66 I am not saying that homosexual parents consciously choose children as a shield from heteronormative hostility. Many other factors could contribute to such a decision. And undertaking to have or acquire a child may expose a homosexual to more hostility from interests opposed to gay parenting. And, providing more unwitting support for sociobiologist E. O. Wilson's thesis that homosexuals serve an evolutionary function as "caretakers" for heterosexuals, many homosexuals do end up "cleaning up" after the

recklessness of heterosexual reproduction by adopting children with medical or other complications that dramatically reduce their value to many prospective heterosexual parents. I just want to point out a special kind of symbolic income that some homosexual parents may derive from children.

67 Dorothy Dinnerstein, The Mermaid and the Minotaur Sexual Arrangements and Human Malaise (1999).

68 Michael Grenfell, Pierre Bourdieu: Agent Provocateur Europe (2004).

Overcoming Mother Nature's discrimination. Israeli Yonatan Gher's first trip to Mumbai was to visit a fertility clinic. Gher, his partner, and their new baby become a family. Markets in sperm, ova, and children help couples to realize their dreams of creating families. Shut out from biological family making because they lack the heterosexual genetic diversity to create children, and often restricted by state laws to adopt, gay women and men can turn to alternatives. Lesbian women now have access to sperm markets, whereas gay men use ova markets. (J. Adam Huggins, International Herald Tribune/Getty Images/Stringer/STR)

9 Transracial Adoption of Black Children: An Economic Analysis

MARY ESCHELBACH HANSEN
AND DANIEL POLLACK

There may be reasons why a difference in race . . . may have relevance in adoption proceedings. But that factor alone cannot be decisive in determining the child's welfare.

– Judge David L. Bazelon, U.S. Court of Appeals, District of Columbia Circuit (*In re* adoption of a minor, 228 F.2d 446 [1955])

Notwithstanding the 1955 opinion of Judge Bazelon, the role of race in determining adoptive placement of black children remains contentious. Opponents to transracial adoption argue that transracial adoption inflicts group harm on the black community.[1] A similar group-harm argument is made by those seeking to limit international adoption. We formerly argued that banning international adoptions is inefficient.[2] In this chapter, we extend this argument to transracial adoption. We provide a brief history of transracial adoption and antidiscrimination law in adoption, and we use administrative data compiled by the Children's Bureau to describe the length of time black children spend as legal orphans before they are adopted.

Adoptions of black children and other children of color have increased since the 1990s. Transracial adoptions have increased as well, but black children continue to experience delays in adoption relative to children of other races. Because a child adopted transracially spends less time as a legal orphan than the average

The data used here were made available by the National Data Archive on Child Abuse and Neglect, Cornell University, Ithaca, New York, and have been used with permission. Data from the Adoption and Foster Care Analysis and Reporting System (AFCARS) were collected by the Children's Bureau. Funding for AFCARS was provided by the Children's Bureau, Administration on Children, Youth, and Families, Administration for Children and Families, U.S. Department of Health & Human Services. The collector of the original data, the funder, the archive, and Cornell University and their agents or employees bear no responsibility for the analysis or interpretation presented here.

Financial support for this research was provided through the NIH/NICHD/Demographic and Behavioral Branch (R03-HD045342-01), through the Mellon Fund at the College of Arts and Sciences of American University, and through the Summer Research Institute at the National Data Archive on Child Abuse and Neglect at the New York State College of Human Ecology at Cornell University. The authors thank the staff at NDACAN for their assistance.

Research assistance was provided by Renata Kochut.

adopted black child, we conclude that greater emphasis on transracial placement is warranted and that more vigorous enforcement of the antidiscrimination law in child welfare would result in gains for black children.

A. RACE AND ANTIDISCRIMINATION LAW IN ADOPTION

In the mid-1950s, the Child Welfare League of America (CWLA) reported that black children were the largest group of children in need of adoption.[3] Between 1958 and 1962, adoptions of black children increased, but the number of black children in need of adoptive families remained large. Agencies revisited the way prospective adoptive families were screened and opted to include more kin, single women, and foster parents in the pool of prospective adoptive parents. The most controversial alternative for adoptive placement was transracial placement.

Racial matching – coordinating placements in foster care and adoption so that the parents and children are of the same race – was considered to be good social work practice and in the best interests of children. Children and families were matched on physical characteristics, including skin color, as well as expected intellectual ability, social status, and religious heritage. Although other matching criteria were abandoned in the 1970s and 1980s in favor of matching criteria that emphasized the ability of families to parent children with specific needs, racial matching remained often used.

The debate over transracial adoption became heated after members of the National Association of Black Social Workers (NABSW) resolved to oppose transracial adoption as a matter of policy and practice. In its position paper of 1972, the NABSW called transracial adoption "a blatant form of racial and cultural genocide."[4] In the late 1970s and 1980s, there emerged a countermovement that sought to remove race and ethnicity from consideration in adoptive placement. In the early 1980s, at least six states permitted race to be a relevant factor in adoption.[5] By 1994, NABSW had softened its position to some extent: transracial adoptions should be a last resort only after a documented failure to find a home with black parents.[6] Reflecting this, from 1990 to 1995, many states included a rank ordering of placement preferences for adoption, which included race as a primary factor. The first preference was for placement with a relative, who was usually of the same race as the child.[7]

The debate over transracial adoption contains several strands of argument. One strand is about whether transracially adopted children exhibit normal social and psychological development. Opponents of transracial placements are concerned that removing the preference for in-racial placement from policy would lead social workers, families, and the public to discount the importance that race and culture play in a child's life. A second strand of argument is about whether allowing transracial placement allows child welfare service providers to avoid equal treatment of blacks. Opponents of transracial adoption are concerned that removing preferences for in-racial placement would reduce efforts to recruit persons of color to be foster and adoptive parents. A third strand of argument is that preferring in-racial placements results in unnecessary and harmful delays or denials of otherwise appropriate placements.

The debate over transracial adoption is part of a larger debate between the advocates of so-called color-blind social policy and so-called racial separatists. After *Loving v. Virginia*,[8] the U.S. Supreme Court case that declared unconstitutional state and local laws prohibiting interracial marriage, some states continued to ban transracial adoptions. The separatists maintained that people of color belong to social groups separated by current and historical discrimination and that interracial family making caused harm to these groups. The advocates of color-blindness maintained that making race a factor in social policy perpetuates racism. Removing race from rules on adoptive placement, they argued, created benefit both for society and for specific children.

Senator Howard Metzenbaum advocated color-blind social policy. In 1993, he introduced the Multiethnic Placement Act (MEPA),[9] which was intended to eliminate the use of racial matching practices in adoptive and foster care placement. Moved by the stories of white foster parents who were prevented from adopting their nonwhite foster children, the proponents of MEPA envisioned an increase in transracial adoption. However, the version of MEPA that was signed in 1994 was not a call for color-blind social work practice. MEPA specifically directed states to recruit of a pool of foster and adoptive families that would reflect the demographics of the population of children in need of care. The final form of MEPA contained the stipulation that racial and ethnic background could still be considered in making a placement, if it was only one among many factors used in the placement decision.

In 1996, Congress passed, and the president signed, the so-called Interethnic Adoption Provisions,[10] which were intended to strengthen MEPA. Although MEPA II did not change the language of the original MEPA on recruitment of a racially representative pool of prospective parents, MEPA II did amend the language of the original MEPA to prohibit discrimination on the basis of race in placement. Race was to be excluded from placement guidelines. Under MEPA II, race may only enter decision making in placement when issues of race are matters of the best interests of a *particular* child. MEPA II also empowered the Department of Health and Human Services to enforce the law through fiscal sanctions.

After more than ten years of social work practice under MEPA, tension still exists in social work practice between the right of the child to a culturally sensitive adoptive placement and the right of a child to a speedy placement regardless of race. The Office for Civil Rights has conducted more than 130 investigations of race discrimination in child welfare practice, but the workaday trade-offs made in social work practice are mostly shielded from direct observation.

B. THE INEFFICIENCY OF A BAN ON TRANSRACIAL ADOPTION

To understand the costs of restricting adoptive placement by race, consider Figure 9.1A. On the horizontal axis is the number of children in foster care who are waiting to be placed in adoptive families, either transracially or within race. On the left-hand vertical axis is the net benefit from same-race adoption, and on the right-hand vertical axis is the net benefit from transracial adoption.[11]

The benefit of same-race adoption may be quite high; if we place special value on cultural preservation, we could even claim that the marginal benefit of a policy that

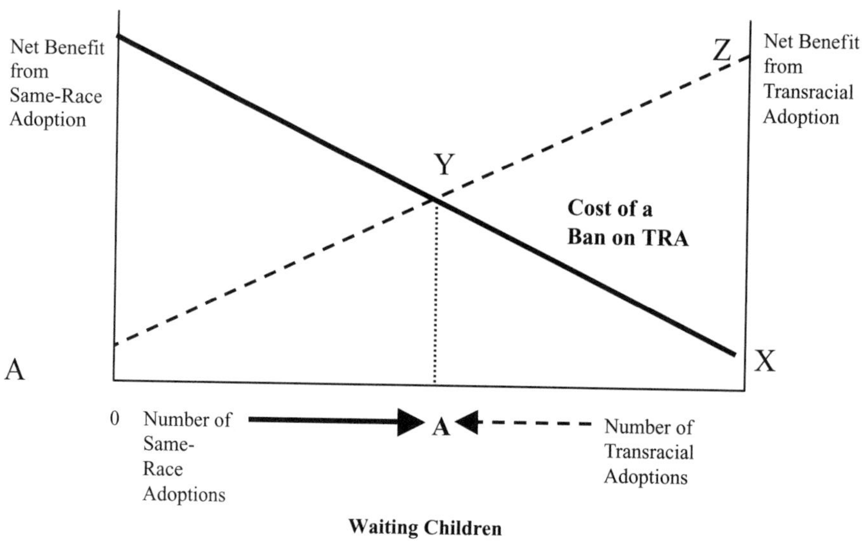

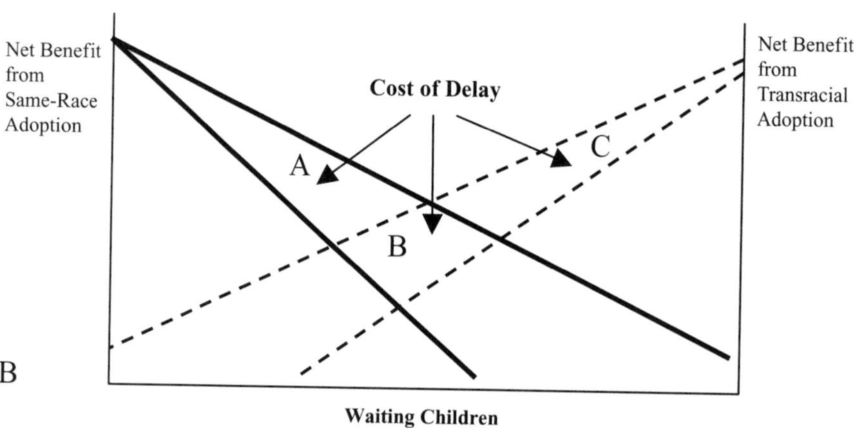

Figure 9.1. **Cost of banning or delaying transracial adoption.** *A*, The cost of banning TRA is the lost benefits to society for adoptions that do not occur. The cost is equal to area *XYZ*. *B*, Delay in adoption due to racial matching policies reduces the benefits of adoption to children and generates costs equal to $A + B + C$.

stresses same-race adoption never declines. Yet the cost of recruiting same-race adoptive parents rises with the number of waiting children placed. The net benefits of same-race placement must fall as the number of waiting children increases. Recruitment costs that increase with the number of children to be placed also cause a declining net marginal benefit of transracial adoption.

If adoption policy aims to maximize social welfare from adoption, then each child should be placed so that the benefit to society from her adoption could not be greater if we changed a child's placement. According to this rule, *A* children should have same-race placements; the remaining children should be placed transracially.

Suppose that same-race placements can be found for all waiting children if we spend enough money to find them. Because the costs of the first transracial adoptions are small compared to the high cost of the last same-race placements, the cost of the ban is area *XYZ* in Figure 9.1A.

Figure 9.1B ignores the costs of delay. Age at adoption is consistently associated with stability and better outcomes, so delay in adoption reduces the net marginal benefits of adoption.[12] The costs of delay are incorporated into Figure 9.1B. Rules requiring or permitting a time period of race preference in adoptive placement slows down adoptions of any race, imposing a cost of $A + B + C$.

The psychic cost of delaying or denying a waiting child placement in a permanent family is inestimable. In dollar terms, the cost of imposing or banning transracial adoption or of denying adoption to maintain a policy of racial matching is likely to be substantial. The net benefits to society of adoption from foster care (without regard to race) are estimated to be 150,000 to 300,000 dollars per child.[13]

Furthermore, facilitating transracial adoption today frees resources that can be used to gain the benefits of adoption in the future. For example, resources used today to house black children in foster care could be used instead to recruit and train more black adoptive families.

C. THE NUMBER OF TRANSRACIAL ADOPTIONS

In fact, the number of families finalizing adoptions across black–white racial lines has never been large. The peak of transracial adoption in the 1944–75 period occurred in 1971, when adoptions of black children by white parents numbered about 1.5 to 2 percent of all adoptions.[14] Some authors claim that, of the group, about one-third of adopted black children were placed with white families.[15] None of these historical data are complete or consistent, and none separate transracial adoptions from same-race adoptions, so the actual percentage of placements that were transracial can never be known.

The National Center for Health Statistics estimated that 1 percent of all adopted children in a 1987 survey were black children adopted by white mothers.[16] In a 1988–9 survey of 625 white adoptive parents in California, 4.6 percent had adopted black children and 15.8 percent had adopted children of Hispanic origin.[17] The North American Council on Adoptable Children reported that a 1989–90 survey of adoption agencies revealed that 22 percent of their placements of black children were transracial.[18]

Whether the MEPAs have had any independent effect on adoption, and especially on the number of adoptions of black children waiting in foster care, is unknown. No systematic or systemic information on transracial adoption was collected prior to MEPA I, and only one survey of agencies, states, and adoption lawyers has been published since the passage of the MEPAs.[19] The implementation of the Adoption and Foster Care Analysis and Reporting System (AFCARS) in fiscal year 1995 provides the first opportunity to examine trends in transracial adoption of children across states over time. The following sections examine recorded races of adoptive children and transracial placement in adoptions with state agency involvement using AFCARS data for 1996–2003.

1. Administrative Data on Adoptions from Foster Care

The Adoption and Safe Families Act[20] required states to document increases in adoptions to qualify for performance bonuses. States had to come into compliance with a federal rule, issued in December 1993, requiring the submission of child welfare data to AFCARS.[21] Information had to be submitted on all children whose adoptions were finalized after any state agency involvement. The Children's Bureau[22] publishes tabulations and makes available a public-use version of the data.

In addition to data on race, the AFCARS data include information on age of the adopted child, the date of finalization of adoption, and the dates of termination of the rights of each birth parent. We calculate the time between termination of parental rights and adoption using the later of the recorded termination dates. The analysis of time from termination to finalization in section C3 also uses as controls data on the gender of the adopted child, adoptive family structure, prior relationship of the child to the adoptive parents, and the primary special needs basis and recorded disabilities of the child. Finally, although AFCARS contains a few observations of private adoptions, our analysis is limited to cases with state agency involvement.

2. Limitations of the Data

The Children's Bureau puts little faith in the AFCARS data for 1995 to 1997.[23] Relatively few states were in compliance with the federal rules on AFCARS before fiscal year 1998. For example, in 1995, just thirty-one states submitted some adoption data to AFCARS. Moreover, the data submitted were incomplete: more than 35 percent of adoption records for fiscal year 1996 and more than 22 percent for 1997 do not include sufficient information to calculate the time between termination of parental rights and adoption.[24] The completeness of the data improves markedly for fiscal years 1998 and 1999, for which about 7 percent of records are incomplete. The data for 2000–3 are nearly complete, with fewer than 2 percent of records missing these benchmark dates.

The data on race of the adopted child are relatively complete. Only about 5 percent of all AFCARS records are missing a code for the child's race or indicate that the child's race is "unable to be determined." The percentage of cases with missing race data is highest in fiscal years 1997–9, for which 6.7 to 9 percent of records have incomplete data on race.

The data on race of the adoptive parents, however, are not very complete. Race of the adoptive mother is missing or "unable to be determined" in 20 to 50 percent of cases before 2000; race of the adoptive father is missing or "unable to be determined" in 43 to 62 percent of cases before 2000.[25] After 2000, race of the adoptive mother is missing in 13 to 14 percent of cases, and race of the adoptive father is missing in 9 to 12 percent of cases. Just over one-third of cases are missing race information on one or more members of the adoptive family.

Although the first three years of data are suspect, AFCARS represents the only source of case-level data on adoptions with state agency involvement that is consistent in format across states and over time. Moreover, the AFCARS count for fiscal year 1996 is highly correlated with data reported by the CWLA.[26]

Table 9.1. *Race of adopted children and transracial adoption (percentage of valid observations)*

	Percentage of adopted children		Transracial adoptions		
	Of color*	Black	All children	White children (not Hispanic)	Black children
1996	51.0	37.6	11.6	3.5	17.2
1997	59.4	45.0	13.2	3.9	17.7
1998	60.6	46.8	12.7	3.7	13.6
1999	60.5	46.0	12.5	5.5	11.2
2000	59.7	42.9	14.0	5.5	14.2
2001	59.5	40.1	15.7	6.5	16.8
2002	59.3	40.3	16.3	8.5	18.6
2003	57.0	38.3	16.9	8.2	20.1
Average	59.0	42.1	14.7	6.4	16.0

Finally, we note that the AFCARS adoption data are not ideal data for studying the movement of all children through the process of termination of parental rights and adoption. Because the adoption data include those children who were actually adopted, there is an inherent selection problem. There is some evidence of individual selection on the observables (discussed later), but the data set offers no way to correct it.

3. Identifying Transracial Adoptions

For fiscal years 1996–9, the race of the child and each adoptive parent is recorded as one of four categories: white, black or African American, Asian or Pacific Islander, and Native American. A separate field records the Hispanic origin of each adopted child and each adoptive parent. The reporting of race in the AFCARS data changed for fiscal year 2000 to conform to the 2000 census format. A separate, binary variable represents races labeled white, black or black, Asian, and Native American. Under this system, adopted children and their parents can indicate multiracial heritage. To address the complication of the change in the coding of the race variable, it was necessary to simplify the data so that the recorded race is more comparable across time. We created a dichotomous variable for each person (i.e., for each adoptee and each adoptive parent) to represent whether the person is a person of color. A person is designated to be of color if he or she is recorded in AFCARS as nonwhite and not of Hispanic origin.[27]

The first columns of Table 9.1 summarize the AFCARS data on the race of adopted children at the national level by year. In 1995, 51 percent were children of color. This percentage rose to 60.6 percent in 1998 and then fell slowly to 57 percent in 2003. The proportion of adopted children recorded as black rose from 37.6 percent of valid observations for fiscal year 1996 to 46.8 percent of valid observations for 1999. Thereafter the proportion of adopted children who were black fell to 38.3 percent.

Table 9.2. *Age and time from TPR to finalization by transracial adoption*

	Average age at finalization		Months from TPR to finalization	
	Same race	TRA	Same race	TRA
1996	6.67	6.16	21.57	14.17
1997	6.43	5.68	16.48	14.68
1998	6.77	5.91	15.30	14.81
1999	6.88	5.79	14.30	13.82
2000	6.93	5.83	14.64	13.97
2001	6.97	5.82	15.35	14.37
2002	7.04	5.94	15.51	14.27
2003	7.02	5.80	15.64	14.27
Average	6.92	5.85	15.37	14.25

Note: TPR, termination of parental rights; TRA, transracial adoption.

The percentage of adoptive parents of color was less than the percentage of adopted children of color; transracial adoptions of children of color occur regularly. Transracial adoption is defined here as the adoption of a child of color by white, non-Hispanic parent(s) only, or adoption of a white, non-Hispanic child by parent(s) of color only. This method purposely underestimates transracial adoptions. For example, the adoption of a child of Hispanic origin by a black parent is not considered transracial, and neither is the adoption of a black child by an Asian parent or a parent of Hispanic origin. No adoption by an interracial couple (where an interracial couple is, by this definition, composed of one white, non-Hispanic partner and one partner of color) is considered a transracial adoption. The method focuses the analysis on the most controversial of transracial adoptions.

The right-hand columns of Table 9.1 show that transracial placements in adoptions with state agency involvement rose from 11.6 percent in 1997 to 16.9 percent in 2003. There were 938 identifiable transracial placements in 1997; there were more than 7,500 identifiable transracial placements in 2003.

Averaging across all years, black children were placed transracially in 16 percent of adoptions with state agency involvement. In 1996 and 1997, more than 17 percent of black children adopted were adopted transracially. As kinship adoption of black children increased, transracial adoption fell to a low of 11.2 percent in 1999. After 1999, transracial placements of black children rose steadily so that in 2003, 20 percent of adopted black children were adopted transracially. White, non-Hispanic children also experienced increases in transracial placement, from 3.5 percent in 1996 to 8 percent in 2002 and 2003.

D. TRANSRACIAL ADOPTEES EXPERIENCE SPEEDIER ADOPTIONS

Table 9.2 shows that, on average, finalization of adoption occurred at a younger age and sooner after termination of parental rights when the placement was transracial rather than same race. Transracially adopted children were more than a year younger, on average, than their counterparts in same-race placements. Although the age of children placed within race rose about six months between 1996–7 and 2003, the age of transracial adoptees fell by a few months. Transracial adoptions happened, on average, one month more quickly after termination of parental rights and were among the most expeditious adoptions finalized from 1996 to 2003. More than 40 percent of transracially placed children were adopted before their third birthdays, and the proportion of infants and toddlers among transracially adopted children about doubled (increasing from 26% to 49%) between 1996 and 2003. Transracial placements were only half as prevalent among adoptions of teens.

We model the length of time a child waits in foster care as a legal orphan:

$$\text{Wait}_i = \alpha + \beta \text{Age}_i + \varphi \text{Black}_i + \delta \text{TRA}_i + \phi \mathbf{X}_i + \varepsilon_i,$$

where Wait is the (natural logarithm of the) wait time of child i measured in months, Age is the (log of the) age of the child in months at the time of termination of parental rights, Black indicates that the child is black, and TRA indicates a transracial adoption. The vector X includes other case characteristics such as the special needs and disabilities of the child, the marital status of the adoptive parent(s), and whether the adoptive parents had a relationship with the child prior to adoption. Interactions, state, and year effects are also included.

The time period between termination of parental rights and finalization of adoption is consistently and positively associated with the age of the child in previous studies.[28] In California, older children and children who experienced abuse or neglect before entering care waited longer for an adoptive family.[29] Furthermore, being adopted at an older age is the primary determinant of disruption and dissolution in adoption.[30]

Table 9.3 confirms these findings at the national level. Age at the time of termination of parental rights remains the single most important determinant of wait time. The model predicts that if termination of parental rights occurs when the child is 5.5 years, rather than 5 years, the wait is likely to be 1.04 years (one year and two weeks), rather than 1 year.

Barth reports that the age and race of a child have significant and independent effects on the odds of adoption and that the race and age effects are equally dramatic.[31] Smith finds that in the cohort of foster children whose birth parents' rights were terminated in October 1997, children who were older and black had longer times between termination and adoption.[32] Black children wait longer for adoption. The standard error of the estimated effect of being black is very small, indicating that there is very little chance that black children and children of other races have identical wait times. Furthermore, the interaction between race and age is positive, indicating that the racial gap in placement grows with age.

One strand of the debate over transracial adoption in the 1980s focused on whether policies favoring in-racial matching add to the time a black child spends as a legal orphan. An analysis of Michigan child welfare data for cases opened in the 1980s indicates that black children were moved more slowly into adoption than children of other races, all other things being equal.[33] The average wait time for black children in the 1996–2003 AFCARS data is 17.7 months, whereas the average

Table 9.3. *Determinants of time from TPR to finalization*

Ln (age at TPR)	0.382**
	(0.003)
Black	0.185**
	(0.019)
Black* ln (age at TPR)	0.008*
	(0.005)
TRA	–0.084**
	(0.033)
Black* TRA	–0.066**
	(0.013)
State effects?	Yes
Year effects?	Yes
Case controls?	Yes
N	226,584
R^2	0.20

Note: Dependent variable is ln (time from TPR to finalization). Robust standard errors are in parentheses. Case controls include special needs and disabilities, family structure (single/married), and prior relationship of adoptive parents to child.
$^{*}p < 0.05$. $^{**}p < 0.01$.

wait time for children of all other races is 15.0 months. And as discussed earlier, wait times recorded in AFCARS are shorter for transracially placed children than for children in same-race placements. The regression results in Table 9.3 confirm that children adopted transracially spend less time as legal orphans; transracial placement speeds the adoption of black children.

E. CONCLUSION

The Office for Civil Rights (OCR) of the U.S. Department of Health and Human Services has the discretion to conduct periodic reviews to determine whether recipients of federal financial assistance operate their programs in compliance with MEPA. In late 2003, in an unprecedented move, OCR issued a Letter of Finding against Hamilton County and the state of Ohio for 1.8 million dollars for blocking white families from adopting black children between 1995 and 2000.[34] According to OCR, it initiated more than 130 investigations of racial discrimination across the country. In the majority of the cases, either no violation was found or the grantee agency was asked to make needed changes in its program. The Ohio case was the first instance in which OCR issued a finding that the civil rights of individual children or prospective adoptive or foster parents were violated. Seemingly, this finding was made because of an extensive history of discrimination and repeated failure of the county to make necessary corrections. In 2005, OCR issued a finding against the South Carolina Department of Social Services, and in 2006, a fine of about 107,000 dollars was imposed.[35]

Although the role of transracial adoption in speeding adoptive placement for black children continues to be questioned in the social work literature, AFCARS data confirm that children adopted transracially spend less time as legal orphans. OCR should enforce the MEPAs to capture all possible gains of adoption for black legal orphans in foster care.

NOTES

1 *See* Jini Roby & Stacey A. Shaw, *The African Orphan Crisis and International Adoption*, Social Work 51, 199–210 (2006).

2 Mary Eschelbach Hansen & Daniel Pollack, *Tradeoffs in Formulating a Consistent National Policy on Adoption*, AMERICAN UNIVERSITY DEPARTMENT OF ECONOMICS WORKING PAPER 2005-14 (2006), http://www.american.edu/academic.depts/cas/econ/workingpapers/workpap.htm.

3 RITA J. SIMON, HOWARD ALSTEIN, & MARYGOLD S. MELLI, THE CASE FOR TRANSRACIAL ADOPTION (1994).

4 National Association of Black Social Workers, *Transracial Adoption* (1972) (position paper).

5 ARIZ. REV. STAT. ANN. § 8-105.C.1, D.4 (1974 & Supp. 1982–3); COLO. REV. STAT. § 19-4-110(2)(a) (1973 & Supp. 1982); OKLA. STAT. ANN. TIT. 10, § 60.12(1)(c) (West 1966); PA. STAT. ANN. TIT. 1, § 1 (Purdon Supp. 1982–3); S.D. CODIFIED LAWS ANN. § 25-6-13 (1976); WASH. REV. CODE ANN. § 26.32.060 (1961 & Supp. 1983).

6 National Association of Black Social Workers, *Preserving African-American Families* (1994) (position statement).

7 JOAN HOLLINGER & THE ABA CENTER ON CHILDREN AND THE LAW, NATIONAL RESOURCE CENTER ON LEGAL AND COURT ISSUES, A GUIDE TO THE MULTIETHNIC PLACEMENT ACT OF 1994 AS AMENDED BY THE INTERETHNIC PROVISION OF 1996, (1998)

8 388 U.S. 1 (1967).

9 P.L. 103-382.

10 P.L. 104-188, Section 1808, also known as MEPA II.

11 Here we assume for simplicity that the waiting children are identical (tantamount to assuming that the most important disability is the disability of being without parents).

12 RICHARD P. BARTH & MARIANNE BERRY, ADOPTION AND DISRUPTION: RATES, RISKS AND RESPONSES (1988).

13 Mary Eschelbach Hansen, *The Value of Adoption*, Adoption Q. 10 (2) (2007).

14 *See* Elizabeth Bartholet, *Where Do Black Children Belong? The Politics of Race Matching in Adoption*, 139 U.PA. L. REV. 1163–1256 (1991); H. FOGG-DAVIS, THE ETHICS OF TRANSRACIAL ADOPTION (2002); Kathy S. Stolley, *Statistics on Adoption in the United States*, 3 Future Children 26–42 (1993); Simon, *supra* note 3.

15 *See* R. G. McRoy, L. A. Zurcher, M. L. Lauderdale, & R. N. Anderson, *Self Esteem and Racial Identity in Transracial and Inracial Adoptees*, Social Work 522–6 (Nov. 1982); Devon Brooks, Sigrid James, & Richard Barth, *Preferred Characteristics of Children in Need of Adoption: Is There a Demand for Available Foster Children?* 76 SOCIAL SERVICES REV. 575–603 (2002).

16 Christine A. Bachrach, K. A. London, & Penelope L. Maza, *On the Path to Adoption: Adoption Seeking in the United States, 1988*, 53 J. MARRIAGE FAM. 705–18 (1991).

17 Brooks, *supra* note 15.

18 T. Gilles & Joseph Kroll, Barriers to Same Race Placement (1991).

19 *See* Rita J. Simon, *Transracial Adoptions: Does the Law Matter?* Am. Experiment Q. 85–94 (1999).

20 P.L. 105-89.

21 *See* Penelope Maza, *Using Administrative Data to Reward Agency Performance: The Case of the Federal Adoption Incentive Program*, 79 Child Welfare 444–56 (2000).

22 The Children's Bureau (CB) is one of two bureaus within the Administration on Children, Youth and Families, Administration for Children and Families, of the Department of Health and Human Services. It boasts an annual budget of more than seven billion dollars and works with state and local agencies to develop programs that focus on preventing the abuse of children in troubled families, protecting children from abuse, and finding permanent placements for those who cannot safely return to their homes. http://www.acf.hhs.gov/programs/cb/aboutcb/about_cb.htm.

23 The User's Guide and Codebook states that "adoptions finalized in years prior to [fiscal year] 1998 are not being updated because most states indicated that those data were not credible" (NDACAN n.d., 9).

24 For fiscal year 1996, eight of the states that submitted AFCARS adoption data omitted one or more of the elements needed to calculate the wait time for at least 90 percent of adoption cases. Only thirteen states submitted enough information to calculate time between termination and finalization for 90 percent or more of adoption cases.

25 These percentages account for single parent adoptions, i.e., if the adoption was completed by a single mother, the adoptive father's race is not applicable, rather than missing.

26 Mary Eschelbach Hansen & Bradley A. Hansen, *The Economics of Adoption of Children from Foster Care*, 85 Child Welfare 559–83 (2006).

27 It could be argued that "unable to determine" considered indicates "person of color," but inconsistencies across states and over time in the use of the "unable to determine" category requires a conservative approach. Occurrences of "unable to determine" are therefore treated as missing.

28 *See* Rosemary Avery, *Adoption Assistance under P.L. 96-272: A Policy Analysis*, 20 Children Youth Services Rev. 29–55 (1998); James A. Rosenthal, *Outcomes of Adoption of Children with Special Needs*, 3 Future Children 77–88 (1993); Toshio Tatara, Characteristics of Children in Substitute and Adoptive Care (1993).

29 Richard P. Barth, Mark Courtney, & Marianne Berry, *Timing Is Everything: Analysis of the Time of Adoption and Legalization*, 18 Social Work Res. 139–48 (1994).

30 *See* Barth, *supra* note 12; Robert M. Goerge, Eboni C. Howard, D. Yu, & S. Radomsky, Adoption Disruption and Displacement in the Child Welfare System, 1976–94 (1997); Victor Groze, Successful Adoptive Families: A Longitudinal Study of Special Needs Adoption (1996).

31 Richard P. Barth, *Effects of Age and Race on the Odds of Adoption versus Remaining in Long-Term Out-of-Home Care*, 76 Child Welfare 285–308 (1997).

32 Brenda D. Smith, *After Parental Rights Are Terminated: Factors Associated with Exiting Foster Care*, 25 Children Youth Services Rev. 965–85 (2003).

33 Sherrie A. Kossoudji, *Racial Aspects of the Move to Adoption, in* Adoption Policy and Special Needs Children (Rosemary J. Avery ed., 1997).

34 *See* Elizabeth Bartholet, *Multiethnic Placement Act Enforcement Decisions 2006*, http://www.law.harvard.edu/faculty/bartholet/mepa.php.

35 *Id.*

Jamie Galbraith, twenty-seven, is paid fifteen thousand dollars for every ova harvest. Jamie is a multiple-harvest egg seller. She has had at least four "donation" procedures, which were successful for purchasers. One of the egg retrievals involved a flight to Boston and having sixty-six eggs suctioned from her uterus. With the funds derived from this work, Jamie has saved for the down payment on a house and supports her family while her husband is away on military duty. Jamie knows that her eggs are in demand because she is naturally blonde and has green eyes. More important, she produces more than twice the amount of eggs than typical women who undergo ovary stimulation processes. (Fabrizio Constantini/Getty Images)

PART THREE. SPECTRUMS AND DISCOURSES: RIGHTS, REGULATIONS, AND CHOICE

> Most of us in this generation grew up believing that we had fantastic, unlimited, freedom of choice. Yet as mothers many women face "choices" on the order of: You can continue to pursue your professional dreams at the cost of abandoning your children to long hours of inadequate child care. Or: You can stay at home with your baby and live in a state of virtual, crazy-making isolation because you can't afford a nanny, because there is no such thing as part-time day care, and because your husband doesn't come home until 8:30 at night.
>
> – Judith Warner, *Newsweek*, February 21, 2005

In Part Three, authors address the thorny issues of privacy, human rights, legal regulation, and choice. These issues expose conflicts of interest that might arise between new parents and their children, in gay parent adoption, in the use of human eggs for scientific research, and in the ethics of using life sources outside of the context of parenting. Do free markets really translate to free choice? Maybe not, but as we have come to see, reproductive markets help individuals who otherwise see their natural rights to parent limited either due to infertility or sexuality. Questions of whether there are limits to free choice and a need for more law in the parenting domain are discussed here.

10 Reproducing Dreams

NAOMI CAHN

Eggs, sperm, and embryos are sold – and they are often sold to the highest bidder. The price of a desirable egg may be more than fifty thousand dollars, although eggs are available for less. X and Y Consulting, which claims to be the "longest operating donor recruiting agency in the U.S.," explains that its donor fee is based on the cost of living and wage rates in the state where the donor lives, so the fee can be quite variable; and in addition to the actual cost of the egg, the consumer will also pay various expenses associated with the donation process, including medical fees as well as transportation.[1] Egg producers can earn sizeable fees. The George Washington University Medical Center pays egg donors a standard four thousand dollars and earnestly explains that the money is earned income, and so it must be reported on the recipient's tax return.[2] The Ethics Committee of the American Society for Reproductive Medicine has even defended payment for eggs, explaining that payment does not discourage the provider's altruistic motivations and also promotes fairness to the providers.[3]

Sperm sales are a transnational market. The price of a sperm vial ranges, but it may cost hundreds of dollars. In 2006, the cheapest vial of sperm available from the Sperm Bank of California, a nonprofit organization, cost 295 dollars, while shipping charges added at least another 190 dollars.[4] A British service, Fertility4Life.com, offers several different options for sperm purchase, ranging from the "Diamond Plan," to the "Beat the Clock Plan," to single donation sales.[5] In Denmark, sperm is more expensive than gold.[6] Although California Cryobank provides its donor catalog for free, a baby photo of the donor costs twenty-one dollars, and a longer profile of the donor costs sixteen dollars.[7] Sperm producers are typically paid less than one hundred dollars per "deposit," although frequent providers can earn significant amounts of money.

Embryo sales represent a new, potentially lucrative market that has not yet reached its price point. Embryos are available through several different options, including through donation that is truly uncompensated for the donors,[8] embryo-selling banks, and embryo "adoption" agencies. Consider the efforts of Jennalee Ryan to establish her new business, the euphonious Abraham Center of Life. At the Abraham Center, "donor-created embryos" are made available for infertile couples.[9] Ryan assembles embryos, and then she sells them for twenty-five hundred dollars per embryo. She provides donor profiles to prospective parents, allowing them to select their embryo of choice from those that she has already manufactured.[10] As an alternative, Nightlight Christian Adoptions allows potential parents to adopt an embryo.[11] Only parents who are committed to offering "a constructive, wholesome, and spiritual home environment" to their child, as verified by a home study, are eligible to participate. As their Snowflakes Embryo Adoption fact sheet explains, for a program fee of eight thousand dollars, parents can help embryos "achieve their ultimate purpose – life."

The mere existence of this extensive, international market in gametes, however, obscures what is, for many, the initial and critical question of whether gametes should be sold at all. For some, eggs and sperm should never be sold. They argue that the sale of eggs and sperm results in exploiting the gamete providers, encouraging eugenics as consumers choose the "best possible" genes, leading down the slippery slope that ends in buying children, and discriminating based on class because of who is able to buy gametes.[12] Others argue that because it interferes with so-called natural reproduction, gamete sales result in unnatural families with two moms or two dads, or only one parent. And political philosopher Molly Shanley observes that a market-based system in gametes "perpetuates an overly individualistic understanding of human society and distorts the liberal commitment to human freedom," suggesting that if we cannot achieve the "ideal" of making "gamete transfer a real 'gift' by forbidding all payment, the main harm of a market system would be avoided if a uniform fee for donating and for receiving gametes was put into effect" along with abolishing anonymity.[13]

On the other hand, marketization facilitates access by marginalized groups, facilitates new family forms, and does not objectify women – at least in the context of sperm sales.[14]

Can this market be saved? Should this market be saved?

The thesis of this chapter is that issues involving commodification – such as market access, price, safety of gametes, exploitation of providers, and sale of children – are intertwined with regulation of the resulting relationships such as whether sperm donors can assert parental rights or whether children will be able to learn the identity of their donors. If, for example, single women, gays, and lesbians are unable to purchase gametes, then the laws governing parenthood will undoubtedly reflect similarly discriminatory attitudes. If the two-heterosexual-parent presumption controls the gamete market, then that same presumption will, as was true when similar presumptions dominated the adoption world, affect the rights of gametic children to discover their biological progenitors, and the rights of those biological providers to learn about their gametic children.

There is, as we know, a continuum of options when it comes to markets in gametes, ranging from prohibiting sales completely to allowing an unfettered market that extends – perhaps – through the sale of embryos. As part of this focus, it may be useful to distinguish the different markets involving eggs, sperm, and embryos. Although the consumers and sellers may be the same, the producers of egg and sperm face quite different experiences. Rather than a single-minded focus on regulating the sale of gametes, we should discuss regulating different actors within the transactions, whether regulations should differ depending on the type of gamete, and the impact of each kind of regulation. Coherent discussions of commodification should begin with parsing out the stakes and interests of each market participant and examining why regulation might be appropriate.[15]

An examination of the rhetoric of commodification shows that suspicions about marketization are tangled up with fears about eugenics, slavery, and personhood. It seems to me that the marketization obsession brings together the most important issues in this debate – identity, parenthood, and the impact of technology – but that any discussion of the sale of gametes must be concerned with the equity of the market for those who are involved in it and want to be involved in it, as well as the implications of any sale for the provider, recipient, and child. Banning the sale of gametes will result in the inequities and inefficiencies that Michele Bratcher Goodwin identifies in the body part sale and, possibly, in the majoritarian rule against single women and lesbians that Martha Ertman fears, but allowing an unfettered market, although perhaps efficient, is inequitable. Because of the nature of what is being sold – reproduction dreams – this is the type of transaction that we, as a culture, want to regulate and where we might want to redefine efficiency to include access and equity. With appropriate regulation concerning gamete safety, nonexploitation of providers, and equal access, then the actual market transactions should pose little danger to human flourishing. Nonetheless, by focusing primarily on the particular set of issues involved in market sales, we obscure the human relationships at the core of these sales: the relationships between gamete providers, children, and ultimate parent(s).

Although I advocate allowing for the continuation of these sales, my proposal argues for fundamental change in the market that recognizes the interrelationship of the technology of gamete provision to identity and parenthood. Indeed, these sales might best be subject to a hybrid model that draws on both private ordering and altruistic donation.[16] Jennalee Ryan's bank can coexist with Snowflake Embryo Adoptions; egg and sperm donations from relatives do not preclude the sale of these gametes by unrelated providers.

Ultimately, the gamete market is already mixing money and identity. Suggesting that the use of money taints otherwise pure relationships ignores the myriad situations in which intimacy and economic transactions already occur. The mere ascription of financial value to these items, the mere use of commodification discourse, does not necessarily destroy all other values they may contain.[17] As Professor Viviana Zelizer points out, "people invest a great deal of effort in creating monies designed to manage complex social relations that express intimacy but also inequality... the point is not that these areas of social life valiantly resisted commodification. On the contrary, they readily absorbed monies, transforming them to fit a variety of values and social relations."[18] There are multiple situations in which people are paid for work that benefits other people, ranging from nannies, to clergy, to medical professionals.[19]

Assuming that the market continues, the question is how "to structure social relationships that involve elements of both,"[20] rather than banning financial transactions altogether. In some ways, commodification is beside the point because, even if it were banned, underground markets would develop.[21] Instead, we should more profitably focus on the relationship between human flourishing and gamete sale.[22]

The extremes of no regulation and complete banning are not viable for different reasons. Instead, we need to expand the purpose of regulation and design interventions that will achieve those purposes. At the least, we need market regulation to ensure the enforceability of contracts relating to sperm provision and physician/clinic services, but we also need to ensure that contracts relinquishing parental rights are enforceable. Moreover, regulations should seek to ensure that providers (particularly egg providers) are not exploited. Third, laws must clearly identify the parents of any child produced through gamete provision, specifying that the recipients are, indeed, those entitled to assert parental rights. Fourth, regulations must ensure equality of access, based on race, income, sex, sexual orientation, or other criteria. Finally, market regulation must ensure that a gamete-provided child has access to identifying information once the child is eighteen. Although a few of these regulations exist piecemeal in a few states, there is no comprehensive scheme that ensures that all these strands – identity, parenthood, access, and exploitation – are bundled together.

Regardless of the pricing system applicable to sperm, eggs, and embryos, the anticommodification arguments are entirely accurate when it comes to the critical issue of what is being sold. Gametes can create people and familial relationships, unlike the sale of kidneys – or potatoes. It is the regulations concerning those resulting relationships that should assume critical importance. These issues are significant, of course, for market purposes (e.g., they may contribute to market efficiency), but also because, even if gamete sales are regulated like potato sales, the underlying products differ. Recognizing these differences does not mean that there should be no market, but rather, that market requires market adjustments. There is a patchwork of state regulation concerning the relinquishment of rights by donors, the establishment of rights for parents, and the need for identity disclosure, each of which inherently affects the existence and operation of a market in gametes. Any discussion of market structure must also examine the need to enforce contracts that both set the terms of a sperm sale and establish the parental role, if any, for gamete providers.[23]

The remainder of this chapter explores two components of market regulation: anonymity of donors and parenting relationships. The focus on pricing works less well when, after a woman or a man has decided what to do with her or his body, there is now a child with separate and independent needs and interests who is deciding what to do with her body. Children have independently recognized rights that exist apart from, and sometimes in conflict with, those of their (different sets of) parents.

A. ANONYMITY

The history of secrecy surrounding gamete provision is complicated: sperm providers are often promised anonymity[24] and may have relied on that promise in agreeing to provide sperm. Similarly, although the identity of egg providers was often well known in early cases, there is now more anonymity and secrecy attached to this process, as well. Moreover, the intending parents in gamete provision cases have generally been subject to much less pressure to disclose the biological backgrounds of their children than have adoptive parents, who have been counseled to tell their children that they are adopted. And outside of cases involving known sperm providers, there is little law on identity disclosure for gamete providers. On the other hand, intermediary banks are increasingly frequently offering the option of known donors, or providers, who agree to disclose their identity at some point in the child's life. Internet registries are also helping to facilitate contact between gamete providers and gamete-formed families.

1. Legal Protections for Anonymity

Outside of private promises, the law has typically supported the anonymity of sperm providers and, as discussed in the next section, distinguished between the rights of known and unknown providers. In one of the first cases to deal with the disclosure of the identity of a sperm donor, the court crafted a compromise.[25] The parents of an eleven-year-old girl with a rare kidney disorder sued California Cryobank, which the parents allege provided them with the defective sperm that led to the kidney disease. As part of their suit, the Johnsons sought to depose the donor himself, who resisted, claiming that disclosure would infringe his privacy interests. The donor's privacy claims were grounded in the contract between the Johnsons and Cryobank, which states that his identity will not be disclosed, as well as in the California and federal constitutions.[26] The court held that the absolute prohibition in the contract was contrary to public policy, which allowed for disclosure based on good cause, and although the court recognized a limited constitutional right to privacy under the California constitution, it held that the identity could be disclosed. Given the particular circumstances of the case, however, the court directed that the donor be deposed without ever revealing his identity.

The *Johnson* court rejected the donor's claim to a physician–patient privilege because there was no evidence that the donor ever consulted California Cryobank for medical diagnosis and treatment; the donor instead sought merely to make money from the sale of his sperm and was thus not subject to the protections offered by the privilege. Sale of the sperm did not subject him to the same privacy rights.[27]

As a policy matter, is this type of transaction entitled to secrecy? Perhaps the answer is yes, except to all of those involved in the transaction itself: the bank, the intending parents, and the child. Just as the initial move to secrecy in adoption records was not designed to protect against disclosure within the relationship, the protection accorded to gamete donors should not extend to disclosure to anyone not directly involved in the transaction. The information could remain private, a secret shared only by the child, her parents, and the provider. Identifying information could be released, on request, once the gamete offspring reach eighteen, or through a confidential intermediary system that would allow for national searches and that would require all donors to register. States should guarantee the release of such information to mature adults through laws that would preempt private agreements (such as between the gamete provider and the intending parents or between the gamete provider and a gamete bank). Although all states have addressed this issue in various ways for adoptees,[28] few states have considered legislation on disclosure of the identity of gamete providers.

2. Why Not End Anonymity?

The primary arguments against information disclosure center on pragmatic concerns about the supply of gametes and more philosophical concerns about the rights of privacy of everyone involved: the parent(s), gamete providers, and the child.

a. Supply and demand. Requiring that gamete providers agree to the possibility of information disclosure may be risky in terms of supply. One of the primary arguments against disclosure of the identity of gamete providers is that it will have a negative effect on the supply of sperm. If sperm providers know that they may be found, then they may be less likely to give gametic material out of fear that an unknown child will come knocking on their door twenty years later. In contrast, current practices appear to protect their ongoing anonymity. Studies have repeatedly shown that about half of both egg and sperm donors would continue to participate even if anonymity were removed.[29] Early studies from countries that have moved toward mandatory donor identification similarly showed that donors were less willing to provide gametes if they knew their identity would be disclosed.[30] Even the future possibility that a law will require such disclosure may have a dampening effect.[31] Indeed, after Sweden enacted legislation in 1985 that mandated the identification of gamete providers when the child reached the age of eighteen, there was some concern that the legislation had caused a severe decline in the number of sperm donors.[32] Subsequently, however, there appears to be an increase in the number of sperm providers, and fears that donor identity release requirements would inhibit semen provision have been allayed.[33] Similarly, after New Zealand mandated the release of identifying information, there was an initial decline; rates stabilized, however, after the first year.[34] Thus, although requiring the release of information may have some initial impact on the number of donors, predictions of drastic long-term effects appear overblown. Moreover, such legislation may result in the development of new methods to recruit other donors.[35]

It appears, then, that the requirement that children receive access to donor information will not necessarily result in a dramatic decrease in donors.[36] The critical policy questions are whether the risk of a temporary shortage in gametic material is balanced by allowing access to this information for gamete donor children and the providers themselves. Although sale of gametes may be a commercial transaction for the seller, it has much broader implications for the children ultimately created; it is their interests and, in many cases, the interests of their parents that are respected through a disclosure regime.

b. Privacy. The argument against providing identifying information relies, in large part, on the history of nondisclosure. The traditional articulation of the fundamental right to privacy does not comprehend the various interests at stake in the gamete provision cases. The cases' discussions of personhood and privacy provide conflicting notions of whose rights and interests merit protection at any one time. In this context, there are a series of possible harms from disclosure of information beyond the anticipated boundaries that one expects to keep secret, including breach of confidentiality and intrusion into decision making.[37] At the same time, there may be harms from nondisclosure such as children who feel betrayed by not knowing their origins. It is, consequently, important to recognize that privacy, while constitutionally protected, is not absolute and requires balancing various interests.

Ultimately, and ironically, a failure to disclose the identity of gamete providers reinforces the notion of the "exclusive"[38] and traditional family. It suggests that recognizing a child's need for disclosure threatens parental rights – instead of acknowledging the validity of the child's interests and the increasing pertinence of genetic information. And it denies the possibilities for connection that biology can create. The secrecy surrounding adoption developed during a period of pronatalism, a celebration of the nuclear family and of heterosexual motherhood and a corresponding condemnation of single mothers.[39] Allowing for the release of identifying information is a rejection of a system that reifies the traditional family.

Children's right to know includes two interrelated parts: the right to know that one has been conceived through donor gametes and the right to know the donor.[40] Requiring that parents tell their children of their donor-conceived status is highly problematic: not only is it difficult to enforce, but it is highly intrusive of intrafamilial relationships. On the other hand, when young children learn that they have third-party gametes, studies have repeatedly shown that this has no effect on their relationship with their parents or adjustments to their environment.[41]

Several studies have examined whether donor offspring experience identity problems that are similar to those of adopted children, and while the studies often conflict, they do indicate that at least some donor children experience a sense of loss for not having information about their biological pasts or being able to establish a relationship with their gamete providers.[42] In fact, a number of groups have formed to work on the issues that the children and their parents confront.[43] In one study of children who were not told until they were adults that they were born through donor insemination, the (now adult) children explained that they were experiencing problems of personal identity in conjunction with some hostility toward their families for not disclosing their origins.[44]

Most heterosexual parents do not disclose to their children that they have been conceived with third-party gametes. It is, of course, far easier to hide the use of third-party sperm or eggs where there is both a mother and a father.

Failing to disclose this information also, and ironically, values contract over connection. We imagine that explicit contracts, between gamete providers and gamete banks and between biological parents and adoption agencies, and implicit contracts, between the ultimate parents, the biological parents, and the state, guaranteeing secrecy, are more important than the children's need for information or the biological parents' later need for contact. We live in a culture that respects kinship based on blood ties.[45] It is perfectly possible and completely desirable to challenge concepts of families based solely on blood by emphasizing intention and nurture, but it is also important to acknowledge that genetic ties may be important for a variety of reasons. Without essentializing the notion of genetic connection, children may still want to know where they came from.

B. THE PARENTING EFFECT

Although most states have some laws concerning the parental rights of sperm providers, few have comparable statutes for egg providers. Many of the statutes covering sperm provision address insemination of married women. But some do not address parenthood issues outside of the marriage context. There are gaps when it comes to the relationship between donors and unmarried parents. Even where the parties agree on parenthood, explicit contracts precluding rights for gamete donors are not necessarily enforceable.[46]

For sperm, the law typically facilitates transactions by allocating parental rights to the intending parents, rather than to the gamete provider.[47] There are three different situations in which women use donated sperm: (1) married women may be artificially inseminated by a known or unknown donor because their husbands have experienced fertility impairments; (2) single women or lesbian couples may use an unknown donor; or (3) single women or lesbian couples may use a known donor. Virtually all states address the first situation.

1. Donor Sperm

Many states have adopted the Uniform Parentage Act (UPA), a model statute originally promulgated in 1973. According to the 1973 UPA, for the husband to become the legal father when the woman becomes pregnant through donor sperm, a doctor must supervise the insemination, the husband must consent in writing to the insemination, and the physician must file the husband's consent with the state health department. Only when these requirements have been satisfied can the husband become the legal father and the donor's legal rights be terminated.[48] For example, Ohio requires both husband and wife to consent in writing before the woman can be inseminated with donor sperm.[49] In Kansas, the consent of a husband and wife can be filed with the court, and it is treated just like consent to an adoption.[50] The law does not seem to contemplate that unmarried couples might use the method.

The original UPA was revised in 2002 and now provides that a donor is not a father unless he signs a consent to paternity or, during the child's first two years of life, lives with the child and holds out the child as his offspring.[51] The revised act, however, has only been adopted in seven states.

If a couple fails to follow the law's requirements, then the results may be disastrous. Consider what happened to three-year-old Alexandria when her parents, Lorraine and Gordon, divorced.[52] Gordon had a vasectomy before he married Lorraine, so they discussed using a donor to have children. Both parents looked at a donor catalog from the Pacific Fertility Medical Center before choosing a man who looked like Gordon. They then signed a consent form that required each of them to treat any resulting child as their child. But California law mandates that a doctor certify the signatures on the consent form; there was no physician certification on their form. When Lorraine requested child support from Gordon, a California court decided that Gordon did not have to support Alexandria because no one had followed the law on how to establish parenthood after artificial insemination. The story is even more complicated; Gordon claimed that he had signed a form so that Lorraine could have a child but that he never wanted to be a father. For Alexandria, the story is simple: she has no father.

When single women or lesbians search for someone they know to provide sperm, they may want the man to continue to be involved in the child's life – or they may not. In the first situation, the parents may enter into an agreement that sets out exactly what rights each participant has. Some men consider themselves coparents and may move to be closer to the children, whereas others arrange for visits throughout the year.[53] One of my single lesbian friends became friendly with Walter, a gay man, in graduate school; she asked Walter if he had any interest in becoming a part-time parent. She became pregnant, and Walter, who lives half a continent away, attended the birth. She now has a room set aside in her house for Walter's frequent visits from a city on the other side of the continent, and she takes the child to visit him and his family. But not all relationships are so harmonious. Known sperm donors have received extensive visitation rights despite the objections of the biological mother and her partner. On the other hand, in Florida, X agreed to provide sperm to a friend but then to relinquish all rights and obligations related to the child. He subsequently decided that he wanted to be a father and sued the mother, trying to establish his paternity.[54] The court refused to grant him any rights, finding that the law governing donation prevented him from establishing any rights.[55]

A few states recognize that a sperm donor can be a father if the parties have agreed on this arrangement. In Kansas, the law provides that a sperm donor who provides sperm to a doctor for the insemination of a woman to whom the donor is not married does not have any parental rights, unless he and the mother have agreed otherwise. In other words, the default rule is that a sperm donor has no rights, even if he is known to the mother. This has not prevented a man from claiming that he is the father of his former girlfriend's twins.[56] Daryl Hendrix and Samantha Harrington were friends when Hendrix provided sperm to a doctor so that Harrington could have children. When Harrington gave birth to twins, Hendrix sued her, asking the Kansas courts to make him the father. He claims that his biological connection is enough for him to be the father.

The case raises the question of a state's authority to define parental rights and also suggests that gamete donors should always have the choice to become involved in children's lives. It also flatly poses the question of whether every child should have two parents.

Texas law similarly provides that sperm donors are not fathers but says nothing about how an agreement might affect parental rights. So what happens when the sperm donor signs an agreement that states that he will be the parent of any child? In 2003, Sharon Sullivan, a lesbian, and Brian Russell, a gay man, signed a coparenting agreement, in which Russell agreed to provide his sperm to Sullivan. Their agreement also said that if Sullivan became pregnant, the baby would be "the child of BRIAN KEITH RUSSELL as if he and SHARON SULLIVAN were married at the time of conception, and that BRIAN KEITH RUSSELL will be named as the father on the child's birth certificate."[57] Although Russell did provide the sperm, other parts of the agreement began to fall apart. Russell asked to attend the birth of their child, but this did not happen. Less than a month after the birth, he sued Sullivan, requesting that he be named the father of her daughter.[58] Faced with a law stating that sperm donors have no parental rights, but with an agreement that explicitly gave Russell paternal rights, the Texas courts allowed him to try to establish his paternity.

Because so many courts have recognized that sperm donors may have rights, some have charged that courts are stretching to find a male and female parent for every child. The laws that currently exist are simply not clear about the paternal rights of sperm donors when a single woman or lesbian gives birth. When the mother knows the sperm donor, the issues become far more complex.

2. Egg-Formed Families

Generally, donors sign an agreement waiving all parental rights and responsibilities with respect to any child conceived from their eggs.[59] Only a few states, however, have enacted specific legislation assigning parental status after egg donation. As a result, the rights of egg providers, recipients, and children are not clear in most states. Even where there are laws, they generally address only a married recipient and her husband, labeling them as the parents of a child from an egg donation. Like sperm statutes, egg statutes fail to deal with legal parentage of children conceived by single women.[60] Although few states have specific legislation with respect to egg donation, other states have adjudicated the parenthood status of an egg donor.

a. Egging on the laws. As of 2006, only six states had specific legislation pertaining to egg donation.[61] The statutory provisions of these states – Colorado, Florida, North Dakota, Oklahoma, Texas, and Virginia – delineate the relationships and responsibilities between egg donors and their offspring and similarly provide, albeit applying different language, that an egg donor relinquishes all maternal rights and obligations with respect to the donation itself and the resulting child.[62]

Florida law, like that of many other states, addresses only the parenting rights of married recipients. If a child is born "within wedlock" as the result of donated eggs, then the husband and wife couple are the parents[63]; Florida law says nothing, however, about whether a recipient who is single is the parent. Florida's domestic relations law permits only reasonable compensation directly related to the donation of eggs and relinquishes egg donors of all maternal rights and obligations with respect to the donation itself or the resulting children.[64] Texas and North Dakota laws, which explicitly include egg providers as "donors," preclude a donor from serving as a parent.[65] Oklahoma's artificial insemination statute[66] addresses parentage issues in the context of both egg and embryo providers, precluding both donors and any resulting children from having any rights with respect to one another.[67] On the other hand, the Oklahoma law covers only marital couples, ostensibly leaving out other types of families that are not married.[68] In Virginia, the intended mother is the legal mother of a child conceived through the assistance of an egg donation, and the egg donor has no parental rights and obligations.[69] Connecticut resolves this issue by restricting the application of its artificial insemination laws to married couples. Under Connecticut law, a physician cannot perform artificial insemination by donor (AID) unless "the physician receives in writing the request and consent of the husband and wife desiring the utilization of A.I.D." and the permission is filed in the local court.[70]

b. Cases of eggs. Although there are very few cases involving egg donors, courts are frequently called on to decide comparable issues involving gestational carriers in alleged breach of surrogacy contracts. The decisions are quite confused when it comes to the rights of the surrogates, the egg and sperm donors, and the so-called intending parents, or the people who initially arranged for the child's birth. Everyone involved typically signs a contract that sets out their understanding that the intending parents are the ones who should be receiving custody.

But things do not always go as planned. Such was the case in a 2006 Pennsylvania case, in which James Flynn and Eileen Donich signed an agreement with a company called Surrogate Mothers Inc. so that they could have children.[71] In the agreement, Flynn was listed as the "biological father or adoptive father" and Donich as the "biological mother, adoptive mother, or partner." The company then found Jennifer Rice, who agreed to serve as the egg donor, and Danielle Bimber, who agreed to serve as the gestational carrier. James promised to pay up to twenty thousand dollars for multiple births, as well as medical and travel expenses for Bimber. In the agreement, Bimber stated that she would not try to act as a parent to any resulting child but would instead give up any parental rights that she might have.[72]

Flynn provided the sperm, Rice the egg, and Bimber became pregnant.[73] She gave birth to Matthew, Mark, and Micah in November 2003, all of whom were then placed in the hospital's neonatal intensive care unit. Donich called the hospital frequently to find out how the boys were doing, but Bimber brought them to her house when the boys were eight days old. Bimber, Flynn, and Rice each went to court, trying to establish their rights to the boys. The first Pennsylvania court gave custody to Bimber because she was the "legal mother" and also found that the surrogacy agreement was not valid. On the other hand, an Ohio court found that Flynn and Rice, who were biologically related to the triplets, were the parents.[74] Ultimately, an appeals court in Pennsylvania decided that Bimber had no legal relationship to the triplets and that Flynn was the father; only he could allow Bimber to take custody of the children.

At the same time, one of the Ohio judges explained that

> there are only a few states that have even begun to address the issue of determining who the parents of a surrogate child may be. Even the few states that have begun to address the issues involved have approached the issues from four different directions. Unless the state legislators begin to address the multiple issues involved, it will be the children that will be caught in a continual tug of war between the egg donor or donors, the sperm donor or donors, the surrogate parent or parents, and those that simply want to adopt a child from what they perceive as the ideal parents.[75]

If the courts were confused, so was the media coverage. One newspaper reported, "Surrogate mother gets custody of 3; Judge Criticizes Sperm Donor," while another concluded, "Surrogate awarded custody of triplets; [man] who fathered babies gets visitation."[76] Who are these people? Is the "sperm donor" the father?

C. CONCLUSION

Ultimately, there is no uniformity on parentage or on identity issues when it comes to families formed through assisted reproductive technology. Even more troubling, however, is that the laws and cases consider parenting in isolation from technology and identity. Resolving some of these conflicts is simple: enact legislation that clarifies the resulting parentage rights whenever third-party provided gametes are used, regardless of the marital status of the consumers, and allow providers and gamete provider children to dissolve anonymity when the children reach the age of eighteen. The private nature of these transactions, however, has allowed them to escape much regulation.

Moreover, in addition to the confusing issues of parenthood and to the lack of regulation, the new reproductive technologies are highly controversial on a series of different levels. Because they involve sex, reproduction, nature, parenting, technology, and money, they touch on many contemporary social debates: the technologies allow children to have only one legal parent, they are contrary to the moral beliefs of many, and they have become confused with political conflicts on cloning and stem cell research. Clarifying the varying interests involved in reproductive technology – including the gamete providers, the children, the family members who raise the child, the market participants, and the state – provides the basis for deciding on the systems for acknowledging, and regulating, those interests.

NOTES

1 *X and Y Consulting Inc. Fee Schedule*, http://eggdonorsnow.com/feeschedule.html.

2 The George Washington University Medical Faculty Associates, *Become an Egg Donor*, http://www.washivf.com/GWIVF-GWIVF_Content_C-Index_Page_Template_1143644787796.html.

3 Ethics Committee of the American Society for Reproductive Medicine, *Financial Incentives in Recruitment of Oocyte Donors*, 74 Fertility & Sterility 216 (2000).

4 The Sperm Bank of California, *Fee Schedule for Recipient Services*, http://www.thespermbankofca.org/pdf/feeschedule2006.PDF.

5 Fertility4Life.com, *Price Plans*, http://www.fertility4life.com/hi/price.asp.

6 Will Pavia, *The Vikings Are Coming*, The Times (London), Nov. 27, 2006, at 4.

7 California Cryobank Sperm Bank, http://www.cryobank.com/fees_ds.cfm?page=9.

8 Penn Fertility Care, *Donor Embryo Program*, http://pennhealth.com/fertility/embryo_donor.html.

9 *World's First Donor Created Human Embryo Bank – The Abraham Center of Life – Opening in San Antonio*, EWorldwire Press, July 28, 2006, http://www.eworldwire.com/pressreleases/15132.

10 Nicola Foy, *Embroyo Broker Gets the Once-Over*, San Antonio Express-News, Jan. 13, 2007, at http://www.mysanantonio.com/news/MYSA011307_03B_embryo_265802d_html6870.html; William Saletan, *The Embryo Factory*, Slate Mag., Jan. 15, 2007, http://www.slate.com/id/2157495.

11 Nightlight Christian Adoptions, http://www.nightlight.org/snowflakeadoption.htm.

12 These last four concerns are nicely articulated in Martha Ertman, *What's Wrong with a Parenthood Market? A New and Improved Theory of Commodification*, 82 N.C. L. Rev. 1, 26–34 (2003).

13 Mary Lyndon Shanley, Making Babies, Making Families: What Matters Most in an Age of Reproductive Technologies, Surrogacy, Adoption, and Same-Sex and Unwed Parents' Rights 94–5, 98 (2001).

14 Joan Williams and Viviana Zelizer differentiate between commodification, which "blurs the distinction between proposals to bring market institutions and strategic, self-interested behavior into family life, and proposals to end domesticity's erasure of women's economic contribution," and marketization, which "allocate[s] a certain set of social relations to the market." Joan C. Williams & Viviana A. Zelizer, *To Commodify or Not to Commodify: That Is Not the Question, in* Rethinking Commodification, 362, 370–1, 376 (Martha Ertman & Joan Williams eds., 2006). Allowing a market to exist in games is marketization.

15 In discussing the possibilities for private ordering of reproductive tissue sales, there are critical issues involving nondiscriminatory market access as well as commodification of babies. The access issues are more easily addressed than the commodification issues, e.g., expanding insurance coverage of infertility, an approach used in some other countries, would enhance equity within the system and allow more people of color to use gametic reproduction. *See* June Carbone & Paige Gottheim, *Markets, Subsidies, Regulation, and Trust: Building Ethical Understandings into the Market for Fertility Services*, 9 J. Gender, Race & Just. 509 (2006).

16 Michele Goodwin, Black Markets: The Supply and Demand of Body Parts 20–2 (2006).

17 *See* Viviana A. Zelizer, The Social Meaning of Money (1997); Naomi Cahn, *The Coin of the Realm: Poverty and the Commodification of Gendered Labor*, Iowa J. Gender, Race & Just. 1–20 (2001).

18 Zelizer, *supra* note 17.

19 Williams, *supra* note 14.

20 Ellen Sarasohn Glazer & Evelina Weidman Sterling, Having Your Baby through Egg Donation (2005).

21 *See* Goodwin, *supra* note 16.

22 Goodwin, *supra* note 16; Joan Williams & Martha Ertman, Rethinking Commodification 304 (2005).

23 Ertman, *supra* note 12.

24 It appears that state law did not actually regulate this promise of nondisclosure. Similarly, in the adoption context, state law never guaranteed complete anonymity to the biological parents.

25 Johnson v. Superior Court, 80 Cal. App. 4th 1050 (Cal. App. 2. Dist., 2000) *rev. denied*, 2000 Cal. LEXIS 6741 (2000).

26 The contract between the provider and the cryobank provided for confidentiality "unless a court orders disclosure for good cause." Johnson v. Superior Court, 80 Cal. App. 4th at 1057. The contract between the sperm recipients and the cryobank stated that the Johnsons would "not now, nor at any time, require nor expect [cryobank] to obtain or divulge... the name of said donor, nor any other information concerning

characteristics, qualities, or any other information whatsoever concerning said donor"... "it being the intention of all parties that the identity of said donor shall be and forever remain anonymous." *Id.* at 1064–5.

27 Although we might think differently about privacy in connection with a sale of "goods" than in connection with a sale of "personhood," treating sperm and eggs as the sale of goods might help allay concerns about the identity of the providers. This is an example of how the concept of commodification may be useful because it allows us to separate out the good from the privacy interests of the provider. If we view gametes as quasi-commodities, this may diminish privacy concerns. Professor Rhadika Rao suggests that the right of privacy protects individuals' relationship to their frozen embryos where the individuals attempt to establish a personal relationship with the embryos, whereas the law of property applies more appropriately where individuals want to sell frozen embryos because they have no personal relationship to the embryos. On these issues, *see* Rhadika Rao, *Property, Privacy, and the Human Body*, 80 B.U. L. Rev. 359, 456–9 (2000).

28 *See, e.g.*, Elizabeth J. Samuels, *The Idea of Adoption: An Inquiry into the History of Adult Adoptee Access to Birth Records*, 53 Rutgers L. Rev. 367, 368 (2001).

29 *E.g.*, Eric D. Blyth, Lucy Frith, & Abigail Farrand, *Is It Possible to Recruit Gamete Donors Who Are Both Altruistic and Indentifiable?* 84 Fertility & Sterility S21 (2005) (Supp. 1).

30 *E.g.*, K. Daniels & O. Lalos, *The Swedish Insemination Act and Availability of Donors*, 10 Human Reprod. 1871 (1995).

31 June Carbone & Paige Gottheim, *Markets, Subsidies, Regulation, and Trust*, 9 J. Gender Race & J. 509 (2006).

32 Daniels, *supra* note 30; F. Shenfield, *Privacy versus Disclosure in Gamete Donation: A Clash of Interest, of Duties, or an Exercise in Responsibility?* 14 J. Assisted Reprod. & Genetics 371, 371 (1997); A. Lalos, K. Daniels, C. Gotlieb, & O. Lalos, *Recruitment and Motivation of Semen Providers in Sweden*, 18 Human Reprod. 212 (2003).

33 Shenfield, *supra* note 32, at 371.

34 Marilyn Gardner, *Sperm Donors No Longer Bank on Anonymity*, Christian Science Monitor, March 30, 2005, http://www.csmonitor.com/2005/0330/p11s02-lifp.html.

35 Blyth, *supra* note 29.

36 In the adoption context, the two states – Alaska and Kansas – that never prevented disclosure have experienced higher than average adoption rates. *See* Naomi Cahn & Jana Singer, *Adoption, Identity, and the Constitution*, 2 U. Pa. J. Const. L. 150, 187 (1999).

37 Daniel Solove, *A Taxonomy of Privacy*, 154 U. Pa. L. Rev. 477, 490–1 (2006).

38 *See* Alison Harvey Young, *Reconceiving the Family: Challenging the Paradigm of the Exclusive Family*, 6 Am. U. J. Gender & L. 505, 554–5 (1998); Naomi R. Cahn, *Reframing Child Custody Decisionmaking*, 57 Ohio St. L. J. 1 (1997) (arguing that it may be appropriate to recognize the caretaking rights of more than two adults).

39 *See* Rickie Solinger, Wake Up Little Susie: Single Pregnancy and Race before Roe v. Wade 13 (1992).

40 Lucy Firth, *Beneath the Rhetoric: The Role of Rights in the Practice of Non-anonymous Gamete Donation*, 15 Bioethics 473, 476 (2001).

41 S. Golombok *et al.*, *Families Created by Gamete Donation: Follow Up at Age 2*, 20 Hum. Reprod. 286 (2005); Joann E. Scheib & Alice Ruby, *Impact of Sperm Donor Information on Parents and Children*, 4 Sexuality, Reprod. & Menopause 17, 17 (2006).

42 *See* A. J. Turner & A. Coyle, *What Does It Mean to Be a Donor Offspring? The Identity Experience of Adults Conceived by Donor Insemination and the Implication for Counseling*

and Therapy, 15 HUM. REPROD. 2041, 2050 (2000) (contrasting their study, which did find such psychological issues, with other studies that did not).

43 *See* Celia Hall, *Torment of Children with Donors for Fathers*, DAILY TELEGRAPH, Aug. 31, 2000, at 5 (Donor Conception Network provides support for parents and some children).

44 *See id.*

45 *See* JUDITH S. MODELL, KINSHIP WITH STRANGERS: ADOPTION AND INTERPRETATIONS OF KINSHIP IN AMERICAN CULTURE (1995).

46 *E.g.*, E.G. v. K.M., 37 Cal. 4th 130 (Cal. 2005); Serpico v. Urso, 469 N.E.2d 355 (Ill. App. Ct. 1984).

47 *See* Nancy Polikoff, *Breaking the Link between Biology and Parental Rights in Planned Lesbian Families: When Semen Donors Are Not Fathers*, 2 GEO. J. GENDER & L. 57, 63 n. 28 (2000). Most of these statutes address situations involving the obligation of married parents and unknown donors.

48 If, under the supervision of a licensed physician and with the consent of her husband, a wife is inseminated artificially with semen donated by a man not her husband, the husband is treated in law as if he were the natural father of a child thereby conceived. The husband's consent must be in writing and signed by him and his wife. The physician shall certify their signatures and the date of the insemination and file the husband's consent with the state department of health, where it shall be kept confidential and in a sealed file. However, the physician's failure to do so does not affect the father and child relationship. All papers and records pertaining to the insemination, whether part of the permanent record of a court or of a file held by the supervising physician or elsewhere, are subject to inspection only on an order of the court for good cause shown. Nat'l Conf. of Commissioners on Uniform State Laws, UPA § 5 (1973), http://www.law.upenn.edu/bll/ulc/fnact99/1990s/upa7390.htm.

49 OHIO REV. CODE ANN. § 3111.92 (2006).

50 KAN. STAT. ANN. § 23-130 (2006). The consent provided for in this act shall be executed and acknowledged by both the husband and wife and the person who is to perform the technique, and an original thereof may be filed under the same rules as adoption papers in the district court of the county in which such husband and wife reside. The written consent so filed shall not be open to the general public, and the information contained therein may be released only to the persons executing such consent, or to persons having a legitimate interest therein as evidenced by a specific court order.

51 NCCUSL, Uniform Parentage Act §§ 703-704 (2002), http://www.law.upenn.edu/bll/ulc/upa/final2002.htm.

52 The following facts are drawn from Alexandria S. v. Pacific Fertility Med. Ctr., Inc., 55 Cal App. 4th 110 (Cal Ct. App. 1997).

53 John Bowe, *Gay Donor or Gay Dad?* N.Y. TIMES, Nov. 19, 2006, at §6, 66.

54 L.A.L. v. D.A.L., 714 S.2d 595 (Fla. Dist. Ct. App. 2d 1998).

55 Michael E. Eisenberg, *What's Mine Is Mine and What's Yours Is Mine: Examining Inheritance Rights by Intestate Succession from Children Conceived through Assisted Reproduction under Florida Law*, 3 BARRY L. REV. 127, 134–5 (2002) (citing L.A.L. v. D.A.L., 714 S.2d at 597).

56 Steve Fry, *Court Weights Parental Rights*, TOPEKA CAPITAL-JOURNAL, Dec. 5, 2006, at 1A.

57 *In re* Sullivan, 157 S.W.3d 911, 913 (Tex. Ct. App. 2005).

58 Michael Serazio, *Seminal Case: How Donated Sperm Spawned a Child*, HOUSTON PRESS, March 10, 2005, http://www.houstonpress.com/2005-03-10/news/seminal-case/.

59 Helen M. Alvaré, *The Case for Regulating Collaborative Reproduction: A Children's Rights Perspective*, 40 Harv. J. Legis. 1, 15 (2003) (citing voluntary ASRM guidelines advising that "donors and recipients and their partners should execute documents that define or limit their rights and duties with regard to any offspring").

60 *Id.* at 27 (noting that Florida statute requires donors to relinquish all rights and obligations with respect to resulting children and citing that North Dakota, Oklahoma, Texas, and Virginia make the intended mother the legal mother, while relieving the egg donor of all rights and obligations); Laura M. Katers, *Arguing the "Obvious" in Wisconsin: Why State Regulation of Assisted Reproductive Technology Has Not Come to Pass, and How It Should*, 2000 Wis. L. Rev. 441, 448 (2000) (stating that the legal relationship of the egg donor to the child is uncertain in most states).

61 *See, e.g.*, Alvaré, *supra* note 59. *See also* Ami S. Jaeger, Assisted Reproductive Technologies Model Act (1999); Anne Reichman Schiff, *Solomonic Decisions in Egg Donation: Unscrambling the Conundrum of Legal Maternity*, 80 Iowa L. Rev. 265, 271 (1995).

62 *See* Colo. Rev. Stat. § 19-4-106(1), (2) (2006) (specifically legislating parentage with respect to egg donation); Fla. Stat. Ann. § 742.14 (2006) (amended Oct. 20, 2005, and providing that "the donor of any egg, sperm, preembryo, or embryo, other than the commissioning couple or a father who has executed a preplanned adoption agreement... shall relinquish all maternal or paternal rights and obligations with respect to the donation or the resulting children simultaneously upon the completion of the donation by operation of law. Only reasonable compensation directly related to the donation of eggs, sperm, preembryos, and embryos shall be permitted"); N.D. Cent. Code § 14-20-60 (2005) (stating that "a donor is not a parent of a child conceived by means of assisted reproduction," defined under § 14-20-02(4)(b), (c) as a method of causing pregnancy other than sexual intercourse and including the donation of eggs or embryos); Okla. Stat. Ann. tit. 10, § 555 (providing that "an oocyte donor shall have no right, obligation or interest with respect to a child born as a result of a heterologous oocyte donation from such donor. A child born as a result of a heterologous oocyte donation shall have no right, obligation or interest with respect to the person who donated the oocyte which resulted in the birth of the child"); Okla. Stat. Ann. tit. 10, § 556(B)(2) (2007) (further providing that "the husband and wife donating the human embryo shall be relieved of all parental responsibilities for any child or children resulting from the human embryo transfer"); Okla. Stat. tit. 10, § 556(B)(2) (2007) (further providing that "the husband and wife donating the human embryo shall be relieved of all parental responsibilities for any child or children resulting from the human embryo transfer"); Tex. Fam. Code Ann. § 160.702 (2007) (setting forth the parental status of a donor by governing that "a donor is not a parent of a child conceived by means of assisted reproduction"); Va. Code Ann. § 20-158 (2007) (providing that unless the donor is the husband of the gestational mother, "a donor is not the parent of a child conceived through assisted conception").

63 Fl. Stat. Ann. § 742.11 (2006)

64 *See* Fla. Stat. Ann. § 742.14 (2006).

65 N.D. Cent. Code § 14-20-02, 60 (2006); Tex. Fam. Code Ann. § 160.102(6), 160.702 (2007).

66 Okla. Stat. tit. 10, § 556(B)(2) (2007).

67 *Id.* at §§ 555, 556(B)(2), (C), (D).

68 *Id.* at § 556 (A)(1), (2). *See also* at § 556(A)(3) (requiring the original written consent of the husband and wife donating the human embryo to be filed with the court by the physician).

69 Va. Code. Ann. § 20-158 (2007).

70 Conn. Gen. Stat. §§ 45a-772-773 (2006).
71 J.F. v. D.B., 897 A.2d 1261 (Pa. Super. Ct. 2006).
72 *Id.*
73 John Horton, *Triplets' Custody Awarded to Father, Toddlers in Tug of War between Dad, Surrogate*, Cleveland Plain Dealer, April 22, 2006, at A1.
74 Rice v. Flynn, 2005 Ohio 4667, P37, 32 (Ohio Ct. App. 2005).
75 J.F. v. D.B., 848 N.E. 2d 873, 881 (Ohio App. 2006) (Slaby, Presiding Judge, concurring).
76 John Horton, *Surrogate Awarded Custody of Triplets, CSU Professor Who Fathered Babies Gets Visitation*, Cleveland Plain Dealer, Jan. 8, 2005, at A1; Barbara White, *Surrogate Mother Gets Custody of 3; Judge Criticizes Sperm Donor, Cuts Back His Visitation Rights*, Pittsburgh Post-Gazette, Jan. 8, 2005, at A1.

11 Why Do Parents Have Rights?: The Problem of Kinship in Liberal Thought

MAGGIE GALLAGHER

Let us begin with a thought experiment: a nineteen-year-old single, pregnant, black high school dropout walks into a government hospital in Harlem to deliver a baby. After the birth, a married, black, college-educated couple from Scarsdale shows up, offering to claim the baby and raise it as their own. To whom will the government hospital hand over the baby?

Under current law, the answer is, of course, clear: the unmarried teenage high school dropout who gave birth is the mother and gets to keep her baby. But *why*? After all, we live in an era in which the very idea of parental rights is viewed with increasing disfavor and in which mere biology is viewed with suspicion as a source of legal parenthood. The canon of family law declares that we no longer accept the discredited idea that biology gives parents rights over their children, which is described as viewing children as chattel. "The best interests of the child" are supposed to trump parental rights grounded in "mere biology."[1]

Certainly the answer cannot be in the best interests of this particular child. Everything we know from social science evidence – about the importance of class, resources, family structure, and the success of adoption – points in the opposite direction. If the child's best interests are the dominating criterion, this baby would be materially, emotionally, and educationally better off if raised by two affluent, educated, married parents in Westchester than by one poor, single mother in Harlem. Why should we privilege mere biology in this case?

Let me be clear: I offer this thought experiment as a comment on the limitations not of the laws that give the mother her baby, but of legal theories underlying parenthood and the family. In my view, for the government to take children away from legally competent mothers because they happen to be single, or poor, or live in Harlem, would be a human rights abomination.[2] But why?

Conceptually, how and why, under prevailing norms in liberal societies, are we to understand and take into account human biology, in which powerful obligations and externally imposed identities arise out of the acts of bodies, not minds, in accounts of parenthood increasingly theoretically grounded in choice, desire, acts of caretaking, or alternatively, in the best interests of the child?

For the purpose of this volume, the question is particularly acute. After all, before one can have a so-called baby market, one must have transferable interest (i.e., "property right"). The current debate in this volume is thus deeply tied to the problem of parenthood and is grounded in problems, puzzles, and contests within liberal (including classical liberal, i.e., conservative) thought over the family as a social and legal institution.

The family is a problem for liberal societies. (I use *liberal* in this chapter in the overarching sense that includes "classical liberal," i.e., conservative.) It is a problem practically, in the sense that it is our least successful institution. Our economic and political institutions command widespread respect and an equally widespread desire for emulation, at least in their fruits of a high degree of stability, affluence, political legitimacy, and personal choice. But many who yearn to emulate these aspects of liberal societies would like to do so without simultaneously adopting the associated late-twentieth and early-twenty-first-century family culture: our high rates of family fragmentation, fatherlessness, unmarried child bearing, and sustained below-replacement fertility.[3] Yes, families in liberal societies are celebrated and admired for taking on new burdens – meeting adults' desires for intimacy, fulfillment, gratification, and gender equality to a degree unprecedented in human history. At the same time, families in liberal societies are widely perceived as getting weaker and are objectively failing more often to do what was once perceived as their core function: getting men and women together to make and raise the next generation.[4]

Today in the United States, one-third of children are born outside of marriage, and close to half of all new marriages end in divorce.[5] Outside the United States, most developed nations are dealing with sustained below-replacement fertility, as well, leading to widespread new concern about the future of the welfare state in rapidly aging nations and, in some cases, the end of the society itself:

> A growing number of countries view their low birth rates with the resulting population decline and ageing to be a serious crisis, jeopardizing the basic foundations of the nation and threatening its survival. Economic growth and vitality, defense, and pensions and health care for the elderly, for example, are all areas of major concern.[6]

But more important (at least for the purposes of this chapter), the family is a problem for liberal societies, *in theory*. In part, this is an offshoot of the problems liberal theory has wrestling with group identity generally. As Frances Fukuyama writes in the current issue of the British magazine *Prospect* (adapted from an earlier essay in the *Journal of Democracy*), "modern identity politics springs from a hole in the political theory underlying liberal democracy. That hole is liberalism's silence about the place and significance of groups."[7]

In the case of family, this general problem in liberal theory is exacerbated by the unusually powerful role families play in the identity formation of individuals, with long-lasting effects typically inflicted on them when they are hapless and vulnerable children, before the age of reason and without their express consent. The classic moral narrative celebrated by and in liberalism is the liberation from just such externally imposed social identity. As Fukuyama puts it, "one's social status was now achieved rather than ascribed; it was the product of one's talents, work and effort rather than an accident of birth. One's life story was the search for fulfillment of an inner plan, rather than conformity to the expectations of one's parents, kin, village or priest."[8]

The family thus belongs with that category of things that the romance of liberalism, in some deep sense, seeks to escape, rebel, and overthrow. Although there are many elements of choice in family systems that make economic analysis appropriate, and many ways that our own family system has adapted to liberal political ideals in particular, there is a persistent tension between the self-chosen liberal individual and the family as a concept. For conceptually, what distinguishes family and kinship as a category from other kinds of human relations and endeavors is that it is the realm of unchosen relation, of socially supported identities that impose substantial obligations on individuals, whether they like it or not.

Although marriage and the family have always been expected to generate close feelings of love, they are not conceptually, as a category, founded on the presence or absence of these emotions. *Friendship* is the generic term for human relationships founded on affection and affinity – on the profound moral good of intimate choice. *Family* is the place where we find ourselves in a web of relationships we never fully choose and cannot (conceptually, at least) escape. My brother remains my brother, even if I hate his guts and swear never to see him again. I may hate my wife and love my mistress, but that does not make my mistress my wife. My child is my child, and regardless of how fulfilling or unfulfilling I find the relationship, I owe him powerful obligations that circumscribe my liberties and even my identity; in other words, I may choose to be a deadbeat dad, but I'm still a dad, whether I like it or not. We may choose who to marry; we do not wholly choose what marriage is (or else "marriage" as a category would dissolve into "any close personal relationship"). We may (or sometimes may not) choose to have children; we do not choose what "being a parent" means. As children, we do not get to choose our families at all.

Liberal theory has coped conceptually with the anomalous nature of the family in two ways. The first way is by conceptualizing children as part of the weak and vulnerable, who must be protected by government from oppression. Here, liberalism adopts its familiar role of using government power to rescue individuals from injustice of private action. In this mode, liberalism also generates a surprisingly traditional model of state-supported moral norms regarding parenthood; parents are tied to children by the state and regulated in the performance of their preconceived and state-prescribed duties, often reconceived as fostering the kind of citizen appropriate to the liberal state.[9]

This view, which is based in important human realities and serves important human goods, allows liberal theory to consent to externally imposed obligations, both cultural and legal, on parents; these tensions are softened, for liberal theory, by the technological, legal, and cultural developments of modern life (such as legal, safe abortion and better contraception) that allow us to understand parenthood as a choice made by adults. If you do not want the externally imposed legal or social parental obligations to meet children's needs, then do not choose to become a parent. However, the state is also, in this view, justified in imposing obligations on those who did not, in any meaningful sense, choose to become parents (e.g., the vast majority of unmarried fathers). Here, older, unreflective understandings of parenthood as rigidly grounded in mere biology are allowed to continue to give rise to state-enforced obligations, accompanied by considerable tolerance for old-fashioned social stigma when these obligations are not met (e.g., so-called deadbeat dads).[10]

The second way in which liberal theory copes with the family is to celebrate and widen the degree of adult choice in the formation of families, often now reconceptualized as an important personal right (e.g., "love makes a family").[11] Just as liberal societies resolve the tension between religious identity and liberalism by means of so-called religious liberty or adult choice in religion, many voices seek to reconcile liberalism and the family by expanding the range of adult choice in family life. Let Katherine Bartlett, a reporter for the prestigious American Law Institute's *Principles of the Law of Family Dissolution*, speak for many when she says her work is driven by "the value I place on family diversity and on the freedom of individuals to choose from a variety of family forms."[12]

There is an obvious, at least surface tension between these two modes of conceptualizing the place of families in liberal thought – between a state that seeks to impose moral obligations on parents and a state that seeks to expand individuals' right to form families as they choose – but more on that later.

Liberal theories of the family did not begin by embracing family diversity in the largest Bartlettian sense. The first step in the drama of the liberal theory's encounter with kinship is the liberation of the adult child – often presenting first as an adolescent, or embryo adult – from the expectations of his or her parents, with regard to all the sources of identity: economic activity, religion, marriage, and kinship. *Fiddler on the Roof* represents the immigrant drama in the quintessential American fashion: as a series of love stories, in which each daughter successively liberates herself from some aspect of convention in the choice of her marriage partner, with the third daughter ultimately choosing the right to disaffiliate (by marrying a non-Jewish spouse) from the kinship group itself. A contemporary example of the same general narrative is the movie *Bend It Like Beckham*, although here, the question is not free choice of a marriage partner, but rather, the freedom to choose playing soccer over marriage, symbolically expressed in the protagonist's success in winning her South Asian father's consent to leave her sister's wedding to play in a soccer game.

This genre has a predictable narrative structure, in which the tension is provided by the young people's determined efforts to overcome conventional obstacles that keep them apart – reflected and represented by the parents' objections; the parents' profound attachment to and love for the child, in turn, carries the parents across the cultural divide into acceptance of individualism, including in the realm of love and marriage. *Romeo and Juliet* gets replayed, but this time as a comedy, in which the young couple triumphs.

My father-in-law, who came as a professor from India to Long Island in the mid-1960s, put his finger on the essential story line when he asked me (after viewing *Bend It Like Beckham*, in fact), "Why is it that the parents are *never* right?" One would think that, odds are, human nature being what it is, occasionally, the young would come to be impressed by the wisdom of the older generation. But somehow, in the stories we tell each other in our culture, this never happens. The young people are never taught by their trials and tribulations the wisdom of listening to their parents in the matter of loving and choosing a spouse. Instead, youthful love reeducates the parents in recognizing and overcoming their inherited (and therefore not freely chosen) biases, in learning how to love their individual child enough to let go of their cultural norms.

For a while, the liberal narrative was content with celebrating free choice of a marital partner – a long-standing distinctive trait of American marriage systems. The sexual revolution of the 1960s expanded the story line to liberate individual choice from marriage itself – to celebrate the right of the individual to choose his own identity-conferring forms of sexual relationships; conventional structures like marriage were themselves obstacles to be overcome on the path to the individual's liberation from unchosen obligation and externally imposed norms.

Both the success of the sexual revolution and its inherent limitations (i.e., of trying to seek identity from meaningless sexual encounters, an especially difficult undertaking once the social and legal restrictions that allowed one to experience meaningless sex as a revolutionary, meaningful act have been largely overthrown) have led to new efforts to reconcile marriage with liberal theory and practice.[13] New social science evidence on marriage (and divorce) affirms the personal experience of many: that commitment is better for both children and adults than a series of disconnected emotional and sexual relationships.[14] And the push for gay equality in marriage has tended to subordinate the older liberal narrative of marriage as confining and oppressive (because it is a socially chosen form that comes with norms and expectations generated by society that are imposed as an ideal on individuals) to a new narrative of marriage as an individual right and personal choice, which the wider law and society is obliged to respect and support for all.

The push for gay equality has also turned renewed attention to the rights of adults to form not just adult relationships, but families of choice. Liberal theory's effort to reconceptualize the family has taken two seemingly contradictory forms: a renewed effort to liberate the child, as an individual, from the power and authority of parents, and a renewed emphasis on the right of adults to form families however they choose. Neither of these conceptual models leaves much room for the classic experience of kinship, which has, at its center, a man and a woman, who, by a sexual act, create a child to whom both are bound (along with their kin), whether or not they have consciously chosen to do so and be so. Moreover, the act of the mother and father, in creating the child, creates both a powerful social identity and concentric webs of obligations to caretaking. This is the complex human phenomenon that I have called *generativity*, in which bodies, not minds, create heavy obligations, and which, in turn, generates social respect (and resources) for those who meet them. As far as I can see, there is little place (theoretically, I mean) for this human phenomenon in liberal theories of either the Right or the Left.

Partly as a result of these tensions in liberal thought about the family, and partly as a result of dynamic social changes to which the law seeks to respond, there is one word to sum up the current state of the law of parenthood: confused. As David D. Meyer has written,

> On one front, the growing number of families raising children in informal or unconventional settings has put pressure on law to recognize parentage outside

> its traditional boundaries, on the basis of caregiving wholly apart from biology, marriage, and adoption. At the same time, the ready availability of DNA testing has spurred efforts to place new weight on biology, pushing parentage back toward a narrower and more traditional core. Courts and legislatures have responded to these developments often impulsively and in isolation, introducing a new and fundamental incoherence into the law's conception of parenthood.[15]

On one hand, biology as the sole independent source of parenthood (for men) has received an unprecedented degree of new institutionalization, as society attempts to cope with the fragmenting effects of the sexual revolution and the retreat from marriage: never before in our history have men had more publicly enforceable legal obligations to a child, simply because they once had the sex that biologically produced the child. Never have more public resources been devoted to actually enforcing the obligations of legal paternity. These governmental efforts have received unusually wide support, from traditionalists who believe in fatherhood (and fear unrestrained male sexual drives), from feminists who seek greater gender equity in parenting, from social liberals who seek to improve the well-being of poor mothers, and from economic conservatives who understand that what fathers do not pay, taxpayers will.

On the other hand, biological parenthood as an irrevocable obligation for single men who have sex with women has become entirely irrelevant in other social contexts: the common law principle that parents cannot negotiate away the child's right to the support and care of both his natural parents has been entirely abrogated in the case of reproductive technologies. What I cannot do, even by written contract with the advice of an attorney, in the case of a sexual relationship with a woman (create a child without legal responsibility), I can easily do with the consent of a medical clinic, for an infertile couple, a single mom, or a same-sex partnership.

The October 28, 2006, *New York Times* carried one example of a quartet carrying out the new logic of choice in parenthood:

> The Vandenbergs, who live in Mill Hill, a gentrifying neighborhood in downtown Trenton, have formed a family with another gay couple, John Hatch, 44, and David Henderson, 48, who live a block and a half away and have been together 18 years.[16]

In a twenty-page parental contract signed by all four of them, Mr. Hatch and Mr. Henderson each agreed to be the biological father of one of the Vandenbergs' children, to give up his parental rights so the biological mother's partner could adopt the child, and to share in parenting responsibilities.[17]

The point we are rapidly reaching in our conceptual models is not whether biology will be allowed to trump any other material or moral consideration in the care of children, but whether and how so-called natural parenthood will matter at all in our core legal understanding of parenthood – and if so, *why*?

Of course, we are a long way, in practice, from discounting kinship itself as a category, but we are increasingly challenged and taxed to explain why and how kinship matters. The challenge comes not from those who would say "the family is bad," but rather, from those who say the much more attractive thing: "love makes a family." For although kinship ordinarily generates the experience of love and is tightly bound to obligations to care, it is not, as a conceptual category, defined by the inner emotions of the people who inhabit it. Kinship as a category creates obligations (some of them enforceable by law) quite distinct from and apart from any emotional ties the parties may have to each other. It is "friendship" that, historically speaking, was the category used to define those intimate relationships created by and defined through the affection we have for one another.

We live in times in which social elites (those with power "to define reality"[18] in a society) find it increasingly puzzling to explain or value generativity: the ongoing reality that in the normal instance, children must be physically made, and the people who make them must have a profound sense of obligation and connection to their biological children. Although alternate social processes may substitute for generativity in the particular, no other system besides natural parenthood will generate the norms and social energy needed to actually reproduce a society.

A. GENDER ASYMMETRY AND GENDER JUSTICE

Moreover, there is a profound gender asymmetry at work in the process of generativity. The people who physically make children in the most intensive meaning of the word are called "women," and this process of physical labor is extremely costly for them (us). A culture that downgrades, suppresses, and demystifies biology will therefore necessarily decline to value a significant portion of the work, risk, and opportunity costs that women do in choosing to become mothers.

Even the idea of so-called biological relationship to children differs profoundly for men and for women. The processes by which parents become attached to their children are clearly different in nature and kind for men and for women. If we wish children to have actual substantive connections of care and support to the male humans who physically made them, *something* must be done to make this happen, and that something is necessarily profoundly different for men than for women. Reducing biological kinship to genetic relations disguises some very real gender asymmetries in the process through which men and women become parents.

For natural mothers, the biological and social processes are the most tightly and inextricably knit. Thanks to the development of reproductive technologies, we are now capable of disaggregating conceptually the phenomenon of motherhood into three categories – genetic motherhood, gestational motherhood, and social (and/or) legal motherhood – in a way that reveals the profound gender differences. Of these three modes of parent formation, the one that is unique to women is gestational – there is no cognate of this part of the process of parent formation in the male repertoire.

Conceptualizing biological parenthood as the "donation of genetic materials" is therefore a profoundly androcentric model. It does not become less so even when a court endorses a man's deliberate effort to "manufacture" a motherless child on gender-equality grounds, as Maryland's highest court recently did.[19]

But paradoxically, the new emphasis on the obligations of biological parents irrespective of marital status produces a profoundly female-centered perspective on parenting: natural parents are obligated to care for their child regardless of marital status. This is the normal experience of women, but it is far from widely reproduced in the experience of men. Attempts out of desire to protect children and to equalize the genders to disaggregate marriage from fatherhood have had some important interim successes as policy. But in the larger perspective, they have dramatically failed. Forty years of experience with unwed child bearing demonstrates conclusively that marriage makes a profound difference in male paternity behavior, even when marriage as a legal construct has been almost entirely severed from paternity as a legal construct.[20] For men, the primary biosocial mechanism for producing reliable fathers is called "marriage." Fifty years of social experimentation with alternative family forms have made it abundantly clear: outside of marriage, relatively few children enjoy the benefits of a reliable father.[21]

Because human reproduction is radically gendered, gender-neutral models of parenting formation (and therefore so-called parental rights) will produce radically asymmetrical outcomes for men and women, and for the children they make together.

B. THE FUTURE OF KINSHIP

Here is my main thesis: the family, as a conceptual and legal category, is in the process of undergoing *isomorphic institutional change*.[22] The term, borrowed from new institutionalist economics, refers to the way in which a dominant institution or institutions tend to remake the norms, values, and habits of thought of a dependent, less powerful institution in its own image. Massimo Sargiacomo, in an essay unrelated to the family, explains the basic processes of isomorphic institutional change:

> Based on the classification proposed by DiMaggio and Powell, institutional isomorphic processes are prompted through three different mechanisms: "coercive," "mimetic" and "normative." Coercive isomorphism usually "stems from political influence and the problem of legitimacy," and it generally comprises the different sources of pressures cascading down on organizations from international, national and regional legislation.... Sometimes uncertainty and ambiguity are also effective forces that push some organizations to imitate practices implemented by successful organizations. Generally speaking, the fewer the number of visible alternative organizational models in a field, the faster the rate of isomorphism in that field. This institutional isomorphism typology is called "mimetic" because when uncertainty reigns organizations are thus encouraged to "adopt forms that are considered legitimate by other organizations in their field, regardless of these structures' actual efficiency."
>
> The last unanimously recognized source of isomorphic institutional change is commonly called "normative" and it is usually triggered by "professionalization." ... This phenomenon results from the continuous effort of some professions to shape organizational action, crafting the educational curricula of potential entrants in the related occupational market. University and training centres, as well as professional associations, are very important vectors of normative isomorphism, thus acting as "change agents" or organizations.[23]

Another scholar defines normative isomorphism as emerging "from pressure to establish common professional norms and identities."[24] Professional discourse (like the one in which we are engaged) is thus a common source of isomorphic institutional change.[25]

The debate taking place here in the pages of *Baby Markets* is a microcosm of one taking place in the larger context, over how to understand the family in a liberal society. It is a classic example of the way that isomorphic institutional change works, with one complicating factor: liberal societies have two different dominant, successful institutions – government and the market – and remaking family according to the norms of either one tugs family law in two opposing directions, generating the poles of a great many interesting intellectual debates in these and other pages. One side argues for reconceiving babies (and parenthood) as markets and using the tools we have to remake these markets so that they function better. The other side looks to apply the classic concerns of liberal political values – such as protecting the weak and vulnerable from the limitations of markets or affirmatively promoting social equality – to this new world of reproductive technology. It is a fruitful, if familiar, tension.

On one hand, in this volume, we have a set of scholars inclined to deconstruct the family into the components most amenable to analysis as a market. To have a market, you need something akin to a property right, and for the market to thrive among strangers (especially strangers who do not engage in repeat business with one another), you need the right set of legal rules to facilitate transparency, enforce contracts, prevent fraud, and so on. Markets thus constructed are engines of abundance: they produce more of whatever good the market is constructed to seek, in this case, primarily babies for couples who cannot produce them themselves, and to a lesser extent, parents for babies who need them.

On the other hand, you have a set of scholars, often, although not exclusively, feminist, who see the family through the lens of the tool used to deconstruct and rebuild the power relationships within the state and government: equality. The goal here is to ensure that those in and those who run the baby market comply with basic norms derived from liberal theories of government theory: equality, protection of dependency, nondiscrimination, and so on. Once again, the point I am making is not that these scholars are doing something wrong, bad, or intellectually inappropriate. On any particular issue, I would often agree that the intrusion of these norms into the realm of the family is appropriate. Rather, the point I wish to make here is that it is, in some profound and primal sense, an intrusion – the importation of external norms that fail to provide tools to enable us to see or define what is distinctive, or conceptually unique, about families.

What is striking to this observer is the extent to which the family (or at least kinship) as a legal and social institution has few intellectual advocates seeking to protect it as its own conceptual category – as something that is different from either the political or the market sphere (or even the close personal relationship) and that therefore generates its own categories, norms, values, habits of thought, and tools of analysis.

Our inherited tradition of marriage and kinship rests on a vision that is primarily integrative and synthetic: it seeks to unite the disparate goods of sexual pleasure, erotic bonding, adult caretaking, physical procreativity, and parenting into an institution called "marriage." Marriage as a kin creator seeks to weave together moral relations and obligations out of the raw materials of human biology, to unite mothers and fathers, parents and children, love and sex, intimacy and economics; it confers social meaning on the accident of biology.

As Musonius Rufus, a Roman Stoic, put it,

> The husband and wife . . . should come together for the purpose of making a life in common and of procreating children, and furthermore of regarding all things in common between them, and nothing peculiar or private to one or the other, not even their own bodies. The birth of a human being which results from such a union is to be sure something marvelous, but it is not yet enough for the relation of husband and wife, inasmuch as quite apart from marriage it could result from any other sexual union, just as in the case of animals.[26]

Our emerging concepts of the family, by contrast, are fundamentally analytic: they seek to break apart the family and kinship into component parts (individual bilateral relationships, market transactions, legal obligations) that are more consistent with the main institutions of liberal societies – to expand the rights and capacity of individuals to pick, choose, and combine these building blocks (pleasure, Eros, commitment, caretaking, parenting) without undue interference from social preferences or norms, except those political norms (equality, protection of the weak, market transparency) congenial to one or the other of the more powerful liberal institutions. In this analytic acid bath, the baby of kinship threatens to dissolve into just one of many close personal relationships.

Whether liberal societies will find a conceptual grounding for taking seriously the biosocial experience of kinship in the world we are busily socially constructing remains an open question. How the biological phenomenon of erotic attraction, male–female bonding, and sexual reproduction should be socially acknowledged, if at all, is no longer clear. Whether a society without such a deep commitment to generativity as the core norm of parenthood can survive over the long run is also an open question.

Liberal societies, I should note, specialize in historically unprecedented triumphs. We shall see.

NOTES

1 "A third story in the family law canon is that common law property norms no longer shape the law of parenthood. The story contends that the law of parenthood is now structured around children's interests, having shed a common law tradition that used property norms to guide the law of parenthood and that granted parents (especially fathers) rights of custody and control over their children that were strong enough to be the functional equivalent of property rights. Much like the story of the end of coverture, this story is presented as a narrative of progress and equality. It asserts that a common law regime that failed to recognize children's legitimate interests has been supplanted by a legal order that prioritizes children's interests. . . . Family law casebooks similarly report that the law of parenthood has 'shift[ed]' from a regime that treated children as 'chattels' rather than 'persons'. . . . Scholars observe that the law of child custody has moved 'from father's property to children's rights.' They declare that child custody determinations are now based on 'the best-interests-of-the-child'. . . But the canonical

story of the demise of common law property norms . . . overstates the changes that have occurred in family law over time. . . . Parents retain substantial elements of many of their common law rights, even where those rights potentially conflict with their children's interests." Jill Elaine Hasday, *The Canon of Family Law*, 57 STAN. L. REV. 825, 848–9 (2004).

2 If forced to choose, I would willingly surrender the right to vote, or to speak freely if I had to, to retain the right to be with and care for my own children, and I suspect most readers and writers of this volume would agree.

3 For rates of family instability in European nations and the United States, *see, e.g.*, Gunnar Andersson, *Dissolution of Unions in Europe: A Comparative Overview*, MAX-PLANCK-INSTITUT FUR DEMOGRATISCHE FORSCHUNG, working paper (Feb. 2003), http://www.demogr.mpg.de. For an overview of fertility rates in developed nations, *see, e.g.*, Francesco Billari and Hans-Peter Kohler, *Patterns of Low and Lowest-Low Fertility in Europe*, 58 POPULATION STUD. 161–76 (2004).

4 *E.g.*, Justice Field, writing for the California Supreme Court, held that "the first purpose of matrimony, by the laws of nature and society, is procreation." Baker v. Baker, 13 Cal. 87, 103 (1859); *see also* Laudo v. Laudo, 197 N.Y.S. 396, 397 (App. Div. 1919) ("The great end of matrimony is . . . the procreation of a progeny having a legal title to maintenance by the father"); Poe v. Gerstein, 517 F.2d 787, 796 (5th Cir. 1975) ("Procreation of offspring could be considered one of the major purposes of marriage"); Singer v. Hara, 522 P.2d 1187, 1195 (Wash. App. 1974) ("Marriage exists as a protected legal institution primarily because of societal values associated with the propagation of the human race"); Baker v. Nelson, 191 N.W.2d 185, 186 (Minn. 1971), *appeal dismissed for want of a substantial federal question*, 409 U.S. 810 (1972) ("The institution of marriage as a union of man and woman, uniquely involving the procreation and rearing of children within a family, is as old as the book of Genesis"); Heup v. Heup, 172 N.W.2d 334, 336 (Wis. 1969) ("Having children is a primary purpose of marriage"); Zoglio v. Zoglio, 157 A.2d 627, 628 (D.C. App. 1960) ("One of the primary purposes of matrimony is procreation"); Frost v. Frost, 181 N.Y.S.2d 562, 563 (Supr. Ct. New York Co. 1958) (discussing "one of the primary purposes of marriage, to wit, the procreation of the human species"); Ramon v. Ramon, 34 N.Y.S. 2d 100, 108 (Fam. Ct. Div. Richmond Co. 1942) ("The procreation of off-spring under the natural law being the object of marriage, its permanency is the foundation of the social order"); Pretlow v. Pretlow, 14 S.E.2d 381, 385 (Va. 1941) ("The State is interested in maintaining the sanctity of marriage relations, and it is interested in the ordered preservation of the race. It has a double interest"); Stegienko v. Stegienko, 295 N.W. 252, 254 (Mich. 1940) (stating that "procreation of children is one of the important ends of matrimony"); Gard v. Gard, 169 N.W. 908, 912 (Mich. 1918) ("It has been said in many of the cases cited that one of the great purposes of marriage is procreation"); Lyon v. Barney, 132 Ill. App. 45, 50 (1907) ("The procreating of the human species is regarded, at least theoretically, as the primary purpose of marriage"); Grover v. Zook, 87 P.638, 639 (Wash. 1906) ("One of the most important functions of wedlock is the procreation of children"); Adams v. Howerton, 486 F. Supp. 1119, 1124 (C.D. Cal. 1980), *aff'd* 673 F.2d 1036 (9th Cir. 1982) (observing that a "state has a compelling interest in encouraging and fostering procreation of the race"); Dean v. District of Columbia, 653 A.2d 307, 337 (D.C. 1995) (Ferren, J., concurring and dissenting) (finding that this "central purpose . . . provides the kind of rational basis . . . permitting limitation of marriage to heterosexual couples"). A New Jersey court: "Lord Penzance has observed that the procreation of children is one of the ends of marriage. I do not hesitate to say that it is the most important object of

matrimony, for without it the human race itself would perish from the earth." Turney v. Avery, 113 A. 710, 710 (N.J. Ch. 1921) (citations omitted).

5 In 2005, 37% of births were outside of marriage. *See* B. Hamilton *et al.*, *Births: Preliminary Data for 2005*, NATIONAL CENTER FOR HEALTH STATISTICS (2006). M. D. Bramlett and W. D. Mosher, *First Marriage Dissolution, Divorce, and Remarriage: United States*, Advance data from VITAL AND HEALTH STATISTICS NO. 323 (2001).

6 Joseph Chamie, *Low Fertility: Can Governments Make a Difference?* (April 2, 2004), unpublished paper, presented at the Annual Meeting of the Population Association of America, http://paa2004.princeton.edu/download.asp?submissionId=42278.

7 Frances Fukuyama, *Identity and Migration*, 131 PROSPECT (2007), http://www.prospect-magazine.co.uk/printarticle.php?id=8239.

8 *Id.* (Note that I, and not Fukuyama, apply this analysis to the problem of families in liberal societies.)

9 *See, e.g.*, LINDA MCCLAIN, THE PLACE OF FAMILIES: FOSTERING CAPACITY, EQUALITY, AND RESPONSIBILITY (2006).

10 "For low-income men, biology (and economic support) has increasingly defined fatherhood under the law. For poor women, the legal definition of motherhood seems to be moving in the opposite direction." Jane C. Murphy, *Protecting Children by Preserving Parenthood*, 14 WM. & MARY BILL RTS. J. 969, 974 (2006).

11 *See* http://www.lmfamily.org/; *see also Beyond Same-Sex Marriage: A New Strategic Vision for All Our Families and Relationships*, a statement released by various scholars and activists in April 2006, http://www.beyondmarriage.org/.

12 Katherine T. Bartlett, *Saving the Family from the Reformers* (Brigitte M. Bodenheimer Memorial Lecture on the Family), 31 U.C. DAVIS L. REV. 817 (1998).

13 *See, e.g.*, DONALD S. BROWNING, MARRIAGE AND MODERNIZATION: HOW GLOBALIZATION THREATENS MARRIAGE AND WHAT TO DO ABOUT IT (2003); MILTON C. REGAN JR., FAMILY LAW AND THE PURSUIT OF INTIMACY (1993); Elizabeth S. Scott, *Marital Commitment and the Legal Regulation of Divorce*, *in* THE LAW AND ECONOMICS OF MARRIAGE AND DIVORCE (A. Dnes & R. Rowthorn eds., 2002); RECONCEIVING THE FAMILY: CRITICAL REFLECTIONS ON THE AMERICAN LAW INSTITUTE'S PRINCIPLES OF THE LAW OF FAMILY DISSOLUTION (Robin Fretwell Wilson ed., 2006); Anita Bernstein, *For and Against Marriage, a Revision*, 102 MICH. L. REV. 129 (2003); *The Marriage Movement: A Statement of Principles*, INSTITUTE FOR AMERICAN VALUES (2000).

14 *See, e.g.*, Norval Glenn & Thomas Sylvester, *The Shift: Scholarly Views of Family Structure Effects on Children*, 1977–2002 (2006), http://www.familyscholarslibrary.org/content/readingrooms/shift/; W. BRADFORD WILCOX ET AL., WHY MARRIAGE MATTERS: TWENTY-SIX CONCLUSIONS FROM THE SOCIAL SCIENCES (2005); LINDA J. WAITE & MAGGIE GALLAGHER. THE CASE FOR MARRIAGE: WHY MARRIED PEOPLE ARE HAPPIER, HEALTHIER, AND BETTER OFF FINANCIALLY (2000); SARA MCLANAHAN & GARY SANDEFUR, GROWING UP WITH A SINGLE PARENT: WHAT HURTS, WHAT HELPS (1994).

15 David D. Meyer, *Parenthood in a Time of Transition: Tensions between Legal, Biological, and Social Conceptions of Parenthood*, 54 AM. J. COMP. L. 125 (2006).

16 Tina Kelley, *For Gay Couples, Ruling Has Cash Value*, N. Y. TIMES, Oct. 28, 2006, at B1, http://www.nytimes.com/2006/10/28/nyregion/28gay.html?_r=1&oref=slogin.

17 *Id.*

18 James Davison Hunter, *To Change the World*, TRINITY FORUM BRIEFING 3(2), http://www.ttf.org/pdf/Bv3n2-Hunter-Text.pdf.

19 *In re* Roberto D.B., _A.2d_ (Md.), 2007 WL 1427451 (May 16, 2007) (http://www.courts.state.md.us/opinions/coa/2007/110a02.pdf). The dissent in this case noted the

implications for unmarried fathers of making "intent to conceive" the new legal standard. As reported by the Associated Press, "Judge Dale Cathell said the father had the twins 'manufactured' and then didn't want them to be listed as having a mother. 'The majority, in essence, holds that if you do not intend to be the mother, you should not be responsible as a mother,' Cathell wrote. 'There are probably tens, if not hundreds of thousands, of fathers (and certainly mothers as well) who did not intend to be parents at the time of the actions that led to conception, who have been judicially determined to be responsible for the support of the child they did not intend to conceive.'" *Ruling May Have Broad Implications for Prospective Gay Dads*, Associated Press, June 2, 2007, http://www.365gay.com/Newscon07/06/060207dads.htm.

20 A review of several national surveys found that by their mothers' estimates, roughly 40 percent of children with nonresident fathers saw their father once a month, whereas nearly the same number did not see their father at all in a given year. Wendy D. Manning & Pamela J. Smock, *New Families and Non-resident Father-Child Visitation*, 78 Social Forces 1 (1999). *See also* Valerie King, *Variations in the Consequences of Nonresident Father Involvement for Children's Well-Being*, 56 J. Marriage & Fam. 963 (1994) (finding that half of children with nonresident fathers see their fathers only once a year, if at all, whereas just 21% see their fathers on a weekly basis).

21 *Id.*

22 Thanks to Daniel Cere of McGill University for pointing out the relevance of this term to the ongoing family debates.

23 Massimo Sargiacomo, *Analysis of Institutional Pressures and Accounting Records of a 17th Century Italian Feudal Community: The Case of the Commune of Penne* (1626–1690), Proc. 11th World Cong. Accounting Historians (July 19–22, 2006), http://palissy.humana.univ-nantes.fr/msh/wcah/textes/sargiacomo.pdf.

24 Per Laegreid *et al.*, *Regulation inside Government: Modern Management Tools in Norwegian State Agencies*, paper presented at the conference A Performing Public Sector: The Second Transatlantic Dialogue (June 1–3, 2006), http://soc.kuleuven.be/io/performance/paper/WS2/WS2_Laegreid_Roness_Rubecksen.pdf.

25 A somewhat different language to describe a similar or related process is *colonization theory*, a term coined by Jurgen Habermas (and applied to the family by sociologist Alan Wolfe), as described by Donald S. Browning: "'Colonization theory,' as I briefly mentioned earlier, teaches that technical rationality enters into daily life from two perspectives – the efficiency goals of the marketplace and the control goals of government bureaucracy. Both disrupt the face-to-face interactions of the 'lifeworld' and the intimate spheres of marriage and family." Browning, *supra* note 13, at 19.

26 Rufus Musonius, Fragment 13A, *What Is the Chief End of Marriage? translated in* Musonius Rufus: The Roman Socrates 89 (Cora E. Lutz ed. & trans., 1947).

12 Free Markets, Free Choice?: A Market Approach to Reproductive Rights

DEBORA L. SPAR

Can markets protect reproductive rights? It sounds like a rhetorical question, or even a patently absurd one, because markets, we are tempted to respond, have nothing to do with reproductive freedom. Markets are about money and prices, about bringing buyers and sellers together in a neutral and impersonal environment. Markets do not care about reproductive rights, or indeed about any rights at all. How could they possibly be used to protect them?

Yet the apparent absurdity of this connection does not necessarily make it untrue. For although markets are clearly not designed to advance reproductive rights, they may still be able, under some circumstances, to provide this critical function. In fact, the very impersonality of markets and their sheer lack of normative content might actually make them uniquely capable of protecting reproductive freedoms.

The remainder of this chapter will explore this counterintuitive proposition, examining whether – and how, and why – markets could be harnessed to the service of this particular right.

A. OF RIGHTS AND MARKETS

The first point to consider is the normative void that lies at the center of commerce. Markets, as already noted, are not inherently defined by a commitment to any set of rights. They have no goals aside from their own function and no particular commitment to any of those who operate along their structure. Instead, markets are entirely impersonal and mechanical constructs, bringing together buyers and sellers, supply and demand, in a chain of interactions mediated by price. As Douglass North has so eloquently elaborated, markets exist at the behest of governments and on the back of appropriate institutions. When they work best, they encompass an intricate bundle of rules, norms, and traditions, all of which are directed at the dual pursuits of efficiency and profit maximization. There is no room in this complex for societal goals like justice or equity, and no reason to suspect that markets will naturally produce these auxiliary benefits.

Just because markets are not committed to rights, however, does not mean that they are inimical to them: it simply makes them neutral. Sometimes, to be sure, markets do produce social bads, outcomes deleterious to social welfare. If, for example, the global fashion industry were to develop a keen taste for baby seal fur, then the normal operation of the market would lead to an increase in the killing of baby seals. If the furniture industry likewise started to prize rare tropical hardwoods, then the market would drive the price of these woods up, increasing incentives for loggers to fell as many trees as they can. In the United States, meanwhile, one might similarly argue that the private provision of health care has pushed prices to unaffordable levels and undermined the right of poor people to enjoy good health. In all these cases, putting something into the market – be it seals, trees, or emergency rooms – arguably leads to a suboptimal, even harmful, outcome.

In other cases, however, the same kinds of markets, serving the same impartial dictates of supply and demand, can produce beneficial outcomes and social goods. Private farms and agribusinesses, for instance, provide nearly all the world's food supply; private corporations supply an increasing amount of the world's fresh water.[1] Private markets generate the energy that lights our schools, the computers that teach our children, and the books we treasure as knowledge. Hospitals around the world are frequently run by for-profit corporations, and most life-saving drugs have been developed by private pharmaceutical firms – massive, undeniably commercial entities that make money while saving lives.

In practice, therefore, it seems difficult to argue that markets themselves are inherently good or bad, or that the development of a market in any specific area would necessarily be either protective or destructive of rights. Instead, markets drive only toward those purposes for which they are so perfectly suited: matching supply and demand, allowing firms to produce products and maximize profits, and offering customers the opportunity to buy. Sometimes this matching and these purchases are socially beneficial; sometimes they are not. But it is difficult, or at least unfair, to blame the market in either case for its social effect.

B. MARKETS AND REPRODUCTION

Let us turn, then, to a second consideration, and to the particular characteristics that are likely to define the market for reproductive products or services. Is there anything about these markets that will tend to make them more or less protective of rights? Is there anything that might push them toward either creating or destroying social value? If markets in general are inherently neutral, capable of creating both social goods and social bads, then we need to examine the specific circumstances under which reproductive markets are likely to exist and the specific pressures that are most likely to operate on them.

Historically and theoretically, we have a rather good idea of what causes markets to fail. We know, for example, that markets are not very good at delivering public goods – things like the classic lighthouse, or clean air, the costs of which are borne by a small number of people but the benefits of which are inevitably and uncontrollably shared by many.[2] Markets are also not very good at producing goods drawn from common pool resources – Atlantic cod, for example, or Scottish salmon. The markets will work in these cases, but they will tend to overproduce the commodity at hand, destroying the underlying resource and creating a clear social bad.

Yet reproduction is neither a public good (at least, in the customary economic use of that term) nor a common pool resource. Instead, reproduction is an innately *private* good, one that draws from a theoretically unlimited resource pool: ourselves.

So, technically, at least, we should expect a market in reproductive services or products to work very well – matching supply and demand through the mechanism of price. Moreover, because competition in markets tends to increase supply over time and reduce price, we might also expect that an active and vibrant market for reproduction would allow individuals to have greater access, at lower prices, to whatever reproductive options are commercially available. This is a critical and often overlooked point. Because if we believe that one of the key aspects of reproductive freedom is access to reproductive choice, then markets – which tend naturally to produce both access and choice – are a natural ally of those who argue for reproductive rights.

Admittedly, a functioning market is not necessarily a good market in normative terms. We could, theoretically, imagine a vast reproductive enterprise composed of all sorts of nefarious and exploitative behavior – women being coerced to sell their wombs or eggs, for example, or desperate couples selling their infants or embryos for a supposedly fair price. Indeed, such stories already populate a whole subgenre of science fiction tales, including such classics as Margaret Atwood's *The Handmaid's Tale* and Aldous Huxley's *Brave New World*.[3] Economic theory, however, is more prosaic. It simply suggests that markets in the field of reproduction – markets for eggs, or sperm, or babies, or wombs, or embryos – are not particularly prone to either market failure or the destruction of limited resources. In commercial terms, these markets should work. Indeed, the basic economics here suggest that enabling and expanding markets for reproduction will simultaneously expand reproductive options and, in the process, the reproductive rights of those with access to those options. What kind of normative outcomes are produced as a result, however, is a more complicated question, and one that leads us directly to a third strand of inquiry.

C. REPRODUCTIVE SALES: A BRIEF HISTORY

In 2009, at a time when the reproductive market seems to be leaping into headlines around the world, it is tempting to believe that this market is brand new, a freshly born product of massive technological change. And to some extent, this is true. Thanks to technologies such as preimplantation diagnosis (PGD) and intracytoplasmic sperm injection, would-be parents have far more options available to them today than they did even twenty years ago. Thanks to the Internet and other modern media, they also have a rapidly advancing stream of information about these new options. This combination of options and information makes it feel as if the market for reproduction – what I have elsewhere called the *baby business* – is a creation of the twenty-first century.[4] Yet the history here actually runs much deeper. In fact, there have been several earlier iterations of the market, instances in which buyers and sellers came together to exchange reproductive goods. How these markets evolved, and how they interacted with reproductive freedoms, provides an interesting insight into the connections between markets and rights in the reproductive sphere.

1. The Market for Contraception

Consider, for example, the case of contraception. Prior to 1873, when it became illegal, contraception was a flourishing industry in the United States.[5] In that year, however, moral crusader Anthony Comstock convinced Congress to pass the Act of the Suppression of Trade in, and Circulation of, Obscene Literature and Articles of Immoral Use.[6] Under the bill's provisions, contraceptives were grouped with other so-called obscene items and were banned as such.[7] Interstate transport of contraceptives was outlawed, as was the use of the postal system for sending contraceptives and related information.[8] The bill also forbade the importation of contraceptives[9] and stated that

> whoever . . . shall sell, or lend, or give away, or in any manner exhibit, or shall offer to sell, or to lend, to give away, or in any manner to exhibit, or shall otherwise publish or offer to publish in any manner, or shall have in his possession, for any such purpose or purposes, any obscene book, pamphlet, paper, writing, advertisement, circular, print, picture, drawing or other representation, figure, or image on or of paper or other material, or any cast, instrument or other article of immoral nature, or any drug or medicine, or any article whatever, for the prevention of conception, or for causing unlawful abortion, or shall advertize the same for sale, or shall write or print or cause to be written or printed, any card, circular, book, pamphlet, advertisement, or notice of any kind, stating when, where, how, or of whom, or by what means, any of the articles in this section hereinbefore mention, can be purchased or obtained, or shall manufacture, draw, or print, or in any wise make any such articles, shall be deemed guilty of a misdemeanor.[10]

The sentence for such crimes was a minimum of hard labor for six months, with a maximum of five years for each offense and a fine of between one hundred and two thousand dollars.[11]

In the wake of what become known as the Comstock law, most U.S. states followed suit with their own mini or little Comstock laws.[12] Twenty-two states, for example, passed local obscenity laws that theoretically made birth control illegal, although the precise determination of illegality was left to the courts.[13] Twenty-four states explicitly passed laws forbidding contraception, including advertising or information related to birth control.[14] Connecticut went the furthest of them all and outlawed the actual use of contraception.[15]

Even as these laws were being imposed and extended, however, contraceptive sales remained strong, driven by the strength of demand from men and women determined not to conceive. Mainstream producers of rubber continued to sell condoms under vague names such as "sheaths, male shields, capotes . . . or rubber goods . . . for gents," while smaller entrepreneurs (known less generously as smut peddlers) offered a wide range of so-called feminine hygiene products, composed primarily of douches and crude spermicides.[16] By 1938, these products with "virtually no names" included more than four hundred options and generated annual revenues of roughly 250 million dollars.[17] Yet technically, advertising these products and selling them across state lines was still illegal.

Writing at the time, many observers noted that the thriving underground industry for birth control had effectively rendered the laws meaningless. "If the purpose of the statutes be to minimize the use of contraceptives," reported a 1939 article in the *University of Chicago Law Review*, "the rapid growth of the industry, particularly in recent years, shows clearly that such a purpose is not being achieved."[18] Others noted that the legal prohibitions had actually encouraged the development of a wholly unregulated market: "The notorious unenforceability of such statutes is evidenced by the flourishing bootleg industry which prospers in spite of them. These laws, by driving the industry underground, have impaired effective government regulation and thus indirectly promote the sale of worthless products at exorbitant prices."[19] There was also dismay that the laws prevented doctors from doing what the bootleggers were: "Year after year this vicious law legally tied the hands of reputable physicians while quacks and purveyors of bootleg contraceptives and 'feminine hygiene' articles and formulas flourished."[20]

Meanwhile, of course, activists such as Mary Dennett Ware and Margaret Sanger were also attacking the prohibitions on more philosophical grounds. Ware, a middle-aged activist and grandmother, tried to get the Comstock laws revoked by striking "for the prevention of conception" from Section 1142 of the New York Penal Law, which made it a misdemeanor for "a person to sell, or give away, or to advertise or offer for sale, any instrument or article, drug or medicine, *for the prevention of conception.*"[21] She failed and was instead convicted, in 1929, of sending obscene material through the mail.[22] In 1918, Sanger similarly went before the New York Court of Appeals, arguing for a doctors-only bill that would have exempted physicians from the Comstock laws.[23]

Eventually, the activists' reasoning gained ground. In a landmark 1930 decision regarding condoms, the Court interpreted the Comstock laws to apply to intent, rather than products, ruling that "there is no federal statute forbidding the manufacture or sale of contraceptives. The articles which the plaintiff sells may be used for either legal or illegal purposes."[24] Three years later, in *Davis v. United States*, the Sixth Circuit Court of Appeals likewise determined (again in a case concerning condom sales) that the sale or advertisement of contraceptive materials was not necessarily illegal – instead, illegality required proof that the contraceptives were to be used for contraception, rather than to combat disease.[25] Finally, in 1936, the Court issued its most liberal ruling on contraception, determining in *United States v. One Package* that physicians could legally both import and prescribe birth control.[26]

Clearly, this belated triumph for contraception was due in part to the efforts of activists like Ware and Sanger and to the noble arguments they had raised on behalf of reproductive freedom and access to birth control. The changing legal status of contraception reflected a growing acceptance of women's rights and of all people's rights to reproductive choice and privacy. Yet it is also critical to realize that much of the legal victory in this ostensibly intimate realm was actually achieved by private firms arguing on commercial grounds. The 1930 decision, for example, was technically a trademark case, brought by one condom manufacturer suing another for trademark infringement. And the Court's reasoning – which had the inevitable effect of widening access to contraception – was nevertheless entirely commercial, focusing, as noted earlier, on "the article which the plaintiff *sells*."[27] *Davis v. United States* was also a commercial suit, brought by a wholesale company that sold rubber goods to druggists. Again, the Court's ruling had the effect of widening access to birth control but an intent based on markets – here, of confirming that the sale or advertisement of contraceptive materials was not necessarily illegal.[28] Finally, the *One Package* case, arguably the most important in terms of limiting the impact of the federal Comstock laws, was again a commercial case, this time involving a gynecologist who had ordered the "one package" of pessaries (diaphragms) from Japan. This time, the Court did make reference to what might be considered a social goal, arguing that federal law "embraced only such articles as Congress would have denounced as immoral if it had understood all the conditions under which they were to be used."[29] Yet the ruling was still undeniably economic in origin, responding to the doctor's commercial right to import and sell diaphragms. Significantly, after *United States v. One Package*, doctor-prescribed contraception was essentially legal everywhere in the United States, except Massachusetts and Connecticut.[30] A year after *One Package*, the American Medical Association "formally recognized birth control as an integral aspect of medical practice."[31]

2. The Market for the Pill

The development of the birth control pill, today one of the most important elements of female reproductive control, was likewise driven largely by private firms and market motives. Although activists and concerns for reproductive rights played a key part in its development, it was ultimately the market – buyers and sellers, supply and demand – that made the pill possible.

Preliminary work on what would become the pill began as early as 1937, when scientists began to demonstrate the potential for progesterone to prevent ovulation.[32] Due to the uncertainty surrounding the Comstock laws, however, the science of contraception was left entirely in the laboratories, with no one attempting to push it toward women or into the market.[33] After two pharmaceutical firms, Syntex and Searle, independently synthesized progesterone in the early 1950s, however, one lone researcher named Gregory Pincus started to use progesterone to experiment with contraception.[34] During this time, his research was funded entirely by the private fortune of Katherine Dexter McCormick, a widow who was determined to provide women with some means of contraception that they alone could control. As his research progressed, Pincus joined forces with John Rock, a path-breaking Boston physician, who, in 1944, had quietly carried out the first critical steps in what would later become in vitro fertilization (IVF). In 1954, Rock and Pincus began experimenting with progesterone, technically exploring its efficacy in treating infertility, but really monitoring its ability to prevent conception by stopping ovulation.[35]

When Rock and Pincus arrived at a formula that worked, they tested their new birth control pill in Puerto Rico, where a largely Roman Catholic population had never found the need for explicit laws condemning contraception.[36] After successful clinical trials there and in Haiti, the scientists published their results in

Science, stating unequivocally that progesterone could be used for contraception.[37] Searle, which manufactured the progesterone that Rock and Pincus had used, struggled briefly to decide whether to use its sell progesterone for contraception.[38] But its struggles were short-lived.[39] In 1957, the Food and Drug Administration (FDA) approved Enovid, Searle's first commercial birth control pill, as a treatment for "gynecological disorders." In 1959, Searle returned to the FDA to market Enovid explicitly as a contraceptive, and in 1960, it received the formal approval. By this point, however, an estimated five hundred thousand women were already using the pill for contraception, taking their cue from information attached to the 1957 drug release, which warned about "possible contraceptive activity."[40]

By 1961, an estimated one million women were using the birth control pill, at a price that had recently fallen from ten to seven dollars per month.[41] By 1963, prices had plummeted to $2.90 a month, and a reported 1.75 million American women were using the pill, producing annual revenues for Searle of roughly sixty-one million dollars.[42] By 1973, just ten years later, the number of users had soared to ten million, and the market – including both the firms that were profiting handsomely from the pill and the consumers who were avidly purchasing it – had triumphed over any remnants of legal and moral opposition.[43]

3. The Market for In Vitro Fertilization

A similar and even more pronounced commercial dynamic surrounded the development of in vitro fertilization, the essential precursor to today's growing range of reproductive options.

In 1974, four years before the birth of Louise Brown, the world's first so-called test-tube baby, the U.S. Congress placed a temporary moratorium on the use of federal funds for fetal research.[44] Although no baby had yet been born from IVF, Congress was apparently concerned about what might happen to aborted fetuses in the wake of the Supreme Court's recent legalization of abortion and thus specifically forbade the federal government from funding any kind of fetal research.[45] Because federal regulations defined the fetus to mean "the product of conception from implantation until delivery," the funding ban technically extended to research on IVF, as well.

In theory, this funding ban could have meant the end of IVF in the United States. Yet, as was the case with contraception, legal restrictions in this area did not, in the end, hamper the development of either IVF technologies or an IVF industry. On the contrary, after the birth of Louise Brown in England, the American IVF industry surged forward, fueled by demand from couples desperate to conceive genetically related children and facilitated by private doctors who were willing to supply them.[46]

In 1980, Drs. Howard and Georgeanna Jones set up the first private IVF clinic in the United States, the Norfolk, Virginia-based Jones Institute for Reproductive Medicine. In December 1981, they helped to produce Elizabeth Jordan Carr, the country's first successful test-tube baby.[47] By this time, four other U.S. fertility clinics had also begun to offer IVF services.[48] Their prices were not cheap: at the Jones Institute, for example, preliminary screening for IVF treatment cost $1,650 in 1983, and the total cost of an IVF procedure, including nonmedical expenses, was around $7,500.[49] Because success rates were quite low, the overall cost for a couple to have a 50 percent chance of delivering a baby via IVF was probably in the range of thirty-eight thousand dollars.[50]

High prices, however, exerted little downward pressure on demand. Indeed, by 1986, test-tube pregnancies had become nearly routine, and more than two thousand children had been born through this recently vilified method. In 1986, there were more than one hundred clinics in the United States, performing ten thousand cycles of IVF and related technologies each year and generating annual revenues of about forty-one million dollars.[51] Sperm donation and embryo donation had become somewhat routine, and even more intricate technologies like surrogacy were starting to emerge.[52] All of this work, meanwhile, was still occurring in the private sector and with wholly private funds.

Today, IVF and related technologies are estimated to generate revenues in the United States exceeding three billion dollars a year.[53] In 2003, the most recent year for which data are available, there were 437 clinics in the United States, which reported carrying out 112,872 cycles and producing, as a result, 48,756 babies.[54]

These three examples are not, of course, determinative, but they do suggest that when markets have encountered reproduction in the United States, their operation has tended to expand reproductive options and enable wider access to them. Commercial markets do not have this effect because they care in a normative sense about either reproduction or reproductive rights. Instead, they simply follow the course of commercial activity, bringing a supply (in this case, of contraceptive devices, birth control pills, and babies) to those who deeply desire them.

D. THE PROBLEM WITH PRODUCERS

In the reproductive market, therefore, it seems relatively safe to conclude that commercial growth and expanded supply have historically brought tangible benefits to the ultimate so-called consumer – to couples hoping not to conceive, individuals trying to avoid sexually transmitted diseases, and would-be parents attempting to conceive a child. As the technologies of assisted reproduction advance, it is also becoming increasingly possible for some parents to use the market to produce a particular kind of child, arguably exercising a parental right (or at least an option) to have a child born without Tay-Sachs or cystic fibrosis, for example, or a child whose cord blood can be used to save a dying sibling.[55] In this context, one could easily argue that the market does indeed protect and expand a parent's reproductive rights.

At the same time, however, the exercise or enjoyment of these rights often drags other individuals into the equation – individuals whose rights are both murkier and more vulnerable to exploitation. Consider, for example, the case of PGD. PGD is the pathbreaking technology that allows parents to select an embryo with particular genetic characteristics: one without the Tay-Sachs gene, for example, or with the blood type to match an older, dying child. In this procedure, parents first create several embryos using IVF. Then, when the embryos are at the eight-cell stage (so early, in fact, that they are traditionally not yet even considered embryos), technicians remove a single cell from each embryo and subject it to screens that reveal the genetic makeup of the child that embryo would become. With this intervention, parents who know they are at risk of passing a genetic mutation on to their offspring can instead produce a healthy child, and parents who already have a sick child can – occasionally – conceive a healthy, perfectly matched sibling to serve as a desperately needed donor. In these cases, and they are growing, parents understandably regard PGD as a godsend – a medical miracle that literally saves their children's lives.

Yet even if the so-called consumers in this case are wholly enthusiastic supporters of the market for PGD, and even if they feel that their rights have been dramatically expanded by its use, the technology does nevertheless raise questions about the rights of others. For instance, has the child born from PGD had her human rights compromised in some way as a result of her parents' choice? Will she suffer from having not been born from the same blind conception that defines most humans? And what about other children, whose parents choose not to choose? Are their rights being imposed on? What about the disabled, whose rights could be undermined by others choosing against their inherited traits? These are tough questions, and troubling ones.

Even more troubling is the realization that new types of producers are also being created in the market for reproduction. They are, of course, the component suppliers: the men who donate sperm, the women who donate eggs and lend wombs. Are their rights being compromised by the reproductive market?

For all these questions, it is easy to answer yes: yes, human rights are compromised when some humans can choose their children's traits; yes, we hurt disabled individuals by letting other individuals choose against disability; and yes, most strongly, we exploit men and (particularly) women when we allow them to sell their genetic material.[56]

It is not entirely clear, however, that yes is always the appropriate answer. How do we know, other than by assertion, that children will feel wronged by having been chosen? We cannot. We could wait until these children grow up, perhaps, and systematically poll their feelings and preferences; we could wait and see if they, as a group, demonstrate beliefs or behaviors that distinguish them from their peers. But without such analysis, it seems foolhardy to assert any wrong on their behalf. After all, a child consciously conceived to be free of Tay-Sachs or cystic fibrosis or sickle-cell anemia is not inherently shorn of any rights we typically assign to individuals. Likewise, it is not obvious that a living deaf person is inevitably deprived of his rights if an unrelated couple decides not to give birth to a deaf child. True, if this couple's individual decision were multiplied thousands of times, creating a society where deafness was either exceedingly rare or concentrated among certain groups, then we would need, as a society, to ensure that the remaining deaf individuals were not deprived of their rights or existing benefits. But again, it is not inevitable that individual choices (even thousands or millions of them) would suffice to eliminate the random mutations that cause deafness or other disabilities, or that a reduced level of these disabilities would cause able-bodied people to behave any differently.

We are left, therefore, with the most vexing question to emerge from the reproductive market – the question of whether the sale of reproductive components (eggs, sperm, wombs, and embryos) constitutes exploitation, or at least commodification, of the sellers. Most observers of this field have argued that it does: that selling body parts, and particularly eggs and wombs, places the sellers (young women) in a relationship that is inevitably exploitative; that, as Margaret Jane Radin has famously argued, "conceiving of any child in market rhetoric wrongs personhood."[57] Yet it is not clear why this relationship necessarily holds, nor why elements of commodification – paying a price for things of value – are inherently wrong. Does paying for eggs demean the egg donors or the children born as a result? Maybe, in some cases. Do surrogate mothers or sperm donors lose dignity in some way that even they cannot identify? We simply do not know. Yes, a handful of surrogate mothers have subsequently regretted their experience and rallied against the practice. A tiny number of sperm donors have sought to discover the children they sired. But in the vast majority of cases, surrogates and egg and sperm donors seem either pleased with their contribution or emotionally unaffected.[58] By what right can we claim degradation on their behalf?

Moreover, because discussions of commodification are inherently subjective and ill defined (just what is a commodity, after all, and how can we tell when it is bad?), the debate over reproductive components might more usefully be framed in terms of more objective and practical considerations. We could begin, for example, with a basic evaluation of safety, examining whether any given procedure is safe for the donor, the prospective parents, and the imagined child. If the procedure is not safe for the donor, or if it exposes her to any long-term risk, then donation, whether paid or not, clearly compromises the donor's human rights. This seems a simpler calculation than commodification, and also a more immediately important one.

Next, we should ask whether the donor is being coerced in any way: by money or praise; doctors or relatives; glossy pamphlets or a lack of information. If the donor is being coerced, then the transaction is unfair and would arguably constitute a violation of the donor's rights. But if it is not, and if the donor is willingly and knowingly entering into a contractual relationship, then it is not clear that this contract necessarily constitutes exploitation.

And finally, we need to think about the relationship between the donor and the child. Too often, reproductive markets and the debates around them concentrate only on the relationship between donor and prospective parent, or between the would-be parents and the still unconceived child. We need to broaden this discussion to consider the born child, and particularly the child who becomes an adult. What rights does he or she have in this process, and what relationship will he or she want to maintain with the donors who provided raw material for his or her birth? Recent revelations by the grown children of sperm donors suggest that they want far more than their parents – contractual, social, and genetic – ever imagined.[59] Any discussion of rights, therefore, must include theirs as well.

E. THE ROLE OF THE STATE

Occasionally, economists and others make the unfortunate mistake of assuming that markets exist in a vacuum and that the only role of governments is to collect taxes and get in the way of business.

Clearly, however, that assumption is totally misplaced and wrong in ways that are directly relevant to the topic at hand because, of course, no one is arguing – or for sure, this chapter is not arguing – that the reproductive market should exist without regulation. On the contrary, all markets, even ostensibly free and competitive markets, are regulated to some extent by government, and it seems obvious, given the sensitivities and social implications involved, that the reproductive market is particularly in need of firm, if flexible, rules.

If, for instance, a given society thinks that gender selection is bad, then they can simply ban that piece of the reproductive market or subject it to some kind of queuing system. If people think that certain reproductive options – mitochondrial transfer, for example, or reproductive cloning – are too dangerous, they can prohibit them. Conversely, if people believe that other techniques – like IVF – are socially or individually beneficial, they can choose to subsidize them, as is already the case in countries such as Denmark and Israel.

Which brings us around to where we began, with a plea for the impartiality of markets. On their own and in the aggregate, markets remain wholly aloof from both rights and reproduction. They do not exist to protect rights and have no natural mechanism by which to consider them. Yet both theory and history appear to suggest that markets can indeed advance reproductive rights, largely by expanding the range of reproductive options available to individuals and by granting them access to these options through the mechanical operation of supply and demand.

But markets do not operate in a vacuum, and they can never be the only source of protection for rights because any movement that they make in this direction happens only as an accident of their normal, profit-maximizing behavior. In the end, therefore, the only market that can fully protect reproductive rights is one that combines commercial forces with the tempering hand of government regulation.

NOTES

1 Maude Barlow, Blue Gold: The Fight to Stop the Corporate Theft of the World's Water (2002).

2 *See* R. H. Coase, *The Lighthouse in Economics*, 17 J. L. & Econ. 2, 357–76 (1974).

3 Margaret Eleanor Atwood, The Handmaid's Tale (2006); Aldous Huxley, Brave New World (1998).

4 *See* Debora L. Spar, The Baby Business: How Money, Science, and Politics Drive the Commerce of Conception (2006).

5 Estimated at thirty thousand dollars in 1892. Andrea Tone, *Making Room for Rubber: Gender Technology and Birth Control before the Pill*, 18 Hist. & Tech. 1, 51, 60 (2002).

6 Act of March 3, 1873, ch. 258, 17 Stat 598.

7 *Judicial Regulation of Birth Control under Obscenity Laws*, 50 Yale L.J. 4, 682 (1941). In fact, one source specifically points out that "the anti-contraceptive laws were not originally passed as a result of controversy over religious doctrine; they were passed as a by-product of an attempt to give legal support to a widespread attitude about obscenity." Carol Flora Brooks, *The Early History of the Anti-contraceptive Laws in Massachusetts and Connecticut*, 18 Am. Q. 1, 3 (1966).

8 J. E. Leonarz, *Validity of Regulations as to Contraceptives or the Dissemination of Birth Control Information*, 96 A.L.R.2d 955 (2001). *See also* 18 U.S.C.S. § 1461 (mailing); 18 U.S.C.S. § 1462. (importation); *previously* 18 U.S.C. §334 (mail) and 18 U.S.C. §336 (interstate commerce). Also, the Tarriff Code of 1930 Section 305(a) of the Tariff Act of 1930 (19 U.S.C.A. § 1305[a]) provided that "all persons are prohibited from importing into the United States from any foreign country any article whatever for the prevention of conception or for causing unlawful abortion." Apparently, this was one of the first examples of how the Congress could use its interstate commerce and postal powers to regulate matters typically left to the states. *See, e.g.*, Harriet F. Pilpel & Theodora S. Zavin, *Birth Control*, 14 Marriage & Fam. Living 2, 118 (1952).

9 *Supra* note 6.

10 *Id.*

11 *Id.*

12 Leonarz, *supra* note 8.

13 *Some Legislative Aspects of the Birth-Control Problem*, 45 Harv. L. Rev. 4, 726 (1932); Mary Ware Dennett, Birth Control Laws (1926), at 7, 10.

14 *26 States According to Some Legislative Aspects of the Birth-Control Problem*, 45 Harv. L. Rev. 4, 723 (1932)

15 Dennett, *supra* note 13, at 10.

16 Andrea Tone, *Black Market Birth Control: Contraceptive Entrepreneurship and Criminality in the Gilded Age*, 87 J. Am. Hist. 2, 445–7 (2000).

17 *The Accident of Birth*, 17 Fortune (1938), at 83–5.

18 *Contraceptives and the Law*, 6 U. Chi. L. Rev. 2, 265 (1939).

19 *Judicial Regulation of Birth Control under Obscenity Laws*, 50 Yale L.J. 4, 686–7 (1941).

20 *The Status of Birth Control: 1938*, New Republic, April 20, 1938, at 324.

21 Carole R. McCann, Birth Control Politics in the United States: 1916–1945 68–9 (1994). *See generally* John M. Craig, *"The Sex Side of Life": The Obscenity Case of Mary Ware Dennett*, 15 Frontiers 145 (1995).

22 The conviction was subsequently reversed on appeal. Craig, *supra* note 21; United States v. Dennett, 39 F.2d 564, 569 (2d. Cir. 1930).

23 McCann, *supra* note 21.

24 Young's Rubber Co. v. C.I. Lee and Co., 45 F.2d 103, 107 (2d. Cir. 1930).

25 *Id.* at 475.

26 United States v. One Package, 86 F.2d 737 (2d Cir. 1936). Section 334 referred to the mailing provision and made it "unlawful for anyone to deposit or cause to be deposited 'non-mailable matter,' and defines that phrase to include any printed circular giving information where and how things designed, adapted and intended for indecent or immoral use, or for preventing conception can be obtained." Section 396 was the similar provision for interstate commerce, making it "unlawful for any one to knowingly deposit, or cause to be deposited, with any express company or other common carrier for carriage in interstate commerce, any 'article, or thing designed, adapted, or intended for preventing conception.'"

27 *Supra* note 24, at 107 (italics added).

28 *Id.* at 475.

29 *Id.* at 739.

30 David Loth, *Planned Parenthood*, 272 Ann. Am. Acad. Pol. & Soc. Sci. 95 (1950).

31 Although a 1936 study by the Journal of the American Medical Association showed that the laws had no effect on physicians. *Report of the Committee to Study Contraceptive Practices and Related Problems Appointed by the Board of Trustees of the American Medical Association*, XX JAMA 1911 (1936)(citation omitted).

32 Loretta McLaughlin, The Pill, John Rock, and the Church 100–1 (1982); Barbara Seaman, *The Pill and I: 40 Years On, the Relationship Remains Wary*, N.Y. Times, June 25, 2000, at 19.
33 McLaughlin, *supra* note 32; *see* Martha Campbell & Malcolm Potts, *History of Contraception*, 6 Gynecology & Obstetrics 1, 17 (2002).
34 McLaughlin, *supra* note 32, at 115.
35 *Id.*
36 *Id.* at 128; Linda Grant, *A Laboratory of Women*, Independent, Sept. 19, 1993, at 14.
37 C. R. Garcia, J. Rock, & G. Pincus, *Effects of Certain 19-Nor Steroids on the Normal Human Menstrual Cycle*, 124 Science 891, 892 (1956).
38 McLaughlin, *supra* note 32, at 135–7.
39 *Id.*
40 Bernard Asbell, The Pill: A Biography of a Drug That Changed the World 163–4, 170 (1995); Irwin C. Winter, *Industrial Pressure and the Population Problem – The FDA and the Pill*, 212 JAMA 1067–8 (1970).
41 *G.D. Searle Reduces Price of Birth Control Pill to $7 a Month*, Wall Street Journal, Feb. 9, 1961, at 8.
42 *Birth Control Push*, Wall St. J., Nov. 1, 1963, at 1.
43 Sharon Snider, *The Pill: 30 Years of Safety Concerns*, FDA Consumer, Dec. 1990, http://www.fda.gov/bbs/topics/CONSUMER/CON00027.html.
44 National Research Act, Pub. L. No. 93-348, § 213, 88 Stat. 342 (1974).
45 Exceptions were made for research designed to protect the fetus itself. *See* National Research Act, Pub. L. No. 93-348, § 213, 88 Stat. 342 (1974).
46 As one source explains, "The diffusion is likely to continue during the next 5 years, as judged by the demand of sterile couples and the heightened efficacies reported by established centers." Clifford Grobstein *et al.*, *External Human Fertilization: An Evaluation of Policy*, 222 Science 12 (1983). For earlier history of IVF attempts, *see generally* Barry D. Bavister, *Early History of In Vitro Fertilization*, 124 Reproduction 181 (2002).
47 Paul Clancy, *A Special Kind of Mother's Day; "In Vitro" Families Celebrate*, USA Today, May 12, 1989, at 3A; Sandy Rovner, *Making Babies: How Science Can Help Infertile Couples*, Washington Post, Aug. 6, 1986, at 13.
48 *See* Clancy, *supra* note 47.
49 Grobstein, *supra* note 46. The estimate of seventy-five hundred dollars is for a woman's first attempt at IVF. Subsequent attempts were less expensive: around five thousand dollars.
50 *Id.* Note that this figure is not adjusted for inflation.
51 Debora Spar, The Baby Business 32 (2006).
52 Rovner, *supra* note 47.
53 Spar, *supra* note 51, at 32–3.
54 U.S. Department of Health & Human Services, Centers for Disease Control & Prevention, 2003 Assisted Reproductive Technology Success Rates (2005), at 13.
55 Spar, *supra* note 51, at 97–127.
56 Classic arguments along these lines include Margaret Jane Radin, Contested Commodities: The Trouble with Trade in Sex, Children, Body Parts, and Other Things 139 (1996); Michael Sandel, *The Baby Bazaar*, New Republic, Oct. 20, 1997, at 25; Gena Corea, The Mother Machine (1977); Leon Kass, Toward a More Natural Science: Biology and Human Affairs 31 (1985).
57 Radin, *supra* note 56.

58 For surrogates, *see* Helena Ragoné, Surrogate Motherhood: Conception in the Heart (1994); Lori Andrews, *Beyond Doctrinal Boundaries: A Legal Framework for Surrogate Motherhood*, 81 Va. L. Rev. 2343 (1995). For sperm donors, *see* David Plotz, *No Nobels, One "Failure," a Few Regrets*, http://slate.msn.com/is/103402/; David Plotz, The Genius Factory: The Curious History of the Nobel Prize Sperm Bank (2005); K. Daniels *et al.*, *Previous Semen Donors and Their Views Regarding the Sharing of Information with Their Offspring*, 20 Human Reprod. 1670 (2005).

59 Mikki Morrissette, *Behind Closed Doors: Moving Behind Secrecy and Shame*, Voices of Donor Conception, Volume 1 (Mikki Morrissette ed., 2006).

13 Commerce and Regulation in the Assisted Reproduction Industry

JOHN A. ROBERTSON

The assisted reproduction field has grown phenomenally since the first in vitro fertilization (IVF) birth in 1978, with more than two million births worldwide. Assisted reproductive technologies (ARTs) and their many variations are now firmly ensconced within the medical care system. In 2003, there were more than 120,000 cycles and 35,000 births annually in the United States,[1] and perhaps 200,000 births throughout the world.[2] These technologies are avidly sought by persons unable to have children and present an attractive career alternative for obstetrician-gynecologists.

ARTs raise both ethical and health policy issues. The ethical questions involve the status and control of extracorporeal embryos, the technologization of family and reproduction, and the ability to recombine genetic, gestational, and social parentage. The health policy issues are less sexy but just as important. These concern the high cost of the procedures and lack of access, the risk that children will be born with congenital defects, and the effects on parenting and the family.

Some people still wonder whether we have proceeded too fast in accepting technological control over conception. They fear that we have paid insufficient attention to the effect of separating and recombining the genetic, gestational, and social aspects of reproduction on children, families, and, indeed, the human narrative. Others are concerned about extensions of ARTs to nontraditional families such as single men and women or gay and lesbian couples. Still others are bothered by the prospect of extensive preimplantation genetic selection and manipulation (PGD), which external access to the embryo makes possible. As a result, new controversies will arise as new techniques come on-line and new uses are made. Despite its naturalization, the use or regulation of reproductive technology will continue to occupy public and professional attention for some time to come.

Others take an industry-wide approach to infertility treatment as a commercial enterprise. The problem is that they use the terms *market* and *business* in such a broad sense that the terms lose their ability to tell us something new. Any exchange of anything for something can be thought of as a market or business. Because babies

I am indebted to Jane Cohen for comments on an earlier draft.

are not yet born, one is literally buying the prospect of a baby, not the baby itself.

This chapter addresses the issues raised by the presence of money and markets in assisted reproductive services. Section A describes the components of a market analysis that would shed light on the field. Section B then examines five ongoing areas of debate or concern about money and the role of commercial or market factors in ART. Section C concludes.

A. THINKING IN MARKET TERMS: SUPPLY, DEMAND, AND COMPETITION

I offer here a more complete look at some of the business- and market-related issues related to supply, demand, and competition in ART-related services. One set of issues involves demand-side issues of who gets access. A second set of issues concerns factors affecting the supply of fertility services.

1. Demand-Side Issues

On the demand side, important questions concern who wants ARTs and who is able to get them. The potential market is infertile couples and individuals who are infertile or who, due to sexual orientation or other special factors, are unable to have children. Yet only a minority of infertile persons get ART services. In some cases, this has to do with personal preference because there are physical and moral costs to using some of these techniques. In other cases, there are resource problems. Some countries treat ART and infertility as a needed medical service that the national health system should pay for. Others treat it like a luxury good available only to those who are able to purchase it.

One may legitimately ask whether such an investment to produce a child is worth it, and whether society should subsidize it. That inquiry would look at the costs and benefits of coverage, what it does to others in the health insurance pool, and whether it is worth subsidizing in a national health system. If not covered, obtaining such children becomes a luxury good of sorts (Debora Spar's luxury model).[3]

In the United States, few states mandate insurance coverage, and health insurance coverage for fertility services is rare. Except in Illinois, Maryland, and Massachusetts, ARTs are rationed by the ability to pay direct out-of-pocket charges.[4] Although infertility affects all economic groups, most people perceive access to basic health care as a more pressing problem. The 1992 Clinton health care plan, for example, specifically excluded IVF, and no one now seriously argues that the financially strapped Medicaid system should cover ARTs. European countries, with their lower birthrates, have to face whether to give subsidies or whether to create barriers on moral grounds, as in Italy.[5]

In addition to access, an important demand-side issue is the so-called captive nature of some patients. For many women and couples, infertility is a source of enormous suffering. Some become desperate to conceive and seem willing to use any technology that has the slightest chance of working. Patients may downplay the true risks and overinflate the likelihood of benefits, insist on additional procedures that have little likelihood of working, or be vulnerable to exploitation by profit-driven providers who overplay the efficacy of their procedures.

But there are built-in constraints here. People will be more careful about incurring out-of-pocket costs for ART than if insurance pays for it, particularly given the rigors of the procedure. There is now a widespread network of support groups, and information about success rates of particular programs is a few mouse clicks away. Paying patients can be more discriminating in what they request and better equipped to question medical recommendations. Also, persons who opt for ART will probably be seen by board-certified reproductive endocrinologists, treated in laboratories with some degree of certification, and thus less likely to receive poor-quality care. But mishaps occur in even the best-regulated systems and may occur more frequently where regulation is absent or only professionally driven.

There are also demand-side limits to adoption of the more exotic procedures that garner the lion's share of public attention and drive a good deal of the concern about commodification such as cloning and genetic engineering. Most infertile persons are driven by the desire to have genetically or biologically related children for rearing. As treatments move further from coital conception and the chance to rear biologically related children, problems increase and demand drops. Safe and effective reproductive cloning is still far off, but even if it worked, it is unlikely that there would be a great rush among fertile couples to use it, and only limited demand from the infertile. Nor will people quickly queue up for embryo screening if coital conception is likely to provide a healthy child. The ease and efficiency of new technologies might eventually change the situation, but learning the genomic secrets of complex traits and manipulating them in advance is still too distant a dream to worry us for at least another decade or two, and perhaps more.

A final demand-side issue is the shift in social norms that supports demand for ART services by unmarried persons. One development is the greater willingness of single or unmarried persons to have and rear children. The second is the growing acceptance of gay and lesbian rights, including the right to use assisted reproduction to have children and rear families. Indeed, the fact that gays and lesbians have and rear children has been a major reason why some courts have been sympathetic to the cause of same-sex marriage. For example, a main factor driving the Massachusetts Supreme Judicial Court's recognition of same-sex marriage was the sense that the children of gays and lesbians should have the same social support and stability structures that the children of opposite-sex marriage have. As the court explained, it "cannot be rational ... to penalize children by depriving them of State benefits because the State disapproves of their parents' sexual orientation."[6] The New York and Washington supreme courts, however, in closely divided opinions, found that the need to promote procreation by heterosexuals required the opposite result.[7] Refusing to recognize same-sex marriage is not likely to stop the march toward gay reproduction, which may increasingly turn to assisted reproduction for help.

The demand for reproductive services from gays and lesbians raises a supply-side problem for infertility professionals. The hallmark of professionalism has traditionally been the right to select one's own clients and to control the technical details of the services provided. State and federal civil rights laws now limit professional choice over clients on the basis of race, sex, ethnicity, and disability,[8] with a few states and cities also banning discrimination on the basis of sexual orientation.[9] In states that have not added sexual orientation to the banned list, doctors are legally free to refuse to provide ART services to gays and lesbians. But professional organizations of fertility specialists have found that discrimination against single or married persons on the basis of sexual orientation is not ethically acceptable.[10] Although not legally enforceable as such, this means that a program or doctor should help a single woman or lesbian couple with donor gametes and IVF. It also means that they should provide egg donation and surrogacy to single or coupled gay males, despite their religious or other beliefs about the desirability of parenting in those circumstances.

2. Supply-Side Issues

There is an ample supply of qualified providers to meet the demand for services presented by paying patients in the United States and, to varying extent, by paying and subsidized patients in other countries (though there may be legal constraints on certain procedures). Success rates are steadily creeping upward, and patients have easy access to comparative data through the Centers for Disease Control and Prevention (CDC). In addition, laboratory accreditation and tissue-handling practices required by the Food and Drug Administration (FDA) for donor gametes protect against infection. If anything, there is less chance of harm to patients than in other areas of medicine, if only because fertility treatment is largely an elective procedure for otherwise healthy patients.

What explains the success of some and the failure of others? Favorable state insurance laws might explain the success of ART clinics in Massachusetts, Maryland, and Illinois programs, but not those from California, New Jersey, and New York. We cannot tell whether more successful programs draw more patients or whether other factors explain their higher activity. Indeed, many smaller, nonacademically affiliated programs have good success rates. CDC annual reports of clinic-specific success rates provide a wealth of information that could be mined for economic or business insight into infertility practice.[11]

Several programs, including the Shady Grove Fertility Center in Maryland, which innovated in this area, have started a so-called shared risk, or money back guarantee, program. For a set fee, the program would offer three cycles, and if no baby was born, it would refund the money.[12] It would be interesting to know whether such insurance programs have reduced costs for patients or otherwise have been a successful business strategy. Shady Grove Fertility Center is the third ranked IVF center in terms of procedures done, whereas the Genetics and IVF Institute in Fairfax, an early leader in egg donation, PGD, and sex selection, does many fewer.[13] One operates in a state with insurance coverage for IVF, Maryland, whereas the other state, Virginia, does not. But one also provides shared risk, and the other does not.

Other than the high cost of ART procedures, the greatest barrier to assisted reproduction in some countries are restrictive laws about what procedures may be done and who may receive them. Moral constraints, however, are less likely to affect basic IVF than procedures such as egg donation, embryo screening, treatment of unmarried and gay persons, and the like. Germany, for example, has laws highly protective of embryos but reported, in 2002, nearly eighty-five thousand ART treatment cycles.[14] Yet Germany does no egg donation or PGD. Ireland and Slovenia appear to have few IVF centers,[15] but infertile couples can easily travel to Switzerland, Germany, or the United Kingdom for treatment. Reproductive tourism, however, is an option only for those who can pay.

3. The Market for Babies

The focus on infertility as the so-called baby business recalls the famous 1978 article by Landes and Posner, "The Economics of the Baby Shortage."[16] They looked at the shortage of babies for adoption and made an economic argument that women should be paid to give up babies for adoption. Among the benefits would be to reduce the abortion rate. Their hardheaded analysis touched off the debate over paying money for children and other contributions that have been a main current of bioethics for at least twenty-five years. The latest kerfuffle about paying women who donate embryos to research testifies to its staying power.

Although Landes and Posner never mention ARTs, which had not yet entered medical practice, their analysis is prescient. A few years later, the question of payment surfaced as an important side issue in the *Baby M* surrogate custody case.[17] In this case, Mary Beth Whitehead, the surrogate mother, fled with the baby fathered by and intended for the Sterns. The courts eventually gave primary custody to the Sterns, with visitation rights to Whitehead. Some states responded to concerns raised by cases like *Baby M* by regulating the compensation paid to surrogates, similar to regulations in the adoption context. The California Supreme Court introduced a bolt of clarity into the field with its favoring an intentionalist approach to rearing rights in a child born from an embryo made with the gametes of the infertile couple and gestated by another.[18] However, it has turned out that surrogacy is but a small part of the infertility industry.

B. SIX CURRENT CONTROVERSIES

The remainder of this chapter delves more deeply into market and commercial aspects of ART, trying to answer questions of what defines the boundary of the market and commerce and how that boundary is decided. The fact that money is paid and there is commerce of sorts is not in itself interesting. Medicine is rife with prices and markets. There are no free lunches, and everyone has to make a living. It is more interesting to explore the problems markets create in particular areas. That calls for a series of more local investigations to identify conflicts and how they might be resolved. I investigate six areas: infrastructure, twinning, paying donors and surrogates, selection, embryo status, and regulation.

1. Market Infrastructure: The Need for Rules

An important requirement for market relations are clearly defined rules of property, contract, and exchange, which enable people to know what they are trading and what the consequences of carrying out agreements will be. Indeed, legal rules, like a highway system, are a subsidy that society provides to facilitate exchange. This is as true for exchanges of reproductive factors and services as for any other sector of the economy. But while the general background rules of property, tort, and contract apply to assisted reproduction, the novel contexts in which they arise do present particular kinds of legal uncertainty. An efficient system of reproductive technology needs an infrastructure of legal rules for how technology affects ownership and control of gametes and embryos and the rearing rights and duties in the offspring generated by ART.

However, the absence of an overarching legal code specifically for assisted reproduction does not mean that all rules are absent or that all questions need be settled in advance. Indeed, if the business or market for reproduction is as robust as Debora Spar claims, there is likely to be sufficient certainty to enable people to invest resources and time in providing and seeking services. With new technologies, the areas that need rules come to light only after experience has identified problems and proposed solutions. We may still be too early in the rule-development cycle for norms for all areas of reproductive technology to have emerged. Most are likely to fall under the domain of principles that apply from other areas of law and morality.[19]

Despite the lack in most jurisdictions of a legislative code for assisted reproduction, an infrastructure of legal rules for dispositional control over embryos and for assignment of parenting rights in offspring is largely in place. Take, for example, ownership and control of embryos. It has long been clear that the gamete providers have joint dispositional authority over the embryo vis-à-vis the ART clinic, which functions as a bailee of the embryo, not an owner in its own right.[20] Thus it is obligated to return the embryo to the couple, subject to whatever terms the parties agreed to as a condition of their providing gametes and producing embryos. If the clinic intentionally, negligently, or even nonnegligently fails to provide it, it is subject to legal remedies.

The other area in need of legal infrastructure is the rules assigning rights and duties in offspring born with the help of donated gametes or surrogates. Although the rules were only hazily limned at the start of the field in the 1980s, the law for assigning parentage in cases of sperm donation to a married couple were already in place. The latest series of cases from California show that we are well on our way toward recognition of the principle of contract between donors and recipients as a hallmark – although not always a guarantee – of resulting parenting relations.[21]

There is also the moral dilemma that the need for legal infrastructure presents to those loathe to accept ART in the first place. Creating infrastructure signals approval, legitimizes the practice, and encourages expansion by reducing the planning costs of those engaging in it. On the other hand, refusing to provide legal infrastructure may increase litigation and uncertainty and end up harming children caught in battles over rearing rights and duties. With these competing concerns, it is not surprising that so few states and countries have a comprehensive code in place. In the meantime, a common law of responses will fill the gap and occasionally spur legislative clarification or codification.

2. Treatment Externalities: Anomalies, Twinning, and Novel Families

Reproduction is generally viewed as an important individual and social good. A main focus is on the personal importance of reproduction to the individuals involved, but attention to the social importance of reproduction is not far behind. Reproduction is necessary to replenish the work force and support previous generations of workers. Whereas high birthrates put pressure on natural resources, low birthrates impair society in other ways. Thus, unsurprisingly, there is generally wide social support for ARTs. Yet some European countries with declining birthrates have policies that undermine or discourage a wider use of ART.

A special problem posed by infertility treatments are the hidden externalities that may be created. Although there is general social support for childless couples reproducing, technologically assisted reproduction might generate greater health care costs and other social costs. One externality is the doubled risk that IVF offspring will have lower birth weight or congenital anomalies.[22] If this is true, then prospective patients need to be informed so they can make a more knowledgeable choice. Because many will still find the risk worth taking, their private action could lead to higher medical and social costs than coital reproduction ordinarily does. Without more data and study, one cannot be sure that the differences are great enough to charge parents with social irresponsibility in using IVF, much less warrant public policies to discourage its use. It is unlikely that ARTs would be banned or taxed because of these externalities. It does, however, provide a further reason, at a time of strained health care budgets, not to subsidize them through insurance.

A second source of externalities from ART is the higher rate of multiple births. About one-third of all IVF births involve multiples, most of them twins. The rate of higher-order multiples has been reduced in the United States and other countries through professional guidelines, but twinning remains a major problem for children, families, and the medical care system. A singleton birth is the most desirable situation for the health of the mother and offspring, and medical and social costs generally. Twins have a higher rate of premature birth, time spent in ICUs, and more medical and social problems.[23] Yet infertile patients often welcome twins. Lowering the rate of twins, however, is a difficult problem.

One way to reduce the rate of IVF twins would be to transfer no more than one embryo to the uterus at a time. Sweden and Belgium have used insurance incentives to encourage patients to accept single-embryo transfer, and some programs have had great success with it.[24] But the issue is a tricky one, especially in the United States, where twins are generally seen as a good outcome. In the American pay-as-you-go funding system, few levers exist to dampen patient enthusiasm for two babies at the price of one, especially because insurance coverage kicks in once the twins are born. ART patients are happier, which may affect the program's reputation, if two children are born, rather than one.

Professional and insurance guidelines and patient education may be more apt policy levers here than legislative action. But even better education of patients may be limited in what it can do. The doctors involved have an interest in satisfying patients. If patients insist on transferring at least two embryos, it will be hard for doctors to say no. Nor will they push too hard to inform them, for example, emphasizing the negative nature of twins from a social policy viewpoint, when other features of that system smile on the birth of twins.

Some persons might also argue that the anomalous family situations that arise with interchanges of gametes and gestation might generate social and emotional complexities that operate as a social externality. Medical, educational, and legal systems must expend time on a new set of issues. Children will face new sets of parenting problems. Despite their great resiliency, they might not do as well in such situations, which could generate social costs for others. The question of social externality requires more discussion elsewhere. Suffice it to say that the application of the concept of social externality in the ART setting may be too fine grained and elusive to merit special attention in policy making.

3. Paying for Gametes and Gestation

Many doctors make a prosperous living from treating infertility, but this appears to be of lesser moral concern than is the practice of paying gamete donors and surrogates for their services in helping an individual or couple to reproduce. The United States follows a market approach, subject to professional guidelines. Abroad, paid gamete donation is often banned, as in the United Kingdom, Canada, Germany, France, and elsewhere. This means that the service is not available, at least not to the extent that it is in the United States. In most countries in Europe, for example, egg donation occurs to a much smaller extent than in the United States.[25] In those countries, few women in need of egg donation (those with premature menopause or in older age groups) will be able to have children because of the rarity of purely altruistic egg donors.

It appears that egg donors are motivated both by the desire to help infertile persons as well as to receive compensation for their time and effort. Few women appear to have been injured or harmed by paid donation, and many older women or couples have been able to have biologically or genetically related offspring as a result. Careful attention to informing the donor of potential medical, legal, and psychological risks, and treating adverse events in the few cases in which they occur, remain essential to an ethical system of egg donation, whether paid or unpaid. Advertisements for fifty thousand dollars or more for blonde, high-IQ, and Ivy League donors have generated much negative publicity, but such practices, if they in fact exist to any significant extent, appear to be a tiny part of donor egg practices in the United States. They can hardly be cited as an example of exploitation of the poor and vulnerable.

The issue of paying for egg donations has taken on renewed attention in the context of the embryonic stem cell (ESC) and nuclear transfer cloning debate. As the field develops, a major policy issue is whether women who provide eggs for ESC research and therapy should be compensated for their time and trouble in addition to compensation for out-of-pocket expenses. The only realistic prospect for obtaining sufficient eggs to meet research and therapeutic needs for the foreseeable future is from live donors (the use of cadaveric or fetal ovaries will require more knowledge of in vitro maturation of eggs than now exists). Some altruistic donors might be available, particularly from relatives of persons with diseases who might be treated with ESC-derived therapies, but it is unrealistic to think that such donations will satisfy the demand for creating embryos for ESC research and therapy.

Given that the system of paid egg donation for treating infertility has worked reasonably well in the United States, the idea of compensating women for the time and effort involved in psychological and physical screening, hormonal stimulation, monitoring, retrieval, and the other steps involved in providing eggs for ESC research has strong appeal. Compensating women for donating eggs for ESC research is not only fair, but also consistent with the deeply embedded practice of paying subjects in biomedical research. Payments to research subjects have long been considered legitimate in the United States, as long as they do not constitute an undue inducement. If the risks and benefits of the research to the patient or others are positive, payment alone to an otherwise competent and informed subject will not be undue. Nor is compensation coercive merely because it provides an incentive to persons to donate.

Despite the likely need to pay women for their efforts to provide eggs for ESC research and therapy, the National Academy of Sciences, in its 2005 "Guidelines for Human Embryonic Stem Cell Research," took the position that no payments should be provided to egg donors other than reimbursement of direct expenses. It listed the arguments on each side of the issue but gave no analysis of why the position against payment was stronger than the position for it. It did note, however, that "this policy should be regularly reviewed and reconsidered as the field matures and the experiences under other policies can be evaluated."[26] In the meantime, two states actively involved in ESC research – California and Massachusetts – have banned paying donors of eggs for research, except for the expenses of donation.[27] California has taken the position that expenses are limited to out-of-pocket expenses,[28] whereas Massachusetts has not yet defined expenses.

Two recent developments suggest that the policy process may be "working itself pure" to permit payment, as well. The first is the publication of guidelines by the American College of Obstetricians and Gynecologists approving of payment for services to donors of eggs for ESC research.[29] The second is the ethical guidelines set by the International Society for Stem Cell Research, the professional organization of ESC researchers. Rather than banning payment altogether, it leaves it up to each host country.[30] That will not help within a particular country, but it avoids setting an international standard against payment that might have developed after the Hwang fraud in South Korea, which involved researchers creating ESCs from eggs obtained by fraud or coercion.[31]

In my view, there are serious problems of efficiency and fairness with a kidney model of nonpayment for egg donation for infertility treatment or research. Bans on payments make it harder to get gametes and are not justified given the time and effort required of the donors. The arguments in favor of a ban would have to be the risk of coercion and undue influence in payment or a moral sense that any payment is per se wrong. If paid donation is acceptable for treating infertile women and recruiting subjects for biomedical research, then it should be acceptable for recruiting donors to provide eggs for ESC research, as well. The key to protecting donors is careful practice and fully informed consent, not bans on compensating women who commit significant time and effort to providing eggs for ESC research.

The same analysis would apply to payments for embryos and gestational surrogacy, but I limit myself here to a discussion of paying for embryos. This issue was recently raised by reports that a made-to-order embryo bank had opened in San Antonio, Texas.[32] Unaffiliated with any medical center, the program purports to make embryos for couples from a catalog of sperm and egg donors. In some cases, those seeking embryos can "buy ready-made embryos matched to their specific requirements – even down to choosing what eye and hair colour they would like their child to have. . . . Buyers get 'portfolios' that include the donors' medical and social histories and usually a picture of them as a baby."[33] But this is not an attractive business model: it requires the development and maintenance of inventory for an unknown set of demanders. A just-in-time supply chain, with the described center acting as a broker for those who need embryos to reproduce, is more likely.

Aside from the sirenic horror of selling embryos, the idea of brokering arrangements between egg and sperm donors and recipients makes sense. Adoption agencies and sperm banks are brokerage agencies. Doctors will be needed to stimulate and retrieve eggs and transfer resulting embryos into a recipient, thus creating fiduciary duties to protect donors and recipients. Duties to offspring are less clear, but professional guidelines and ethical duties require some attention to whether the recipient has the requisite child-rearing abilities.

4. The Market for Selection

An important feature of IVF is that it opens the preimplantation embryo to the medical gaze and hence to screening, selection, and eventually manipulation, resulting ultimately in greater eugenic selection of offspring. In addition to morphology, embryos can be screened for chromosomal anomalies and genetic characteristics. Only healthy embryos or those having particular chromosomal or genetic makeups would then be transferred to the uterus.

The fear that embryo screening will lead to a market in genetically engineered children available only to the wealthy is overblown. Wanting a healthy child is natural, and we already have a well-established system of prenatal screening for many anomalies. With a family history of genetic disease, one can also screen prospective mates to see if they are carriers of genetic traits harmful to offspring. If so, the parents can avoid conception, seek donor gametes or adoption, or become pregnant and then screen the fetus to see if it is positive for the condition, in which case, termination can be considered.

As with other areas of reproductive innovation, an important policy question is whether any regulation is needed here, and if it is, will it be the result of professional guidelines or governmental action? In the highly decentralized U.S. system, state or federal regulation of the acceptable purposes or uses of PGD are likely to be rare. If regulation occurred, such attempts might run into constitutional problems. We must content ourselves with professional self-regulation, with all its gaps and weaknesses. The American Society for Reproductive Medicine, for example, has been unable to clarify whether PGD for gender variety is acceptable, even though it has spoken in favor of sperm sorting for family balancing.[34] As a result, several member programs are conducting or advertising programs of nonmedical sex selection, including two by former presidents of the association.[35]

A more centralized regulatory approach, such as the Human Fertilisation and Embryology Authority (HFEA) in the United Kingdom, could require approval of new uses of PGD such as to enable a family to have a child to serve as a donor to an existing child, to screen for cancer susceptibility genes, or for family-balancing sex selection. The HFEA has approved PGD for chromosomal and genetic abnormalities and to select out embryos that carry genes that make them more susceptible to cancer – even though the risk of cancer does not arise until adulthood – but has an inconsistent history with other uses. Nonmedical gender selection, even for gender variety, is prohibited. Initially, it approved PGD to ensure that a child will be a good tissue match for an existing child only if the screened embryos were also at risk for the condition of the existing child, thus leaving parents of a child suffering from noninheritable disease with no recourse.[36] But the distinction between inherited and sporadic disease was too thin to carry moral weight, and the HFEA relented, allowing PGD for tissue matching for any disease, regardless of whether the embryo screened was also at risk for it.

In the end, the prospect of embryo screening for more precise prenatal selection raises interesting questions about parental rights to select offspring traits and what that does to love for children, societal norms, and understanding of parentage. Leon Kass, Michael Sandel, and others object that any form of selection treats the child as a thing and denies its "giftedness."[37] But the idea of wanting to have healthy children is strong, and the arguments for blocking such practices are weak. A cocaine model of regulation for PGD is unlikely to emerge in the United States. Regardless of how one answers the normative questions, the undeveloped state of technical and genomic knowledge will also forestall regulation. We simply do not know enough about the genomics of desirable traits to subject them to embryo screening in a way that would attract people not otherwise undergoing IVF. Nor do we know how to do safe and effective reproductive cloning or most of the other procedures that raise the greatest ethical hackles. Even if we did, demand for those procedures would still be limited because of the cost and trouble involved.

5. Culture-of-Life Politics and the Market for ARTs

The influence of ethics and politics in the market for ARTs may be much less than one would have expected from the high visibility of culture-of-life partisans in electoral politics, particularly in the abortion, emergency contraception, and ESC funding debates. Assisted reproduction often involves creating, transferring, freezing, or discarding embryos, necessarily implicating right to life issues, which are contested so bitterly in the abortion and ESC settings.

The Warnock Committee in the United Kingdom and the American Fertility Society in the United States took the position that the embryo was not a legal person or entity with interests, but nevertheless deserved special respect, if only on symbolic grounds.[38] As long as creation and use of embryos was for a legitimate purpose, such as medical research or treating infertility, it was acceptable to create, transfer, discard, or donate embryos for research or infertility treatment. This is the ethical or normative position that supports the legal regime of gamete source–dispositional control of embryos that now undergirds assisted reproduction.

Some countries take a much more restrictive view of embryo status, most notably Germany and Italy.[39] They each require that all embryos be transferred to the uterus, that only a limited number be created, that no freezing or research occur, and so on. Whereas Germany's position dates back to 1990, the very conservative Italian position was enacted in 2004 and withstood a referendum to repeal it.[40] Although no doubt a reflection of the importance of the Vatican in Italian politics, the enactment of the Italian law and the failure to reverse it by referendum show the strength of the right-to-life views in contemporary life.

The most recent manifestation of the culture of life's strength in the United States has been in the ESC research debate that has roiled American politics for several years. Because ESCs are derived from early embryos, the question of whether it is ethical to destroy embryos for research or therapy poses a major barrier for some persons. In the United States, the issue has focused on federal funding, not prohibitions per se, and led to former president Bush's first veto, when he refused to sign a law that would have reversed his administratively imposed ban on federal funding of ESC research.[41] But there is no federal law against discarding embryos or using nonfederally funded embryos for research, nor does any state explicitly ban the discarding of embryos, though a few come close.[42]

An interesting facet of the ESC debate is how it has brought questions about the moral status of embryos into the public eye when, for years, embryos have been created and discarded in the course of infertility treatment without much public concern. Logically, right-to-lifers opposed to ESC research should also focus their attention on IVF clinics and their practices in creating embryos. If they are appalled that human lives are being destroyed for ESC research, they should be equally incensed by the great number of embryos created during IVF treatment and the number stored, discarded, and so on. It certainly would be logical for them to demand that only a few embryos be created and all embryos placed in the uterus, as is the case in Germany and Italy.[43]

Continued growth of the power of the culture-of-life forces could lead to more restrictive IVF policies, but these are unlikely to dampen demand for ART services. Indeed, there may be some technical slack in the system so that fewer embryos could be created and fewer discarded without impairing success rates or noticeably increasing costs to paying couples. Also, national guidelines that seem highly restrictive on the surface may not be so in practice. Germany, for example, protects embryos against discard or research but defines an embryo as existing only after syngamy, when the twenty-three chromosomes provided by each parent fuse into a new diploid genome, at roughly twenty hours after fertilization.[44] That enables German doctors and embryologists to freeze fertilized eggs at the pronuclear stage just prior to syngamy and achieve quite respectable success rates with thawed pronuclear embryos.[45] Italian law has not yet clarified its new law on this point.

Culture-of-life forces may, in future election cycles, lose some of their political clout, but a less stringent application of their moral position has wide support. The respect due to embryos and the earliest stages of human life will continue to be a factor in future debates and policy making. It is one of the factors that needs to be balanced in arriving at acceptable public policies for the genomic and reproductive innovations of the future.

6. The Vanishing but Not Extinct Need for Regulation

It has been a standard refrain in discussions of ART to bemoan the lack of regulation and even call for a centralized system of regulatory control, as occurs in the United Kingdom through the HFEA. In fact, a great deal of legal and professional self-regulation already exists. In addition to background tort, contract, and property doctrines and medical licensing laws, at least one state has laboratory and other regulations for ART.[46] If gametes, embryos, stem cells, or tissue from others are involved, the lab must meet FDA requirements.[47] There are also clinic-specific reporting requirements to the CDC.[48] None of these are perfect. Gaps exist, but there are many avenues of information, control, and market discipline by patients and others. The problem is less with regulation than with particular issues of regulation, many of them having to do with moral conflicts over the status of embryos, eugenics, and family affiliation law.

An unusual indicator of the absence of major regulatory problems with ARTs was the difficulty that the conservative President's Council on Bioethics (PCB), under the direction of Dr. Leon Kass, a noted bioethicist and long-time opponent of reproductive technology, had in finding problems or ways to improve the delivery of ART services. After two years of study, it issued a report in 2004, "Reproduction and Responsibility: The Regulation of New Biotechnologies." That report made some useful suggestions for increasing monitoring and information about these practices but found none of the glaring problems said to exist in this so-called wild west industry. We can take the PCB's report as a benchmark for the state of the field and the lack of a compelling case for more extensive regulation. It found that much more research is needed before one can determine whether major changes in current practices and regulatory institutions are justified. Surprisingly, although it discussed commercial issues, it did not recommend against a market for reproductive services or for paying gamete donors and surrogates.[49]

C. CONCLUSION

Whether there is a reproductive market or baby business that needs special attention is itself contestable. But, if there is one, its boundary is unclear and variable and shifts with the procedure in question, needs of infertile couples, societal standards of health and safety, technological developments, and concerns about protecting early human life and children. In a setting with so many cross-cutting issues, it would be unrealistic to expect otherwise.

In the end, the rules that govern the most intimate of decisions will be the same rules, turned to a more narrow focus, that we apply to other activities involving medicine, people, and children and the privacy and autonomy that characterize them. The world of reproductive technology raises many local or specialized problems, but they are not fruitfully encompassed or clarified by calling them collectively a "business" or "industry." They are that, but they are many more things as well. In coming to terms with reproductive technologies, the business side may not be of foremost importance.

NOTES

1 Centers for Disease Control & Prevention, U.S. Department of Health & Human Services, 2003 Assisted Reproductive Technology Success Rates: National Summary and Fertility Clinic Reports 11 (2005).

2 *See* press release, American Society for Reproductive Medicine, *Highlights from the Conjoint Meeting of the American Society for Reproductive Medicine and the Canadian Fertility and Andrology Society: International Numbers on Assisted Reproduction* (Oct. 17, 2005), http://www.asrm.org/Media/Press/2005international_numbers.html (reporting that ART produced between 197,000 and 220,000 live births worldwide in 2000).

3 Deborah Spar, The Baby Business: How Money, Science, and Politics Drive the Commerce of Conception (2006).

4 *See* 215 Ill. Comp. Stat. 5/356m (2000); MD Code Ann., Ins. § 15-810 (Lexis-Nexis 2006); Mass. Gen. Laws Ann. ch. 175, § 47H (West 1998) (requiring certain group policies to include coverage for the diagnosis and treatment of infertility). *See generally* Peter J. Neumann, *Should Health Insurance Cover IVF?* 22 J. Health Pol. Pol'y & L. 1215 (1997) (health insurance coverage of IVF and the various policy issues involved); National Conference of State Legislatures, *50 State Summary of State Laws Related to Insurance Coverage for Infertility Therapy* (July 2006), http://www.ncsl.org/programs/health/50infert.htm.

5 *See* Katherine E. Abel, *The Pregnancy Discrimination Act and Insurance Coverage for Infertility Treatment: An Inconceivable Union*, 37 Conn. L. Rev. 819, 822 (2005) ("In France . . . IVF is fully reimbursed by the social security system, and in Belgium, Denmark, and Norway the state bears most of the cost of IVF"); John A. Robertson, *Protecting Embryos and Burdening Women: Assisted Reproduction in Italy*, 19 Hum. Reprod. 1693 (2004).

6 Goodridge v. Dep't of Pub. Health, 798 N.E.2d 941, 964 (Mass. 2003).

7 By one-vote margins, both the New York and Washington high courts held that the refusal to recognize same-sex marriage did not violate state constitutions. *See* Hernandez v. Robles, 7 N.Y.3d 338, 361 (2006); Anderson v. King County, 138 P.3d 963, 968 (Wash. 2006). *See also* Citizens for Equal Prot. v. Bruning, 455 F.3d 859, 871 (8th Cir. 2006) (concluding that an amendment to the Nebraska state constitution limiting marriage to opposite-sex couples is rationally related to legitimate state interests).

8 *See, e.g.*, 42 U.S.C. § 1395dd (2000) (restricting the discretion hospitals have in refusing individuals emergency medical services); *id.* § 2000d (prohibiting discrimination by programs or activities receiving federal funding); *id.* § 12132 (prohibiting discrimination in public services, programs, or activities); Colo. Rev. Stat. Ann. § 24-34-601 (West Supp. 2006) (prohibiting discrimination in public accommodations including any "dispensary, clinic, hospital, convalescent home, or other institution for the sick, ailing, aged, or infirm"); N.H. Rev. Stat. Ann. §§ 354-A:1, 354-A:2 (Supp. 2006) (including health care providers among public accommodations subject to antidiscrimination laws); Tex. Health & Safety Code Ann. § 311.022(a)(c) (Vernon 2001) (prohibiting the denial of emergency medical services and prohibiting arbitrary discrimination).

9 *See, e.g.*, Cal. Civ. Code § 51(b) (West Supp. 2006); Mass. Gen. Laws Ann. ch. 272, §§ 92A, 98 (West 2000); Minn. Stat. § 363A.02 (2004); N.J. Stat. Ann. §§ 10:5–4, 10:5–5 (West Supp. 2006); R.I. Gen. Laws §§ 11-24-2, 11-24-3 (2002); VT. Stat. Ann. tit. 9, §§ 4501, 4502 (Supp. 2006). *See also* Madison, Wis., Code of Ordinances § 3.23(1) (1992) (declaring that the city's policy is "to foster and enforce

to the fullest extent the protection by law of the rights of all of its inhabitants to equal opportunity to gainful employment, housing, credit and the use of City facilities and public accommodations without regard to . . . sexual orientation").

10 *See* Ethics Committee, American Society for Reproductive Medicine, *Access to Fertility Treatment by Gays, Lesbians, and Unmarried Persons*, 86 FERTILITY & STERILITY 1333, 1333–5 (2006), http://www.asrm.org/Media/Ethics/fertility_gaylesunmarried.pdf. The fact of discrimination is most glaring if a program treats single women but not single men, or lesbian couples but not gay couples. Programs, however, remain free to refuse services if they think that someone, regardless of his or her sexual orientation, will not be a responsible parent. *See* Ethics Committee, American Society for Reproductive Medicine, *Child-Rearing Abilities and the Provision of Fertility Services*, 82 FERTILITY & STERILITY 564, 564 (2004), http://www.asrm.org/Media/Ethics/childrearing.pdf.

11 *See* Centers for Disease Control & Prevention, *Assisted Reproductive Technology Report Commonly Asked Questions* (2004), http://www.cdc.gov/art/art2004/faq.htm.

12 *See* John A. Robertson & Theodore J. Schneyer, *Professional Self-Regulation and Shared-Risk Programs for In Vitro Fertilization*, 25 J.L. MED. & ETHICS 283, 284 (1997) (describing a typical shared-risk plan that charges a set price for three cycles of IVF and offers a 90% refund if there is no delivery).

13 Spar, *supra* note 3, at 54.

14 A. Nyboe Anderson *et al.*, *Assisted Reproductive Technology in Europe, 2002*, 21 HUM. REPROD. 1680, 1681 (2006) (presenting results generated from European registers by the European Society of Human Reproduction and Embryology).

15 *See id.* at 1681 (listing Ireland as having five reporting IVF clinics and Slovenia three).

16 Elisabeth Landes & Richard Posner, *The Economics of The Baby Shortage*, 7 J. LEGAL STUD. 323 (1978).

17 *See In re* Baby M, 537 A.2d 1227, 1249–50 (N.J. 1988) (stating that "there are, in a civilized society, some things that money cannot buy" and discussing the social ramifications of paying for surrogacy services).

18 *See* Johnson v. Calvert, 851 P.2d 776, 782 (Cal. 1993) ("We conclude that . . . she who intended to procreate the child – that is, she who intended to bring about the birth of a child that she intended to raise as her own – is the natural mother under California law").

19 *E.g.*, concepts from property, contract, and informed consent may fill in gaps that arise. *See, e.g.*, York v. Jones, 717 F. Supp. 421 (E.D. Va. 1989) (finding that a bailment relationship existed between plaintiffs and defendant institution, thereby allowing plaintiffs to state a cause of action in detinue when the defendant institution refused to release the plaintiffs' prezygote); Moore v. Regents of the Univ. of Cal., 793 P.2d 479 (Cal. 1990) (addressing principles of personal autonomy, informed consent, fiduciary duties of medical professionals, and the law of conversion when defendant used the plaintiff's cells in medical research without plaintiff's permission).

20 *See York*, 717 F. Supp. at 425. However, this does not hold true when the couple has transferred their joint dispositional control to the clinic. *See id.* at 426–7 (defining the institute's possessory interest in the prezygote by the terms of the cryopreservation agreement).

21 *See* K.M. v. E.G., 117 P.3d 673 (Cal. 2005) (holding that both the woman who donated her ova and her lesbian partner who carried the child are the child's parents); Elisha B. v. Superior Court, 117 P.3d 660 (Cal. 2005) (enforcing the obligation of a woman who agreed to raise children with her lesbian partner to support those children).

22 *See* Michele Hansen *et al.*, *The Risk of Major Birth Defects after Intracytoplasmic Sperm Injection and In Vitro Fertilization*, 346 NEW ENG. J. MED. 725, 725 (2002) ("Infants conceived with use of intracytoplasmic sperm injection or in vitro fertilization have

twice as high a risk of a major birth defect as naturally conceived infants"); Laura A. Schieve *et al.*, *Low and Very Low Birth Weight in Infants Conceived with Use of Assisted Reproductive Technology*, 346 New Eng. J. Med. 731, 733 tbl.4 (2002) ("Singleton infants conceived with assisted reproductive technology had a risk of term low birth weight that was more than twice that of singleton infants in the general population").

23 *See* Lynne S. Wilcox, *Assisted Reproductive Technology: Estimates of Their Contribution to Multiple Births and Newborn Hospital Days in the United States*, 65 Fertility & Sterility 361, 361 (1996); American Society for Reproductive Medicine, *Patient's Fact Sheet: Complications of Multiple Gestation* (Aug. 2001), http://www.asrm.org/Patients/FactSheets/complications-multi.pdf.

24 John A. Robertson, *Reproductive Technology in Germany and the United States: An Essay in Comparative Law and Bioethics*, 43 Colum. J. Transnat'l L. 189, 208 (2004).

25 Aside from the United Kingdom and Spain, relatively few egg donations occur in Europe as compared to the United States. *Cf.* Centers for Disease Control & Prevention, *supra* note 1, at 75 (stating that the number of transfers with donor eggs in the United States for 2003 was 12,996), *with* Anderson *et al., supra* note 14, at 1685 (stating that the number of transfers internationally, not including the United Kingdom or Spain, for 2002 was 2,438).

26 Committee on Guidelines for Human Embryonic Stem Cell Research, National Research Council and Institute of Medicine, *Guidelines for Human Embryonic Stem Cell Research* 87, 101 (2005), http://www.nap.edu/catalog /11278.html#toc.

27 Mass. Gen. Laws Ann. ch. 111L, §§ 2, 8 (West 2006); Act of Sept. 26, 2006, ch. 483, § 7, 2006 Cal. Legis. Serv. 2740 (to be codified at Cal. Health & Safety Code § 125355).

28 *See* Act of Sept. 26, 2006 ("No payment in excess of the amount of reimbursement of direct expenses incurred as a result of the procedure"). *See also* Cal. Code Regs. tit. 17, § 100020(h) (2006), http://www.cirm.ca.gov/laws/pdf/ AdoptedRegs_100010.pdf (defining *permissible expenses*).

29 Committee on Ethics, American College of Obstetricians & Gynecologists, *ACOG Committee Opinion No. 347: Using Preimplantation Embryos for Research*, 108 Obstetrics & Gynecology 1305, 1316 (2006).

30 International Society for Stem Cell Research, *Guidelines for the Conduct of Human Embryonic Stem Cell Research* 15 (draft June 30, 2006), http://www.isscr.org/StaticContent/StaticPages/ISSCRTaskForceGuidelinesDRAFT6-30-06.pdf.

31 *See* Anthony Faiola & Joohee Cho, *S. Korean Stem Cell Expert Apologizes for Ethical Breach*, Washington Post, Nov. 25, 2005, at A24 (reporting that scientist Hwang Woo Suk hid the fact that he used ova samples taken from two junior assistants and purchased from other women in the research that led to the reported cloning of the first human embryo); William Saletan, *Breaking Eggs: The Lesson of the Korean Cloning Scandal*, Slate, Jan. 4, 2006, http://www.slate.com/id/2133745 (suggesting that the scientific breakthroughs claimed by Hwang may not have been entirely truthful).

32 Debra J. Saunders, Editorial, *Embryos Made to Order*, San Francisco Chronicle, Aug. 8, 2006, at B7; Julie Wheldon, *The Embryo Bank Where You Order a Bespoke Baby*, Daily Mail (London), Aug. 5, 2006, at 6; William Saletan, *The Embryo Factory: The Business Logic of Made-to-Order Babies*, Slate, Jan. 15, 2007, http://www.slate.com/id/ 2157495/pagenum/all/#page_start. *See generally* the Abraham Center of Life, http://www.theabrahamcenter oflife.com (detailing the processes for embryo donation, surrogacy, adoption, and egg donation).

33 Wheldon, *supra* note 32.

34 *See* Ethics Committee, American Society for Reproductive Medicine, *Sex Selection and Preimplantation Genetic Diagnosis*, 72 Fertility & Sterility 595, 598 (1999),

http://www.asrm.org/Media/Ethics/Sex_Selection.pdf (concluding that, although "legal prohibition" is not warranted for nonmedical sex selection, "the cumulative weight of the arguments against nonmedically motivated sex selection gives cause for serious ethical caution").

35 Spar, *supra* note 3, at 122; Susannah Baruch, David Kaufman, and Kathy Hudson report data that show a growing use of PGD, at least in major programs. *See* Susannah Baruch *et al.*, *Genetic Testing of Embryos: Practices and Perspectives of U.S. IVF Clinics*, 86 FERTILITY & STERILITY 5 (2006), http://www.dnapolicy.org/resources/ PGDSurveyReportFertilityandSterilitySept.

36 HUMAN FERTILISATION AND EMBRYOLOGY AUTHORITY, REPORT: PREIMPLANTATION TISSUE TYPING ¶ 6, at 2 (2004), http://www.hfea.gov.uk/cps/rde/xbcr/SID-3F57D79BE71326E9/hfea/PreimplantationReport.pdf.

37 *See, e.g.*, LEON R. KASS, LIFE, LIBERTY, AND THE DEFENSE OF DIGNITY 131 (2002); MICHAEL J. SANDEL, PUBLIC PHILOSOPHY 207–9 (2005); Michael J. Sandel, *The Case against Perfection*, ATLANTIC MONTHLY, April 2004, at 51, 62 (arguing that genetic engineering threatens society's appreciation of life as a gift).

38 *See* Ethics Committee, American Fertility Society, *Ethical Considerations of the New Reproductive Technologies*, 46 FERTILITY & STERILITY 30S (Supp. 1 1986) (explaining that each program should develop and announce its policies on the options dealing with embryos and that potential donors should not be coerced into donation).

39 *See* Robertson, *supra* note 5 (Italy's restrictive law on assisted reproduction "situates Italy at the most conservative end of the spectrum in Europe"); Robertson, *supra* note 24, at 195–6 (outlining the grounds and scope of Germany's "strong formal protection of fetuses and embryos"). Ireland, Austria, and Poland are also highly protective of embryos. *See* Robertson, *supra* note 24, at 192.

40 Sophie Arie, *In Europe, Italy Now a Guardian of Embryo Rights*, CHRISTIAN SCIENCE MONITOR, June 14, 2005, at 1.

41 Sheryl Gay Stolberg, *First Bush Veto Maintains Limits on Stem Cell Use*, N.Y. TIMES, July 20, 2006, at A1.

42 *E.g.*, Louisiana seems to come very close. *See* LA. REV. STAT. ANN. §§ 9:122, 9:129 (2000) (stipulating that a human embryo in vitro shall not be "farmed or cultured solely for research purposes" nor be "intentionally destroyed"). IVF clinics in that state have not challenged the law.

43 Germany has finessed the issue by not including pronuclear embryos as embryos. Only at syngamy – emergence of a new genome at twenty hours after fertilization – does an embryo exist. The fertilized egg prior to syngamy can thus be frozen and discarded. *See* Robertson, *supra* note 24.

44 *See* Eve-Marie Engels, *Human Embryonic Stem Cells – The German Debate*, 2 NATURE REV. GENETICS 636, 637–8 (2002).

45 *See* Anderson *et al.*, *supra* note 14, at 1684 tbl.VI.

46 *See* Baruch *et al.*, *supra* note 35, at 7 (noting that "New York has developed standards for laboratories that include oversight of genetic tests associated with" IVF).

47 21 C.F.R. § 1271.45(b) (2006). In addition, tissue banks must be registered and follow a variety of record keeping and good manufacturing practice regulations. 21 C.F.R. §§ 207.20(f), 210.1(c), 807.20(d), 820.1 (2006). The FDA, however, does not specify which genetic mutations or heritable conditions make someone ineligible to be a donor.

48 Baruch *et al.*, *supra* note 35, at 7.

49 *See id.* at 147–57, 205–24.

14 Ethics within Markets or a Market for Ethics?: Can Disclosure of Sperm Donor Identity Be Effectively Mandated?

JUNE CARBONE AND PAIGE GOTTHEIM

The regulation of fertility services involves the creation of norms about a new and rapidly growing technology. Although artificial insemination itself is hardly new,[1] the creation of a global industry supplying fertility services is. This new industry involves decentralized, easily moveable services catering to a growing global demand.[2] The birth of children has historically attracted intense efforts to forge and enforce moral understandings based on the intersection of sex, marriage, and procreation,[3] but the use of medical services to create children from multiple donors, who may or may not be connected to each other, is a different matter.[4] Kelly Weisberg, in her book on surrogacy in Israel, recounts the case of an Italian man and his Portuguese wife, living in France, who arranged for a British surrogate to be inseminated in a Greek laboratory with sperm from an anonymous American donor, who contributed to a Danish fertility bank, and the eggs of another British woman.[5] When the commissioning couple refused to accept the twin girls because they were the wrong gender, the surrogate arranged to have the babies adopted by a lesbian couple in California.[6] No comprehensive rules or norms govern the process or prevent the would-be parents from trying again in another part of the world.

Within such rapidly changing markets, ethical understandings, to the extent that they can be successfully forged at all, must occur within the interstices of market mechanisms. Consider, for example, the issue of mandating disclosure of sperm donor identity.[7] Initially, the practice of artificial insemination by a donor placed a premium on secrecy.[8] Men were embarrassed about infertility, husbands and wives sought to conceal the practice, and children might never be told about the circumstances of their birth, much less about the identity of the donor.[9] Moreover, in jurisdictions in which parental status was uncertain, anonymity protected donors from unwanted contact or child support responsibilities and protected recipients from demands for visitation or parental recognition.[10]

These attitudes have changed as greater emphasis has been placed on genetic identity and the stigma associated with nontraditional families has lessened. Mary

Adapted from June Carbone & Paige Gottheim, *Markets, Subsidies, Regulation, and Trust: Building Ethical Understandings into the Market for Fertility Services*, 9 J. Gender Race & Just. 509 (2006).

Shanley observes that "the right to learn the identity of one's genetic forebear stems from some people's desire to be able to connect themselves to human history concretely as embodied beings, not only abstractly as rational beings or as members of large social (national, ethnic, religious) groups."[11] Moreover, the importance of genetic information to medical decision making has made it more important and more likely that the child will at some point learn whether he is biologically related to the parents who raised him.[12] For the children of single parents or gay or lesbian couples, it will be obvious from an early age that other adults were involved in their creation.[13] These concerns have led some countries to require the disclosure of nonidentifying medical or genetic information[14] and other jurisdictions to require the disclosure of donor identity when the child comes of age.[15]

Nonetheless, some recipients, for a variety of personal, cultural, or legal reasons, may continue to prefer anonymity. If a country attempts to build the disclosure principle into the understandings of acceptable fertility practices, what are the prospects for success? We examined Australia's effort to adopt ethical guidelines mandating disclosure when the child reaches the age of majority.[16] Australia did so in the face of an insufficient supply of sperm donors to meet existing demand, and the new ethical guidelines had the predictable effect of aggravating the existing shortage.[17] To increase supply, a clinic near Sydney applied for permission to recruit sperm donors from Calgary, to whom it offered all-expense-paid trips to Australia if the donors would contribute sperm every other day for two weeks.[18] Although the effort produced a large expression of interest, it did not produce enough donors to end the shortage.[19] In considering the Australian experience, we developed four principles tied to success or failure in locking in ethical understandings.

The first principle involves the relationship between aboveground and underground markets. If regulations are too onerous, too easy to circumvent, or too at odds with accepted practices, they may spur underground markets or fertility tourism that simply bypasses them. The Swedes, for example, responded to legislation that banned gamete payment and mandated disclosure of sperm donor identity by procuring the majority of their donor sperm in Denmark.

The second principle is comparative regulation. Standard accounts of corporate governance describe a "race to the bottom," or competition in laxity, by which jurisdictions compete to attract new industries by providing a favorable regulatory climate. With easily mobile fertility services, providers might seek to specialize in accordance with the background law of the jurisdiction in which they are located, as the Danes become known for their willingness to supply a worldwide trade in sperm or California becomes identified with surrogacy services. Practices in these jurisdictions may then set standards that become industry norms.

The third factor is subsidization. Greater financial support of fertility services might overcome disadvantageous regulations. The background condition for fertility services in Europe and Australia is the generous state subsidization of medical care. If the state health care system offers financial advantages over those services available abroad, the state may be in a better position to lock in its ethical preferences.

Finally, we consider the factor of trust. With disclosure of sperm donor identity, for example, the issue is not just the provision of information, but also the consequences. Can a known donor exercise parental rights? Could he be held liable for child support? Security about the arrangements is likely to influence the construction of markets.

A. TIPPING POINTS: STAY VISIBLE OR SHOP UNDERGROUND?

The first question in assessing the effectiveness of a new ethical regime is considering whether the new rules are likely to prompt compliance or wholesale circumvention. If the net effect of mandatory disclosure, for example, is wholesale deterrence of sperm donation, infertile couples will need to go elsewhere to become pregnant at all, establishing networks to circumvent the requirements. Where disclosure mandates are combined with restrictions on payment (for many, an equally important ethical principle), the most common result has been long waiting lists for the available sperm.[20] In 2004, for example, 336 Swedish women were inseminated with Danish sperm, producing eighty-one pregnancies, thirty more than the number of pregnancies produced by artificial insemination in Sweden itself.[21] The Swedish ban on payment meant that the Swedish market could not adjust supply to meet the new ethical principle, and Swedish women responded by leaving the country for their fertility treatments. Denmark has consolidated its position as the fertility center of choice for sperm donation in Europe. The result not only undermines Swedish clinics, but it also serves to reinforce convictions that donor anonymity is an acceptable practice.

In emphasizing the ease of circumvention, we do not mean to suggest, however, that the development of norms to govern new practices is simply a matter of a cost-benefit analysis, in which the critical factor is the ease of circumvention alone.[22] Cass Sunstein, while he describes norms as "factors that act as taxes on or subsidies to action,"[23] also advances the idea of a "norm bandwagon" that occurs when "the lowered cost of expressing new norms encourages an ever-increasing number of people to reject previously popular norms, to a 'tipping point' where it is adherence to the old norms that produces social disapproval."[24]

Consider, for example, the ban on payment for organs for transplant. Organ donations – hearts, lungs, livers, kidneys, corneas – are legal. The sale of human organs, however, is against the law in every country (with the exception of Iran), and the world's medical associations and political and religious leaders have stated that the practice is morally and ethically irresponsible, inhumane, and unacceptable, and that it violates the dignity of the human person.[25] The ban on payment, however, contributes to a shortage of organs for transplant.[26] Desperate patients, for whom an organ transplant may be the difference between life and death, have sought organs wherever they could find them.[27] The result is an illegal, complex, well-organized, and often cross-continental organ trafficking market, composed of buyers and sellers, conducted with only "a scant nod toward secrecy" in Israel, India, Turkey, China, Russia, and Iraq.[28] If the aboveground market falls too far behind in meeting available demand, then a flourishing black market may effectively supplant it, even where the ethical principle – the ban on organ sales – is itself widely accepted.

The effect can be that much more dramatic where government regulations drive practices underground *after* supply networks are already in place. India, for example, has long been a major supplier of organs, originally without much effort at concealment. Between 1983 and 1988, 131 patients from the United Arab Emirates alone were reported to have traveled to India to buy kidneys from local living donors.[29] By the early 1990s, approximately two thousand kidney transplants from contracted living donors were being performed annually.[30] A 1994 act criminalizing organ sales forced the market underground. It nonetheless continued to thrive, "[producing] an even larger *domestic* black market in kidneys. In some areas this new business is controlled by organized, cash-rich crime gangs expanding out from the heroin trade (in some cases with the backing of local political leaders). In other areas the business is controlled by ever more wealthy owners of profit hospitals."[31]

The original aboveground market made it that much easier for the black market to take hold, and the criminalization of the activity has made it that much harder to police the exploitation of kidney donors that the criminalization was designed to prevent. Moreover, the combination of a flourishing black market with the failure to address the inadequacies of the aboveground market risks approaching a tipping point, where payment for kidney donations from live donors becomes the only possible way to effectively curtail the growth of a global black market in organs.[32]

It is, of course, far easier to create an underground market for sperm than for kidneys. The donor need experience no discomfort, medical complications, or follow-up care. And sperm, whether frozen and shipped or inserted directly into the recipient, is easy to transport without detection. Commercial sperm banks in the United States, Denmark, and elsewhere are sufficiently well established that creation of a network to circumvent inconvenient restrictions could be easily established,[33] and indeed, in the unlikely event commercialization were effectively curtailed, women could simply return to use of the turkey baster. The drawback to use of a known donor has always been the risk that the donor could insist on and obtain parental status; travel abroad or use of informal domestic networks makes official norms banning payment or requiring donor identity disclosure easy to circumvent in the absence of widespread acceptance. To a much greater degree than with organ sales, strict domestic regulation runs the risk of fueling international or illegal supply.

B. COMPARISON SHOPPING: ESCAPE OR BUY IN?

The second factor is comparative regulation. Framing norms involves not just choices between compliance and circumvention, but escape from or opting into regulatory regimes that express divergent values. Standard accounts of corporate governance describe a race to the bottom, or competition in laxity, by which jurisdictions compete to attract new industries by providing a favorable regulatory climate.[34] With mobile fertility services, providers might seek to specialize in accordance with the background law of the jurisdiction in which they are located. Although outright bans or mandatory provisions often drive out potential patients, supportive regulation can attract new customers, and these customers may be particularly attracted to legal regimes that simultaneously police domestic providers in that country and express support for values that may encounter a hostile reception elsewhere. The competition need not necessarily be one for laxity.

South Africa, for example, has sought to promote so-called fertility tourism as a boon to its domestic economy by capitalizing on looser regulations for access to fertility services.[35] Since the 1997 change in law permitting single women access to donated sperm,[36] South Africa has celebrated a "gaybe (as opposed to baby) revolution."[37] The term *gaybe* was coined to express South Africa's openness to gay and lesbian couples from abroad, who may be barred from such services in their local jurisdictions.[38] "Baby-on-Safari" is now an entry in South Africa's official tourism guide, and the very visibility of South African advertising may aid those who would like to undermine discrimination against gays and lesbians in the provision of fertility services.[39]

The expression of religious values creates obvious opportunities for adventures in regulatory comparison shopping. The creation of the European Union (EU) eliminated many of the restrictions on travel and purchases within the EU.[40] Yet attitudes toward fertility techniques within the EU vary not only by religion, but in accordance with national differences in the respective roles of religious versus secular values.

Italy provides a dramatic case in point. Italian fertility services once followed a laissez-faire model of live and let live.[41] Partly in response to the celebrity of Italian fertility specialists, who produced a pregnancy in a sixty-three-year-old woman and joined in controversial cloning efforts, and partly in response to pressure from the Vatican, Italy adopted the most restrictive fertility regulations in Europe.[42] Although the vast majority of Italians might have agreed to ban reproductive cloning and overage pregnancies, the Vatican-dictated 2004 law restricted fertility services to married couples with proven infertility, outlawed gamete donation and surrogacy, and curtailed freezing and screening of embryos in accordance with Roman Catholic religious beliefs that treat human life as sacred starting with the joinder of sperm and egg.[43] The result not only restricts access for single women, lesbians, and other unmarried couples, but it also reduces the effectiveness of the available services because of the requirement that all embryos be implanted.[44] Prospective patients who do not share the religious beliefs underlying the law may find more compatible regimes abroad, and clinics in Spain, Austria, and Switzerland quickly reported a 20 percent increase in Italian patients.[45] Additionally, Italian doctors frustrated by the legislation have declared intentions to set up fertility treatment clinics right outside the border to take advantage of less stringent regulations in neighboring countries.[46] Although many may agree with the effort to curb the so-called wild west atmosphere of Italian fertility services before the law, the net effect may be to encourage international comparison shopping for efficacy and price as well as a different brand of ethics.[47] Once fertility tourism takes hold, opt-in values may be become more effective than top–down restrictions in the creation of shared norms.

C. STATE SUBSIDIZATION: BUYING LOYALTY OR ACQUIESCENCE?

The background for fertility services in Europe, Australia, and Israel is often generous state subsidization of medical care. By the late 1980s, Belinda Bennett reports that the estimated cost of "IVF for 5000 infertile couples in Australia was $A30 million: $A17 million paid by the Federal Government, $A6 million by patients, and $A7 million by health insurance funds."[48] Unlike the United States, where such funding overwhelmingly comes from patient payments or insurance, or the United Kingdom, where funding has been cut, the Australians recognize "that infertility is a serious disability and that the alleviation of its effects by the various forms of reproductive technology should be supported by public health care resources in the same way as other medical (surgical, hormonal, etc.) treatment for infertility."[49] As a result, Australians may be more reluctant to travel abroad for services unavailable on terms of their choosing at home.

Although state subsidization clearly makes it easier to secure compliance with official norms, the coexistence of public and private networks can have a complex interaction in the creation of norms. The out-of-control character of Italian fertility services, for example, dates back to an administrative regulation issued in 1985 that required public hospitals to only perform fertility procedures that involve the sperm and egg of married couples.[50] The regulation spurred the creation of private clinics, which supplied most of Italy's fertility procedures.[51] These private clinics, in turn, were more financially dependent than state hospitals on their ability to secure paying patients. Mary Canoles observes,

> Since private clinics receive no government funding, there has been no legal limit to what private clinics can accomplish. Such policies have allowed older women, who are no longer theoretically capable of conceiving, to have children with the assistance of private clinics.[52]

The freewheeling doctors who helped women over the age of sixty to conceive and give birth to healthy children prompted the later crackdown, but only after large portions of the Italian public got used to the idea that they could seek out and pay for the services of their choice.[53] Allowing public hospitals to provide sufficient services to undercut the market for alternatives might have done more to encourage public acceptance than the seesaw nature of Italian regulation.

In contrast with Italy, the United Kingdom has been a pioneer in the provision of fertility services through the combination of careful oversight, which has instilled public confidence in the procedures, and integration into the more general provision of state-subsidized medical care. The Human Fertilisation and Embryology Authority, which licenses all British fertility clinics,[54] reports that

> over the last 14 years the UK has become a world leader in fertility treatment and research. We are proud of the huge advances which have helped people to create the families they wish for and help the treatment of serious disease.

Much of this owes to the fact that public confidence in the checks and controls on the sector has allowed the researchers and health professionals to take their work forward.[55]

Public confidence, however, may also reflect the fact that British law provides for one free in vitro fertilization cycle, encouraging the British public to at least start with domestic clinics that are licensed by the authority.[56] It is only when treatment is unavailable that British citizens are tempted to endure the hazards of seeking treatment abroad.[57] They are increasingly finding, however, that Eastern European countries offer fertility services with equal success rates, less stringent regulation, and lower prices than their western European counterparts.[58] From a single cycle of IVF treatment, Slovenian clinics produced a 36 percent chance of pregnancy, compared with 31.9 percent in Hungary and 28.4 percent in Britain.[59] Yet the cost of treatment in Britain (between $3,630 and $7,260)[60] is, on average, double that in Hungary and Slovenia.[61] Funding restrictions may threaten the careful ethical balance British authorities have tried to strike as people look farther afield.[62]

State subsidization, however, if it is generous enough, may also generate countervailing pressures to soften harsh restrictions. Kelly Weisberg tells the fascinating story of Israel's approval of the first legislation anywhere in the world approving surrogacy in the face of mounting public demands to assist infertile couples.[63] Critical to the Israeli story is the most generous system of state-subsidized fertility services anywhere in the world. The government provides universal health care, and all Israeli women, irrespective of religion or marital status, may receive free unlimited access to in vitro fertilization up to the birth of two live children.[64] In a society in which the pressures to reproduce are enormous, Israeli doctors are at the forefront of fertilization techniques, and Israel has the highest per capita concentration of IVF clinics in the world.[65] Israeli women, facing an Israeli ban on surrogacy enacted in the aftermath of *Baby M*,[66] began to seek services in California, but the costs, which could run as high as one hundred thousand dollars, were prohibitive for all but the wealthiest Israelis.[67] Couples began to lobby to at least have the in vitro fertilization performed in state-subsidized Israeli facilities, and the Knesset, under pressure from the Israeli High Court,[68] eventually passed surrogacy legislation that satisfied the rabbinical authorities. After difficulties with the initial cases, regulators supplemented the legislation with procedures that better protected surrogates.[69] The net effect was a public discussion that ultimately limited surrogacy to cases in which the intended father provided the sperm and the surrogate was not genetically related to the child and regulated provisions for payment to limit the potential for exploitation. The values debate, however, and the resulting compromises, could only occur because of the need to operate within the ambit of state-subsidized services.

D. THE CREATION OF TRUST: ARMS-LENGTH DEALS OR COMMUNITY FORMATION?

The final factor that helps shape broader normative understandings is trust. Trust is increasingly seen as an important element of market function. Economists have demonstrated that interpersonal trust has a considerable effect on economic growth as it affects the transaction costs associated with investment. Stephen Knack and Paul Zak observe, "If trust is sufficiently low, so little investment will be undertaken that economic growth is unachievable, resulting in a low-trust poverty trap."[70] Interpersonal trust can be a powerful economic stimulant: a 15 percent increase in the proportion of people who report that others in their country are trustworthy raises per capita output growth by 1 percent for every year thereafter.[71] Moreover, income gains further enhance interpersonal trust in a virtuous circle that helps facilitate market transactions.[72]

The process of establishing norms can help build circumstances of trust.[73] Particularly with respect to a new technology or new practices, norms may take a while to establish.[74] Creating trust requires a measure of predictability[75]; that predictability may be difficult if attitudes are changing or if customs have yet to be established.

Donation of sperm easily creates grounds for mistrust, especially if the accompanying laws or norms are in flux. With the first cases of sperm donation, legal paternity was an uncertain matter. A husband who consented to his wife's use of sperm to circumvent his infertility might find that he was not the legal father of the child he raised.[76] Conversely, a sperm donor with no intention of playing a parental role might find himself subject to a suit for child support or subject to a knock on the door from a child looking for a father to play a role in his life.[77] Anonymity could shield both – creating a greater level of confidence between donor and recipient that their intent to sever the donor's parental status will be honored.[78] Laws clearly terminating the donor's parental status could also create such confidence.[79] The greater the participants' ability to secure enforcement of their understandings, the greater their confidence in newly established norms and agreements.

Trust can also be established through personal relationships and the identification of others with shared values. Rainbow Flag Health Services, a "Known Donor Sperm Bank" in Alameda, California, built on the provisions of California law permitting donors to sever their parental standing to establish a sperm bank expressly catering to clients who share its commitment to core ethical principles.[80] Its Web site contains a lengthy statement of philosophy, which begins,

> Rainbow Flag Health Services' founding goal is building a stronger Lesbian & Gay community by assisting Lesbians and Gay Men to bring children into their families. Toward this end we are guided by two principles, respect for all the parties involved and truthfulness toward those children born of our endeavors.[81]

The sperm bank seeks to establish the principle of identity disclosure, in this case, when the child turns three months old, by recruiting donors and recipients committed to the practice. Lesbians, to a greater extent than other fertility patients, may prefer a known donor. An infertile heterosexual couple may have the option of leading the child to believe that he or she is the biological offspring of the adults who raised him. Lesbian parents often find that the child begins to wonder who her father is by the age of three, and they do not have the option of suggesting that two women produced the baby on their own. Instead, Rainbow Flag emphasizes, "Your child will grow up without secrets. They will not grow up fantasizing that their 'father' is the lost King of Bavaria or Charles Manson. Your child will know that their donor is a regular guy who they will meet and maybe become friends with."[82]

Rainbow Flag Health Services effectively uses the Internet to create a private niche for those who share its philosophy. It tailors its message and its services to meet the special needs of the gay and lesbian community.[83] It does not pay sperm donors, except for expenses, and emphasizes that the child will know that the donor contributed sperm because he wanted to bring a child into the world, and that "his motivation was [*not*] the $50 per visit most sperm banks pay donors."[84] Rainbow Flag effectively acts as a yenta, screening potential applications and matching donors and recipients who want to create a child.

Leland Traiman, Rainbow Flag's director, emphasized in an ART symposium at the University of Iowa that his clients' confidence in his service was justified, however, only because of the background law in California. The Web site states,

> We operate under California law [California Family Code Section 7613(b)] which legally separates Donor and Mother. Clients from outside of California are still covered by this law under the full faith and credit clause of the United States Constitution. We hold a [tissue banking license] from the State of California as well as [laboratory licenses] from the Federal Government (CLIA) and the State of California.[85]

The California Family Code provision to which the Web site refers severs the parental status of the donor when the parties use a physician to perform the insemination.[86] This ensures that the donor will not be able to claim a legal father's right to visitation or custody. The Web site also refers to the organization's federal and state licenses as seals of approval, certifying its reputability.[87]

Rainbow Flag Health Services seeks to facilitate the identification of those who share their philosophy, rather than to change social norms. The process, however, is one that creates mutual trust based on the ability to solidify understandings about the donor's and recipient's respective roles.[88] This way, the donor can participate in the child's life without raising the legal parent's fear that the donor will try to claim parental standing inconsistent with their agreement.

E. CONCLUSION: THE AUSTRALIAN EXPERIMENT

The Australian experience in attempting to mandate disclosure of sperm donor identity in the context of a subsidized system that bans donor payment provides a case study in the effort to lock in new norms.[89] Ethical guidelines by the National Health and Medical Research Council,[90] Section 6.1, adopted in November 2004, provided that

> persons conceived using ART are entitled to know their genetic parents. Clinics must not use donated gametes in reproductive procedures unless the donor has consented to the release of identifying information about himself or herself to the persons conceived using his or her gametes. Clinics must not mix gametes in a way that confuses the genetic parentage of the persons who are born.[91]

The immediate effect was to aggravate the country's existing shortage of donor sperm. The Albury clinic near Sydney responded by proposing a seven-thousand dollar package that included airfare, accommodations, and per diem expenses.[92]

The donor must spend two weeks in Australia, donating sperm every other day. The National Health and Medical Research Council conducted a six-month investigation into the practice and concluded that the clinic's proposal involved expenses, not payment, and therefore did not violate the Prohibition of Human Cloning Act or the human tissues acts.[93]

As of our last inquiry, no Canadians had arrived at the clinic in Australia.[94] The larger issue, however is whether any of the Australian initiatives will help reverse the declining donations – and stem the long-term prospects of encouraging circumvention of the state system and its ethical norms. What the Canadians' recruitment represents, with the specific approval of the payment of expenses in the face of a ban on more direct compensation, is an effort to create acceptance of the new principle of donor identity disclosure in the context of Australian fertility services. Does it have any hope of success?

The scale may not be large enough to solve the problem entirely, but the approach reflects the analysis we have articulated.[95] The prohibition of payment invites creation of either an underground market, perhaps involving freeze-dried shipping; local networks of private donors who stay away from public clinics[96]; or fertility tourism to jurisdictions offering a better mix of services.[97] Limiting these developments, however, are several countervailing considerations. First, unlike Italy, Australia does not seem to have private clinics that can readily move abroad, and unlike Sweden, it is not adjacent to another country offering easily accessible comparable services. Instead, Australians have relatively more attachment to their health services because of the level of subsidization and may be more likely to travel to neighboring states or seek assistance from private networks than to go to another country.[98]

Within this context, recruitment from Canada – in addition to alleviating shortages – could promote the creation of trust. Martha Ertman observes that in the United States, "technological innovations (such as medical testing, the world wide web, overnight delivery services, and liquid nitrogen to preserve frozen sperm) have facilitated a large, national market, in which geographic and social distance between donors and recipients provide further anonymity."[99] A major advantage of Canadian sperm donors is distance. Even if the child ultimately learns of the donor's identity, he is less likely to seek an ongoing relationship with someone half a world away. Furthermore, the risk of changing laws, accidental discovery, or incest between siblings unaware of their ancestry diminishes with distance. Ertman's insights, although they suggest a broader ambit for the growth of anonymous donations in the United States, explain much of the appeal of the Albury efforts, as well.

The final issue is whether the Australian efforts have the potential to change Australian preferences, that is, to build acceptance of a principle of disclosure into fertility practices. The ethical guidelines suggest that clinics "should help potential gamete donors to understand and accept the significance of the biological connection that they have with the persons conceived using their gametes"[100]; that is, the clinics should conduct a public education campaign designed to build support for the new principles and ensure the consent of those directly involved.

The success of these efforts, however noble the ethical principle at the core, is likely to rest on the success of the Australians in building a *market*, not a charity. The offer of an Australian holiday, rather than the commitment to altruistic provision, may succeed in bringing donors from abroad. If the numbers become large enough or sufficient alternative sources become available, Australia will reverse the fertility tourism at play in other places. It will have brought the tourists to donate, rather than to receive, and to help establish, rather than circumvent, its ethical restrictions. Only by relaxing its anticommodification principle can Australia succeed in winning acceptance of the competing principle of identity disclosure.[101]

NOTES

1 Jeffrey M. Shaman, *Legal Aspects of Artificial Insemination*, 18 J. FAM. L. 331 n.1 (1980) (citing W. FINGOLD, ARTIFICIAL INSEMINATION 6 [1964], crediting the English surgeon John Hunter with performing artificial insemination in humans as early as 1790).

2 June Carbone, *Toward a More Communitarian Future? Fukuyama as the Fundamentalist Secular Humanist*, 101 MICH. L. REV. (2003) (reviewing FRANCIS FUKUYAMA, OUR POSTHUMAN FUTURE: CONSEQUENCES OF THE BIOTECHNOLOGY REVOLUTION [2002]). For a comprehensive examination of fertility tourism, *see* Richard Storrow, *Quests for Conception: Fertility Tourists, Globalization, and Feminist Legal Theory*, 57 HASTINGS L.J. 295 (2005).

3 *See, e.g.*, JUNE CARBONE, FROM PARTNERS TO PARENTS: THE SECOND REVOLUTION IN FAMILY LAW (2000) (arguing that family obligation has shifted from a system based on marriage and legitimacy to one based on regulation of the parent–child relationship).

4 For a review of these issues in the context of surrogacy, where Australia also bans payment, *see* Anita Stuhmcke, *Looking Backwards, Looking Forwards: Judicial and Legislative Trends in the Regulation of Surrogate Motherhood in the UK and Australia*, 18 AUSTL. J. FAM. L. 13 (2004).

5 KELLY D. WEISBERG, THE BIRTH OF SURROGACY IN ISRAEL (2005).

6 *Id.* at 263, n.45.

7 For debate on the principle of disclosure of sperm donor identity, *see* K. R. Daniels & P. Thorn, *Sharing Information with Donor Insemination Offspring: A Child-Conception versus a Family-Building Approach*, 16 HUM. REPROD. 1792 (2001). Lucy Frith, *Gamete Donation and Anonymity: The Ethical and Legal Debate*, 16 HUM. REPROD. 818 (2001). Glen McGee *et al.*, *Disclosure to Children Conceived with Donor Gametes Should Not Be Optional*, 16 HUM. REPROD. 2033 (2001). A. McWhinnie, *Gamete Donation and Anonymity: Should Offspring from Donated Gametes Continue to Be Denied Knowledge of Their Origins and Antecedents?* 16 HUM. REPROD. 807 (2001). Pasquale Patrizio *et al.*, *Disclosure to Children Conceived with Donor Gametes Should Be Optional*, 16 HUM. REPROD. 2036 (2001).

8 *See* Gaia Bernstein, *The Socio-legal Acceptance of New Technologies: A Close Look at Artificial Insemination*, 77 WASH. L. REV. 1035, 1057, 1072, 1081 (2002).

9 *Id.* at 1093 (doctors advised patients to keep the process secret for the benefit of the child); Mary Lyndon Shanley, *Collaboration and Commodification in Assisted Procreation: Reflections on an Open Market and Anonymous Donation in Human Sperm and Eggs*, 36 LAW & SOC'Y REV. 257, 266 (2002).

10 *Id.* at 266.

11 *Id.* at 268.

12 BBC News, *Call to End Sperm Donor Anonymity*, http://news.bbc.co.uk/1/hi/health/2065329.stm (poll shows that 83% believe medical and health records of sperm donors should be disclosed).

13 BBC News, Poor Couples Want IVF Anonymity, http://news.bbc.co.uk/1/hi/health/4205661.stm (referring to a Dutch study indicating that forty of the sixty-four heterosexual couples chose an identifiable donor, while forty of the forty-one lesbian couples did).

14 Gordana Kovacek Stanic, *The Significance of Biological Parentage in Yugoslav Family Law*, 31 Cal. W. Int'l L.J. 101, 111 (2000) (describing disclosure rules in Spain, Britain, and Victoria).

15 BBC News, *Sperm Donor Anonymity Ends*, http://news.bbc.co.uk/1/hi/health/4397249.stm (noting a new British law to take effect and predicting shortage of sperm as a result). In the United States, although most sperm banks provide anonymity, some voluntarily supply identifying information. *See* Marta M. Ertman, *What's Wrong with a Parenthood Market? A New and Improved Theory of Commodification*, 82 N.C. L. Rev. 1, 20 n.82 (2003).

16 *See* Helen Szoke, *Australia – A Federated Structure of Statutory Regulation of ART, in* The Regulation of Assisted Reproductive Technology 78 (2003).

17 State law governs Australian fertility treatments, and a variety of state laws have banned payment for more than twenty years, which has limited efforts to increase supply. *See* N.S.W. Stat. 164 § 32 (1983); N.S.W. Stat. 164 § 38 (1983); Vict. Acts 10163 § 13(7) (1984); Vict. Acts No. 63 § 57 (1995); *see also Reproductive Technology Code of Ethical Clinical Practice*, 1995 (S. Austl.); Stacy Fara, *Sydney Sperm Shortage*, Sydney Star Observer, Dec. 11, 2003. Intended Parents Inc., http://www.intendedparents.com/News/Sydney_sperm_shortage.html (waiting list of six months for anonymous donor sperm).

18 National Health & Medical Research Council, *Ethical Guidelines on the Use of Assisted Reproductive Technology in Clinical Practice and Research*, 16–17, § 6.1 ("Uphold the Right to Knowledge of Genetic Parents and Siblings") (Sept. 2004), http://www.nhmrc.gov.au/publications/_files/e56.pdf.

19 *IVF Clinic Still Favors Aussie Sperm*, National Nine News, July 10, 2004, http://news.ninemsn.com.au/article.aspx?id=12199. *See also Where Are the Children's Rights in Holiday Deals for Sperm Donors?* Australian Children's Rights News, Issue 36 (Dec. 2003) at 30, http://www.dci-au.org/acrn/ACRNDecember2003.pdf (reporting that the Albury clinic advertised in the sports section of Calgary University's student newspaper, offering a seven-thousand dollar package that included airfare, accommodations, and per diem).

20 Marc Bygdeman, *Swedish Law Concerning Insemination*, Ippf Med. Bulletin, at 3 (Oct. 1989) (discussing the decline in both the number of donors and the number of couples choosing artificial insemination by donor [AID] treatment following the enactment of the mandatory disclosure law). *See also* Linda Nielson, *Legal Consensus and Divergence in Europe in the Area of Assisted Conception – Room for Harmonization? in* Creating the Child 305, 306–8 (1996). *See also* Matthew Hill, *Sperm Donors Want to Keep Anonymity*, BBC News, Oct. 15, 2002, http://news.bbc.co.uk/1/hi/health/2329675.stm.

21 Hill, *supra* note 20.

22 For a discussion of the relationship between law and norms more generally, *see* Lawrence Lessig, *The Regulation of Social Meaning*, 62 U. Chi. L. Rev. 943, 956–8 (1995) (observing that "social meaning" provides "a semiotic resource" that members of a society or subculture can use to induce others to behave in a certain way); Eric A. Posner, *Law,*

Economics, and Inefficient Norms, 144 U. PA. L. REV. 1697, 1699–1701 (1996) (defining a "norm" as "a rule that distinguishes desirable and undesirable behavior and gives a third party the authority to punish a person who engages in the undesirable behavior"); Cass R. Sunstein, *Social Norms and Social Roles*, 96 COLUM. L. REV. 903, 914 (1996) (defining norms as "social attitudes of approval and disapproval, specifying what ought to be done and what ought not to be done"). For a representative sample of social norms scholarship, *see Symposium: Law, Economics, and Norms*, 144 U. PA. L. REV. 1643 (1996); *see also* Lawrence Lessig, *The New Chicago School*, 27 J. LEGAL STUD. 661 (1998) (*hereinafter* Lessig, *The New Chicago School*) (outlining "old" and "new" schools of law and economics and explaining the emphasis of the new school on norms).

23 Sunstein, *supra* note 22, at 912.

24 *Id.*

25 Michael Finkel, *Complications*, N.Y. TIMES MAG., May 27, 2001, at 26 (the Human Tissues Act of 1961 outlawed organ donor sales in Great Britain).

26 Nancy Scheper-Hughes, *The Global Trade in Human Organs*, 41 CURRENT ANTHROPOLOGY 191 (2000); Shelby E. Robinson, *Organs for Sale? An Analysis of Proposed Systems for Compensating Organ Providers*, 70 U. COLO. L. REV. 1019 (1999) (stating that tens of thousands of Americans are on waiting lists). *See also* Human Tissues Act of 1961 (outlawing organ sales). In the United States, the National Organ Transplant Act, 42 U.S.C.A. §§ 273, 274(e) (1991) (banning payment).

27 BBC News, *Patients Warned over Buying Organs*, http://news.bbc.co.uk/1/hi/health/2275807.stm.

28 Finkel, *supra* note 25, at 26.

29 Scheper-Hughes, *supra* note 26, at 191.

30 *Id.*; *see also* Nancy Scheper-Hughes, *The End of the Body: The Global Traffic in Organs for Transplant Surgery*, http://sunsite.berkeley.edu/biotech/organswatch/pages/cadraft.html.

31 *See* Scheper-Hughes, *supra* note 30.

32 For a comprehensive discussion of these issues, *see* MICHELE GOODWIN, BLACK MARKETS: THE SUPPLY AND DEMAND OF BODY PARTS (2006).

33 Aurhus, Denmark, is home to the largest sperm bank in the world, shipping frozen sperm to more than forty different countries around the globe as diverse as Spain, Kenya, Paraguay, and Hong Kong. Cryos, the sperm bank set up in 1987, reported trading both in bulk orders to countries such as Britain, supplementing waning domestic supplies, and to individual clientele in such disparate countries as Israel, Ghana, and the United Arab Emirates. Cryos is not just taking advantage of the low restrictions in Denmark, which, unlike many countries, permits payments; it has utilized the freedom afforded by loose regulation domestically to supply an international market with tighter restrictions. CryoBank, another sperm bank, set up an affiliate dissemination center in New York City in December 2003, capitalizing on the market for donated Scandinavian sperm.

34 *See* Alvin K. Klevorick, *The Race to the Bottom in a Federal System: Lessons from the World of Trade Policy*, 14 YALE J. REG. 177 (1996).

35 Barbara Cole, *Come to SA – and Go Home Pregnant*, PRETORIA NEWS, May 10, 2004, http://www.iol.co.za/index.php?set_id=1&click_id=13&art_id=vn20040510050511176C495920#jump.

36 *Id.*

37 *Id.*

38 *Id.*

39 For a more general discussion of the use of jurisdiction shopping to create gay- and lesbian-friendly services and environments, *see* Jennifer Gerarda, *Competitive*

Federalism and the Legislative Incentives to Recognize Same-Sex Marriage, 68 S. Cal. L. Rev. 745 (1995).

40 *European Union Enlargement Could Lead to Fertility Tourism from West to East*, Medical News Today, July 1, 2004, http://www.medicalnewstoday.com/medicalnews.php?newsid=10145 (reviewing the report put out in June 2004 by the European Society for Human Reproduction and Embryology).

41 Rosario M. Isasi *et al.*, *Legal and Ethical Approaches to Stem Cell and Cloning Research: A Comparative Analysis of Policies in Latin America, Asia, and Africa*, 32 J.L. Med. & Ethics 626, 632 (2004) (explaining that after decades of enjoying a laissez-faire model, the Assisted Reproductive Technology [ART] law was passed in Italy, shifting the model to one of the most prohibitive or conservative regulatory approaches in place in the world. The ART law prohibits embryo research, embryo cryopreservation [freezing], and gamete donation. It also restricts access to fertility treatments to "stable heterosexual couples who live together and are of childbearing age"); *see* Italy Medical Assisted Procreation Law, no. 40 (2004).

42 *Id.*; *see also* BBC News, *Italian Fertility Treatment Curbed*, http://news.bbc.co.uk/1/hi/world/europe/3545421.stm.

43 Isasi *et al.*, *supra* note 41.

44 Tamsin Smith, BBC News, *Fertility Laws Frustrate Italians*, http://news.bbc.co.uk/1/hi/world/europe/3548242.stm (reporting a drop in the success rate from one in four to one in nine).

45 *Id.*

46 *Supra* note 42.

47 Smith, *supra* note 44.

48 Belinda Bennett, *Resource Allocation and the Beginning of Life*, 9 J. Contemp. Health L. & Pol'y 77, 81–2 (1993).

49 *Id.* at 84 (citing National Bioethics Consultative Committee, *Access to Reproductive Technology: Final Report for the Australian Health Ministers' Conference* 40 [March 1991]) (background paper for Australia Health Ethics Committee).

50 Mary E. Canoles, *Italy's Family Values: Embracing the Evolution of Family to Save the Population*, 21 Penn St. Int'l L. Rev. 183, 193–4 (2002).

51 *Id.*

52 *Id.* at 194.

53 *See more generally* Richard Storrow, *Quests for Conception: Fertility Tourists, Globalization, and Feminist Legal Theory*, 57 Hastings L.J. 295, 306 (2005) ("Under the Medically Assisted Reproduction Law, infertility services have been sweepingly curtailed. The new law bans sperm and egg donation, embryo freezing, and surrogate motherhood and severely limits the number and type of fertility services available to 'stable' heterosexual couples").

54 Debora Spar, *Reproductive Tourism and the Regulatory Map*, 352 New Eng. J. Med. 533 (2005).

55 Human Fertilization and Embryology Authority, *HFEA Statement Following the House of Commons Science and Technology Select Committee Report*, http://www.hfea.gov.uk/cps/rde/xchg/SID-3F57D79B-D21A4D0D/hfea/hs.xsl/1070.html.

56 Spar, *supra* note 54, at 533.

57 In the United Kingdom, the government funds only about one-fourth of otherwise eligible fertility procedures. Funding availability varies regionally, and long waiting lists are common. *See* HFEA Directory of Clinics, *Your Guide to Infertility* 19 (2003–4), http://www.hfea.gov.uk/HFEAPublications/YourGuidetoInfertility/DoC%20text%20version%20%28for%20website%29.pdf.

58 *Id.*
59 Caroline Ryan, *EU Faces Fertility Tourism Threat*, http://news.bbc.co.uk/1/hi/health/3853237.stm.
60 MSNBC News, *Fertility Tourism May Be Next European Boom*, http://msnbc.msn.com/id/5334082.
61 *Id.*
62 *Demand Is Rising for Scandinavian Babies*, NATIONAL VANGUARD, June 6, 2005, http://www.nationalvanguard.org/story.php?id=5210.
63 Weisberg, *supra* note 5.
64 *Id.* at 182.
65 *Id.* at 189.
66 *Id.* at 38.
67 In the late 1980s, at a time when the average gross monthly salary in Israeli was less than two thousand dollars, surrogacy fees in the United States were forty thousand dollars for a case without medical complications and without including the potentially substantial travel costs. *Id.* at 57.
68 *Id.* at 127. *See* Zabaro v. Minister of Health, H.C.J. 5087/94 (filed Sept. 18, 1994) (invalidating the surrogacy ban and giving the government five and a half months to enact new legislation).
69 *Id.* at 30–1. They require the contract to specify the number of attempts (no more than seven), the maximum period for those attempts (no more than eighteen months), and the number of embryos the surrogate is willing to carry. They also provide for psychological counseling at the commissioning couple's expense and for payment into an escrow account that separates the parties from direct contact over the financial terms.
70 Stephen Knack & Paul J. Zak, *Building Trust: Public Policy, Interpersonal Trust, and Economic Development*, 10 S. CT. ECON. REV. 91, 92 (2002).
71 *Id.*
72 *Id.*
73 Francis Fukuyama, *Differing Disciplinary Perspectives on the Origins of Trust*, 81 B.U. L. REV. 479, 480 (2001) (trust appears only after norms are established).
74 *See, e.g.*, Judith F. Daar, *The Future of Human Cloning: Prescient Lessons from Medical Ethics Past*, 8 S. CAL. INTERDISC. L.J. 167, 171 (1998) (discussing historic rejection of artificial insemination by donor because of potential emotional dangers to sperm donor, child, and husband).
75 Fukuyama, *supra* note 73, at 485–6 (repeat transactions help build trust).
76 Bernstein, *supra* note 8, at 1056–8, 1069–70 (discussing uncertainty about legal paternity).
77 For cases affirming the parental status of sperm donors who wanted visitation, *see* Thomas S. v. Robin Y., 209 A.D.2d 298, 306–7 (Sup. Ct. 1994); C.M. v. C.C., 377 A.2d 821 (N.J. Juv. & Dom. Rel. Ct. 1977); Welborn v. Doe, 394 S.E.2d 732 (Va. Ct. App. 1990).
78 *See, e.g.*, Ertman, *supra* note 15, at 18 (the provision by banks of both contractual and practical donor anonymity to protect the integrity of the new family that the recipient intends to create is a "social safeguard"); *see also* Nancy D. Polikoff, *Raising Children: Lesbian and Gay Parents Face the Public and the Courts*, *in* CREATING CHANGE: SEXUALITY, PUBLIC POLICY, AND CIVIL RIGHTS, 305, 325–6 (John D'Emilio *et al.* eds., 2000); Ellen Lewin, *Wives, Mothers, and Lesbians: Rethinking Resistance in the U.S.*, *in* PRAGMATIC WOMEN AND BODY POLITICS, 164, 168–70 (Margaret Lock & Patricia A. Kaufer eds., 1998) (describing four lesbians' alternative insemination strategies, all of which involved assuring donor anonymity to protect their new families).

79 Bernstein, *supra* note 8, at 1084 (noting that laws passed in the 1960s permitting sperm donors to terminate their parental status helped win acceptance of the procedure).
80 Cal. Family Code § 7613 (1994).
81 Rainbow Flag Health Services, http://www.gayspermbank.com/index.html.
82 *Id.* The Web site cites the Code of Practice of the Human Fertilisation and Embryology Authority of Great Britain to argue that Rainbow Flag Health Services believes in truthfulness to the child about the "child's potential need to know about his or her origins and whether the prospective parents are prepared for the questions which may arise while the child is growing up."
83 *Id.*
84 *Id.*
85 *Id.*
86 *Supra* note 80.
87 Rainbow Flag Health Services, *supra* note 81.
88 Other sperm banks also try to create trust through extensive screening for the qualities clients value. *See* Ertman, *supra* note 15, at 18–19.
89 *See Reproductive Technology Code of Ethical Clinical Practice, 1995* (S. Austl.), http://www.nhmrc.gov.au/publications/synopses/e56syn.htm. The Australian laws also require licensure, screening, and reporting.
90 National Health & Medical Research Council, *supra* note 18, at 16–17, § 6.1 (proclaiming, "Uphold the Right to Knowledge of Genetic Parents and Siblings").
91 *Id.*
92 *Where Are the Children's Rights, supra* note 19.
93 *IVF Clinic Still Favors Aussie Sperm, supra* note 19.
94 *See id.* (emphasizing preference for Australian donors).
95 National Health & Medical Research Council, *supra* note 18 (summarizing the Prohibition of Human Cloning Act 2002, Pt. 2, Div. 2, Sec. 23 § 6.3) (declaring, "Limit the Number of Persons Born from a Single Donor"). The supply of overseas sperm may potentially be quite large, but the Albury clinic by itself is likely to remain small scale, and the new ethics guidelines limit the number of sperm from each donor.
96 Carol Nader, *Laughing all the Way to the Bank, but It's Black Humour*, Age, April 26, 2006, http://www.theage.com.au/news/national/last-man-standing/2006/04/25/1145861348250.html.
97 Ertman, *supra* note 15, at 14–20. Victorian women, who must be married to avail themselves of services there, already travel to New South Wales to take advantage of the more liberal state regulations of that state. Of the eighty-five women treated at the Albury Clinic in New South Wales in 2004–5, thirty-eight were lesbians, thirty-six were single, and eleven were married; seventy-five were from Victoria.
98 Bennett, *supra* note 48.
99 Ertman, *supra* note 15, at 19–20.
100 Ethical Guidelines, *supra* note 18, at 16, § 6.1.1.
101 For a more general discussion of commodification, *see* Ertman, *supra* note 15.

PART FOUR. THE ETHICS OF BABY AND EMBRYO MARKETS

> The Brave New World no longer is just fiction. A grandmother in South Africa gives birth to her own grandchildren. An Australian judge orders that two frozen embryos "orphaned" when their millionaire parents are killed in a plane crash must be thawed and brought to term if a surrogate mother can be found. In the U.S., a daughter plans to become pregnant, have an abortion and donate the fetal tissue to save her ailing father's life.
>
> – Stephen Budiansky *et al.*, U.S. News & World Rep., April 18, 1988

In Part Four, authors expand the discourse on baby markets to embryo and stem cell selling. They unpack contemporary debates on the topic, revealing the gaps in congressional and state discourses. They expose the irony in a legal system that ignores and refuses to regulate assisted reproductive technology, and yet is hostage to special interest groups on the issue of stem cell research and technology. These chapters challenge us to think about the appropriate legal response to stem cell usage. More important, they remind us of the unique role the contributor – the embryo maker – plays in these public discourses and whether she should be paid for her services.

15 Egg Donation for Research and Reproduction: The Compensation Conundrum

NANETTE R. ELSTER

Nobel Prize winner George Bernard Shaw was quite prophetic when he wrote, "Science... never solves a problem without creating ten more." The development of assisted reproductive technologies (ARTs) and the subsequent emergence of embryonic stem cell therapy (EST) have illustrated the multitude of questions raised by technological advancement.

This chapter will focus on the dilemmas raised by payment for oocytes extracted from one woman either to assist another individual or couple build their family through ART or to assist researchers in pursuit of the promises of EST. Section A will provide a brief overview of egg donation. Section B will provide a brief overview of EST and how donated oocytes may become integral in stem cell research. Section C will examine the issue of payment to or compensation of donors of oocytes in both the reproductive and the research contexts and why the issue of payment for the same physical act seems so divisive depending on the ultimate purpose for which the oocytes will be used. Finally, the chapter will conclude with a discussion of autonomy and paternalism and the need to reconcile these positions to ensure that the benefits and ART and EST are both maximized and the harms are minimized to women and society overall.

A. A BRIEF OVERVIEW OF EGG DONATION

Aging in women impacts the quality of their eggs and thus their fertility and ability to conceive a child. In 1984, however, all that changed with the first successful egg donation, in which a younger woman's eggs were extracted from her body and fertilized in vitro with the sperm of the husband of the older woman, resulting in the creation of an embryo that was successfully transferred to the older woman's uterus for gestation. In 2006, the most recent year for which data are available, nearly 17,000 ART cycles were performed using donor eggs.[1] This is more than three times more cycles using donated eggs than nearly a decade ago, in 1996, when just over five thousand cycles utilized donor eggs.[2] Increased use and increased success have made egg donation commonplace in the world of ART.

Recipients of donor eggs are typically women with ovarian failure, due to early menopause, disease, or disease treatment; women whose ovaries have been removed; or women born without ovaries.[3] Donors are generally between the ages of twenty-one and thirty-four years old, healthy, and emotionally stable.[4] To determine if a donor satisfies these criteria, she is medically and psychologically screened.[5] Screening recommendations have been developed by the American Society for Reproductive Medicine, the professional society of reproductive endocrinologists, andrologists, and other reproductive medicine professionals. Additionally, the Food and Drug Administration has regulations requiring screening and subsequent testing for donors of reproductive materials.

Donors are typically recruited through newspaper advertisements. This is done either directly by the fertility center or by agencies that act as brokers between donors and intended recipients. Donors can either be anonymous to the recipient(s) or they may be known such as a friend or a family member. Additionally, donors are often compensated between three thousand and ten thousand dollars per donation attempt. It is estimated that nearly three-fourth of those donating eggs are college-aged.[6] The fact that so much recruiting is done in college newspapers and that, at times, premiums are being paid to donors who are well educated suggests, if nothing else, that those donors are educated and capable of understanding what it is they are undertaking.

The egg donation process itself involves the donor taking hormone medications, usually by injection, to stimulate her ovaries to produce multiple eggs in one cycle, mature those eggs, and ultimately release those eggs when mature.[7] The mature eggs are then retrieved under anesthesia in a minor surgical procedure, in which an ultrasound-guided probe with a needle attached is inserted into the vaginal wall to retrieve the eggs.[8] The retrieved eggs are then fertilized in a Petri dish with the sperm of the intended father or a sperm donor to create embryos. This procedure, with the exception of the combination of egg and sperm, is the same whether a woman is donating her eggs for research or for reproductive purposes.

Current guidelines regarding the medical and psychological profile of those donating eggs were developed with an eye toward the use of those eggs in reproduction, but more recently, a need has developed for egg donors to donate their eggs for research purposes, and it is unclear what qualifications are most desirable in research donors and if the same criteria are or should be applied. What is clear is that payment to donors donating for research is less acceptable than payment to donors donating for reproductive purposes, which will be discussed later. Also evident is that many donors will be needed for research, which will likely deplete the already scarce supply of donated eggs available for reproduction.

The vast number of eggs needed for such research became clear amid the scandal involving South Korean researcher Hwang Woo Suk. Hwang, using oocytes donated by his junior scientists and paid donors, published research indicating that he and his team had created patient-specific stem cells through the technique known as somatic cell nuclear transfer. The researchers' report was later retracted, and it was learned that during the course of his research, Hwang used more than two thousand eggs extracted from 129 women,[9] igniting a storm of controversy about oocyte donation for research purposes and the demand that may be placed on women in pursuit of the goals of EST research. As stem cell research continues in the United States and abroad, this controversy continues to grow.

B. A BRIEF OVERVIEW OF STEM CELL RESEARCH

Stem cells are unique among our bodies' cells in that they are not specialized and they can become many different types of body cells. In addition, stem cells are self-renewing so that large quantities can continue to be reproduced for medical purposes.[10] The hope is that by capturing this power of stem cells, researchers will be able to create specific types of tissue, such as heart, lung, and kidney tissue, which could help repair damaged organs or lead to development of alternatives for organ transplant as well as the development of treatments for conditions like spinal cord injury, Alzheimer's disease, Parkinson's disease, and juvenile diabetes. Stem cell research may also help us gain a better understanding of how cells divide and differentiate into specific types of cells and tissues and thus learn how to develop drugs and other treatments specifically targeted to a particular individual's condition.

Stem cells currently can be derived from three sources: embryos donated by individuals or couples who have undergone infertility treatment, embryos specifically created through donated egg and sperm, and embryos created through nuclear transfer.[11] Nuclear transfer involves taking DNA from one person, likely the patient, and transferring it to an enucleated donated egg, which is then coaxed into acting as if it has been fertilized.[12] Two of the ways to create ESTs involve the use of donated eggs, making them a significant component for such research.

From the very outset of stem cell research, confusion, be it intentional or actual, has existed over the distinction between reproductive cloning and therapeutic cloning, with much of the public not recognizing that there is not just a semantic discrepancy, but a significant difference in intent and outcome. Reproductive cloning involves creating a nearly genetically identical human being. Therapeutic cloning, however, involves creating embryonic stem cells that are identical to those of the person being treated so as to be able to avoid problems of rejection and to assist with identifying and developing treatments and cures.[13] Neither the purpose nor the intent of therapeutic cloning is to create a human being.

In 1998, James Thomson and his colleagues at the University of Wisconsin reported that they had derived embryonic stem cells from an embryo donated by an infertile couple who had previously undergone in vitro fertilization (IVF). The federal law in existence at that time (and currently) prohibited federal funding of "the creation of a human embryo or embryos for research purposes; or research in which a human embryo or embryos are destroyed, discarded, or knowingly subjected to risk of injury or death."[14] In 1999, however, it was determined that the National Institutes of Health (NIH) could fund research that utilized embryonic stem cells but could not fund the creation or derivation of embryonic stem cells.[15] It took until August 2000 for the NIH to issue its final guidelines titled "Research Using Human Pluripotent Stem Cells"; however, no funds were ever awarded because of a change in administration.

On August 9, 2001, in his first national address, President Bush announced his plan to allow funding for limited embryonic stem cell research. The compromise position presented by Bush is that federal funding be made available for research on approximately sixty cell lines already in existence at the time of his announcement. (To note, as of today, fewer than one-half of those stem cell lines are actually useable.[16]) President Bush's rationale for the limitation was that "the life and death decision" had already been made with respect to the existing cell lines – the embryos had already been destroyed.[17]

The Bush plan does *not* allow for the funding of research using stem cells derived from embryos previously created for IVF and no longer intended for reproductive purposes by the couple or individual, nor does it allow for the creation of embryos that would necessitate the use of donated oocytes. The issue of funding is so important because with federal funding comes accountability of researchers, widespread application and accessibility of the fruits of research, and a regulatory framework that operates to prevent potential research abuses and protect research participants.

As research regarding embryo stem cells develops, an increasing need for donated eggs has arisen or will arise. As the now retracted research in South Korea demonstrated, hundreds of eggs are currently needed to create just one stem cell line.[18] If research then becomes practice, will there be an even greater demand for women to donate their eggs? What criteria will be used to select donors for research or, eventually, for treatment of others? Will the criteria be the same or different than the criteria used for donors in the context of reproduction? Is altruism a sufficient incentive for women to undergo a medical regime of injections, blood tests, and a surgical procedure requiring anesthesia?[19] These questions have reignited the debate about how, when, why, and even more significantly, if women should be compensated for donating their eggs, whether for reproduction or for research.

To gauge the risks of oocyte donation – long term, short term, medical, and psychological – the California Institute for Regenerative Medicine contracted with the National Academy of Sciences to convene a meeting of experts to discuss the known risks, potential risks, and ways to minimize risks for oocyte donors.[20] The panel concluded that a great deal remains unknown about the potential risks to donors and that more research must be carried out to more accurately identify the risks.[21] The panel did, however, suggest that minimizing potential risks is possible and cited two ways to accomplish this goal: "The first is to identify which potential donors have particular risk factors and exclude them from the donor pool."[22] The other way to screen donors would be based on age.[23] Finally, the panel discussed that because all risks cannot be eliminated, alternative sources for oocytes should also be considered.[24]

The uncertainty of the medical risks is just one of the reasons why assessing the appropriate level of compensation, let alone the appropriateness of compensation itself, is so difficult. However, this is not vastly different than payment to research participants. Payment to research participants in clinical trials, for example, is permissible, as long as it is not coercive or an undue influence, as determined by an institutional review board.[25] The next section will examine current positions on the ethical and social acceptability of payment of women for the donation of their eggs and whether the purpose of the donation should dictate the appropriateness of compensation.

C. THE COMPENSATION CONUNDRUM

As discussed previously, concerns regarding egg donor compensation arise in the context of both donation for reproduction and for research. In the United States, compensation to egg donors donating for reproductive purposes, although often raising an ethical eyebrow, has yet to be prohibited by law. It has been argued that "the widespread use of egg donation in the United States is due to the legal and social permissibility of paying women to donate eggs."[26] The acceptability of payment to donors, however may be changing. In February 2007, House Bill 873 was introduced in Maryland. The bill allows for reimbursement of direct expenses incurred by an oocyte donor only and would make "a person who offers to compensate or compensates an individual to encourage the donation of oocytes . . . guilty of a misdemeanor and on conviction . . . subject to imprisonment not exceeding 90 days or a fine not exceeding $10,000 or both."[27]

Compensation for research, however, has garnered far more legislative attention, with a number of states introducing and/or actually enacting legislation that would prohibit any compensation but would allow for reimbursement of expenses directly incurred as a result of participation. The legislative reaction is likely in response to the 2005 "Guidelines for Human Embryonic Stem Cell Research" published by the National Academy of Sciences. One major recommendation is that

> women who undergo hormonal induction to generate oocytes specifically for research purposes . . . should be reimbursed only for direct expenses incurred as a result of the procedure, as determined by an Institutional Review Board. No cash or in kind payments should be provided for donating oocytes for research purposes.[28]

States, such as California and Connecticut, that have made state funds available for embryonic stem cell research have enacted legislation that essentially mirrors this recommendation.[29] Despite legislative enactments based on this recommendation, it is a recommendation that has received numerous commentary and criticism. In a recent prepublication copy of the 2007 amendments to the National Academy's "Guidelines for Human Embryonic Stem Cell Research," the Advisory Committee acknowledged that this is an issue that may be dealt with after future deliberation and information gathering has occurred.[30]

The international approach to compensation of egg donors differs markedly from that in the United States, and not surprisingly, the number of egg donation cycles occurring outside the United States is dramatically lower.[31] Many countries outside the United States explicitly prohibit payment to egg donors for reproductive purposes but view donation for research purposes quite differently. Just recently, the United Kingdom's Human Fertilisation and Embryology Authority granted permission to allow recruitment of egg donors participating in research.[32] The United Kingdom will now also permit women undergoing IVF for their own reproductive purposes to obtain a reduction in payment for such treatment by donating some of their retrieved eggs for research,[33] a practice raising its own ethical dilemmas and concerns about coercion and/or undue influence.

1. What Is Being Paid For?

The issue of money and eggs begs the question, what are these women actually being paid for? Are they being paid for their time, their pain and suffering, their genetic material, the number of eggs they produce, their looks, their intelligence, their ethnicity? The answers to these questions, and even posing them, cause a type of social queasiness, if you will, harkening back to the unpalatable images of the eugenics era or far into the future of a Brave New World, in which the distinction between person and product becomes blurred.

The guidelines of the American Society for Reproductive Medicine regarding donor criteria, however, do not specify physical characteristics, academic achievements, or athletic feats that might make some donors more desirable than others. While health, both physical and mental, is paramount, the importance of screening is for the donor's health and well-being, that of the recipients, and arguably, that of the potential offspring. Traits such as a high SAT score, athletic prowess, and beauty are arguably an outgrowth of the commercialization of the field of ART, or it may merely be human nature in selecting those traits for breeding that are what one finds most appealing – after all, that is little different than how one selects a mate with whom to reproduce. It is when these subjectively desirable traits, however, seem to have a monetary value placed on them that ethical dilemmas arise, at least in the context of donation for reproductive purposes.

2. Rationale for Prohibiting Payment to Egg Donors

Payment to egg donors for research or for reproduction raises a number of ethical and philosophical concerns, including the potential exploitation of women; unduly influencing those who may be financially needy; coercion of those seeking to reduce the costs of their own infertility treatment; and the potential commodification not only of the oocytes and the women who provide them, but also of the children created if women with certain traits are paid more because of those characteristics, when the donation is for reproductive purposes. The Ethics Committee of the American Society for Reproductive Medicine, cognizant of these very real concerns, issued a statement in 2000 (reviewed in 2004), in which they determined that "payments to women providing oocytes should be fair and not so substantial that they become undue inducements that will lead donors to discount risks."[34] They set the outer acceptable limits of such compensation at ten thousand dollars, finding that sums above that amount "go beyond what is appropriate."[35]

In the reproductive context, the demand for egg donors far exceeds the supply, which is one factor contributing to the concern that young women are being induced, if not enticed, to undergo the rigors of an ovarian stimulation and egg retrieval process. In part, the shortage of egg donors in the reproductive context has increased the concern that pursuing therapeutic cloning would even further increase the demand for egg donors to the point where eggs would become commodities and women would become exploited in the process because they are so lured by large dollar amounts that they do not, or cannot fully, evaluate the risks of their participation.

Whether the same type of qualifications desirable in eggs donated for reproduction are equally desirable for research is unclear, but that in itself may add fuel to the debate in that academically, economically, or socially disadvantaged women may be candidates to donate for research, but not for reproduction. This is where the questions and concerns regarding exploitation may actually lie. Beeson and Lippman assert that "biotechnology may have great potential for advancing healing, but in the context of inadequate regulation and extreme social inequality, it threatens to convert the bodies of women into instruments for use by the more privileged."[36]

In testimony on May 15, 2002, before the Subcommittee on Criminal Justice, Drug Policy, and Human Resources of the Committee on Government Reform, Judy Norsigian, executive director of the Boston Women's Health Book Collective, expressed her concern that there are many potential risks to women who donate their eggs for therapeutic cloning purposes, and none of the proposed legislation at that time provided appropriate protection for these women. In prior testimony, she lamented that a lack of data on the health effects of ovulation-inducing drugs, as well as the absence of regulation in the area of infertility services, posed potential dangers to the women donating their eggs. She stated, "While some altruistic volunteers may be willing to be egg donors, the reality is that women with limited financial resources will be the primary providers of human eggs to enterprises that offer what appear to be lucrative payments." Additionally, due to the heightened demand for donors, "it is likely that many women will become repeat donors, and that there will be a massive expansion in the use of women as paid 'egg producers.'"[37] For some, this is more acceptable in the reproductive context because the ultimate outcome is a human life, but in the research context, this is not the case. If ESTs result in effective treatments, however, the outcome may be the saving of human life.

Ms. Norsigian is not alone in her concern. An advocacy group known as Hands Off Our Ovaries has formed to limit the risks placed on women contributing to the research enterprise. In the group's manifesto, they assert that "left uncontrolled, research demands will place undue burdens on young, poor women. . . . The ends do not justify these sorts of means."[38] Their message came across loud and clear during the 2006 election season, with *Everybody Loves Raymond* actress Patricia Heaton appearing in ads campaigning against a Missouri proposal to provide state funds for stem cell research. The organization has more than three hundred signatories from around the world and asks for a moratorium on egg extraction until more information about the risks are known and a worldwide dialogue has occurred to ensure that truly informed consent can be obtained by women participating in EST by providing their eggs.[39]

More recently, the governor of California signed into law Senate Bill 1260, which prohibits "payment in excess of the amount of reimbursement of direct expenses incurred as a result of the procedure [egg removal, processing, disposal, preservation, quality control, and storage] to any subject to encourage her to produce human oocytes for the purposes of medical research."[40] The law does not seem to prohibit payment to women donating eggs to others for reproductive purposes, but can the law be interpreted as prohibiting couples or individuals utilizing donated eggs to create their embryos from donating their excess embryos for medical research?

3. Rationale in Favor of Payment to Egg Donors

"Although the physical and psychological risks entailed in oocyte donation are real, they are not so severe as to justify intervention to limit the decision-making authority of adult women."[41] The same concerns certainly have not been raised regarding payments to men for their time and effort as sperm donors, yet men do not take medication or undergo a surgical procedure, nor is their time commitment comparable to the time commitment required from women donating eggs. Women are no less able to evaluate risks and benefits than men, and to treat the two so completely opposite suggests a certain level of paternalism, if not potential discrimination. The risks to women are, without a doubt, greater than those to men, given the surgical intervention and medication regime required of the women, which sperm donors do not undergo, but the screening for women is more rigorous as well. Rather than prohibiting payment to women who choose to knowingly and voluntarily assume these risks, would it not be equally worthwhile to determine ways to reduce those risks and to ensure that women have all the information necessary to make a truly informed and voluntary choice?

The financial incentives to donate cannot be overlooked, though, especially given the uncertain risks that women may be assuming, "but it is not the sole or often central reason for donating."[42] As such, to deny women the opportunity to experience personal satisfaction, satisfy an altruistic motive, or help because of an experience of infertility with a friend or family member[43] reflects a patent disrespect for the autonomy of women. This is not to suggest that safeguards are not necessary or important to protect against potential risks to women; however, denying payment for time, effort, and inconvenience may be more punitive than protective.

University at Albany, State University of New York, philosophy professor Bonnie Steinbock, in discussing payment of donors in reproductive arrangements, argues that "if excessive payments exploit donors, so do payments that are too low. Justice would seem to require that the women who go through the rigors of egg donation be fairly compensated."[44] The aspect of commodification wherein women with subjectively more desirable traits are paid more money, however, may best be addressed by treating all egg donors similarly, compensating them for the time and effort involved in their participation, regardless of whether the donation is for research or for reproduction. If nothing else, the eugenic concerns of picking and choosing the most socially desirable genetic characteristics in a donor may be reduced. The concept of limiting payment may be one way to reach a compromise and avoid at least this one significant concern about the commercialization of reproduction.

4. Should the Purpose of the Donation Matter?

In resolving the compensation conundrum, we must consider whether the purpose of the donation matters – whether donation for research or donation for reproduction makes a difference in the acceptability of payment. Bioethicist Dan Brock thinks that "we should admire these egg donors and respect their choice to donate to help others, not seek to prevent them from doing so."[45] Given that both involve the same extraction process, it would seem that one solution might be "equal pay for equal work," and to allow payment for one and not the other has many implications. It might suggest, for example, that one is more important than the other, or it might suggest that it is acceptable to commodify women and the products of their bodies for reproduction, but not for research; it may lead to discrimination, with intelligent, beautiful, and athletic women commanding high rates for their eggs, whereas those without the same advantages will be further disadvantaged by only having the option to donate their eggs for research without compensation and only reimbursement of direct expenses. There seems to be some injustice in allowing an Ivy League student to earn tens of thousands of dollars donating her eggs to an affluent infertile couple, yet a single mom on welfare, who may be willing to donate her eggs, may only be eligible to donate for research and would thus only be reimbursed for actual expenses. This would exacerbate, rather than eliminate, the potential for exploitation of women.

5. What Is the Solution?

One solution would be no payment at all, no matter what the purpose of the donation. This, however, might limit the number of donors willing to donate to help others build their families, and it does seem a bit late to try to squeeze the genie back into the bottle. This might also further limit progress in EST research. Another solution might be to allow compensation in both contexts, but to set limits on or standardize the level of payment to reasonably reflect all that is involved in the actual process of egg donation. Most important, however, would be to ensure that women are truly informed about what it is that they are choosing to do: the purpose of their donation; the medical, psychosocial, and legal risks that might be involved in their participation, both immediately and in the future, including a description of both known and unknown considerations; and the alternatives to participation.

Informing and educating potential donors is essential no matter why they are providing their eggs to another. Efforts have been made to accomplish this. For example, in 1998, the New York State Task Force on Life and the Law developed a guidebook titled *Thinking of Becoming an Egg Donor?*,[46] and the Boston Women's Book Collective, on their *Our Bodies Ourselves* companion Web site, lists questions that any woman should ask when deciding whether she should become an egg donor.[47] The recent National Academies report "Assessing the Medical Risks of Human Ooctye Donation for Stem Cell Research" lays out the range of risks – long term, short term, medical, and psychological – and although not drafted for a lay audience per se, the information contained in the report is information to which donors should have access to be able to make truly informed and voluntary choices; additionally, such information must be continually updated as new research occurs and new information becomes available.

D. CONCLUSION

Both sides of the debate raise important considerations, yet the debate, like most, seems more focused on differences in viewpoints, rather than on similarities. Neither side can truly disagree about the number of healthy and happy families that have been built only because of what is often the kindness of strangers (i.e., egg donors) in the reproductive context, nor is it likely that there will be such vehement disagreement if and when a treatment or cure results from stem cell research. No one can disagree that women should not bear all of the burdens and risks for something that may benefit all humanity. Resolution does not have to be an all-or-nothing proposition, and any solution must carefully weigh the implications for both family building and research, and above all, women should be provided with enough information about the medical, social, and psychological risks of egg donation to make an informed choice; likewise, researchers, physicians, and mental health professionals should use every means possible to reduce these risks.

Should women not only be able to make the choice about whether to donate their eggs, but also, for what purpose? Why is it more acceptable for one to be paid to contribute to the creation of life but not to the sustaining of life? And what drives this growing distinction – politics, culture, money? The questions abound, yet the answers are not so readily available. On one hand, the questions boil down to a simple balancing of autonomy versus paternalism, but on further consideration, more seems to be at issue. Is it possible to protect women, while at the same time developing this potentially life-saving technology, and will eliminating payment to women for their time, effort, and inconvenience truly protect the interests of all women?

NOTES

1 Centers for Disease Control & Prevention, *2006 Assisted Reproductive Technology (ART) Report* (2008).
2 Centers for Disease Control & Prevention, *1996 Assisted Reproductive Technology Success Rates* (1998).
3 American Society for Reproductive Medicine, Patient Information Series, *Third Party Reproduction: A Guide for Patients* (2006).
4 Practice Committee of the American Society for Reproductive Medicine, *2006 Guidelines for Gamete and Embryo Donation*, 86 FERTILITY & STERILITY S44 (2006).
5 American Society for Reproductive Medicine, *supra* note 3.
6 CBS Evening News, *Inside the Business of Egg Donation*, May 17, 2006.
7 American Society for Reproductive Medicine, *supra* note 3.
8 *Id.*
9 Robert Steinbrook, *Egg Donation and Human Embryonic Stem-Cell Research*, 354 NEW ENG. J. MED. 324–6 (2006).
10 *See, e.g.*, Committee on Guidelines for Human Embryonic Stem Cell Research, National Research Council and Institute of Medicine, National Academy of Sciences, *Guidelines for Human Embryonic Stem Cell Research* (2005) [hereinafter National Academies].
11 *Id.* at 2.
12 Richard Mollard, *Nuclear Transfer – Stem Cells or Somatic Cell Nuclear Transfer*, http://www.isscr.org/public/therapeutic.htm.
13 National Academies, *supra* note 10, at 2.
14 42 U.S.C. § 289g-1(b)(2).
15 National Bioethics Advisory Committee, *Ethical Issues in Human Stem Cell Research* (1999).
16 National Academies, *supra* note 10, at 18.
17 *Text of President Bush's Position on Stem Cell Research*, http://www.washingtonpost.com/wp-srv/onpolitics/transcripts/bushtext_080901.htm.
18 Steinbrook, *supra* note 9.

19 *See, e.g.*, D. W. Brock, *Is a Consensus Possible on Stem Cell Research? Moral and Political Obstacles*, 32 J. Med. Ethics 36–42, 41 (2006).

20 Committee on Assessing the Medical Risks of Human Oocyte Donation for Stem Cell Research, *Assessing the Medical Risks of Human Ooctye Donation for Stem Cell Research: Workshop Report* (2007).

21 *Id.* at 52.

22 *Id.* at 55.

23 *Id.*

24 *Id.*

25 *See, e.g.*, Brock, *supra* note 19, at 41.

26 John Robertson, *Compensation and Egg Donation for Research*, 86 Fertility & Sterility 1573–5, 1573 (2006).

27 Maryland House Bill 873, introduced Feb. 9, 2007.

28 National Academies, *supra* note 10, at 10.

29 *See, e.g.*, Conn. Gen. Stat. sec. 19a-32d (2006) and Cal Health & Saf Code sec. 125355 (2007).

30 Human Embryonic Stem Cell Research Advisory Committee, *2007 Amendments to the National Academies' Guidelines for Human Embryonic Stem Cell Research* (2007), prepublication copy.

31 *See, e.g.*, Robertson, *supra* note 26, at 1573.

32 *See, e.g.*, *Payment to Egg Donors OK'd for Stem Cell Research in UK*, Medical Device Week, Aug. 4, 2006.

33 Human Fertilisation and Embryology Authority, *HFEA Statement on Donating Eggs for Research* (Feb. 21, 2007), http://www.hfea.gov.uk/cps/rde/xchg/SID-3F57D79B-37C4DF/hfea/hs.xsl/1491.html.

34 Ethics Committee, American Society for Reproductive Medicine, *Financial Incentives in Recruitment of Oocyte Donors*, 82 Fertility & Sterility S240 (2004).

35 *Id.*

36 Diane Beeson & Abby Lippman, *Egg Harvesting for Stem Cell Research: Medical Risks and Ethical Problems*, 13 Reprod. Biomed. Online 573–9, 578 (2006).

37 Statement of Judy Norsigian, Senate Health, Education, Labor, and Pensions Committee, March 5, 2002.

38 *See* http://www.handsoffourovaries.com/manifesto.htm.

39 *Id.*

40 1005 CA S.B. 1260.

41 American Society for Reproductive Medicine Ethics Committee, *supra* note 34.

42 Andrea Braverman, *Exploring Ovum Donors' Motivations and Needs*, 1 Am. J. Bioethics 16–17 (2001).

43 *See, e.g.*, *id.*

44 Bonnie Steinbock, *Payment for Egg Donation and Surrogacy*, 71 Mount Sinai J. Med. 255–65, 262 (2004).

45 D. W. Brock, *Is a Consensus Possible on Stem Cell Research? Moral and Political Obstacles*, 32 J. Med. Ethics 36–42, 41 (2006).

46 New York State Task Force on Life and the Law, Advisory Group on Assisted Reproductive Technologies, *Thinking of Becoming an Egg Donor? Get the Facts before You Decide!* (1998), http://www.health.state.ny.us/community/reproductive_health/infertility/eggdonor.htm.

47 Boston Women's Book Collective, *Infertility and Assisting Reproduction: Being or Using an Egg Donor*, *at* Our Bodies Ourselves companion Web site, http://www.ourbodiesourselves.org/book/companion.asp?id+25&compID=76.

16 Eggs, Nests, and Stem Cells

LISA C. IKEMOTO

For the past few years, stem cell research has been all the news in biomedical research, bioethics, U.S. elections, and on Wall Street. Government, public and private academic institutions, and private corporations are contributing financial support and other resources to pursuing the therapeutic and economic dream of regenerative medicine. Not surprisingly, the news has included calls for regulation. Proposed research moratoriums, funding restrictions, and funding expansions, in turn, have been premised on a volatile mix of public policy concerns. The discourses of both abortion and therapeutic hope heavily influenced the initial policy debate in the United States. Both these discourses remain dominant influences, but because some states are now funding human embryonic stem cell research, the debate is beginning to address other concerns. This shift comes as the interdependence between human embryonic stem cell research and the fertility industry becomes apparent. Eggs and embryos are the raw materials for both human embryonic stem cell research and the fertility industry. Eggs and embryos thus form the reason for the interdependence. In the process, the emerging debate has broadened to include concerns about women's agency, status, and health.

In the U.S. stem cell research context, payment restrictions and informed consent standards for providing eggs have become two key points in the regulatory debate. Major players, including the National Academy of Sciences (NAS) and the California Institute for Regenerative Medicine, have taken positions against payment for providing eggs and for detailed standards in egg donor informed consent.

The apparent trend toward regulating egg and embryo procurement practices in the research context could increase pressure to regulate the same practices in the largely unregulated fertility industry. The fertility industry has proven adept at forestalling substantial regulation of its practices. Much of that success has depended on the sympathetic and thus politically treacherous nature of its product – family formation.

This chapter examines the formidable mix of market norms and family formation discourse in light of the regulatory needs highlighted by stem cell research. Section A sketches egg procurement as practices in the fertility industry and describes the interface forming between the fertility industry and the stem cell research enterprise over their need for the same raw materials – human eggs.

Section B addresses the legal regulation of egg procurement. Egg procurement for fertility purposes is substantially unregulated. In the stem cell research enterprise, however, there has been some regulatory response to concerns raised by procurement practices. Section C focuses on the commodification concern and on the role of regulatory and market mechanisms in mixing, rather than segregating, commercial from intrinsic value. Despite my argument that the egg payment ban and heightened informed consent standards fail to prevent the commercialization of donation for research, I support regulation. I do so with understanding that rules such as payment bans can only address the most obvious aspects of commodification, and with faith that regulation can preserve space for ways of defining value in measureless, intrinsic terms. Section D concludes, briefly.

A. WOMEN AND THEIR OVARIES AT THE INTERFACE

Much of the hope – and the hype – of stem cell research lies in the combination of two technologies: the creation of stem cell lines with the potential to become any type of cell or tissue in the human body and the use of nuclear transfer to make the resulting cells and tissues compatible with a particular patient's immune system. In 1998, James Thomson and associates at the University of Wisconsin reported their success at creating the first stem cell lines using inner mass cells from human blastocysts.[1] The inner mass cells from human blastocysts are pluripotent because they have not yet become specialized.[2] Each such cell still has the potential to become any type of cell or tissue in the body. Creation of the blastocysts requires human eggs. Pursuit of this hope, therefore, requires egg procurement from women.

1. Egg Procurement for Fertility

The fertility industry created the practices that routinized human egg procurement. Commercial surrogacy in the United States was started by entrepreneurial types in the late 1970s.[3] Initially, surrogates became pregnant by assisted insemination. Thus traditional surrogacy offered eggs, gestation, and birth as one inseparable package. In vitro fertilization (IVF) became available in the United States in the early 1980s.[4] It enabled the separation of fertilization and gestation and, with that separation, a greater range of egg sources. As a normative matter, IVF was first used with eggs obtained from women undergoing IVF in hope of becoming pregnant, giving birth, and raising a child. In other words, eggs were extracted from a woman for the woman's own use. The reunification of woman and egg may have helped make acceptable the in vitro aspect of this technological intervention in conception. As a practical matter, other egg sources emerged soon after, if not simultaneously with, normative IVF use. Family and friends became egg sources for fertility patients undergoing IVF or for those using IVF with surrogacy.[5] Thus the trade in eggs as eggs began.

Within the fertility industry, egg procurement is a commercial activity, despite the rubric of gift. When family or friend provides the eggs, the personal relationship between provider and recipient frames the transfer as gift and the provider as donor. By the late 1980s, however, egg procurement became a commercial practice that accompanied gestational surrogacy.[6] Altruistic donation has become the exception. Now, most egg donors and recipients are strangers to each other. The so-called donors sign formal agreements, in which they agree to relinquish dispositional authority over the eggs and claims to parentage over any resulting children, and to receive thousands of dollars in return.

Egg retrieval is a medical procedure that has become intertwined with the commercial, legal, and cultural practices that form the egg procurement process. From the donor's perspective, the process begins in the commercial realm – the solicitation for so-called egg donors. The intended recipient of the eggs may directly solicit, or a third-party broker may solicit on behalf of intended recipients. A typical solicitation is made through an advertisement in a newspaper, magazine, poster, or Web site. The role of law shows in the agreements the donor signs and the consent she gives to undergo egg retrieval. The retrieval procedure is fairly elaborate. It requires a sustained series of injections of various drugs that, respectively, stop the ovaries from releasing eggs; stimulate the ovaries to produce extra follicles, and hence eggs; and trigger ovulation and maturation of the eggs. This takes place over two or more weeks and is accompanied by monitoring via blood testing and ultrasound imaging. When the blood tests and ultrasound images indicate that the eggs are ready, the woman undergoes egg retrieval surgery. Medical professionals typically retrieve the eggs transvaginally, using a long, specially designed needle, while the woman is under local anesthesia and intravenous sedation.[7] The eggs are handed off to an embryologist for screening and in vitro insemination. When the egg retrieval is complete and the woman wakes up, she receives a check and aftercare instructions.

2. Egg Procurement for Research

Assuming one accepts the therapeutic hope of stem cell research, the explanation for why the research must use human eggs as well as blastocysts created solely for research goes something like this. First, the embryos created for fertility purposes, then donated to research, are too few and, often, too poor in quality for use in creating a self-perpetuating stem cell line. Many more embryos are needed for research. Therefore researchers must use eggs to create embryos. Second, researchers have not yet succeeded in performing somatic cell nuclear transfer on a human egg and then prompting that reconstituted cell into becoming a cell line. The one claimed success at this has since become a well-known fraud.[8] The combination of nuclear transfer with embryonic stem cell technology is considered the greatest hope of regenerative medicine. If genetically modified cell lines can be created, and if those cell lines can be engineered into implantable cells or tissue, those cells or that tissue could be designed as a genetic match for a specific patient. In theory, then, the implanted cells or tissue would fool the patient's immune system into treating the engineered as homegrown. Eggs are needed to figure out the first step – the creation of genetically tailored cell lines. If that is achieved, then the successive steps may depend on egg supply, as well.

Egg procurement for research has not yet become standardized. Generally speaking, there are two possible sources. One is women who provide eggs directly to research. The other is women (or couples) who provide eggs left over from or rejected for IVF use. Thus far, human embryonic stem cell researchers have used both sources.[9] But the type of brokers used; the means of solicitation; the content of the agreements made and consents given; the role of the medical professionals who perform the egg retrieval; the payment of money to women; and the other legal, medical, cultural, and commercial elements of egg procurement have not become settled.

3. The Interface

The fertility industry will play a role in stem cell research. Both the fertility industry and research enterprise create demand for human eggs and embryos. But their relationship is more likely to be collaborative than competitive. At a minimum, some of the eggs and embryos used as the raw materials of producing stem cells will be fertility spares. Women undergoing IVF and women who provide eggs for others' use in IVF will be source and conduit for at least some of those materials. Fertility centers will be the site of those retrievals. It is possible, even necessary, that women providing eggs directly to research will also undergo retrieval at fertility centers. Fertility centers house the expertise and facilities needed for efficient retrieval of eggs, whether they are intended for fertility services or for research.

It is harder to predict how much of egg procurement, as a set of intertwined practices formed within the fertility industry, will inure to the process of procuring eggs for research. The fertility industry measures success in numbers – the number of embryos produced, pregnancies started, and children born.[10] These numbers depend, in part, on efficient egg procurement. Efficient egg procurement requires recruitment of young healthy women with saleable looks, medical histories, SAT scores, and other attributes; retrievals that yield high numbers of eggs; and the ability to persuade the super donors to repeat their services on demand.[11]

Some of these efficiencies would serve the demand for eggs in research well. Solicitation methods might be easily adapted to seek research donors. The methods used to encourage women to persist through the physical discomfort, pain, and psychological challenges of egg retrieval might prove useful. And certainly, the choice of drugs and the dosages, timing, retrieval techniques, and other means used to obtain high yields of high-grade eggs could be adopted, with little or no change for egg procurement in research.

But these practices have raised concerns. The concerns most often raised point out the health risks to women and the commodifying effects of egg selling on women and their bodies. These concerns have had greater resonance in the context of stem cell research than in the context of fertility treatment. One result is that using law to address these concerns is, so far, more feasible, or at least, discussible, in the stem cell research debate context than it is in the fertility context.

B. THE REGULATION OF EGG PROCUREMENT PRACTICES

Egg procurement practices for fertility purposes have emerged naked, as it were, of regulation. The practices have been substantially constituted by and constitutive of the supply of and demand for fertility services. In part, because the funding of the services and the function they serve – family formation – are primarily private, the public has been willing to leave the practices, and the concerns they raise, alone. Or perhaps more accurately, legislatures have been unwilling to intervene in the business of making families. On the other hand, egg procurement practices for stem cell research are emerging in the midst of an intense debate about the ethics of the research. The framing of that debate is expanding. It now includes concerns about the health risks to donors and the potential for coercion and exploitation of donors. These concerns, in turn, have prompted a regulatory response. Guidelines, and in some jurisdictions, regulations, are significantly shaping egg procurement practices for research.

1. Regulation of the Fertility Industry

Egg procurement for fertility purposes is substantially unregulated in the United States. Professional guidelines address some practices. For example, the American Society for Reproductive Medicine recommends a five thousand dollar limit on payment to women who provide eggs.[12] Food and Drug Administration (FDA) regulations address laboratory health and safety issues.[13] The basic principle of informed consent applies to women who undergo ovarian stimulation and egg retrieval, as is true for patients undergoing any other medical procedure. A few states have a law here or a law there, but most of the other practices, including dispositional control, parental rights, and compensation, are formed by a combination of carefully orchestrated human need and profit motive, and then are formalized in agreements made among the donor, recipients, and clinic.

A few states have enacted legislation that facilitates the formation of these practices.[14] In most states, neither the legislatures nor the courts have addressed the issues raised by the terms of egg procurement agreements or, more generally, the enforceability of the agreements. The content of the agreements largely reflects the egg recipient's desire for control and familial security and the clinic's need to protect itself against liability in case the medical or relational aspects of the procurement process go awry. The expectation of law's intervention may shadow egg procurement practices, but so far, demand, supply, and profit are the primary drivers.

2. Regulation of the Research Enterprise

Egg procurement for research purposes has provoked a call for regulation in the United States and abroad. Feminists and others have called for regulation of the fertility industry.[15] But so far, legislatures have been reluctant to respond. On the other hand, the intense debate about stem cell research and the use of public funds to support it have already prompted a nascent regulatory response.

In the United States, the NAS has taken a lead in evaluating the need and content of those regulations.[16] Its recommendations are shaping the regulatory debate. Because California was one of the first states to provide state funding in response to the Bush administration's 2001 restriction on federal funding of stem cell research,[17] it is also among the first to regulate stem cell research. The California

Institute of Regenerative Medicine (CIRM), established by a 2004 voter initiative,[18] has followed the NAS lead closely. CIRM regulations for CIRM-funded stem cell research address risks to the autonomy and health and safety of women who provide eggs for research, and they protect the financial interests of the research enterprise.[19] As a result, egg procurement for research in California is more highly regulated than egg procurement for fertility.

CIRM regulations contain six types of provisions that apply to egg procurement for stem cell research that is CIRM funded. The first type requires and specifies the content of informed consent by those who provide human cells or tissues for research use. The second type addresses the health risks to women who provide eggs for research. The third aims at potential conflicts of interest by those who interact with persons who provide cells or tissues for research use. The fourth and most controversial provision prohibits purchase or sale of cells and tissues for research use. The fifth type allocates access to information and dispositional control between the researchers and the donors. The sixth type might be called "long-arm" requirements: they restrict research materials to those that meet the procurement standards, even if obtained outside the state.

The informed consent provisions are tailored to stem cell research. They use the federal human subject research regulations to set a baseline.[20] However, they add a list of specific disclosures, which include, among others, known health risks of the egg retrieval process, the potential uses of the cells, and the information that "stem cell lines derived as a result of their oocyte donation may be patented or commercialized, but donors will not share in patent rights or in any revenue or profit from the patents."[21] In sum, the informed consent requirements express the goal of allowing the prospective donor to evaluate the known risks to her health and bodily integrity in light of competing scientific and commercial interests.

Other provisions place certain responsibilities for protecting the donor's health and safety on the research institution or the researcher. For example, CIRM regulations require that the "institution shall develop procedures to ensure than an individual who donates oocytes for CIRM-funded research has access to medical care that is required as a direct and proximate result of that donation."[22] The stem cell research oversight committee – a structural mechanism that adds a level of institutional review to stem cell research – is required to confirm that the clinic performing the retrieval "is a member of the Society for Assisted Reproductive Technology"[23] and that the procurement of eggs originally intended for fertility purposes did "not knowingly compromise the optimal reproductive success of the woman in infertility treatment."[24] In addition, conflict-of-interest provisions prohibit the principal investigator from performing the egg retrieval or the physician who performs the retrieval from having a financial interest in the research.[25] Collectively, these provisions acknowledge that the benefits and risks of egg donation for stem cell research are not shared. The procurement process allocates the benefits to the researcher and research institution and the risks to the donor.

As mentioned, the most controversial aspect of the egg procurement regulations prohibits payment of valuable consideration for eggs.[26] The regulations do allow for reimbursement of "permissible expenses," defined as "necessary and reasonable costs directly incurred as a result of donation or participation in research activities."[27] The ban on egg selling, however, is strict. Eggs originally procured for fertility purposes from women who were paid more than "permissible expenses" cannot be used for CIRM-funded research.[28] As a practical matter, this prohibition limits the use of fertility spares in stem cell research to those given by family and friends and to those retrieved from the woman undergoing fertility treatment. The payment prohibition has arms, as well. The regulations classify stem cell lines that originated with eggs procured in violation of the payment prohibition as not "acceptably derived" and therefore not to be used in CIRM-funded research.[29] These prohibitions limit the use of eggs or research materials derived from eggs to those procured in jurisdictions with regulations substantially similar to California's.[30]

The CIRM regulations allocate some dispositional control to egg donors. The regulations state, "CIRM-funds may not be used for research that violates the documented preferences of donors with regard to the use of their donated materials."[31] The informed consent provisions require disclosure of possible uses. These include the use of "cell lines for future studies, some of which may not be predictable at this time,"[32] the use of derived cells or cell products in "research involving genetic manipulation,"[33] or transplantation "into humans or animals."[34] Donors may also consent or refuse to be recontacted in the future.[35] Yet the same list of required disclosures contains the one mentioned previously – "that the results of research may be patentable or have commercial potential, and that the donor will not receive patent rights and will not receive financial or any other benefits from future commercial development."[36] The allocations of control carefully distinguish between protecting the donors' ethical priorities and identity interests, on one hand, and the commercial interests of the research enterprise, on the other.

C. ETHICS AND NORMS AT THE INTERFACE

The NAS-California regulatory approach may prove indicative of the role of U.S. law in stem cell research. The existence and effects of the regulations may also strengthen the call for regulation of egg procurement practices in the fertility industry. The industry and others would, no doubt, resist regulation. In the ensuing debate, the fertility industry's market model and research enterprise's regulatory response may become touchstone and fodder. I argue that both perform well in protecting the interests of the industry at issue and that neither successfully decommercializes egg procurement, and hence women's reproductive capacity. Despite that, I conclude that the regulations are more likely than market mechanisms to protect women against the risks of egg procurement.

1. The Regulatory Approach

The regulatory approach that the research enterprise has taken clearly acknowledges two sets of concerns. For example, the informed consent and conflict of interest provisions respond to concerns that egg retrieval poses health risks to women providing eggs[37] and that existing human subject research regulations would be insufficient to protect women because they are not research subjects in the usual sense.[38] The payment ban responds to a set of linked concerns about coercion and exploitation of women.

The efficacy of the rules in addressing those concerns is subject to debate. Women's health advocates argue that requiring disclosure of known health risks does not go far enough. Most of the health risks arising from egg retrieval are linked to the use of drugs to manipulate the ovaries and endocrine system of the woman undergoing retrieval. Yet there is little long-term data on the safety of these drugs. For one drug, there is little or no safety data at all. Lupron is the drug of choice to prevent ovulation. Although Lupron is FDA approved, its use to prevent ovulation is an off-label use. Because of that, the available safety data have little relevance to its use in egg retrieval.[39] Therefore some argue that disclosing only the known risks fails to enable women to make self-protecting decisions. Some would require that "eggs be obtained without hormonal stimulation."[40] Others have called for a complete ban on egg procurement until the safety of the procedure, or lack thereof, has been ascertained.[41]

Not surprisingly, some have criticized the prohibition on payment for providing eggs. Two often raised bases for the criticism are that the ban is paternalistic and that without payment for eggs, the supply will be insufficient to meet research needs.[42] The more sophisticated objection to the payment ban acknowledges that the health risks and risk of coercion are real, but that women would be better armed as sellers, than as donors, to respond to those risks.[43]

The criticisms of the payment ban overlook how the regulatory approach serves the research enterprise. In the context of a fiercely debated and highly politicized divide over the ethics of human embryonic stem cell research, the regulatory approach allows the research to go forward with the imprimatur of the state. The existence of the rules normalizes the activities subject to regulation. In addition, to the extent that the rules provide boundaries, the boundaries provide security for those within the research sector as well as for those outside. They set up legal, and perhaps ethical, safe harbors for researchers. The existence of regulation will reassure not all, but a substantial portion of the public. This, in turn, may smooth the way for the next scientific innovation that challenges our assumptions and our faiths.

What the critics of the payment ban illuminate is that the regulations substantially fail to address the concern that egg procurement will commodify the woman as well as her eggs. The concern, more specifically, is that the use of contracts and the monetization of egg procurement will not only result in providing eggs for research, but will also normalize a trade in bodily integrity, and in particular, women's reproductive capacity – the primary difference used to justify gender subordination. The fear is that the resulting understanding of women will consist of a little more commodity and a little less humanity.

Those who support the regulatory approach might argue that the payment ban eliminates the monetization, and hence the commercialization. They might also argue that the beefed-up informed consent requirements preserve women's agency. The payment ban, then, serves as a barrier between the commercial and the personal, between market value and intrinsic value. Informed consent and the ability to preempt specific uses of her eggs position the woman to control the meaning of her donation.

The reliance on the payment ban and informed consent to hold the line against commodification overlooks the way in which informed consent effects a transfer of possession.[44] Consent to egg retrieval is also consent to relinquish the eggs to another. The CIRM regulations carefully distinguish between the donor's power to refuse consent to specific research uses of the eggs and her inability to claim any rights or financial interests in any resulting research products. The payment ban, then, does not decommercialize the transfer; rather, informed consent preserves the commercial interests of the egg recipient.

These two accounts attribute different meanings to informed consent. The meanings are not mutually exclusive. Informed consent may enable the woman to make a self-protective decision and to control the meaning of her donation – for herself. Her claim of altruism, for example, is perfectly consistent with the transfer of possession and value. However, if to her, the act of providing eggs for research signifies only intrinsic value, her account may not gain traction against the characterization of the eggs as property.

The issue, then, is whether egg procurement without money, but embedded in a commercial context, would lead down the commodification path. The commodification concern expresses a deep-seated fear that the market is nearly inescapable. From this perspective, commercialization, no matter how it occurs, puts us on a one-way path to commodification. Yet some scholars of commodification have argued that commodification is not inevitably harmful.[45] Margaret Radin has used examples of "incomplete commodification" to locate points at which personhood is preserved in the same space as the sale.[46] Viviana Zelizer has shown not only how market value and intrinsic value intermingle in the most intimate realms of our lives,[47] but also how that which is valued primarily in market terms can and has been transformed almost wholly into the personal and intrinsic.[48]

If there are some acceptable mixes, the issue, then, becomes whether there is a line that must not be crossed. Is there a point of commodification that dilutes human value so much that society will be harmed by the dilution? We have crossed that line before. At this point, with this issue, it may not be necessary to identify the exact location of the battle line. It may be that the battle is the most important thing – the fight against the homogenizing power of the market, the attempt to shore up a cultural bulwark against market hegemony and its effects on the disempowered.[49]

2. The Market Approach

The fertility industry, as mentioned previously, has remained relatively unregulated. Market mechanisms, including cultural norms and the potential for public outrage, are what protect women who provide eggs to others. Egg procurement for fertility is commercial, but private. It is privatized because, unlike stem cell research, the funding is substantially private. In addition, the official purpose of egg procurement in the fertility setting is family formation. That purpose has powerful effects. Among others,[50] it reframes a commercial exchange as an intimate act.

Consider the use of the term *egg donor* in the fertility context. Despite the fact that most women who provide eggs for IVF are strangers to the recipients, "gift" persists as a rubric for commercial egg procurement. *Egg donor* may be a holdover from the period in which family and friends provided eggs for IVF. A more plausible explanation is that *egg donor* positions commercial egg procurement outside the ethical prohibition on treating humans and human body parts as property. In commercial surrogacy, this has resulted in a distinction drawn between baby and services. In *Baby M*, perhaps the most famous surrogacy case, the New Jersey Supreme Court premised its rejection of commercial surrogacy on the prohibition of baby selling in adoption law.[51] To avoid both the legal and moral force of the baby-selling ban, surrogacy contracts characterize the exchange as one of money for services, not baby. Similarly, *egg donor* claims that the money paid is for the time and effort of providing eggs, not human gametes.

The egg market relies on women who assert altruistic as well as pecuniary motives. They want to help others have a child. Expressed altruism is used as a psychological screening criterion for egg donors. This account reinforces the claim that the transaction comports with the ethical prohibition on treating the human body as property. It also implicitly characterizes the purchasers in blameless, sympathetic terms. It removes them from the sanction of the ethical prohibition, as well. The corollary to the prohibition on baby selling is the assumption that parental decisions should be selfless. Adoption discourse often explains voluntary parental termination as a sacrifice committed for the sake of the child and adoption as a selfless act of providing a home for a child in need. The stated altruism of the donor and the implied altruism of the recipients shift egg procurement into the intimate space of family formation.

In the framework of family formation, the so-called donor occupies a blind spot, a space made blind by its position between the commercial and the intimate. Even if the woman providing eggs claims a profit motive, her account rubs up against normalizing imputation of gift. This is the corollary, in a sense, to the effect of informed consent on the truer gift, the egg transfer without payment. In the research context, however, the beefed-up informed consent, in combination with the other regulatory provisions, does provide some protection against health risks and the risk of coercion. In the fertility context, the donor's location between the family and the market may obscure the need for protection. To the extent that she is perceived as a seller in a market characterized by high demand, her position may be conflated with agency. In the market, that attribution often places the burden of addressing the risk on the market participant.

If we rely primarily on market mechanisms to address the risks of egg procurement, the point made earlier may still be relevant. Often, it is the battle that matters, and the enemy is not commercialization per se, but rather, its potential for reducing the range of ways in which we define value. With that in mind, it becomes possible to rethink the potential of the gift rubric and its protective device: family formation.

The term *egg donor* is not simply instrumental. It expresses discomfort with the practices that constitute egg procurement. It evidences concern about commercialization of that which is both normatively priceless and private. It may also indicate unease with a technology use that breaks baby making into components and implements an assembly approach to family formation.[52] The question is whether this discomfort could and should be leveraged into a market mechanism that would address the risks of egg procurement?

Consider an approach that promotes so-called green baby making. Environmentalists have co-opted the meaning of *green* as a market mechanism for interjecting environmentally protective ethics into consumer practices. It accepts consumerism but rejects its excesses. Women's rights activists might adapt the model to interject donor-protective ethics into the fertility industry. Green baby making might be marketed, as it were, as a means of alleviating the discomfort of consumer-based family formation. It might provoke the industry and buyers to address the health and coercion risks of egg procurement. It might also prompt the formation of alternative ways of valuing the women who provide eggs for fertility. Perhaps the biggest risk is that this approach will prove successful, and that in the process, it will soothe a discomfort that signifies something important; that is, instead of taking up the challenge of examining the source of that discomfort, green baby making may cause us to miss a point at which we dilute our own humanity.

D. CONCLUSION

Because context makes a difference, the regulatory approach will not have the same effects on egg procurement for fertility as it might have on egg procurement for research. Yet in different contexts, the experiences of the egg donors are corollary to each other. In the research setting, informed consent purports to protect the personal rights of the donor but also affects a transfer of possession, and hence access to commercial value. In the fertility setting, the ostensible goal of family formation shifts a commercial transaction into the private realm of the family, thus shielding the egg provider and recipient from apparent ethical breach and legal intervention. Neither egg donor nor society is shielded from commercialization of the transfer she makes. But the regulatory approach acknowledges and responds to some of the other risks – the risks to health and the risks of coercion and exploitation. In the market, the woman is left to market mechanisms, which may (or may not) serve donors well, but which may also result in the loss of important moments for considering the meaning of *human.*

NOTES

1 James A. Thomson, *Embryonic Stem Cell Lines Derived from Human Blastocysts*, 282 Science 1145–7 (1998).

2 National Institutes of Health, Regenerative Medicine 2006 1–3 (2006).

3 Debora L. Spar, The Baby Business: How Money, Science, and Politics Drive the Commerce of Conception 75–7 (2006).

4 *See* Jean Cohen, *The Early Days of IVF outside the UK*, 11 Hum. Reprod. Update 439, 449 (2005).

5 Katheryn D. Katz, *Ghost Mothers: Human Egg Donation and the Legacy of the Past*, 57 Alb. L. Rev 733, 773 (1994).

6 Spar, *supra* note 3, at 79–80.

7 American Society for Reproductive Medicine, Assisted Reproductive Technologies: A Guide for Patients 6–7 (2003).

8 *See* Nicholas Wade & Choe Sang-Hun, *Human Cloning Was All Faked, Koreans Report*, N.Y. TIMES, Jan. 10, 2006, at A1.
9 Find stem cell research articles that describe ova sources in the methodology section.
10 *See 2004 Assisted Reproductive Technology (ART) Report: Introduction to Fertility Clinic Tables*, http://www.cdc.gov/art/ART04/ifct.htm.
11 *See* JULIA DEREK, CONFESSIONS OF A SERIAL EGG DONOR 96, 138–9 (2004) (describing the characteristics of a super donor and the increase in income that accompanies them).
12 ASRM committee reports.
13 *See generally* 21 C.F.R. §§ 1271.1–1271.440 (2007). *E.g.*, 21 C.F.R. 1271.220(a) requires that human cells, tissue, and cellular and tissue-based products be processed in a way that prevents the introduction, transmission, or spread of communicable disease.
14 *See, e.g.*, FL STAT. 742.14 (allows reasonable compensation to women who provide eggs for fertility purposes and provides that the woman will not have any material rights and obligations for any resulting children); LA REV. STAT. 14:101.2 (prohibiting the use of an ovum "through the use of assisted reproduction technology, for any purpose other than that indicated by the . . . ovum . . . provider's signature on a written consent form"); VA CODE ANN. 32.1–189.1 (excepts ova from the prohibition on the sale or purchase of human body parts).
15 *See* Spar, *supra* note 3, 217–24; Judith F. Daar, *Regulating Reproductive Technologies: Panacea or Paper Tiger?* 34 HOUS. L. REV. 609 (1997); Weldon E. Havins & James J. Dalessio, *The Ever-Widening Gap between the Science of Artificial Reproductive Technology and the Laws Which Govern That Technology*, 48 DEPAUL L. REV. 825 (1999).
16 *See* National Research Council and Institute of Medicine of the National Academies, *Guidelines for Human Embryonic Stem Cell Research* (2005).
17 Press release, President George W. Bush, *President Discusses Stem Cell Research* (Aug. 9, 2001), http://www.whitehouse.gov/news/releases/2001/08/20010809-2.html.
18 http://www.cirm.ca.gov.
19 *See generally* CIRM Medical and Ethical Standards Regulations Title 17 California Code of Regulations Section 100010–100110 (rev. Jan. 31, 2008), http://www.cirm.ca.gov/laws/default.asp.
20 *Id.*, Section 100100(a).
21 *Id.*, Section 100100(b)(vii).
22 *Id.*, Section 100095(c).
23 *Id.*, Section 10095(a).
24 *Id.*, Section 100095(b)
25 *Id.*, Section 100095(d) and (e).
26 *Id.*, Section 100080(e)(2).
27 *Id.*, Section 100020(h).
28 *Id.*, Section 100095(b)(5).
29 *Id.*, Section 100080(e)(2).
30 The CIRM regulations identify two countries – the United Kingdom and Canada – as two such jurisdictions. *Id.*, Section 100080(b)–(d).
31 *Id.*, Section 100100(b)(1).
32 *Id.*, Section 100100(b)(1)(C).
33 *Id.*, Section 100100(b)(1)(D).
34 *Id.*, Section 100100(b)(1)(E).
35 *Id.*, Section 100100(b)(1)(B).
36 *Id.*, Section 100100(b)(1)(I).
37 *See Statement of Judy Norsigian*, Executive Director, Our Bodies Ourselves, Subcommittee on Criminal Justice, Drug Policy and Human Resources, Government Reform

Committee, U.S. House of Representatives, Hearing on Human Cloning and Embryonic Stem Cell Research after Seoul: Examining Exploitation, Fraud, and Ethical Problems in the Research, March 7, 2006. *See also* Basil C. Tarlatzis & Evangelos Papanikolauou, *Multifollicular Ovarian Stimulation for IVF: More May Not Be Better* (review article of research indicating that high doses of the drugs that produce a high egg yield result in chromosomal damage in the eggs, and hence in the resulting embryos).

38 *See* David Magnus & Mildred K. Cho, *Issues in Oocyte Donation for Stem Cell Research*, 308 Science 1747, 1747–8 (2005).

39 Statement of Judy Norsigian, *supra* note 37.

40 *Id.*

41 *See* Hands Off Our Ovaries, *Mission Statement*, http://handsoffourovaries.com/mission.htm.

42 *See, e.g.*, Judith Daar & Russell Korobkin, *Selling Eggs Isn't Selling Our Souls*, L.A. Times, Aug. 30, 2006, at B13.

43 *See* Chapters 2 and 17 in this volume.

44 Catherine Waldby & Robert Mitchell, Tissue Economies: Blood, Organs, and Cell Lines in Late Capitalism 71 (2006).

45 For an excellent set of writings that challenge the either-or approach to the commodification concern, *see* Rethinking Commodification: Cases and Readings in Law and Culture (Martha A. Ertman & Joan C. Williams eds., 2005).

46 Margaret Jane Radin, Contested Commodities 102–14 (1996).

47 Viviana A. Zelizer, The Purchase of Intimacy (2005).

48 Viviana A. Zelizer, Pricing the Priceless Child: the Changing Social Value of Children (1985).

49 *See* Margaret Jane Radin & Madhavi Sunder, *The Subject and Object of Commodification*, *in* Rethinking Commodification, *supra* note 45, at 17 (calling on scholars to "contend with existing material and social inequalities that reinforce dominant meanings over subversive ones").

50 As discussed in section B, the family formation purpose has probably played a significant role in deterring legislatures from enacting regulation of the industry.

51 In the Matter of Baby M, 537 A.2d 1227 (N.J. 1988).

52 For a richer discussion of this phenomenon, *see* Charis Thompson, Making Parents: The Ontological Choreography of Reproductive Technologies 255–8 (2005).

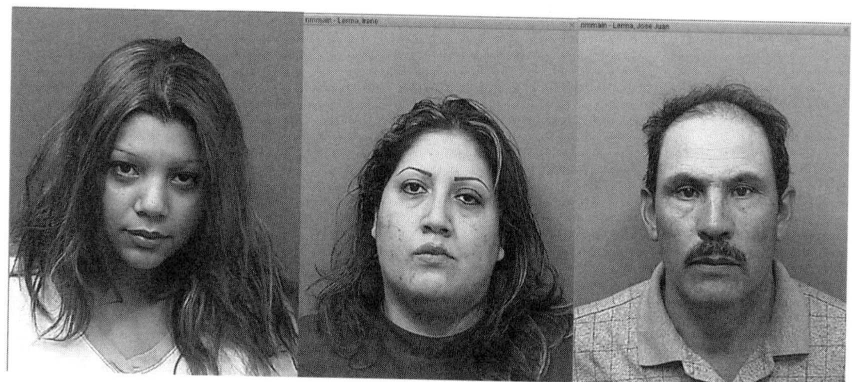

Baby bandits: Nicole Uribe-Lopez and Irene and Jose-Juan Lerma caught in a scheme to sell a baby. Nicole Uribe-Lopez, twenty-three, negotiated the sale of her baby for hard cash and a down payment for a used car. She reduced the original selling price from five thousand to fifteen hundred dollars. A part of the proceeds were to pay for the car. Reporters speculated that some of the money would be sent back to Mexico for the care of her other two children. The Lermas decided to acquire a child on the black market (from Nicole), rather than go through the adoption process, because it was less expensive and more expedient than dealing with an agency. (Pueblo, Colorado Police Department)

17 Where Stem Cell Research Meets Abortion Politics: Limits on Buying and Selling Human Oocytes

MICHELLE OBERMAN, LESLIE WOLF, AND PATTI ZETTLER

Today, there is a sound consensus among countries pursuing stem cell research in favor of limiting the extent to which women can be paid for providing oocytes[1] for research.[2] In addition to U.S. federal guidelines and state laws prohibiting compensation, Canadian law prohibits the "sale, offer to sell, or advertising to sell for money or exchange of property or services of sperm or ova."[3] The United Kingdom currently limits payment to gamete providers to fifteen pounds plus "reasonable" expenses.[4] Even in Israel, which has an extraordinarily active stem cell research community, the report of the Bioethics Advisory Committee of the Israel Academy of Science and the Humanities on the use of embryonic stem cells for therapeutic research endorses only "voluntary donations" of oocytes.[5]

This consensus against compensating women for oocytes is puzzling when considered against the broader backdrop of more commonplace market exchanges involving oocytes that proliferate in the context of assisted reproduction. This chapter undertakes a critical analysis of policies limiting compensation for women who provide oocytes to stem cell researchers.

To engage in this analysis, we begin with some background. First, we provide a brief overview of the manner in which oocytes are used in stem cell research. Second, we discuss the various laws and policies governing compensation for oocytes in two distinct contexts: stem cell research and assisted reproduction. This contrast reveals significant discrepancies in the way oocytes are treated. The following section examines the justifications invoked in support of these distinct policies governing oocytes and concludes that they are untenable and, indeed, incoherent on their own terms.

In section D, we suggest a more plausible justification for the divergent treatment of oocytes in the reproductive and stem cell contexts: abortion-related politics regarding the termination of life. This section evaluates the analogy between stem cell research and abortion, revealing it to be spurious. In the end, we conclude that the ban on compensating women who provide oocytes for use in stem cell research emerges as little more than a vestige of paternalism and a misguided effort by supporters of stem cell research to curry favor among abortion opponents.

A. THE OOCYTE'S ROLE IN HUMAN EMBRYONIC STEM CELL RESEARCH

Human embryonic stem cells are at the center of what many medical researchers believe to be the most promising avenue for developing treatments and even cures for human maladies and ailments ranging from organ failure, to genetic abnormalities, to diseases such as Parkinson's, Alzheimer's, and cancer. These cells, derived from embryos, are particularly interesting to scientists because they are resilient and also possess the capacity to develop into various specialized cells of the body. In other words, once the cell line is cultured, its ability to reproduce itself means that it can be used indefinitely as a source of new cells in the laboratory setting. Moreover, their undifferentiated state means that these stem cells can be made to develop into almost any sort of cell found in the human body (red blood cells, brain cells, muscle cells, etc.).

Present techniques for deriving human embryonic stem cells generally necessitate the destruction of a human embryo. The embryo, created from the union of a human egg and sperm, is permitted to develop outside of the womb for seven to eight days (until it has reached the one hundred- to two hundred-cell, or blastocyst, stage of development). At that point, stem cells are extracted from the developing embryo, and the embryo is destroyed.[6] Researchers can manipulate the stem cells by culturing them and can encourage the replication of these cell lines via somatic cell nuclear transfer (more generically known as cloning).

Human oocytes are essential to the stem cell research enterprise. First, as explained previously, they are used, along with sperm, to form the embryos from which stem cells are derived. Ultimately, stem cell researchers hope to use oocytes in a second way: to create new cells with so-called customized genetic material implanted in the cells by researchers.[7] To do so, researchers will take normal oocytes, from which the nuclear, or genetic, material has been removed. They will replace the nucleus with the genetic material from an adult cell from the body such as a skin, muscle, or blood cell. They will then use that cell to derive stem cells. Such customization is desirable for two reasons: first, it permits researchers to create stem cell lines with specific genetic characteristics, such as sickle-cell anemia, for further research; and second, it ultimately may permit physicians to customize therapeutic treatments to the recipient by using her own cells for derivation and thus eliminate the risk of rejection.

Regardless of whether oocytes will be used in stem cell research or for reproductive ends, identical methods are used to obtain them from women's bodies. Standard protocols require that women who wish to provide oocytes undergo extensive medical and psychological screening before retrieval.[8] If eligible, they receive daily hormone stimulation, typically for eight to fourteen days, to produce multiple oocytes.[9] This requires a series of medical visits as well as the self-injection of ovulation hormones at home. Physicians administer blood tests and ultrasound to determine when the oocytes are ready to be removed.[10] Finally, oocytes are extracted using transvaginal ultrasound aspiration, a procedure in which a physician uses an ultrasound-guided needle to retrieve the oocytes through the woman's vagina.[11] This thirty-minute procedure is performed in a physician's office or outpatient facility, usually with some kind of anesthetic.[12]

The production of surplus oocytes is not risk-free. In the short term, women who take ovulation drugs are at risk for ovarian hyperstimulation syndrome (OHSS).[13] OHSS is characterized by symptoms such as swollen ovaries, bloating, nausea, depressed appetite, and vomiting. In addition, fluid might accumulate in the abdominal and chest cavities. Severe OHSS, which occurs in 2 to 5 percent of all women undergoing ovarian stimulation, is characterized by weight gain, electrolyte abnormalities, and, infrequently, blood clots or kidney failure. Approximately 0.2 percent of donors experience severe OHSS, which requires hospitalization.[14]

The long-term risks of exposure to ovarian stimulation drugs have not yet been thoroughly studied. Long-term effects may include an increased risk of ovarian cancer, although it is unclear whether this risk, if it indeed exists, is due to the ovulation drugs or to the underlying infertility in many IVF patients who use ovulation drugs.[15]

In addition to the hormone-related risks, there are risks connected to the retrieval process. Typical side effects of transvaginal ultrasound aspiration include cramping on the day of the procedure and a feeling of fullness or pressure for a few weeks following the procedure. Between 0.002 and 0.7 percent of donors experience serious side effects that require surgery to correct due to the retrieval procedure.[16]

B. POLICIES REGULATING COMPENSATION FOR OOCYTES

The extent to which the necessary components of human conception, sperm and oocytes, are available as market commodities varies greatly across countries. Although sperm donors long have been compensated for their contributions to assisted reproduction, many countries ban the sale, or purchase, of human eggs.[17] In the United States, it is legal to buy and sell human zygotes, both egg and sperm, for reproductive purposes. This market stands in sharp contrast to policies and laws limiting compensation for the provision of oocytes in the context of stem cell research.

1. The Market in Human Oocytes for Use in Assisted Reproduction

A robust market operates to facilitate the procurement of human oocytes for use in reproduction. For a number of important reasons, lawyers, policy makers, and market participants have avoided conceptualizing the market as expressly involving the buying and selling of human eggs. Identifying eggs as a market commodity triggers familiar concerns such as those that have led to prohibiting the buying and selling of children. These concerns inform debates over practices that guide adoption laws as well as gestational contracts or surrogacy. In those areas, as in the context of contracting for human eggs, contracts tend to stress the service- or labor-based contribution of the women who provide access to their reproductive services.

Thus, although it is clear that the purpose of asking women to undergo ovarian stimulation is not simply to make their ovaries produce surplus eggs, but also to procure the surplus eggs from them, contracts typically do not frame the exchange as "money for eggs." Indeed, most contracts provide that a woman will be paid for her trouble even if her body does not produce any useful eggs for retrieval.

In the United States, women who provide oocytes for reproductive purposes typically are paid. The American Society for Reproductive Medicine, along with numerous medical ethicists and other experts, has endorsed a flat-fee rate of compensation in the range of five thousand dollars.[18] Because the market is not regulated, payments vary considerably. Indeed, women who have characteristics thought to be genetically desirable, such as high academic achievement or athletic ability, can receive considerably more than five thousand dollars.[19] Such payments are in addition to expenses, such as medical expenses and travel, which are commonly borne by the recipient couple.

Some scholars have argued in favor of regulating these exchanges, noting that these transactions tend to reinforce racist norms and reflect a pernicious embrace of genetic determinism. At least one commentator suggests that a ban on such payments might be unconstitutional.[20] At present, however, state laws do not prohibit such payments; indeed, the sale of oocytes is carried out in an open manner with seemingly little stigma for market participants.

2. Limiting Compensation for Oocytes in Stem Cell Research

In contrast with the market in oocytes for reproductive purposes, in the United States, virtually every policy that attempts to govern stem cell research either recommends or requires that women donate their eggs, rather than being paid for them. The first such policy was California's Proposition 71, a three billion dollar bond measure passed in 2004, which established the California Institute for Regenerative Medicine (CIRM). By statute, CIRM oversight bodies must establish standards that prohibit "compensation to research donors," but expenses may be reimbursed.[21] The statute does not define "expenses."[22] Although many interpreted Proposition 71 as permitting only payment of out-of-pocket expenses, such as parking and child care, and not other costs of participation, such as lost wages,[23] CIRM regulations allow for payment of actual lost wages, in addition to travel, housing, child care, medical care, and health insurance.[24]

Other states go further toward limiting compensation. Many states prohibit payments of any kind for providing oocytes for research.[25] In some states, compensation is permissible only to the extent that one is able to argue that oocyte compensation should be governed by existing policies. For instance, if oocytes are considered "nonrenewable organs," then one might argue that Minnesota law should permit payments of "actual expenses such as medical costs, lost income, or travel expenses" incurred directly from the donation.[26]

In late 2005, the U.S. National Academy of Sciences (NAS) followed the lead of these states when articulating federal guidelines for the conduct of stem cell research. NAS recommended against incentives – financial or in kind – for providing oocytes for research, except for reimbursement of direct expenses.[27] Those drafting the guidelines acknowledged that "paying research subjects is 'a common and long-standing practice in the United States'" but pointed to concerns about how much to pay gamete providers and for what ("for example, time, inconvenience, discomfort, or level of risk") and expressed a concern that such payments would compromise informed consent.[28] It concluded that its "recommendation will ensure consistency between procurement practices here and in other countries" as well as being consonant with the limitation imposed by California's Proposition 71.[29]

C. JUSTIFICATIONS FOR THE DISTINCTION BETWEEN OOCYTES FOR REPRODUCTION AND OOCYTES FOR RESEARCH

The explanations that are offered in support of the regulation of oocyte donation in the context of stem cell research, as opposed to reproduction, not only fail to justify the reason for distinguishing between these two end uses of oocytes, but are, on their own terms, incoherent. These justifications tend to fall into one of two categories: first, there are claims that permitting compensation would generate perverse incentives, effectively coercing women into selling their eggs; and second, there are claims that buying and selling oocytes reflects an embrace of the morally reprehensible trade of human bodies and body parts.

1. Oocytes for Research and the Problem of Undue Influence

One concern voiced by those who object to paying women for oocytes in the context of stem cell research is that an offer of money, or other inducement, will exert too much pressure on donors, thereby undermining informed consent or threatening the voluntary nature of participation in research.[30] This claim resonates with literature governing clinical research, generally. The goal of ensuring voluntariness is a central ethical tenet of research with human subjects.[31] In a stratified class society, however, there is no way, short of banning compensation altogether, to ensure that those who agree to participate as research subjects are not motivated, at some level, by the prospect of remuneration.

A brief review of the literature on the risks of paying research participants reveals little support for a complete ban on payments. Moreover, to the extent that one nonetheless supports such a ban on payment for oocyte donation, there is no rational justification for limiting that ban to the stem cell research context. Thus the problem with coercion-based arguments against paying women for oocytes is that they prove both too little and too much.

a. Payment and coercion in research. The ban on payment for oocytes conflicts with widespread practices permitting participants in research to be compensated for their participation. Research participants – whether they are patients or healthy volunteers – commonly are paid for their study participation.[32] Indeed, the matter of payment to research subjects is so uncontroversial that federal regulations and state laws governing human subjects research mention the subject only in passing.[33] Accordingly, decisions about payments are left largely to investigators, whose determinations regarding compensation are reviewed by those charged with research oversight.

The *common rule* (which is the term used by the seventeen federal agencies and departments who have adopted U.S. regulations governing human subjects of research) does not mention compensation.[34] Instead, the various agencies offer "ethical guidelines" to those who design research protocols and who determine rates of compensation for participants. For example, the guidelines of one consist, in part, of the following suggestions:

- Researchers should be careful about paying compensation to subjects who are placed at risk, so that the payment is not seen as coercive. A high payment may induce a needy participant to take a risk that they normally would clearly prefer not to take. That concern would not exist when the risk is minimal.
- Advertising the amount of compensation, in order to give information to potential subjects, poses no risk or ethical problem.[35]

Investigators and institutional review boards (IRBs) justify paying research participants on grounds of fairness ("participants should be compensated for their time and effort") as well as pragmatism.[36] Payments are widely understood to offer an incentive to participate in research trials.[37] For example, studies that require participants to return multiple times for study visits often pay a bonus to participants who complete all their visits. Investigators and IRBs also openly acknowledge that higher payments are necessary when the study involves invasive procedures, such as a bronchosopy, in a population of healthy volunteers than when a study involves noninvasive procedures, such as surveys. Finally, payments may be made as a token of appreciation.[38] Studies may pay participants based on any or all of these grounds; however, the vast majority of studies do not specify the reasons for which payments are made.[39]

To be sure, the ethical guidelines invoked by the National Science Foundation and others might be read to endorse some limit on the amount of compensation offered. For example, the following caution might pertain to the stem cell context: "A high payment may induce a needy participant to take a risk that they normally would clearly prefer not to take."[40] Nonetheless, to the extent that one views stem cell research as simply another instance of research with human subjects, current practices in no way militate in favor of *banning* compensation and would seem, on the contrary, to favor payments to women who are willing to provide oocytes to support such research endeavors. Indeed, given the invasiveness of the oocyte retrieval process, one might even argue that policies limiting compensation to lost costs are too restrictive.

b. Undue influence and the oocyte market. Even if one were to accept the argument that paying women for their oocytes in the stem cell research context would pose too great an incentive, thereby undermining voluntariness by causing them to make irrational choices, one would be required to explain why offering payment for eggs to be used in assisted reproduction does not pose a similar threat. The procedure for removing the oocytes is identical, and thus the medical risks are the same in both contexts. To the extent that one is motivated by concerns about the health and well-being of oocyte donors, such concern would, of course, support a complete ban on payment for oocytes, regardless of their proposed end use.

Furthermore, it seems inherently inconsistent to ban compensation for oocytes, in the research context, based on concerns that payment would lead women to take on unreasonable research risks, in the absence of laws or regulations barring men from receiving compensation for participating in research involving invasive procedures. At present, at least in the United States, there is nothing to stop researchers from offering payment to men (or women) who are willing to undergo, say, a bronchosopy, or to take a previously untested experimental medication, for research purposes. Such procedures carry risks that are at least as significant, and arguably much graver, than those associated with oocyte retrieval. Given that the norm is to pay research participants, even for risky and time-consuming procedures, these differences do not explain why oocyte retrieval should be singled out as the one research procedure for which participants cannot be compensated.

Finally, one might note that there is a disparity, even within the stem cell research context, in terms of current regulations governing compensation for those who provide gametes. Presently, women cannot be compensated for providing oocytes, but it remains legal to compensate men for sperm. To be sure, there are differences in the risk factors relevant to the provision of sperm, as opposed to oocytes. This is a meaningless distinction, however, in view of the fact that researchers routinely compensate study participants for agreeing to undergo risky procedures.

Perhaps the distinction between the law's treatment of sperm and oocytes in the stem cell research context is simply an oversight. Stem cell scientists have paid relatively little attention to the need to collect sperm for research as researchers currently are interested in developing stem cell lines with particular characteristics, whether for research or clinical treatments. In pursuing this line of inquiry, they expect to use somatic cell nuclear transfer, which requires oocytes, but not sperm.[41] Moreover, a single sperm donation provides many more gametes than any oocyte donation possibly could, so there is little reason to anticipate a shortage of sperm, whereas one might reasonably fear a shortage of oocytes. Nonetheless, it is reasonable to anticipate the need for sperm in future research endeavors. The absence of prohibitions against payment for sperm further underscores the irregularity of policies governing oocytes.

The argument that women should not be paid for their oocytes in the stem cell research setting because they are uniquely susceptible to coercion is unsupportable. That women are singled out for such so-called protective treatment in the name of the risk of undue influence seems to testify to the possibility that these policies have been shaped by traditional stereotypes of women – women cannot be trusted to make sound moral judgments about their bodies; women are expected to be altruistic, particularly when it comes to issues involving their reproductive ability; left to their own devices, women are incapable of making reasoned decisions about their own lives and bodies. Reliance on such stereotypes is an insufficient basis for treating women differently with respect to decisions about research participation.

We turn now to a second argument: that payment must be banned because oocytes should not be treated as commodities.

2. Oocytes and the Trade in Human Body Parts

To date, policies limiting compensation for those who provide research-related oocyte donations have not been viewed as controversial. Given the extent to which these limits diverge from current research norms, the lack of debate must reflect a view that this particular form of research is somehow different from other research endeavors. This concern may be seen in the NAS guidelines' suggestion that paying these research subjects raises concerns not only in terms of how much to pay, but also "for what."[42] In essence, the argument is that the body parts in question are human eggs – which, along with embryos and fetuses, are elemental aspects of human life.[43] Allowing human eggs to be bought and sold taps into the broader debate about the risks posed to individuals, and to the collective, by the commodification of human bodies and body parts. As is the case with arguments based on undue influence, the commodification worry proves both too little and too much.

There are both individual and societal harms that may be incurred by permitting the proliferation of a market in human bodies and body parts. As a result, societies routinely ban transactions deemed to undermine the value of human life. Common examples of these are the prohibition against selling babies or human organs. There is less consensus, however, about the extent to which individuals should be permitted to regard themselves as having ownership, and a corresponding right to alienate, body parts such as human tissue and gametes. Even in countries that outlaw the sale of kidneys, there may be little controversy occasioned by the sale of other body parts or tissue. Few object to the selling or buying of renewable body parts, such as human hair, for example, or to the sale of blood or blood products such as platelets.[44]

The underlying impulse behind commodification-based arguments against permitting women to be paid for oocytes to be used in stem cell research derives from a belief that buying and selling oocytes is akin to buying and selling embryos, which, in turn, is akin to buying and selling babies. Of course, as Professor Bonnie Steinbock notes, "eggs are not children, and buying eggs (or even embryos) is not buying children."[45] Moreover, those who adhere to this argument must contend with the fact that there is no real consensus in contemporary jurisprudence regarding the extent to which people should be permitted to sell, or to rent, the parts of their body that are used in reproduction.

Consider the practice of contracts for gestational carriers, otherwise known as surrogacy agreements. The *Baby M* case was the first in a series of cases in which a court was asked to enforce a contract involving the payment of money to a woman who agreed to be inseminated by a man to whom she was not married, for the purposes of producing and surrendering a child to him.[46] Although the New Jersey court in *Baby M* refused to enforce the contract, arguing that it was void against public policy,[47] numerous courts since that time have granted enforcement to similar agreements.[48] Indeed, state legislatures have changed their laws to make it clear that such practices are legal.[49]

Even if one objects to the so-called sale of babies implicit in gestational carrier contracts, one might nonetheless find it acceptable to countenance the exchange of money for oocytes. The market for human eggs and sperm to be used in assisted reproduction is so well entrenched that one hardly considers advertisements for gametes to be noteworthy.

It bears noting that reproduction-related transactions might be seen as raising legitimate commodification-based concerns. Unlike organs, or gestational carriers, in which there is a baseline sense that almost any healthy, willing participant will do, the market in human gametes is shaped by faith in genetic determinism. As previously mentioned, those seeking eggs or sperm for reproductive purposes will pay higher prices for donors who have markers for success such as academic achievement, height, and athletic ability.[50] These transactions arguably constitute both the reification and the instantiation of the stratification of human society according to immutable attributes such as race or eye color. Thus the market in gametes engages in a pernicious grading process, undermining the essential belief that all humans possess equal worth and dignity.

In contrast with the commodification-based arguments that arise from the buying and selling of gametes for reproductive ends, transactions involving oocytes to be used in stem cell research pose less of a threat of commodification. The principal negative societal risk associated with paying for oocytes for infertility treatment is the reification of a genetic caste system. Unlike infertility treatment, with its goal of producing a baby, the goals of stem cell research are much more generic and far-reaching. It is safe to assume that, ultimately, researchers will want to obtain the broadest possible cross section of genetic material to ensure the wide-scale applicability of their findings.[51] Indeed, women who carry genetic mutations that might keep them from providing oocytes for reproduction may be highly desirable for stem cell research because their oocytes might enable disease-specific research. The only reason that one might find significant price differentials in the amount of money that women might be paid for their oocytes would stem from the unwillingness of a certain significant genetic subpopulation to allow access to their oocytes absent higher rates of compensation. Responding to this shortage by offering differential payments likely would raise questions of fairness for IRBs, but it is far from clear that employing such strategies would trigger the dehumanization of those whose oocytes are particularly coveted.

Given the absence of a concerted effort by lawmakers and private industry actors to regulate the market in oocytes for reproductive purposes, it is interesting to revisit the collective determination that women should not be fully compensated for providing oocytes to be used in stem cell research. Such a ban must reflect the belief that stem cell research is different in some significant way. Moreover, because the ban is on payment to women, rather than on the research itself, those endorsing such a ban must agree that, unlike infertility-related transactions, women need to be discouraged from participating in these stem cell research-related transactions. After all, every other participant in stem cell research is compensated for his or her involvement (the technicians, the investigators, the physicians, and the sponsors, to name a few).

In view of the fact that the sale of gametes for reproduction occurs throughout the world, without significant restriction or stigma, it is irrational to argue that paying women for oocytes to be used in stem cell research marks an impermissible step toward the commodification of human beings. The inability of these ostensible justifications to withstand scrutiny suggests that there is some other motive informing the policy limiting compensation to women who would provide oocytes to stem cell researchers. The most plausible motive lies in abortion-related politics regarding the termination of life.

D. ABORTION POLITICS AND THE OOCYTE AS FETISH

The process for procuring oocytes is the same, regardless of whether they will be used in research or in reproduction. The difference lies in the end use of the oocytes. In the context of assisted reproduction, they will be fertilized, and if all proceeds as intended, they will be used to bring about the birth of a child. In contrast, in the context of stem cell research, the oocytes will be used to create an embryo that, ultimately, will be destroyed. Even if it fosters treatments for human diseases, stem cell research does not take an oocyte and use it to help produce a child.

From an antiabortion perspective, which holds that so-called potential human life is sacred, stem cell research might be seen as falling along the abortion spectrum. As such, offering money to women in exchange for providing oocytes to researchers might be analogized to offering money to women in exchange for aborting their pregnancies. Such a practice likely would be considered morally impermissible, alongside a long list of illegitimate reasons for terminating a pregnancy (sex selection, sale of fetal products, etc.).

This analogy to abortion helps to explain the otherwise bizarre distinction between policies limiting payment for oocytes in stem cell research and those permitting payment in the context of assisted reproduction. It also helps to explain the extent to which policies have focused on oocytes, rather than on sperm. The abortion debate historically has concerned itself with the need to monitor women's choices with regard to pregnancy. This is revealed when one considers that relatively few countries actually ban abortion under all circumstances – which is what one would expect if there were widespread agreement that an embryo was human life and that abortion was therefore tantamount to murder.[52]

Even a quick review of abortion laws from around the world demonstrates the law's distrust of women's choices in that the laws overwhelmingly represent lawmakers' efforts to dictate the circumstances under which a woman should be permitted to terminate her pregnancy. For example, some countries permit women to terminate their pregnancies in the event of incest or rape.[53] Such laws reflect the consensus of lawmakers that some women are not "to blame" for having become pregnant and therefore should not be made to carry their pregnancies to term. Other countries' laws permit women to terminate their pregnancies to the extent that their fetuses are severely disabled or if the woman's life is threatened by virtue of the pregnancy.[54]

Most of the world's abortion laws specify the limited conditions under which abortion is permissible, rather than banning it outright.[55] These laws implicitly assert the state's authority to determine the morality of abortion; by definition, they deny a woman's capacity to make her own moral judgment about abortion.

Working by analogy to abortion, those who favor banning compensation for stem cell research are motivated by a belief that this particular use of oocytes should be disfavored. In essence, they reason that stem cell research represents the termination of potential life and that, even if the law permits such research, women should not be encouraged to take such action. It is easy to see why such an analogy is both irrational and misogynistic.

It is irrational to view stem cell research as a variant of abortion because stem cell research does not involve the termination of potential human life.[56] Human gametes might merit treatment with dignity in the laboratory setting, but absent implantation into a woman's uterus, whatever dignity is accorded to gametes in a Petri dish should not be interpreted as a reflection of our collective understanding that these gametes are alive, or even potentially alive. Furthermore, it is incoherent to invoke dignitary justifications for a ban on compensating women for providing oocytes to stem cell researchers in a legal regime in which sperm can be bought and sold, whether for stem cell purposes or otherwise. It simply defies logic to argue that oocytes are more potentially alive than are sperm.

More troubling than the extreme views of a small minority of abortion opponents, however, is the willingness of those who support stem cell research to accede to the demand that women must donate, rather than be compensated for, their contribution to the enterprise. The widespread acquiescence on the issue of compensation is little more than a gesture of deference to those who oppose stem cell research in general. Advocates of limiting compensation offer up women's labor at below-market value – indeed, for free – as a preemptive effort to appease those whose might otherwise be swayed to oppose stem cell research in general. This is precisely what was meant by the British government's explanation that their decision to limit compensation to oocyte donors was "practical, rather than moral."[57]

Surely stem cell research would grind to a halt were the law to require that all those involved in this research volunteer their efforts. As such, the refusal to compensate women for their eggs emerges as not protective of women, but rather, as exploitative.

E. CONCLUSION

Stem cell research is fraught with controversy, but it is a controversy that is informed by the politics of abortion. Proponents of stem cell research have paid homage to abortion opponents by agreeing to limit payments to women who would provide oocytes to researchers. The justifications for such limitations cannot withstand intellectual scrutiny, and the resulting policy emerges as but a new incarnation of an age-old bias against women.

NOTES

1 *Oocytes* is the technical term for human eggs. The human female is born with a finite number of oocytes – typically approximately seven hundred thousand. Erik Block, *A Quantitative Morphological Investigation of the Follicular System in Newborn Female Infants*, 17 Acta Anat. (Basel) 201 (1953).

2 Many countries ban such research altogether. These include Ireland, Germany, Austria, Hungary, Poland, Tunisia, Switzerland, Italy, Brazil, Argentina, Ecuador, Peru, and Costa Rica, among others. *Stem Cell Research*, http://robby.nstemp.com/photo6.html.

3 Canada S.C. 2004, c. 2, s. 7.

4 Human Fertilisation & Embryology Act 1990, Section 12 [hereinafter HFEA].

5 "The sources of human oocytes for nuclear transfer should be carefully considered. Voluntary donations of oocytes could be considered from either human donors or from frozen ovarian tissues, in accordance with existing regulations or legislation." The Bioethics Advisory Committee, Israel Academy of Science and the Humanities, *The Use of Embryonic Stem Cells for Therapeutic Research*, http://www.academy.ac.il/bioethics/english/report1/Report1-e.html [hereinafter BAC Israel].

6 Current research suggests that ultimately, it may be possible to cultivate human embryonic stem cells without destroying the embryo. To date, that research is preliminary and has been successful only in mice. Irina Klimanskaya *et al.*, *Human Embryonic Stem Cell Lines Derived from Single Blastomeres*, 444 Nature 481 (2006). *See also* Young Chung *et al.*, *Embryonic and Extraembryonic Stem Cell Lines Derived from Single Mouse Blastomeres*, 439 Nature 216 (2006).

7 This process is known as somatic cell nuclear transfer (SCNT). To date, no human cell lines have been created through SCNT. This process has been successful, however, in a number of nonhuman animals, including sheep, cats, dogs, and mice. *See* Ian Wilmut *et al.*, *Viable Offspring Derived from Fetal and Adult Mammalian Cells*, 385 Nature 810 (1997) (describing the creation of the lamb "Dolly" through SCNT); Teruhiko Wakayama *et al.*, *Full-Term Development of Mice from Enucleated Oocytes Injected with Cumulus Cell Nuclei*, 394 Nature 369 (1998); Taeyoung Shin *et al.*, *Cell Biology: A Cat Cloned by Nuclear Transplantation*, 415 Nature 859 (2002); Byeung Chun Lee *et al.*, *Dogs Cloned from Adult Somatic Cells*, 436 Nature 641 (2005).

8 American Society for Reproductive Medicine, *Assisted Reproductive Technologies: A Guide for Patients*, http://www.asrm.org/Patients/patientbooklets/ART.pdf; National Research Council & Institute of Medicine (U.S.) Committee on Assessing the Medical Risk of Human Oocyte Donation for Stem Cell Research, Assessing the Medical Risk of Human Oocyte Donation for Stem Cell Research: Workshop Report (2007) [hereinafter NAS Medical Risk].

9 American Society for Reproductive Medicine, *supra* note 8.

10 *Id.*

11 *Id.*

12 *Id.*

13 NAS Medical Risk, *supra* note 8.

14 *Id.*

15 *Id.*

16 *Id.*

17 *See, e.g.*, HFEA, *supra* note 4 (banning compensation exceeding fifteen pounds in the United Kingdom); BAC Israel, *supra* note 5 (recommending the use of only "voluntary" egg donations in human embryonic stem cell [hESC] research conducted in Israel).

18 Oocyte donors spend approximately fifty-six hours completing the procurement process, including interviews, procedures, and counseling. Compensating these women at an hourly rate comparable to that paid to sperm donors would result in payments ranging from $3,360 to $4,200 (as of 2000). The American Society for Reproductive Medicine's Ethics Committee concluded that payments in this range are acceptable, and payments exceeding five thousand dollars would need to be justified. Ethics Committee for the American Society of Reproductive Medicine, *Financial Incentives in Recruitment of Oocyte Donors*, 74 Fertility & Sterility 216 (2000).

19 Gina Kolata, *$50,000 Offered to Tall, Smart Egg Donor*, N.Y. Times, March 3, 1999, at A10. *See also Classified Ad*, Stanford Daily, June 8, 2006, at 19 (offering one hundred thousand dollars for "attractive, intelligent donor of East Indian decent [*sic*]"); *id.* at 13

(offering eighty thousand dollars to a "special egg donor"); Bonnie Steinbock, *Payment for Egg Donation and Surrogacy*, 71 Mt. Sinai J. Med. 255 (2004).

20 Steinbock, *supra* note 19.

21 Cal. Health & Safety Code § 125290.35 (2006).

22 Cal. Health & Safety Code § 12592.10 (2006).

23 Edie Lau, *Stem Cell Rule Riles Critics: They Say State Should Compensate Women for Donating Their Eggs*, Sacramento Bee, July 7, 2005, at A3.

24 17 Cal. Code of Regs. § 100020 (2007).

25 Burns Ind. Code Ann. § 35-46-5-3 (2006); 2006 MD S.B. 144 (signed by the governor April 6, 2006); Mass GL ch. 111L, § 8 (2006); Conn. Gen. Stat. § 19a-32d (2006).

26 Minn. Stat. § 145.422 (2005).

27 National Research Council & Institute of Medicine (U.S.) Committee for Human Embryonic Stem Cell Research, Guidelines for Human Embryonic Stem Cell Research (2005) [hereinafter NAS Guidelines for hESC].

28 *Id.* at 85–6.

29 *Id.* at 87.

30 *See, e.g., id.* (suggesting that payments would compromise informed consent). *See also* David Brown, *South Korean Researcher Is Said to Admit Stem Cell Fakes; Team Will Ask Journal to Retract Its Report*, Washington Post, Dec. 15, 2005, at A01 (description of the Hwang scandal, in which research results were discredited not only on the basis of fabricated data, but also because the women who provided oocytes either were paid or were junior-level employees in Hwang's laboratory).

31 The Nuremberg Code, from United States v. Karl Brandt *et al.*, Trials of War Criminals before the Nuremberg Military Tribunals under Control Council Law 10. Nuremberg, October 1946–April 1949, Volumes I–II, http://www.hhs.gov/ohrp/references/nurcode.htm. The Belmont Report, *Belmont Report: Ethical Principles and Guidelines for the Protection of Human Subjects of Research*, http://www.hhs.gov/ohrp/humansubjects/guidance/belmont.htm. Although payment for research participation raises the issue most directly, questions of undue influence also may arise when a patient's own physician is serving as a primary investigator in a research project. If the physician-investigator attempts to recruit his or her patient directly into the study, the patient may feel pressure to participate. This concern has not been addressed by banning payments, but rather, by requiring IRB oversight and specific disclosures to prospective participants.

32 Neal Dickert *et al.*, *Paying Research Subjects: An Analysis of Current Policies*, 136 Ann. Intern. Med. 368 (2002); Christine Grady, *Payment of Clinical Research Subjects*, 115 J. Clinical Investigation 1681 (2005); Christine Grady *et al.*, *An Analysis of U.S. Practices of Paying Research Participants*, 26 Contemp. Clinical Trials 365 (2005).

33 *See, e.g.*, Dickert, *supra* note 32; U.S. Food & Drug Administration, *Payment to Research Subjects*, http://www.fda.gov/oc/ohrt/irbs/toc4.html#payment.

34 The text is identical for each of the seventeen federal agencies. For the language of the common rule, *see* 45 C.F.R. 46.101–24.

35 *See, e.g.*, National Science Foundation, *Frequently Asked Questions and Vignettes: Interpreting the Common Rule for the Protection of Human Subjects for Behavioral and Social Science Research*, http://www.nsf.gov/bfa/dias/policy/hsfaqs.jsp [hereinafter NSF FAQs]; U.S. Food & Drug Administration, *Recruiting Study Subjects*, http://www.fda.gov/oc/ohrt/irbs/toc4.html#recruiting.

36 NAS Guidelines for hESC, *supra* note 27; Steinbock, *supra* note 19.

37 The amount of money paid to research subjects varies considerably from study to study and from location to location. It is not uncommon for participants to receive hundreds

or thousands of dollars for their research participation. Grady, *An Analysis*, *supra* note 32.

38 Grady, *Payment*, *supra* note 32.

39 Grady, *An Analysis*, *supra* note 32.

40 NSF FAQs, *supra* note 35.

41 *See, e.g.*, Wilmut, *supra* note 7; Wakayama, *supra* note 7; Shin, *supra* note 7; Lee, *supra* note 7.

42 NAS Guidelines for hESC, *supra* note 27.

43 Radhika Rao, *Property, Privacy, and the Human Body*, 80 B.U. L. Rev. 359 (2000); Steinbock, *supra* note 19.

44 Along these lines, one might argue that the prohibition against commodifying oocytes relates to their finite nature. Because they are nonrenewable, one might reason that they are more akin to kidneys than to blood or sperm. The logic behind this analogy founders, however, in view of the fact that fertile women have many hundreds of thousands of oocytes in the ovaries – far more than they will be able to use in even those most prolific of reproductive lives. Block, *supra* note 1.

45 Steinbock, *supra* note 19.

46 *In re Baby M*, 109 N.J. 396 (1988).

47 *Id.*

48 *See, e.g.*, Johnson v. Calvert, 5 Cal. 4th 84 (1993).

49 *See, e.g.*, 750 Ill. Comp. Stat. Ann. 47/1–75 (2005) (the Illinois Gestational Surrogacy Act).

50 Steinbock, *supra* note 19. *See also* Paul Olding, *The Genius Sperm Bank*, http://news.bbc.co.uk/2/hi/uk_news/magazine/5078800.stm.

51 *See, e.g.*, Ruth R. Faden *et al.*, *Public Stem Cell Banks: Considerations of Justice in Stem Cell Research and Therapy*, 33 Hastings Center Rep. 13 (2003).

52 For a comprehensive summary of the world's laws governing abortion, *see The World's Abortion Laws*, http://www.crlp.org/pub_fac_abortion_laws.html.

53 *Id.* ("A number of countries explicitly recognize three other grounds for abortion: when pregnancy results from rape; when pregnancy results from incest; and when there is a high probability of fetal impairment").

54 *Id.*

55 *Id.*

56 The Bioethics Advisory Committee of the Israel Academy of Science and the Humanities recognized this distinction in its report on stem cell research. Noting that abortion in Israel is prohibited except in the event that a mother's life or health is in jeopardy, they explain that, therefore, a developing embryo cannot be removed from a woman's uterus at will. Research with hESC is permitted, however, because the embryo is not developing within the mother's womb. Instead, because it exists in a laboratory, it is similar in status to the ova and the sperm. "The status of the embryo outside the womb is comparable to that of gametes, sperm and oocytes: namely, they should not be wasted in vain but may be manipulated for therapeutic purposes." BAC Israel, *supra* note 5.

57 Robert Steinbrook, *Egg Donation and Human Embryonic Stem-Cell Research*, 354 New Eng. J. Med. 324 (2006).

(Courtesy of Keith Kamholz.)

PART FIVE. TENUOUS GROUNDS AND BABY TABOOS

> A survey of in-vitro fertilisation clinics seeking recalled instances of serious morbidity and known fatalities revealed a wide variety of complications, including two deaths because of the accidental failure to deliver oxygen during general anaesthesia, visceral injuries during egg retrievals, pelvic abscesses, serious infections, five serious vascular complications (one with residual hemiplegia), torsion of the ovary, and cancers discovered during or after treatment.
>
> – Sandra Coney, 345 LANCET 976 (1995)

In Part Five, the contributors consider whether we should give in to baby markets. Some of these exchanges are risky. High rates of multiple births, low success rates, and medical risks to women who use assisted reproductive technology (ART) demand a public response. Yet what the authors realize is that baby selling already exists, and we can either stand on the outside looking in or actively shape the regulatory future of the domain. The pitfalls and ethical challenges in the reproductive domain are discussed in earlier parts of this volume. Here the authors conclude the book by examining how the risky exchanges in ART should be handled and what giving in to baby markets really means.

18 Risky Exchanges

VIVIANA A. ZELIZER

In October 2006, icon pop singer Madonna attracted international headlines by adopting David Banda. David was a motherless one-year-old boy residing at the Home of Hope Orphan Care Centre in the isolated village of Mchinji, Mali. The boy's father, reportedly unable to support his child, expressed great pleasure that the boy should escape local poverty and receive such great care. At the same time, Madonna pledged about three million dollars to help orphans in Malawi. Meanwhile, Malawian advocacy groups objected to what they apparently saw as Madonna's impulse purchase. "It's not like selling property," protested Eyes of the Child, a child rights organization.[1]

The advocacy group sounded a familiar theme: some market transactions go beyond the boundary of decency. Similar objections arise with regard to transfer of sperm, eggs, body parts, and even personal care. What do critics worry about? Typically, they voice two logically distinct objections: first, that some goods and services should never be sold, and second, that some market arrangements are inherently pernicious. These two concerns differ starkly. The first focuses on what is being exchanged, and the second on the terms of the exchange.

This brief statement does no more than sketch a way of thinking about these issues. To clarify what is at stake, it stresses the analogy between exchanges of personal care and exchanges of babies. Let us call this class of transactions *risky exchanges*. I will draw especially on my own work concerning baby markets and on a rapidly expanding literature concerning the economics of care.

I argue that to explain how commercial markets for these risky exchanges actually work, we need to go beyond standard approaches to commodification. Those approaches often rely on simplistic equations of market exchange with moral degradation. Instead, I argue that we need to identify and explain multiple ways of organizing commercial exchanges. Some market arrangements do indeed have pernicious consequences, but others offer benefits to all participants. Only by getting rid of prejudices can we start identifying good matches among objects of exchange, terms of exchange, and welfare of parties to exchange.

On the way to identifying such good matches, we must dispose of two obvious but misleading ways of justifying bans on risky exchanges: (1) that the objects

I have adapted a few paragraphs from VIVIANA A. ZELIZER, THE PURCHASE OF INTIMACY (2005).

of exchange deserve protection because of the strong emotions they involve, in contrast to other commodities, and (2) that they require special treatment simply because they are more important than other exchanges. Risky exchanges are not unique in arousing strong emotions: think of purchasing homes, life insurance policies, or engagement rings. Surely these and many other emotionally charged transfers pass through the market without disrupting or demeaning social life. Nor can we justify bans on body parts or babies because they are more important than other goods. Few people, after all, now suppose that payment for medical treatment to save lives somehow demeans the treatment.

Some more substantial obstacles to understanding also block our way to clear analysis of risky exchanges. Two opposite clusters of beliefs about markets in general stand in the way. On one side stand paired beliefs we can call separate spheres and hostile worlds: first, that social relations divide sharply into spheres of sentiment and solidarity, on one side, and rational, self-interested calculation, on the other; second, that any contact between these hostile worlds tends to produce mutual contamination: corruption of sentimental solidarity into narrow self-interest, introduction of obfuscating sentiment into a sphere better served by efficient means-end rationality.

Another version of the separate spheres–hostile worlds view identifies a continuum from total market immunity to complete commodification. For some sorts of exchanges, runs the argument, any monetary compensation pushes the transaction down a slippery slope toward corruption. "If a free-market baby industry were to come into being," Margaret Jane Radin predicts,

> how could any of us, even those who did not produce infants for sale, avoid measuring the dollar value of our children? How could our children avoid being preoccupied with measuring their own dollar value? This measurement makes our discourse about ourselves (when we are children) and about our children (when we are parents) like our discourse about cars.[2]

At the opposite extreme of separate spheres–hostile worlds beliefs, we find an economistic nothing-but belief: all social relations ultimately reduce to expressions of rational self-interest mediated by one sort of market or another. A generation of work in economics and sociology has undermined both extreme beliefs by documenting and analyzing the incessant interplay of economic activity with solidarity-sustaining interpersonal relations. As applied to markets for body parts, such as blood and organs, Kieran Healey's book *Last Best Gifts*[3] has shown that a number of different intersections between commercial transactions and personal connections actually transfer human goods without the widely feared mutual corruption of markets and human solidarity.

We can usefully approach risky exchanges by considering a class of exchanges for which opinions and practices divide even more widely than with regard to body parts and babies: the paid provision for personal care. Personal care qualifies as a valuable analogy because its commercial provision regularly elicits all the obfuscating beliefs:

- that the objects of exchange deserve special protection because of the strong emotions they arouse

- that they deserve special protection because they are more important than other exchanges
- that they belong intrinsically to mutually exclusive separate spheres
- that contact between the spheres corrupts them
- that, on the contrary, they are nothing but market commodities like anything else

When it comes to personal care, all these widely held but fallacious principles obscure both recognition and the creation of good matches.

A. THE ECONOMICS OF CARE

With the aging of the population, and as more mothers are involved in the labor market, the problem of who cares for children, the ill, and the elderly has emerged as a serious policy concern. Over the last century or so, unquestionably, a higher proportion of personal care has become commercialized. That trend shows no sign of reversing. Nevertheless, the bulk of interpersonal care in Western countries still occurs outside the market. That raises two important questions: first, under what conditions does market-based care provide adequate support for both the recipients and the providers of care? Second, to what degree is the quality of care given via the market and outside the market fundamentally different?

Critics, advocates, care providers, and recipients of care disagree vociferously about these questions. Separate spheres–hostile worlds and nothing-but ideas often arise in those disagreements. One side, at the extreme, declares that genuine care requires insulation from the market, while the other insists that care should be a commercial service just like the rest. In fact, personal care ranges from relations whose ample compensation no one disputes, to others whose commercialization people often abhor. Consider this range of caregivers:

- mothers
- grandmothers
- siblings
- children
- other relatives
- babysitters
- servants
- day care workers
- home aides
- teachers
- nurses
- psychotherapists
- physicians
- pharmacists

By and large, nobody objects to financial compensation for the professionals on this list. These days, no one raises objections to paying physicians and nurses for their professional care of either babies or body parts. On the contrary, almost everyone seeks expensive medical attention for an ailing infant or a defective kidney, nor does it seem strange to pay pharmacists for their crucial contributions to personal care.

Clearly, payment for care as such does not offend fundamental principles. Yet many people insist that financial compensation for care threatens interpersonal relations either because the prospect of material benefit corrupts those relations or because the quality of unpaid care is intrinsically superior to that of paid care. To sort out beneficial from pernicious versions of compensation for care, we must look at the social arrangements by which such risky exchanges occur.

Including markets for care in the debate clarifies the issues, precisely because critics of existing arrangements for care have often voiced both of the classic objections: that some goods and services should never be sold, and that some market arrangements are inherently pernicious. Applied to care of babies, for example, we hear the claim that mother–child relations are too sacred, delicate, or consequential for delegation to paid helpers and the further claim that rich parents have no right to hire vulnerable immigrants as baby tenders at starvation wages because it cheats the babies of proper care, while exploiting their caretakers.

From both perspectives, many people have worried that payment for personal care degrades it, by rationalizing and marketizing what should be based on altruism and affection. Yet accumulating evidence indicates that effective care and financial compensation are perfectly compatible. For example, pointing to the child care market as thickly social and relational, Julie Nelson notes that parents or caregivers seldom define that market "as purely an impersonal exchange of money for services . . . the parties involved engage in extensive personal contact, trust, and interpersonal interaction." "The specter of the all-corrupting market," she argues, "denies that people – such as many child-care providers – can do work they love, among people they love, and get paid at the same time." Paid care, Nelson insists, should not be treated as "relationally second rate."[4]

What is more, experimental programs make it feasible, equitable, and personally acceptable to compensate family members for care they would otherwise have to provide without payment at great cost to household welfare. A 1999 study of the California system, funded at the University of California, Los Angeles, by the U.S. Department of Health and Human Services, concluded that family members actually provided higher-quality service than unrelated workers.[5] Specifically, the study found that clients employing family care workers "reported a greater sense of security, having more choice about how their aides performed various tasks, a stronger preference for directing their aides, and a closer rapport with their aides."

Other experimental public programs have tried paying poor women for the care of their own sick or disabled children, thus formalizing them as paid providers of care. Consider Tasha's case, as reported in a study of strategies used by welfare-reliant mothers caring for children with chronic health conditions or disabilities after the welfare reforms of the early 1990s. Tasha, a forty-five-year-old, unmarried African American living in Cleveland with her two children, had first dropped out of Ohio State University to care for her sick father. She then became primary caregiver for her daughter, who had a severe seizure disorder. Pushed out of welfare, she managed to get hired by an agency that paid her a low hourly wage without medical benefits for thirty hours of weekly care work. The meager salary helped redefine Tasha's social standing:

> I feel good, good you know because like I said, I feel fortunate that I can still do things at home. I went to look at some living room furniture the other day and the guy said: "Are you employed?" And I said: "Yes, I'm employed." You know my social security number, you know, you check it out. So, that kinda thing, it makes you, it makes you feel good.... You know, you're in a different status [when] you're not considered unemployed.[6]

In this case, the entry of paid care into the household by no means undermined its moral economy – quite the contrary.

Persistent hostile worlds assumptions portraying love and care as demeaned by monetization may in fact underpin unjust policies and lead to economic discrimination against those allegedly intangible caring activities, for example, lack of economic security for unpaid caregiving, low pay for caregivers such as nannies and home health aides, resistance to compensating relatives for care work.

Consider the painful impact of the 1996 U.S. welfare reform introducing stringent work requirements for recipients on the mothers of chronically ill children. A comprehensive study found that these women were caught in a terrifying dilemma: if they worked, their sick children did not get proper care, but if they stopped working to care for their children, the mothers lost their welfare benefits.

To compound the difficulties, few American child-care facilities are prepared to receive such children. A dozen concerned medical organizations proposed a solution: change welfare policy to make the care of sick children count as work, thus permitting mothers to meet the work requirement. But their proposal was turned down. Instead, the Bush administration called for increases in work requirements.[7]

What practical implications does this approach imply? To direct our search toward just, noncoercive sets of economic transactions for different types of caring relations. The goal is not therefore to cleanse intimacy from economic concerns: the challenge is to create fair mixtures. We should stop agonizing over whether money corrupts, and instead analyze what combinations of economic activity and caring relations produce happier, more just, and more productive lives. It is not the mingling that should concern us, but rather, how the mingling works. If we get the causal connections wrong, we will obscure the origins of injustice, damage, and danger.

B. BABY MARKETS

The same principle applies to baby markets. As in the case of personal care, widespread misunderstandings about baby markets block us from seeing variations in the organization of commercial exchanges involving babies. As a result, we fail to distinguish between pernicious markets and monetary arrangements that actually enhance the welfare of children and their families.

Recall the two objections to risky exchanges: first, that some goods and services should never be sold, and second, that some market arrangements are inherently pernicious. Both apply to baby markets. Think first about babies as commodities.

Separate spheres–hostile worlds purists – as we saw with the uproar over Madonna's baby adoption – insist on an impermeable division between babies and market transactions: we should never mix babies with monetary interests. The exchange of children should be regulated by altruism, not profit.

Economists, nothing-but enthusiasts, on the other hand, hail a baby market as an efficient solution to imbalances between demand and supply of babies. Most famously, Elizabeth Landes and Richard Posner argued in 1978 for the outright legalization of baby selling as the best solution to the baby shortage. But Landes and Posner fail to say that concrete organization of the baby market would simultaneously promote efficiency, welfare, and active participation of their "producers" and "consumers."

Ironically, despite their conflicting agendas, moral objectors and market enthusiasts similarly overlook the remarkable variety of existing baby market arrangements. When it comes to the second common objection about inherently pernicious market arrangements, the most common concern about baby markets is the creation of an impersonal competition for personal attributes. Here the critics have two valid points: first, the terms of exchange are absolutely crucial for the pernicious or beneficial effects of baby markets, and second, no baby market will be beneficial if it does not take into account the prevailing understandings of childhood in their context.

C. PRICELESS BABIES

For me, current discussions of payments for infants call up a strong sense of déjà vu. Variation and change in markets for babies have preoccupied me for years. My book *Pricing the Priceless Child*,[8] for example, documented the long history and versatility of commercial exchanges involving babies in the United States between the 1870s and 1930s. Most important, the history illustrates that seemingly predetermined separate spheres domains are in fact cultural and social constructs. Those constructs, in turn, shape the organization and legitimacy of economic practices.

The changing U.S. baby market was intimately tied to the profound cultural transformation in children's economic and sentimental value at the turn of the twentieth century, specifically, the emergence of the economically worthless but emotionally priceless child. Whereas in the nineteenth century, the market value of children was culturally acceptable, the new twentieth-century normative ideal of the child as an exclusively emotional and affective asset made any instrumental or fiscal consideration offensive. In an increasingly commercialized world, children were assigned a separate noncommercial space, extra commercium. The economic and sentimental values of children were thereby declared to be radically incompatible.

The creation of this priceless child deeply affected the exchange value of children. Nineteenth-century foster families took in useful children, expecting them to help out with farm chores and household tasks. It was considered a fair bargain. Not surprisingly, the premium went to children (preferably boys) older than ten, old enough to be useful. In this context, babies were "unmarketable" and hard to place, except in foundling asylums or commercial baby farms.

After the 1920s, adoptive parents were only interested in (and willing to wait several years for) a blue-eyed baby or a cute, two-year-old, curly-haired girl. Whereas nineteenth-century mothers who could not afford to raise their illegitimate child were forced to pay to get rid of the baby, by the 1930s, unwanted babies were selling for one thousand dollars or more. As a result, the value of a priceless child became increasingly monetized and commercialized. Ironically, the new market price for babies was set exclusively by their noneconomic, sentimental appeal.

As demand for adoptable children grew, it became a seller's market, and a wide range of commercial arrangements emerged, some of which persist today. They include black-market baby sales with cash payments for the mother and profit for the broker; gray markets, where placements are arranged without profit by parents, friends, relatives, doctors, and lawyers (although professional fees for legal and medical services are part of the arrangement); "gratitude donations" from adoptive parents to child placement agencies; adoption fees; and board payments to foster parents.

D. BABIES TODAY

My own analysis of American baby markets stops around 1950. Fortunately, Debora Spar has provided a fine survey of recent developments in the same field. She documents extensive, varied payment arrangements in contemporary baby markets. As Spar concludes,

> Parents acquire children all the time, and we generally regard it as a fine thing to do. What differs, of course, is the mode of acquisition in the baby business; it is the entry of commerce into what many regard as an entirely noncommercial affair. This argument, though, does not carry any kind of natural weight. If we think that markets are good and children are good, then it's not obvious why mixing the two is inherently vile. Instead, we can just as easily turn this argument on its head, examining how market mechanisms might help to produce a socially desirable outcome.[9]

Here Spar directly parallels my own conclusions about earlier markets. Similar principles apply to adjacent baby markets, ranging from surrogacy fees paid to women for so-called made-to-order babies to the multiple payments involved in the growing global market of international adoptions. In addition to an application fee, home study fee, and program fee, agencies assisting foreign adoptions include fees to the agency's local representative, driver, and interpreter, and sometimes a required donation to a local orphanage.[10]

At the edge of baby markets appear paid exchanges for eggs and sperm. Rene Almeling[11] has beautifully documented these two paired but gender-differentiated markets. She makes three keen observations: first, that beyond the expected biological distinctions, these transactions differ significantly for men and women donors; second, that agencies, recipients, and donors mark those distinctions with differential recruitment, advertising, and compensation arrangements; and third, in a paradoxical reversal of the standard gendered wage gap that penalizes women, Almeling finds that in the reproductive market, women are better paid than men.

As Almeling notes, the organizational structures of both egg and sperm markets are similar: in both cases, commercial agencies rely on advertising and careful screening to match paying customers with paid donors. The two are also complex markets: the bulk of prospective donors on each side turn out to be ineligible. What is more, both markets require extensive adaptation by the donors, for example, egg donation involves invasive and risky medical procedures.

Despite such similarities, Almeling shows that sperm and egg markets operate differently, as agencies, donors, and recipients negotiate distinct and varied definitions of their relationships to each other. While sperm donation is often categorized as an ordinary job, involving legitimate financial incentives, egg agencies emphasize donors' altruistic motivations, minimizing women's desire for monetary gain. Agencies extol the caring dimensions of providing eggs to childless clients to the point of sometimes rejecting donors who appear overly greedy. Egg donation is further personalized by providing donors' photographs and by matching specific donors to recipients, thus reducing the anonymity of the transactions.

Payment systems mark these distinctions: men's compensation is typically standardized so that donors receive similar payment per usable sample. They do not get paid for substandard samples. Women, on the other hand, get paid regardless of the number of eggs produced, and their compensation is negotiated at the time when the agency matches donor to recipient: pay varies depending on such factors as experience (first-time donors get less); education (higher education gets more); and in some cases, race (often minorities get more because of recruitment shortages). Pay also hinges on the donor's physical appearance and, to some extent, on the agency's perceptions of a donor's caring motivations.

Significantly, gifts reaffirm the personalized quality of the egg donor–recipient connection. Grateful egg recipients, Almeling reports, often send their donor flowers, jewelry, or so-called gift money. Sometimes the giftlike quality of the transactions is formalized: one of the egg agencies Almeling studied defines the donor's fee as a nontaxable gift.

Thus, in egg and sperm markets, young men and women are involved in selling their reproductive materials, yet these risky exchanges do not result in identical rationalized markets. What is fascinating in Almeling's account is how similar commercial arrangements produce different outcomes. They do so precisely because they incorporate different kinds of interpersonal relations, in this case, strongly marked by gender. Far from becoming standardized exchanges, each market depends on different kinds of relationships among donors, recipients, and agencies.

As elsewhere, we cannot understand markets for sperm and eggs without taking into account the meanings assigned by participants in the exchange. These differential meanings, Almeling argues, produce the unexpected economic advantages of egg donors. Despite the difficult process of extracting eggs, the supply of donors, she shows, outstrips the supply of sperm donors. Why, then, are egg donors better paid and more highly valued? Both high pay, and the simultaneous definition of a giftlike exchange, Almeling argues, results from "cultural norms of caring motherhood." Here gender trumps supply and demand.

Of course, one could read Almeling's account of egg and sperm markets as confirming nothing-but economist accounts. The altruistic rhetoric could be nothing more than camouflage for a maximizing exchange no different than the purchase of any other consumption good. That would be a mistake. Most of the time, donors, recipients, and commercial agencies are organizing the market to reflect the particular meanings and characteristics of the social relations established by the exchange of reproductive goods. Indeed, Martha Ertman, critic of current limits on baby markets, argues that the market for artificial insemination provides a model for more equitable access to parenthood by same-sex and single parents.[12]

For separate spheres–hostile worlds advocates, all such risky exchanges threaten the sacredness of children. To be sure, in many cases, babies and parents do suffer from these market arrangements: there are dangers of exploiting poor women, there is rampant inequality in the kinds of children who are produced or acquired. But a lot of the time, participants in these exchanges work out a morally acceptable set of conditions for the exchange, which involve severe restrictions as to who gets what, when, and for what.

These multiple baby markets also refute the nothing-but arguments that hold out the possibility of an impersonal rational market that extends into the world of baby exchanges. Both hostile world and nothing-but arguments miss the creation of morally contingent relational markets. The involvement of money does not necessarily convert all exchanges into ordinary sales. Take the surrogacy payment: it can be a venal and dehumanizing payoff, but it can also symbolize acceptable retribution.

E. RISKY ASSUMPTIONS

Analysts of these sorts of risky exchanges often rely on strong, if largely implicit, assumptions about human nature and politics:

- that people in general – givers and recipients of care alike – operate uniformly on self-interest
- that both governmental and market interventions in the provision of care simultaneously attack legitimate interests and corrupt valued interpersonal relations
- that existing political alignments therefore forbid – and should forbid – thoroughgoing governmental and market transformations of current arrangements for exchanges involving babies and care

Given accumulating evidence of widespread human preferences for fair arrangements that produce secure collective goods, all those assumptions deserve scrutiny and debate.

In particular, critics of risky exchanges worry about effects of market solutions. They warn against three classes of perverse effects from market interventions:

1. exploitation of the poor
2. decline in altruism
3. negative impact on other social relations

All three do sometimes occur in markets. But the question is, do all kinds of market arrangements entail these negative outcomes?

My general answer runs as follows: markets vary enormously in the extent to which and the way in which they actually produce such perverse effects. Let me make the case briefly in three major points:

1. Widespread but false beliefs about universal properties of markets make it seem that the perverse effects themselves are likewise universal.
2. The feasibility of alterations in market arrangements does indeed depend on connections between the internal organization of markets and existing configurations of power and culture.
3. A variety of markets analogous to those of babies and care demonstrate the possibility of benign market effects.

Of course – to take up my second main point – the extent to which various market arrangements actually produce efficient, equitable, and politically viable outcomes depends heavily on connections between internal market structures and existing configurations of power and culture. Within economics and sociology, institutional analysts have been insisting on the point for two decades or so.

In general, institutional analysts have drawn from this observation not a conservative pessimism based on the immutability of politics, culture, and human nature, but rather, a cautious belief that all three change in response to shifting circumstances, including deliberate policy interventions. In the case of transfers of body parts, as Healey shows, various organizational structures involving different mixtures of economic and moral incentives sometimes produce relatively efficient and equitable connections between supply and demand.[13]

My third point is that a variety of markets analogous in some respects to those of babies and provision of care demonstrate the possibility of benign market effects. Consider just two analogies: life insurance and monetary compensation for disaster such as 9/11. Life insurance initially raised the same sorts of moral objections as payments for babies or care, as a violation of the sacredness and integrity of human life. In fact, people called life insurance "blood money." But eventually, Americans, and Westerners more generally, came to accept it as a prudent provision for welfare, one so important that it should be universal and backed by government regulation.

Although one might offer the 2005 Katrina disaster as a counterexample, the 9/11 Victim Compensation Fund overcame objections to the financial evaluation of lost lives by instituting public and equitable rules for compensation of loss.

Does this mean that market solutions unfailingly deliver equity, efficiency, and political viability? On the contrary, it means that inventing market-based systems for equitable, efficient, and politically viable transfers of delicate assets requires all the craft that social planners can summon up. Remember the two classic objections to risky exchanges: that some goods and services should never be sold, and that some market arrangements are inherently pernicious. Fixation on the first – the sale of sacred objects – blocks serious consideration of the second.

A similar lesson applies to compensation for replacement of organs and to exchanges of blood. As Healey claims about these markets in his superb study,

> While we should worry about exploitation in the exchange of human goods, it is a mistake to think that commodification as such is the reason exploitation

> happens. Commodified exchanges may well be exploitative, but market exchange does not automatically make it so. Both gift and market systems depend on their specific institutional realization for their effects. The choice is not between morally worthwhile gift giving and morally suspect markets.[14]

Considering the highly exploitative gray market for kidneys and corneas, Healey notes that the problem is not created by organ sellers contracting a sale. Instead, "it is the wider social context in which they find themselves – their dominated class position, long-term disadvantage, and poor life chances – that puts them in a situation that invites their exploitation by 'transplant tourists.'"[15] The question is not contamination, but rather, fairness.

When it comes to markets for babies and care, we need better law and public policy. Instead of worrying about market-based corruption, designers of public policy in these areas should be promoting just, attractive, and life-enhancing economic arrangements. Clear analysis of how existing economic arrangements actually operate provides a significant first step toward that goal.

NOTES

1 *Madonna Adoption Bid Challenged*, http://news.bbc.co.uk/go/em/fr/-/1/hi/entertainment/6048674.stm.
2 Margaret Jane Radin, Contested Commodities 138 (1996).
3 Kieran Healey, Last Best Gifts (2006).
4 Julie A. Nelson, *One Sphere or Two?* 41 Am. Behav. Sci. 1467, 1470 (1998).
5 Pamela A. Doty, E. Benjamin, Ruth E. Matthias, & Todd M. Franke, *In-Home Supportive Services for the Elderly and Disabled: A Comparison of Client-Directed and Professional Management Models of Service Delivery*, http://aspe.hhs.gov/daltcp/reports/ihss.htm.
6 Andrew S. London, Ellen K. Scott, & Vicki Hunter, *Children and Chronic Health Conditions: Welfare Reform and Health-Related Carework*, *in* Childcare and Inequality: Rethinking Carework for Children and Youth 109 (Francesca M. Cancian, Demie Kurz, Andrew S. London, Rebecca Reviere, & Mary C. Tuominen eds., 2002).
7 Wendy Chavkin, *Mothers of Ill Children*, 53 N.Y. Rev. Books 76–7 (2006); *Doctors Speak Out about Welfare Reform*, http://www.findingcommonground.hs.columbia.edu/speakout.pdf.
8 Viviana Z. Zelizer, Pricing the Priceless Child (1985).
9 Debora Spar, The Baby Business: How Money, Science, and Politics Drive the Commerce of Conception 196 (2006).
10 *Id.* at 182; Sara K. Dorow, Transnational Adoption: A Cultural Economy of Race, Gender, and Kinship 81 (2006).
11 Rene Almeling, *Selling Genes, Selling Gender: Egg Agencies, Sperm Banks, and the Medical Market in Genetic Material*, Am. Soc. Rev. (June 2007).
12 Martha M. Ertman, What's Wrong with a Parenthood Market? A New and Improved Theory of Commodification, 82 N.C. L. Rev. 1 (2003).
13 Kieran Healy, Last Best Gifts (2006).
14 *Id.* at 124.
15 *Id.*

19 Giving In to Baby Markets

SONIA SUTER

I come to the issue of baby markets[1] with reservations. Drawing on a relational conception of autonomy and self-definition, I argue that commodification of reproductive material is intrinsically harmful. Moreover, such commodification poses a number of consequential harms. Nevertheless, in spite of these concerns, I "give in" to baby markets, which is to say I do not argue for the prohibition of these markets, but instead for their regulation and oversight. In other words, I am not willing to accept completely free and unfettered markets. I give in to baby markets in part because of the great impracticality of prohibiting markets given how well entrenched they are. In addition, although markets present risks, the risk–benefit calculus calls for allowing markets to exist, provided there is careful and serious regulation of such markets. Thus I take a pragmatic approach that suggests we should (reluctantly) accept baby markets as long as we offer measures to counteract the negative effects of commodification so that baby markets work equitably, safely, and in a way that protects the interests of all involved: seller, buyer, and future child. In a country with limited regulation of the reproductive industry, this may be a tall order.

In section A of this chapter, I use a relational theory of personhood to suggest that reproductive material can be relationally self-defining to varying degrees. The more self-defining such material is, the more intrinsically harmful it is to buy and sell it. I emphasize, however, that baby markets do not exist in a world where all things are equal and that there are numerous consequential effects of baby markets, some of which are even more troubling than the intrinsic harms. In section B, I explain why I nevertheless "give in" to baby markets, and in section C, I focus specifically on the consequential harms of distorted decision making, coercion, and power imbalances. Section D concludes by offering some suggestions for enhancing decision making, with particular emphasis on remedying the inadequacies of informed consent law.

A. COMMODIFICATION AND INTRINSIC HARMS

The concern that baby markets are intrinsically harmful builds on the theory that market valuation is inherently corruptive if we treat certain goods as reducible to monetary measures of value.[2] Whether commodification poses intrinsic harms or degrading effects depends on the "character of the particular good in question" and "the ideals at stake."[3] We potentially do harm to ourselves and to human flourishing if we treat something integral to ourselves as a commodity, that is, as separate and fungible.[4] Whether and to what degree commodification is problematic therefore depends on whether and to what degree the putative "commodity" is integral to the self.

I contend that because embryos and gametes are severable and separable from us, they are not per se integral to us. But the possibility of severability and separation is not sufficient to assess whether something is essential to human flourishing. Some things that are severable and separable, such as employment, can sometimes be deeply integral to the self. To assess how integral something is to the self, we must consider other factors such as our intentions and actions regarding the commodified item, that is, whether we want to separate from it or whether we see it as integral to us.[5] Equally important is the nature of our relationship to the commodified item as understood culturally, legally, and biologically.

What makes embryos, and to a lesser extent, gametes, integral to personhood interests is their centrality to decisions about reproduction and the creation of families. They occupy a unique place in the world of "things" because of their reproductive potential.[6] As one court and many ethicists have recognized, embryos are neither property nor persons, but tissues that deserve special respect because they implicate people's procreative interests.[7] Gametes do not, in and of themselves, have the same capacity, but they are, of course, essential to the reproductive process in a way that ordinary cells are not.

The nature of our relationship with gametes and embryos and their role in self-definition depend a great deal on context and our intentions regarding them, specifically the procreative decisions we make and the relationships that we choose or do not choose to form with the people they may become. But their role in self-definition also depends on the biological, social, and cultural importance of our intergenerational relationships to them. This assessment is rooted in a notion of selfhood that is relational, where self-discovery unfolds "in relation to others with whom we confront our thoughts against their thoughts," where "my life is always embedded in the story of those communities from which I derive my identity," as opposed to an "atomistic conception of self-definition, in which the individual shapes herself without reference to others."[8]

Under this relational notion of self-definition, the extent to which embryos and gametes are self-defining depends on whether they will become people who form part of the community from which we derive our identity. Embryos and gametes may be the origins of families and intimate relationships. Even when genetic relatedness is absent – as in the case of a couple or individual who obtains an embryo for implantation – the embryo, which will become their child, defines them in very real and deep ways and thus is integral to the self. Alternatively, embryos or gametes may be something from which we intentionally separate (whether or not for money) with little or no possibility of future connection: we might donate them to unknown infertile couples or researchers, or we might request that extra reproductive material be destroyed.[9] The fact that we treat these embryos as separable from us diminishes the extent to which they are integral to us. How much depends on why we choose to separate from them. If just profit motivates this separation, we are treating them "as essentially fungible and interchangeable,"[10] and our personhood interests are lessened. But if altruism prompts us to separate from embryos (whether or not we are paid) to help infertile couples or promote research, then these decisions are more relationally self-defining because such decisions are based on our membership in and commitment to the community writ large. In cases in which we donate gametes or embryos to friends or family as part of our commitment to these relationships, an even more significant relational interest would exist. In all these cases, however, separability is the main intention, and therefore these actions are not as self-defining as decisions to use embryos or gametes to become a parent to the future child.[11]

A recent case involving "a colossal mix-up" of sperm at a fertility clinic demonstrates how intent and actions regarding gametes can implicate strong personhood interests.[12] In this case, the clinic accidentally used a man's sperm to inseminate not his girlfriend, as intended, but a woman who had arranged for artificial insemination by an anonymous donor.[13] The man's goal was to use his gametes to create his own family, not to help an unknown woman conceive. His is not the case in which the sperm donor considers his sperm severable and separable. In fact, "when asked about the common assumption that men regard their sperm as expendable, he begins to cry."[14] In short, he had strong personhood and relational interests in his gametes. As a result, he went to court to ask to be declared the legal father if a child was born and turned out to be his.[15]

When someone intends to use reproductive material to create a family, commodification is particularly threatening to human flourishing, as was discussed in the famous case *In re Baby M.*[16] In that case, an infertile couple, William and Elizabeth Stern, entered into a contract with Mary Beth Whitehead, a gestational surrogate who agreed to conceive a child through artificial insemination with the husband's sperm, to carry the child to term, and to relinquish her parental rights so the couple could adopt the child. In exchange, she was to be paid. Originally, Mrs. Whitehead's personhood interests in the fetus were minimal: she intended and contracted to separate from the future child. But in the course of the pregnancy, she formed the kind of relational attachment that implicates personhood interests and that led her to change her mind. Of course, the Sterns, who desperately wanted a family, also had strong, relationally self-defining interests in the future child. They entered into the contract and agreed to pay money with the specific goal of bringing a child into the world whom they intended to raise.

Among the concerns that led the *Baby M* court to invalidate the contract was the exchange of money. The court reasoned that commodification was harmful to all involved: the future child, the gestational surrogate, the natural father, and the adoptive mother. It concluded that "there are, in a civilized society some things that money cannot buy."[17] In so doing, the court drew on the kind of discomfort many feel regarding certain financial exchanges such as paying a spouse for sex, paying for a baby, or paying for a mail-order bride.

Baby M was, we hope, the rare case in which the ultimate intention of one of the contracting parties changes.[18] Assuming sellers do not change their minds, their actions and intentions with respect to the embryos, gametes, or future child are usually severability and separation. As a result, in most instances, although the sellers of the embryo, gamete, or surrogacy service[19] will have a relational interest in the gametes or embryos, their interest will be less than that of buyers who intend to establish a lifelong relationship as parents of the future child.

Self-definition, however, is shaped not only by our subjective choices regarding which relationships to embrace, but also by objective relational factors. Relationships that have social, cultural, and intergenerational importance define us in part, even if we do not choose these relationships. For example, a woman may give birth to a child and ultimately choose not to have a relationship with that child. But until the child has been legally adopted, we recognize that child as the woman's, even if her intention is to part with it. Even afterward, we think of the child as her child, biologically. Biological parents themselves may still feel like parents in one sense, even if they intend to relinquish parental rights.[20]

Unless the biological relationships are complex (e.g., when intended parents use in vitro fertilization (IVF), donor gametes, and/or a gestational surrogate to bring a child into the world), we have long-established cultural and legal understandings that a parent–child relationship exists given certain biological connections. Of course, these understandings are not set in stone, and our society and laws allow people to redefine these relationships through adoption.[21] That this redefinition requires legal recognition and does not occur solely because of one's intentions and experiences attests to the fact that biological connections can create self-defining relationships of sorts between two individuals. As a result, gamete or embryo donors are defined in part by the genetic relationships that exist between them and the people who will develop from those gametes or embryos.[22]

Because embryos and gametes are integral to the self, albeit to differing degrees, depending on intention, actions, and objective recognition of certain relationships, commodification of this reproductive material is potentially intrinsically harmful. This claim, however, presumes a world in which the only variable at issue is whether money should change hands in exchange for an embryo, gamete, or surrogacy service. It presumes no other threats to human flourishing such as unequal bargaining power, unequal access to reproductive options, or limited availability of gametes and embryos. In this theoretical world, widely divergent from the real world, it seems particularly unsettling and improper to engage in financial transactions with respect to the relationally, self-defining decisions associated with baby markets.[23]

To demonstrate fully the kind and extent of harm to human flourishing that baby markets present would require a well-developed normative vision of human flourishing that is beyond the scope of this chapter. I do not offer such a vision beyond my claims about the concerns regarding relational, personhood interests for a few reasons. First, the notion that some things are so central to personhood and human flourishing that they would be corrupted by markets challenges the market-oriented view that all goods are commensurable. But as Sandel has pointed out, "it does not seem . . . possible, in general, to prove or refute the thesis of commensurability, which is one of the reasons that arguments by analogy play such an important role in debates about commodification."[24]

Second, and more important, all things are not equal. Commodification here, as in any other context, occurs against the backdrop of many factors that influence the conditions of the exchange. If these background conditions meant, for example, that such markets enhanced the ability of or opportunities for individuals to create families,[25] prohibiting such markets would be damaging to human flourishing. In those cases, being unable to engage in such commerce would be much more degrading than commodification itself.

Markets might enhance options for buyers and/or sellers, but they also might negatively affect them. This raises empirical questions as to whether and when being able to buy or sell embryos, gametes, or surrogacy services increases opportunities for relationally self-defining actions on the part of both buyers and sellers. So although we may worry about the damaging effects of baby markets on human flourishing, we cannot evaluate baby markets as if the only issue is the intrinsic harm of commodification. It is impossible to separate out completely the intrinsic harms of commodification from the consequential effects (positive or negative) of commodification that turn on "background conditions within which market exchanges take place."[26]

My final reason for not offering a fully developed theory of human flourishing is that the consequential harms of baby markets are equally, and in some cases even more troubling than the intrinsic harms. As I argue in a longer version of this piece,[27] numerous consequential harms exist. Coercion, distorted decision making, and power imbalances made worse by an unregulated infertility industry motivated by profit all potentially impact the self-defining choices associated with baby markets even more than the mere fact of commodification. Market preferences that favor anonymity of sellers and prevent the child from learning her genetic heritage also threaten the child's relational autonomy. Market preferences may also exacerbate the tendencies to use assisted reproductive technologies (ART) for so-called eugenic ends. Finally, even if baby markets increase access to gametes and embryos, they cannot alone overcome the various barriers to ART that its proponents imagine.

As a result, the consequential effects of commodification can be especially threatening. Yet, in spite of these many concerns about intrinsic and consequential harms, I reluctantly accept baby markets. Because I aim to remedy the consequential harms of baby markets, I first explain my pragmatic response to baby markets before I turn to perhaps one of the biggest consequential harms – distorted decision making. In short, I explain why I "give in" to baby markets.

B. GIVING IN TO BABY MARKETS

Despite my unease regarding baby markets, the reality is that markets (black or otherwise) do exist in embryos, gametes, surrogacy services, and other aspects of assisted reproductive technologies.[28] Approaches that try to theorize out the market are insufficiently attentive to real problems, which must be dealt with. In addition, the elimination of commodification in baby markets is highly impractical.[29] Recognizing the costs and impracticalities of prohibiting markets, how entrenched baby markets are, and the possible benefits they offer, I give in to baby markets. That is to say, I reluctantly resist the prohibition of markets, in spite of the many consequential harms of markets. Recognizing that "ideal theory... may have to give way to nonideal theory,"[30] I argue strongly in favor of mechanisms to address many of the threats of such markets. If baby markets are inevitable, better that we allow them, but not that we accept them warts and all.

My goal in advocating the regulation of baby markets is to bring the world as close to ideal as possible. Of course, some of the intrinsic concerns I raised will still exist. But given both the impracticalities and costs of prohibiting markets, as well as the fact that certain background conditions that can affect human flourishing will not disappear simply by banning markets, this may be the price we have to pay. Since my response to baby markets is not grounded in practical realities, we should not let the best be the enemy of the good. As a result, we must choose the next best approach – one in which we tend to the many consequential harms as well as we can. Prohibiting commodification may not actually alleviate many of the background conditions that raise the consequential harms. Instead, it may increase the vulnerability of the disempowered because we will have washed our hands of markets, effects and all. As I suggest in the longer article and, to some extent, in the remainder of this chapter, the consequential harms of unfettered baby markets can threaten the well-being, and even sometimes the human flourishing, of the various participants of baby markets.[31] I turn now to explore this problem with respect to one of the most important effects of baby markets: their potential to distort decision making unduly through coercion and power imbalances.

C. DISTORTED DECISION MAKING

As is true of all the consequential harms, distorted decision making in baby markets is not context-specific in the way that intrinsic harms are.[32] In other words, this harm does not depend entirely on the moral importance of the good being sold, but rather, on the ways in which markets can influence behavior. The concern is that commodification may lead people to make choices they might not otherwise make – in particular, choices that are not in their best interests. Such coercion may be further exacerbated in the face of underlying inequities, where those who are neediest may make choices they would not otherwise make because of a need for money.[33] Such a result would aggravate existing inequities by increasing the flourishing of the advantaged at the expense of the disadvantaged.[34]

Concerns regarding coercion are heightened when the reproductive choices are tied to one's sense of self. We might worry, for example, about the surrogate who originally intended to part with the baby she has carried for nine months and now has a change of heart. Would financial necessity, in some cases, drive her to relinquish her parental rights in spite of bonding with the fetus and wanting to raise the child? The harm would be especially serious. Not only would money have influenced a choice, but it would have done so with respect to a choice that strongly implicates relational autonomy and that is deeply integral to the self.

Coercion is troubling even if lesser personhood interests are at stake. The woman who wants to sell her ova may not have as deep a relational connection to the ova.

Nevertheless, she might not have otherwise chosen to endure the burdensome process of taking hormones, undergoing anesthesia, and facing possible long-term health risks to retrieve the ova had she not needed the money.

An additional concern with markets here (and in other areas of commodification) is their potential to exacerbate power imbalances, which can distort decision making. Sellers in baby markets are, by and large, more economically disadvantaged than buyers. Women with plenty of economic resources, for example, are far less likely to go through the physically arduous process of producing ova for sale or carrying a child for another couple, whereas women in need of money may find this to be a reasonable trade-off.[35] Socioeconomic differences as well as the circumstances of negotiating some of these sales may lead to further power imbalances. For example, in the negotiation of surrogacy contracts, the intended parents and their agents pay many of the relevant expenses and control many aspects of the process. The buyers therefore are in a position to "exert undue influence on the potential surrogate."[36] In short, "the party who holds the most resources is the party who has the greatest ability to manipulate the situation."[37]

But the power relationships in baby markets are complicated. As Martha Ertman has described, the alternative insemination market inverts feminist concerns about gender power imbalances when men are sellers of gametes and buyers include gay women.[38] Moreover, the kinds of structural imbalances that often arise in other contexts, where the buyers are institutions or corporations and the sellers are individuals, are not always present here.[39] The end-point buyers and sellers in baby markets are usually individuals.[40]

Buyers in baby markets, however, are also vulnerable participants. The desire for a child can be overwhelming precisely because of the deep personhood and relational autonomy interests at stake. Many buyers in baby markets are willing to go to great lengths and pay huge sums to have a baby.[41] For this reason, they may arguably be even more invested in the sale of reproductive material than the seller, which can tip the power balance in favor of the seller. Obviously, this power imbalance is less likely to occur when buyers are not the end-point individual purchasers, but are instead sophisticated brokers, whose only stake in the transaction is profit.

Buyers in baby markets are also dependent on the sellers of infertility services to disclose the risks and limitations of the procedures generally and at the particular facility. Many are willing to undergo infertility treatments, even in the face of low (and often uncertain) chances of success and uncertainty regarding long-term safety.[42] The profit incentives in an unregulated infertility industry create conflicts of interest that can exacerbate this problem. Despite legal duties to disclose the risks associated with fertility treatment or limited success rates, the desire to remain competitive may lead some providers or fertility clinics to minimize the risks of fertility drugs or to overstate the prospects of success with fertility treatments.[43] It may also, as seems to have occurred in the *Baby M* case, discourage fertility clinics from disclosing information about participants' vulnerabilities that might make them poor candidates for participating in the buying and selling of fertility services or products.[44] Profit motives can even prevent some buyers from accessing fertility services when clinics "striving for high 'success' rates tend to refuse to take complicated fertility cases, thereby decreasing the risks of a 'low' success rate or, conversely, increasing their statistical pregnancy 'success' rates."[45] In the context of infertility services, the power clearly resides with the sellers.

The sellers of reproductive material, such as ova, may also fall prey to power imbalances vis-à-vis providers of fertility services. Although physicians owe them the same obligation they owe any patient to promote their best interests,[46] the fact that the women are not being treated for a condition and that they offer the prospect of financial benefit to the fertility clinics can create a conflict of interest.[47] This conflict of interest may reduce the extent to which physicians promote these women's best interests in general. Clinics that profit from ovum donors may minimize or even fail to disclose certain risks associated with ovum donation.[48] For example, one clinic has been reported to include information about potential links to cancer in consent forms for IVF patients, while leaving such information out of consent forms for oocyte donors.[49] In addition, donors might be pressured to undergo procedures that maximize the number of eggs retrieved, which can potentially increase the side effects of the procedure.[50] Finally, some clinics try to maximize compliance from donors by holding them legally responsible for the buyers' expenses if the women do not complete the donation process.[51]

D. OVERCOMING DISTORTED DECISION MAKING

Given underlying inequities, various power imbalances between the participants in baby markets, conflicts of interest, and the potentially coercive influence of money, we should be concerned about commodification of embryos and gametes in transactions that implicate varying degrees of relational, personhood interests. We might prohibit baby markets for fear that the coercive influences make consent inherently invalid and market exchanges de facto involuntary. But while women driven by economic necessity to sell eggs might not have made such a choice if everything else were equal, they might well prefer selling eggs over taking a job that pays poorly and offers few rewards. Similarly, while infertile couples desperate to have a child might not have purchased reproductive material if they could have had a child naturally, they might well prefer being buyers in this market over having limited reproductive options. These psychological and economic pressures create a double bind. Circumstances may make otherwise undesirable choices compelling, but prohibiting commodification does not overcome those circumstances.[52] Prohibition of baby markets would merely limit the options for dealing with economic need or infertility. It would limit choices integral to the self, which can also threaten human flourishing.

Rather than prohibit markets, we should bolster informed consent law and impose certain safeguards to minimize the power imbalances and distorted decision making that can arise with baby markets. Of course, the potentially coercive influence of financial necessity or desperation in baby markets cannot be entirely overcome through regulation. For example, we cannot realistically level the economic playing field to remove the economic pressures that may influence decisions to sell eggs or surrogacy services, and we cannot regulate away deep and strong desires to have biologically related children. Some buyers and sellers will necessarily participate in baby markets in the face of such economic and/or emotional pressures.

1. Informed Consent Law and Its Limitations

We are left, then, with the next best approach in a world of imperfection, where we do all we can to enhance the decision-making process so that the participants in baby markets can make self-defining choices based on full awareness and understanding of the implications of these choices. The kind of information essential to truly informed consent for buyers of fertility services and sellers of ova, for example, would, of course, include the physical risks associated with the procedures such as ovarian hyperstimulation syndrome,[53] bleeding and infection,[54] stroke,[55] and "very rarely, death."[56] In addition, they should know about the "controversial risk of ovarian cancer"[57] as well as the fact that many long-term risks are unknown.[58] Ova sellers also need to know about the risks of unintentional pregnancy[59] and the potential for secondary infertility.[60]

But physical risks are not all that is material. To make a truly informed decision to participate in these markets, individuals must also understand the known or possible *psychological* risks.[61] This is an area that has not been adequately researched. One study of ovum donors found that 8 percent of those who were later unable to conceive experienced some distress knowing that someone else was possibly raising a child genetically related to them.[62] Research of anonymous sperm donors or people who relinquished their children for adoption suggests that the psychological impact of selling or donating ova might lead to "experiences of dislocation from genetic offspring, [as well as] desires to learn about these children [and] to meet these children."[63] Selling gametes might affect future relationships in which having children is contemplated.[64] In addition, because these market transactions are intended to create families, they have important legal implications regarding parental rights, the enforceability of contracts, and the amount of information and contact allowed between the various parties: intended parents, donors, and future child.[65]

To ensure that both buyers and sellers can consent to these transactions as meaningfully as possible, we need mechanisms to promote deliberative decision making and to bolster the narrow protections of informed consent. When buyers and sellers in baby markets interact with the medical profession, they are protected by the legal requirements of informed consent.[66] But existing informed consent law cannot achieve the goals of full informed consent in this context for two reasons: (1) it only requires the disclosure of a limited range of information and (2) it goes only so far in ensuring full *comprehension* of risks and benefits.

First, the law of informed consent only requires the disclosure of a narrow range of information, excluding certain types of information that would be crucial to a truly informed decision in baby markets. Ordinarily, physicians are required to disclose information relevant to medical interests, but not nonmedical information.[67] Thus, although physicians must disclose material medical risks associated with ovum retrieval, for example, they may not be legally bound to discuss the legal implications of selling or buying a gamete or embryo.

In addition, it is not clear whether physicians are legally required to disclose the psychological consequences or risks associated with donating an egg or embryo, acting as a surrogate, or undergoing implantation of another's embryo. The law has had very little to say about whether psychological risks should be disclosed to obtain informed consent.[68] Depending on the jurisdiction, the standard of disclosure is based on either what would be material to the reasonable patient or what reasonable professionals would disclose (the standard of care).[69] In jurisdictions that use the reasonable-patient standard, a jury might be persuaded that reasonable patients would consider this information material. To my knowledge, however, no published case has so held. If, instead, the scope of disclosure is based on the professional standard, much will depend on whether such disclosure has become the standard of care, and whether courts would consider psychological risks to be the sort of information physicians should legally be obligated to disclose. In spite of the fact that some commentators and professional organizations call for such disclosure,[70] the lack of oversight makes it difficult to determine how frequently this information is included as part of the disclosure process.[71] Nevertheless, evidence suggests that informed consent is lacking in this area generally.[72]

To promote deliberative decision making, we should focus not only on the information that participants in these markets consider at the moment they give consent, but also on what information they receive (or do not receive) even before they step into a clinic. Ads soliciting ovum donors, for example, encourage egg donation but "never portray the real-life activity" and its risks.[73] One study of nineteen oocyte donation programs found serious inadequacies in the disclosure process during the initial phone interviews with prospective donors, including failure to volunteer information, provision of inaccurate information, reluctance to answer questions, and failure to send written information to prospective donors.[74] These initial encounters may influence the decision-making process in ways that lead donors to minimize the risks.

Finally, in addressing the problems of coercion and decision making in baby markets, we must also focus on helping participants *comprehend* the information they receive. Deciding what should be disclosed is far easier than ensuring that patients fully understand what has been disclosed. It is no surprise, therefore, that the law has focused primarily on the former. Physicians are not required to confirm that patients *understand* the risks associated with a procedure, merely that physicians *disclose* the relevant risks.[75] As many have noted, the legal protections have led to a thin process of obtaining consent that does little justice to the underlying goals of informed consent.[76]

2. Recommendations

All these problems require some retooling of informed consent law in baby markets. First, we should ensure that the obligations of disclosure are sufficiently broad to encompass the kind of information that is central to these decisions. Statutes might require the disclosure of certain kinds of information. For example, buyers and sellers should be told of the known short- and long-term risks, the potential physical risks, and the possible psychological implications of selling or buying reproductive material as well as the legal implications of these decisions, including instances in which the law is unclear about such things as parental status and the enforceability of certain arrangements.[77]

In addition, we need mechanisms to minimize the potential coerciveness of recruitment efforts. One solution is to prohibit ads and other solicitations from trying to entice prospective ova sellers or infertility patients by describing, respectively, only the financial benefits or the success rates of infertility treatment.[78] They must also disclose the risks. Similarly, we should require clinics to provide prospective ova, sperm, or embryo donors with standardized information regarding the physical, emotional, and legal consequences of such decisions even before they step into a clinic.[79] New York, for example, developed a guidebook for egg donors titled *Thinking of Becoming an Egg Donor? Get the Facts before You Decide!*[80] Requiring all egg donors to receive such a document before attending a clinic would enhance the decision-making process.

Legally mandating the scope of material information to be disclosed is only the first step. In addition, we must consider mechanisms to make the *process* of informed decision making as meaningful as possible and to promote *deliberative* informed consent.[81] New York again offers a useful model. A task force drafted model consent forms to ensure some uniformity in the informed consent process among fertility clinics.[82] Unfortunately, not many other states have followed suit.[83] These model consent forms are helpful in creating professional norms and educating providers. But in the context of a largely unregulated infertility industry, mere guidelines may not adequately protect patients.[84] We need some teeth associated with these guidelines.

If we want decision making to be even more deliberative here, however, the system must not rely solely on physicians, particularly given their potential conflicts of interest and the fact that some of the material information is not just medical. For example, the legal implications of these financial transactions extend beyond the medical sphere. We cannot expect physicians to understand, let alone adequately disclose, the full legal implications of the decisions that buyers and sellers are making in baby markets. Thus we should consider requiring consultation with attorneys so that participants in these markets can better understand the legal implications.

Psychologists are appropriate participants, as well. Professional guidelines require psychological screening of ovum donors, for example.[85] Ideally, however, psychologists would do more than just screen potential donors. As a psychologist from a major IVF clinic described it, given the financial conflicts of interest inherent in ovum donation, "my job is to talk donors out of it. That's not because we don't need them, but we want to sleep at night."[86] Psychologists should help donors understand their motivations (e.g., financial or altruistic) and the implications of participating in this process (e.g., the child's or donor's future interest [or lack thereof] in contact and the impact on their fertility). We might borrow from the field of genetic counseling, which sees its role as not only providing information, but helping individuals make decisions consistent with their values and life plans.[87] In addition, information gleaned from such a psychological evaluation that is relevant to the donor's ability to cope with the decision must be disclosed to the donor.[88] Finally, we might also (or alternatively) rely on patient advocates to raise similar questions, while also focusing on elements that are not overtly psychological.[89] They might, for example, ask women to consider other potential sources of income if financial motives are driving their decisions.

My suggestions for enhancing consent in this context will not satisfy everyone. Some have suggested that informed consent in this context is highly problematic. The *Baby M* court reasoned, for example, that the surrogate's consent was "irrelevant" – that a surrogate can never make a totally informed decision prior to the child's birth.[90] Nevertheless, although we may never perfectly comprehend in advance the implications of making many important decisions, we are better equipped to make such important decisions if we are informed, deliberative, and self-aware.

Although I believe informed consent is an important element in overcoming some of the coercive effects of baby markets, it is not sufficient. As I suggest in a longer version of this piece, an enormous contributing factor to coercion, distorted decision making, and power imbalances in baby markets is the fact that the infertility industry in America is motivated by profit and is essentially unregulated.[91] Enforceable reporting requirements would help us gather essential data to begin addressing unanswered questions about the risks and benefits of fertility procedures. Expanding the scope of federal regulations that protect human subjects to encompass the private infertility sector would protect buyers and sellers from experimental and potentially risky procedures. Regulations allowing sellers of reproductive materials and services to withdraw without financial or legal penalties, just as human subjects can withdraw from research protocols without penalty, would also reduce some of the power imbalances. So would regulations to protect the safety of both sellers and buyers against the threats to their well-being that can arise where there are conflicts of interest. For example, we might set limits on hormone doses used to retrieve eggs[92] or on the number of cycles of egg donation a woman may undergo. Admittedly, these recommendations are a tall order. They go against cultural norms that favor free, unfettered markets. They also threaten the fertility industry's self-interest in avoiding regulation, and they do not prevent the possibility of black markets emerging to escape some of these regulatory controls. Too much is at stake, however, to expect the market to address all the consequential harms that arise given the background conditions in which markets exist. Clearly the market has not resolved these consequential harms. In giving in to baby markets, I am willing to accept the intrinsic harms only if we try to minimize the consequential harms that exist because of, and exacerbate, the inequities of our culture. We live in an imperfect, nonideal world. My pragmatic approach offers an admittedly imperfect solution that nevertheless tries to bring us closer to an ideal world.

NOTES

1 In most of this chapter, I primarily refer to the buying and selling of gametes and embryos, although I make some reference to surrogacy services, as well.
2 Michael J. Sandel, *What Money Can't Buy: The Moral Limits of Markets*, 89 Tanner Lectures Human Values 94–5 (1998).
3 *Id.* at 104.
4 Margaret Radin has been influential in this discussion, and I draw, to a large extent, on her analysis in such works as Margaret J. Radin, Contested Commodities (1996) and Margaret J. Radin, *Market Inalienability*, 100 Harv. L. Rev. 1849 (1987) [hereinafter Radin, *Market-Inalienability*].
5 Radin, *Market-Inalienability, supra* note 4, at 1880–1.
6 *Cf.* Radika Rao, *Property, Privacy, and the Human Body*, 80 B.U. L. Rev. 359, 458 (2000).
7 Davis v. Davis, 842 S.W.2d 588, 592–7 (Tenn. 1992) (describing this view among commentators).
8 Sonia M. Suter, *Disentangling Privacy from Property: Toward a Deeper Understanding of Genetic Privacy*, 72 Geo. Wash. U. L. Rev. 737, 772, 773 n.175 (2004) (quoting Alasdair MacIntyre, After Virtue: A Study in Moral Theory 221 [1981]).
9 *See* National Research Council & Institute of Medicine, Guidelines for Human Embryonic Stem Cell Research 81 (2005) [hereinafter NAS Guidelines].
10 Rao, *supra* note 6, at 458–59.
11 The line of cases that protect decisional privacy in reproduction, marriage, and child rearing are consistent with the view that decisions regarding whether and how to create certain relationships enhance and foster self-definition. *See* Planned Parenthood v. Casey, 505 U.S. 833, 923 (1992).
12 Angela Valdez, *The Wrong Egg*, http://www.salon.com/mwt/feature/2006/11/16/fertility_mix_up/index.html.
13 *Id.* For purposes of ease and space, I, like many others, refer to sellers of eggs and gametes as *donors*, a misnomer to be sure. Technically, when they receive money for this reproductive material, they are *sellers. See* Bonnie Steinbock, *Payment of Egg Donation and Surrogacy*, 71 Mount Sinai J. Med. 255, 255–6 (2004).
14 Valdez, *supra* note 12; *see also In re* K.M.H., 169 P.3d 1025, 1040 (Kan. 2007).
15 Valdez, *supra* note 12. Although sperm donors typically sign away their rights to custody, he had not intended to be an anonymous sperm donor. Instead, he planned to use his sperm to create his own child and therefore never signed away parental rights.
16 *In re* Baby M, 537 A.2d 1227, 1234–5 (N.J. 1988).
17 Baby M, 537 A.2d at 1249. The irrevocability of the gestational surrogate's agreement to terminate her parental rights prior to conception was equally problematic to the court. *Id.* at 1248, 1250.
18 Lori Andrews, *Beyond Doctrinal Boundaries: A Legal Framework for Surrogate Motherhood*, 81 Va. L. Rev. 2343, 2351 (1995).
19 Surrogacy is tougher because of the fact that the fetus is not severable from the individual in the way that an embryo is. Thus, although the surrogate may ultimately decide to separate from the child at birth, a relationship is potentially unfolding within her body, making any change of heart all the more compelling from a personhood context. However, Lori Andrews discovered from interviews with surrogates that they "did not refer to the fetus as 'my baby,' . . . but as the intended parents' baby." *Id.* at 2352. Nevertheless, one study found that 22 percent of surrogates considered separating from the baby to be the most emotionally troubling part of the arrangement, while 25 percent considered it to be separating from the intended parents. *Id.* at 2353. This suggests that

the relational interests for surrogates exist but are less than those for the intended parents.

20 Naomi Cahn & Jana Singer, *Adoption, Identity, and the Constitution: The Case for Opening Closed Records*, 2 U. PA. J. CONST. L. 150, 176–7 (1999).

21 June Carbone & Naomi Cahn, *Which Ties Bind? Redefining the Parent-Child Relationship in an Age of Genetic Certainty*, 11 WM. & MARY BILL RTS. J. 1011, 1024 (2003).

22 Lest I be misunderstood, let me be clear that I am not suggesting that the biological connection is greater or more significant than the relationship between the adopted child and adoptive parents or between the child born through gamete donation and the intended parents. My point is simply that being genetically related to another is one, but certainly not the only or most important, aspect of self-definition.

23 This is consistent with the fact that to preserve and protect certain kinds of intimacy, the law does not condone certain financial exchanges, particularly those that help define the level of intimacy. Jill E. Hasday, *Intimacy and Economic Exchange*, 119 HARV. L. REV. 491 (2005).

24 Sandel, *supra* note 2, at 104.

25 *E.g.*, they may increase the supply of reproductive material and theoretically reduce prices. *See, e.g.*, June Carbone & Page Gottheim, *Markets, Subsidies, Regulation, and Trust: Building Ethical Understandings into the Market for Fertility Services*, 9 J. GENDER RACE & JUST. 509, 52 (2006). *But see* Gregory Stock, *Eggs for Sale: How Much Is Too Much?* 4 AM. J. BIOETHICS 26, 27 (2001); Martha Ertman, *What's Wrong with a Parenthood Market?* 82 N.C. L. REV. 1 (2003–4).

26 Sandel, *supra* note 2, at 95.

27 Sonia M. Suter, *Giving In to Baby Markets: Regulation without Prohibition*, 16 MICH. J. GENDER & L. 169, 185 (2009).

28 Julia D. Mahoney, *The Market for Human Tissue*, 86 VA. L. REV. 163, 213 (2002); Michele Goodwin, *Altruism's Limits: Law, Capacity, and Organ Commodification*, 56 RUTGERS L. REV. 305 (2004); Carbone, *supra* note 25, at 520.

29 *See* Suter, *supra* note 27, at 185, for a more detailed discussion of these impracticalities.

30 Margaret Radin & Madhavi Sunder, *Introduction: The Subject and Object of Commodification, in* Ertman, *supra* note 25, at 14.

31 *See* Suter, *supra* note 27, at 193.

32 Sandel, *supra* note 2, at 94–5.

33 *Id.*; *see also* JULIA DEREK, CONFESSIONS OF A SERIAL EGG DONOR 164 (2004); Suzanne Holland, *Contested Commodities at Both Ends of Life: Buying and Selling Gametes, Embryos, and Body Tissues*, 11 KENNEDY INST. ETHICS J. 263, 272 (2001); Steinbock, *supra* note 13, at 258.

34 Radin, *Market-Inalienability*, *supra* note 4, at 1916.

35 *See, e.g.*, Ethics Committee of the American Society for Reproductive Medicine, *Financial Incentives in Recruitment of Oocyte Donors*, 74 FERTILITY & STERILITY 216, 217 (2000) [hereinafter Ethics Committee]. Of course, this will not always be true. As the court noted in *In re* Baby M, "[the intended parents] are not rich and [the surrogate and her spouse] not poor." *In re* Baby M, 537 A.2d 1227, 1249 (N.J. 1988). Nevertheless, the court speculated "that it is unlikely . . . that infertile couples in the low-income bracket will find upper income surrogates." *Id.* at 1249. *See also* Derek, *supra* note 33, at 164.

36 Molly J. W. Wilson, *Precommitment in Free-Market Procreation: Surrogacy, Commissioned Adoption, and Limits on Decision Making Capacity*, 31 J. LEGIS. 329, 341 (2005).

37 *Id.*

38 Ertman, *supra* note 25, at 41.

39 With respect to genetic information, e.g., individuals are much more likely to be sellers than buyers because their information has economic value to those who want it for research, underwriting, etc., whereas the genetic information of others does not usually have the same economic value to individuals. Some genetic information may, however, be of *personal* value to individuals who want to know, e.g., about health risks to their future partners.

40 Debora Spar, The Baby Business: How Money, Science, and Politics Drive the Commerce of Conception 35–46 (2006). Of course, agents may become involved in the transactions, complicating the power balances.

41 *Id.* at 4. Such desperation has led to women trying to have children at significantly advanced ages, in spite of the medical risks (*see* Patrick White, *Woman, 60, Gives Birth to Twins – and Ethics Debate*, Globe & Mail, Feb. 6, 2009, at A1) or, as in the case of Nadya Suleman, to have six embryos implanted, in spite of the fact that the national average number of embryos implanted is 2.3 (*see* Alan Zarembo *et al.*, *Octuplet Doctor's Record Dubious*, L.A. Times, Feb. 10, 2009, at A1).

42 Michele Goodwin, *Assisted Reproductive Technology and the Double Bind: The Illusory Choice of Motherhood*, 9 J. Gender Race & Just. 1, 21 (2005) [hereinafter Goodwin, ART].

43 Goodwin, ART, *supra* note 42, at 22.

44 Although a psychologist from the fertility clinic, who screened Mary Beth Whitehead before she signed the surrogacy contract, warned that Mrs. Whitehead might have difficulty surrendering the child, this issue was not pursued because it might have "jeopardized the Infertility Center's fee." *In re* Baby M, 537 A.2d 1227, 1247–8 (N.J. 1988).

45 Goodwin, ART, *supra* note 42, at 23.

46 Ethics Committee, *supra* note 35, at 219; Mark V. Sauer, *Egg Donor Solicitation: Problems Exist, but Do Abuses?* 1 Am. J. Bioethics 1, 2 (2001).

47 Andrea L. Kalfoglou, *Navigating Conflict of Interest in Oocyte Donation*, 1 AM. J. Bioethics 1a, 1a (2001).

48 *See* M. Jones, *Donating Your Eggs*, Glamour, July 1996, at 170.

49 *Id.* at 168, 170.

50 Kalfoglou, *supra* note 47, at 2; Steinbock, *supra* note 13, at 263.

51 Kalfoglou, supra note 47.

52 Radin, *Market-Inalienability*, *supra* note 4, at 1915–16. *See also* Mahoney, *supra* note 28 (describing the outlaw of payment as a "curious strategy").

53 Gareth Cook, *Ethical Questions Complicate the Recruitment of Egg Donors*, Boston Globe, June 7, 2006, at A18; Sauer, *supra* note 46, at 1–2.

54 Luigi Mastroianni, *Risk Evaluation and Informed Consent for Ovum Donation: A Clinical Perspective*, 1 Am. J. Bioethics 28, 28 (2001).

55 Holland, *supra* note 33, at 270.

56 Michelle A. Mullen, *What Oocyte Donors Aren't Told*, Bioethics, Dec. 2001, at 1c.

57 Andrea D. Gurmankin, *Risk Information Provided to Prospective Oocyte Donors in a Preliminary Phone Call*, 1 Am. J. Bioethics 3, 3 (2001).

58 Cook, *supra* note 53, at A18.

59 Ethics Committee, *supra* note 35, at 217.

60 Kalfoglou, *supra* note 47, at 1a; Mastroianni, *supra* note 54, at 28.

61 *See* Ethics Committee, *supra* note 35, at 218.

62 *Id.* at 217.

63 Mullen, *supra* note 56, at 1c.

64 *Id.*; Ethics Committee, *supra* note 35, at 218.

65 Naomi R. Cahn, Test Tube Families: Why the Fertility Market Needs Legal Regulation 73–129 (2009) [hereinafter Cahn, Test Tube Families].

66 The requirements of informed consent exist in all physician-patient relationships regardless of the specific medical procedures. *See* Barry R. Furrow *et al.*, Health Law: Cases, Materials and Problems 230–88 (6th ed. 2008).

67 *See* Arato v. Avedon, 858 P.2d 598, 600 (Cal. 1993) (rejecting the notion that "a physician is under a duty to disclose information material to the patient's *nonmedical* interests").

68 Virtually all of the case law addressing informed consent and psychological risks examines a different issue: the constitutionality of state laws that mandate the disclosure of psychological risks associated with abortion. *See, e.g.*, Planned Parenthood Minn. v. Rounds, 467 F.3d 716 (8th Cir. 2006) *vacated and remanded* 530 F.3d 724 (8th Cir. 2008). Even the American Bar Association's Model Act, which includes elaborate informed consent provisions, does not discuss disclosure of psychological risks associated with ART. Model Act Gov'g Assisted Reprod. Tech. § 201(2)(a) (2008) [hereinafter ABA Model Act].

69 "A slight majority of courts has adopted the professional disclosure standard [over the reasonable-patient standard], measuring the duty to disclose by the standard of the reasonable medical practitioner similarly situated." Furrow, *supra* note 66, at 240. Of the courts that use a patient-based standard, the vast majority of courts use an *objective* test. Only a few courts apply a subjective patient-based standard, and even then, "the courts tend to leave room for deference to physicians." Jamie S. King & Benjamin W. Moulton, *Rethinking Informed Consent: The Case for Shared Decision-Making*, 32 Am. J. L. & Med. 429, 444 (2006).

70 See Ethics Committee of the American Society for Reproductive Medicine, *Financial Incentives in Recruitment of Oocyte Donors*, 74 Fertility & Sterility 216, 218 (2000) [hereinafter Ethics Committee]; *The Practice Committee of the American Society for Reproductive Medicine and the Practice Committee of the Society for Assisted Reproductive Technology*, 86 Fertility & Sterility S272–3 (2006) [hereinafter Practice Committee]. *But see* ABA Model Act, *supra* note 68 (failing to discuss a need to disclose the psychological risks associated with ART).

71 Sauer, *supra* note 46, at 1. The fact, however, that a professional organization like the American Society for Reproductive Medicine believes that such information should be disclosed could persuade a jury that this is the standard of care, even if many physicians do not in fact disclose such information.

72 *Id.* at 2; *see also* Kalfoglou, *supra* note 47, at 1c.

73 Sauer, *supra* note 46, at 1.

74 Gurmankin, *supra* note 57, at 4, 10 (noting, however, that the study sample was "small and potentially biased").

75 Canterbury v. Spence, 464 F.2d 772, 780 n.15 (D.C. Cir. 1972).

76 *See, e.g.*, Jay Katz, *Informed Consent: Must It Remain a Fairy Tale?* 10 J. Contemp. Health L. & Pol'y 69, 77–81 (1993).

77 *See* Andrews, *supra* note 18, at 2358; ABA Model Act, *supra* note 68, at § 201(2)(c). In the context of genetic testing, some states mandate the disclosure of specific information to ensure that consent to genetic testing is informed. *See* 16 Del. C. § 1220(4) (2009); MCLS § 333.17020 (2009); R.R.S. Neb. § 71–551 (2009).

78 *See* Ethics Committee, *supra* note 35, at 219.

79 Gurmankin, *supra* note 57, at 12; Stock, *supra* note 25, at 26, 27.

80 New York State Task Force on Life and the Law, Advisory Group on Assisted Reproductive Technologies, *Thinking of Becoming an Egg Donor? Get the Facts before You Decide!*

(1998), http://www.health.state.ny.us/community/reproductive_health/infertility/eggdonor.htm.

81 Barbara Atwell, *The Modern Age of Informed Consent*, 40 U. Rich. L. Rev. 591, 597 (2006).

82 Sauer, *supra* note 46, at 2.

83 *Id.*

84 *Id.*; Cahn, Test Tube Families, *supra* note 65, at 193. In spite of federal reporting requirements, Fertility Clinic Success Rate and Certification Act of 1992, 42 U.S.C. § 263a-1 (1992); Cahn, Test Tube Families, *supra* note 65, at 53–4. The only sanction for failing to report success rates is to be listed "as a non-reporting reporting clinic in the CDC's annual report." Alicia Ouellette *et al.*, *Lessons from Across the Pond: Assisted Reproductive Technology in the United Kingdom and the United States*, 31 Am. J. L. & Med. 419, 427 (2005).

85 Practice Committee, *supra* note 70, at S272; *see also* ABA Model Act, *supra* note 68, at § 301(1).

86 Jan Hoffman, *Egg Donations Meet a Need and Raise Ethical Questions*, N.Y. Times, Jan. 8, 1996, at A1.

87 *See* Sonia M. Suter, *The Routinization of Prenatal Testing*, 28 Am. J. L. & Med. 233, 243 (2002).

88 ABA Model Act, *supra* note 68, at § 203(4).

89 Atwell, *supra* note 81, at 608.

90 *See* Suter, *supra* note 27, at 178; Baby M, *supra* note 16, at 1249. Whether one can ever make such life-altering, irrevocable changes before experiencing the realities of one's choice is a very difficult problem, although not unique to exchanges in baby markets. End-of-life decision making is fraught with such dilemmas, and yet the law allows a now-competent individual to make legally enforceable medical decisions in the event one's future self becomes incompetent, even if such determinations result in the end of one's life. *See* Alan Meisel & Kathy L. Cerminara, The Right to Die 7–20 (3d ed. 2004) (§7.02[A]).

91 See Suter, *supra* note 27.

92 See Cook, *supra* note 53, at A18.

Concluding Thoughts

MICHELE BRATCHER GOODWIN

Baby Markets is published at a pivotal time; a year after Nadya Suleman's controversial birth of octuplets, shortly after President Barack Obama lifted federal restrictions on stem cell research, and in the midst of nations changing their adoption laws as a response to allegations of child trafficking and selling. These issues inform us of the urgency for an international discourse on creating families. Implicated in all of this are the ways in which markets have come to dominate how children come into families. As we have learned, markets can help families overcome discrimination. Gay couples suffer from the laws of nature in their inability to naturally reproduce within a couple, which is exacerbated by state laws that limit their ability to adopt. The laws of infertility do not help couples, passionate to parent, who learn that their bodies cannot help their dreams come true. Markets help these couples achieve their dreams. Often, children are benefited by their decisions, but sometimes not.

The lengths to which men and women venture to acquire a child are at times heart-wrenching. Anecdotal accounts of couples surmounting the heaps of adoption papers, extensive reference checks, and home visits offer not only glimpses of the tangled bureaucratic side of adoption, but also reveal layers of inefficiency that affect children languishing in U.S. foster care systems. For too many children in foster care, waiting for a stable home to materialize is tantamount to waiting for the stork to arrive or the lottery to be won. Indeed, needy children without the loving support of mothers and fathers are too often relegated to group homes, and some facilities that more closely resemble asylums than loving families.

In the spheres of assisted reproduction and adoption, many argue that the systems need overhaul. Such assessments spill forward quite easily and persistently. More difficult to answer are the questions regarding the scope of our solutions, which often involve markets and monetary exchanges. If a celebrity removes a poverty-stricken child from her domestic community, is society really benefited? Maybe. But how would we assess that?

There are pitfalls to baby markets. Sometimes adult interests overwhelm and obscure the rights and best interests of children. At times, assisted reproductive technology and adoption seem to serve adult interests and needs more than those of children. In *Baby Markets*, the authors debate these issues and offer thoughtful reflections about how law and society should address these concerns. To be sure, the authors do not all agree on what approach the law should take or what is in the best interest of society. Indeed, many disagree on these issues. What we attempt to do here is invite you into the discourse and offer different views of the reproductive space.

Author Bios

Elizabeth Bartholet: ebarthol@law.harvard.edu
Professor Bartholet is Morris Wasserstein Public Interest Professor of Law and faculty director of the Child Advocacy Program at Harvard University Law School. She holds a JD from Harvard University and a BA from Radcliffe College. Her chapter is a revised version of "International Adoption: Thoughts on the Human Rights Issues," published in *Buffalo Human Rights Law Review* (vol. 13, pp. 151–203, 2007), which contains extensive documentation for the claims made. For other writings on international adoption by the author, see Elizabeth Bartholet publications listed at http://www.law.harvard.edu/faculty/bartholet/pubs.php. The author has been deeply involved in issues related to international adoption since 1985 and draws on this experience as well as cited materials throughout the chapter.

Naomi Cahn: ncahn@law.gwu.edu
Professor Cahn is John Theodore Fey Research Professor of Law, George Washington University Law School. She is a Senior Fellow at the Evan B. Donaldson Adoption Institute and a member of the Yale Cultural Cognition Project. Professor Cahn holds an LLM from Georgetown University, a JD from Columbia University, and a BA from Princeton University. Professor Cahn's chapter is adapted from her book *Egg and Sperm* (2008).

June Carbone: carbonej@umkc.edu
Professor Carbone is the Edward A. Smith/Missouri Chair of Law at the University of Missouri–Kansas City School of Law. She holds a JD from Yale University and an AB from Princeton University's Woodrow Wilson School of Public and International Affairs.

Mary Anne Case: macase@law.uchicago.edu
Professor Case is the Arnold I. Shure Professor of Law at the University of Chicago School of Law. She holds a JD from Harvard University and a BA from Yale University.

Sara Dorow: sara.dorow@ualberta.ca
Professor Dorow is an associate professor of sociology and the director of the Community Service–Learning Program at the University of Alberta. She holds a PhD in sociology from the University of Minnesota.

Nanette R. Elster: nelster@ivflaw.com
Ms. Elster is a partner with Spence and Elster, PC, in Lincolnshire, Illinois. She also serves on the adjunct faculty at several Chicago-based universities and on the board of the Chicago Center for Jewish Genetic Disorders. Ms. Elster holds a JD from Loyola University of Chicago, a MPH from Boston University School of Public Health, and a BA from the University of Illinois at Urbana-Champaign.

Martha Ertman: mertman@law.umaryland.edu
Professor Ertman teaches contracts and commercial law at the University of Maryland Law School. She was previously a professor at the University of Utah, S. J. Quinney College of Law, and the University of Denver College of Law. She holds a JD from Northwestern University and a BA from Wellesley College.

José Gabilondo: gabilond@fiu.edu
Professor Gabilondo is associate dean for academic affairs and associate professor of law at Florida International University School of Law. He holds a JD from the University of California, Boalt Hall School of Law, and a BA from Harvard University.

Maggie Gallagher: Maggie@imapp.org
Ms. Gallagher is president of the Institute for Marriage and Public Policy and the National Organization for Marriage. She is also a nationally syndicated columnist. Ms. Gallagher holds a BA from Yale University.

Michele Bratcher Goodwin: mgoodwin@umn.edu
Professor Goodwin is the Everett Fraser Professor in Law at the University of Minnesota, Walter Mondale School of Law. She holds joint appointments at the University of Minnesota Medical School and the University of Minnesota School of Public Health. She is co-chair of the Women's Faculty Cabinet, and former chair of the American Association of Law Schools Section on Law, Medicine, and Health Care and a Fellow of the Institute of Medicine of Chicago. Professor Goodwin was a Gilder Lehrman postdoctoral Fellow at Yale University after completing her LLM from the University of Wisconsin, a JD from Boston College Law School, and a BA from the University of Wisconsin.

Paige Gottheim: pgottheim@uva.edu
This project is the second collaboration between Paige Gottheim and Professor June Carbone.

Mary Eschelbach Hansen: mhansen@american.edu
Professor Hansen is an associate professor at American University College of Arts and Sciences, Department of Economics. She is also the director of Undergraduate

Studies for the Department of Economics and American University general education assessment coordinator. Professor Hansen holds a PhD in economics from the University of Illinois at Urbana-Champaign and a BS in economics from Saint Louis University.

Ruth-Arlene W. Howe: howeru@bc.edu
Professor Howe is Professor Emerita at Boston College Law School. She holds a JD from Boston College, an MSW from Simmons College, and an AB from Wellesley College.

Lisa C. Ikemoto: lcikemoto@ucdavis.edu
Professor Ikemoto is a professor of law at the University of California, Davis, School of Law. She is also on the board of directors of the Reproductive Health Technologies Project. She holds an LLM from Columbia University, a JD from the University of California, Davis, and a BA from the University of California, Los Angeles.

Kimberly D. Krawiec: krawiec@email.unc.edu
Professor Krawiec teaches securities, corporate, and derivatives law at the Duke University School of Law. She holds a JD from Georgetown University and a BA from North Carolina State University. Professor Krawiec would like to thank Scott Baker, Mary Ann Case, Andrew Chin, Adrienne Davis, Maxine Eichner, Adam Feibelman, Mitu Gulati, David Hyman, Melissa Jacoby, Julia Mahoney, Hiroshi Motomura, Eric Muller, Elizabth Scott, and Mark Weisburd; workshop participants at the universities of Alabama, North Carolina, Illinois, Vanderbilt, and Washington and Lee law schools; and round table participants at Baby Markets: Money, Morals, and the Neopolitics of Choice for their helpful comments on earlier drafts.

Michelle Oberman: moberman@scu.edu
Professor Oberman is a professor of criminal law and contracts at the Santa Clara University School of Law. She holds a JD and an MPH from the University of Michigan and a BA from Cornell University.

Daniel Pollack: dpollack@yu.edu
Professor Pollack is a tenured professor at Yeshiva University Wurzweiler School of Social Work and Senior Fellow at the University of Massachusetts Medical School, Office for Foster Care and Adoption. Professor Pollack holds a JD from Cleveland State University, an MSW from Case Western Reserve University, and a BA from Oberlin College.

John A. Robertson: jrobertson@law.utexas.edu
Professor Robertson is the Vinson and Elkins Chair at the University of Texas School of Law at Austin and the chair of the Ethics Committee of the American Society for Reproductive Medicine. He holds a JD from Harvard University and an AB from Dartmouth University.

Debora L. Spar: Professor Spar is the president of Barnard College. She formerly served as Spangler Family Professor of Business Administration and senior associate dean for faculty research and development at Harvard Business School. She holds both a PhD and an AM in government from Harvard University and a BS from Georgetown University.

Sonia Suter: ssuter@law.gwu.edu
Professor Suter is an associate professor of law at George Washington University Law School. She holds a JD and an MS from the University of Michigan and a BA from Michigan State University.

Leslie Wolf: lwolf@gsu.edu
Professor Wolf is an associate professor of law at Georgia State University College of Law. She was the Class of 2006 Assistant Adjunct Professor, Program in Medical Ethics, at the University of California, San Francisco. She is a graduate of Stanford University, Harvard University Law School, and the Johns Hopkins School of Public Health.

Viviana A. Zelizer: vzelizer@princeton.edu
Professor Zelizer is professor of sociology at Princeton University. She holds a PhD, an MPhil, and an MA in sociology from Columbia University and a BA from Rutgers University.

Patti Zettler: Ms. Zettler is the 2008 Law Fellow for the National Institutes of Health Department of Bioethics. She is a graduate of Stanford Law School.

Index